MUSIC IN THE TWENTIETH AND TWENTY-FIRST CENTURIES

Western Music in Context: A Norton History

Walter Frisch SERIES EDITOR

Music in the Medieval West, by Margot Fassler

Music in the Renaissance, by Richard Freedman

Music in the Baroque, by Wendy Heller

Music in the Eighteenth Century, by John Rice

Music in the Nineteenth Century, by Walter Frisch

Music in the Twentieth and Twenty-First Centuries, by Joseph Auner

MUSIC IN THE TWENTIETH AND TWENTY-FIRST CENTURIES

Joseph Auner

Tufts University

W. W. NORTON AND COMPANY

NEW YORK • LONDON

W. W. Norton & Company has been independent since its founding in 1923, when William Warder Norton and Mary D. Herter Norton first published lectures delivered at the People's Institute, the adult education division of New York City's Cooper Union. The firm soon expanded its program beyond the Institute, publishing books by celebrated academics from America and abroad. By midcentury, the two major pillars of Norton's publishing program—trade books and college texts—were firmly established. In the 1950s, the Norton family transferred control of the company to its employees, and today—with a staff of four hundred and a comparable number of trade, college, and professional titles published each year—W. W. Norton & Company stands as the largest and oldest publishing house owned wholly by its employees.

Editor: Maribeth Payne
Associate Editor: Justin Hoffman
Editorial Assistant: Michael Fauver
Developmental Editor: Harry Haskell
Manuscript Editor: Courtney Hirschey
Project Editor: Jack Borrebach
Electronic Media Editor: Steve Hoge
Marketing Manager, Music: Amy Parkin
Production Manager: Ashley Horna
Photo Editor: Stephanie Romeo
Permissions Manager: Megan Jackson
Text Design: Jillian Burr
Composition: Jouve International—Brattleboro, VT
Manufacturing: Quad/Graphics—Fairfield, PA

Library of Congress Cataloging-in-Publication Data

Auner, Joseph.
    Music in the twentieth and twenty-first centuries / Joseph Auner. — First edition.
        pages cm. — (Western music in context: a Norton history)
    Includes bibliographical references and index.
    ISBN 978-0-393-92920-1 (pbk.)
    1. Music—20th century—History and criticism.   2. Music—21st century—History and criticism.   I. Title.
    ML197.A87 2013
    780.9'04—dc23

                                                                                    2013011902

W. W. Norton & Company, Inc., 500 Fifth Avenue, New York, NY 10110-0017
wwnorton.com
W. W. Norton & Company Ltd. 15 Carlisle Street, London W1D 3BS

3 4 5 6 7 8 9 0

For Edie, Eric, and Mary

CONTENTS IN BRIEF

CONTENTS

ANTHOLOGY REPERTOIRE

1. Gustav Mahler: Symphony No. 3 in D Minor, Movement 4
2. Claude Debussy: *Estampes, Pagodes*
3. Arnold Schoenberg: *Pierrot lunaire*, Op. 21, *Mondestrunken*
4. Alban Berg: *Wozzeck*, Act III, Transition and Scene 3
5. Charles Ives: Symphony No. 4, Movement 1
6. Igor Stravinsky: *Le sacre du printemps*, Part I, Introduction
7. Kurt Weill: *Der Lindberghflug*, "Introduction of the Pilot"
8. Igor Stravinsky: *Symphonie de psaumes*, Movement 2
9. Maurice Ravel: Concerto in G for Piano and Orchestra, Movement 1
10. Arnold Schoenberg: Piano Piece, Op. 33a
11. Anton Webern: Symphony, Op. 21, Movement 2, Variations
12. Béla Bartók: *Music for Strings, Percussion, and Celesta*, Movement 1
13. Aaron Copland: *Billy the Kid* Suite, "Street in a Frontier Town" (excerpt)
14. William Grant Still: *Africa*, Part 2, *Land of Romance*
15. Benjamin Britten: *War Requiem*, Op. 66, Requiem aeternam
16. Dmitri Shostakovich: String Quartet No. 8, Op. 110, Movement 3
17. Pierre Boulez: *Le marteau sans maître*, Movement 5, *Bel édifice et les pressentiments*
18. Pauline Oliveros: *Traveling Companions*
19. Mario Davidovsky, *Synchronisms No. 6* (excerpt)
20. Kaija Saariaho: *NoaNoa*
21. György Ligeti: *Continuum*
22. Elliott Carter: String Quartet No. 5, Introduction, Giocoso, Interlude I, Lento espressivo

SERIES EDITOR'S PREFACE

Western Music in Context: A Norton History starts from the premise that music consists of far more than the notes on a page or the sound heard on a recording. Music is a product of its time and place, of the people and institutions that bring it into being.

Many music history texts focus on musical style and on individual composers. These approaches have been a valuable part of writing about music since the beginnings of modern scholarship in the later nineteenth century. But in the past few decades, scholars have widened their scope in imaginative and illuminating ways to explore the cultural, social, intellectual, and historical contexts for music. This new perspective is reflected in the volumes of Western Music in Context. Among the themes treated across the series are:

- The ways in which music has been commissioned, created, and consumed in public and private spheres
- The role of technology in the creation and transmission of music, from the advent of notation to the digital age
- The role of women as composers, performers, and patrons
- The relationships between music and national or ethnic identity
- The training and education of musicians in both private and institutional settings

All of these topics—and more—animate the pages of Western Music in Context. Written in an engaging style by recognized experts, the series paints vivid pictures of moments, activities, locales, works, and individuals:

- A fourth-century eyewitness report on musical practices in the Holy Land, from a European nun on a pilgrimage
- A lavish wedding at the court of Savoy in the mid-fifteenth century, with music by Guillaume DuFay

- Broadside ballads sung on the streets of London or pasted onto walls, and enjoyed by people from all levels of society
- A choral Magnificat performed at a church in colonial Brazil in the 1770s, accompanied by an organ sent by ship and mule from Portugal
- The barely literate impresario Domenico Barbaia making a tidy fortune at Italian opera houses by simultaneously managing gambling tables and promoting Gioachino Rossini
- A "radio teaching piece" from 1930 by Kurt Weill celebrating the transatlantic flight of Charles Lindbergh

Each volume of Western Music in Context is accompanied by a concise anthology of carefully chosen works. The anthologies offer representative examples of a wide variety of musical genres, styles, and national traditions. Included are excerpts from well-known works like Aaron Copland's *Billy the Kid*, as well as lesser-known gems like Ignacio de Jerusalem's *Matins for the Virgin of Guadalupe*. Commentaries within the anthologies not only provide concise analyses of every work from both formal and stylistic points of view, but also address issues of sources and performance practice.

StudySpace, Norton's online resource for students, features links to recordings of anthology selections that can be streamed from the Naxos Music Library (individual or institutional subscription required), as well as the option to purchase and download recordings from Amazon and iTunes. In addition, students can purchase access to, and instructors can request a free DVD of, the Norton Opera Sampler, which features over two hours of video excerpts from fourteen Metropolitan Opera productions. Finally, for readers wanting to do further research or find more specialized books, articles, or web-based resources, StudySpace offers lists of further readings that supplement those at the end of each chapter in the texts.

Because the books of the Western Music in Context series are relatively compact and reasonably priced, instructors and students might use one or more volumes in a single semester, or several across an academic year. Instructors have the flexibility to supplement the books and the accompanying anthologies with other resources, including Norton Critical Scores and *Strunk's Source Readings in Music History*, as well as other readings, illustrations, scores, films, and recordings.

The contextual approach to music history offers limitless possibilities: an instructor, student, or general reader can extend the context as widely as he or she wishes. Well before the advent of the World Wide Web, the renowned anthropologist Clifford Geertz likened culture to a spider's web of interconnected meanings that humans have spun. Music has been a vital part of such webs throughout the history of the West. Western Music in Context has as its goal to highlight such connections and to invite the instructors and students to continue that exploration on their own.

Walter Frisch
Columbia University

AUTHOR'S PREFACE

The one thing you can count on when you attend a concert of music branded as "contemporary," "modern," or "new" is that there is very little you can count on. It would not be surprising to hear works that challenge every assumption about traditional compositional practice, the boundaries of music and noise, and the roles of the composer, performer, and listener. Yet those expecting or fearing such unusual sounds and experimental styles may encounter pieces that seem unexpectedly familiar, evoking earlier epochs or borrowing from popular forms. The most surprising aspect of such a concert may be just how unsurprising much of the music is.

There has never been less agreement than there is today about how to draw boundaries between musical styles, how best to study music, and how to measure ideas such as historical importance, originality, and progress—or even whether such concepts still have validity. Some have found this situation profoundly exhilarating and stimulating; for others, it has provoked anxiety, despair, or the understandable desire to return to an innocent "golden age," before all the trouble started. That there would be strong disagreements about precisely what the trouble was, who was responsible for it, and when or if a "golden age" had occurred is one of the most distinctive features of musical life in the early twenty-first century.

To provide a starting point for understanding where we are and where we might be going, this book offers a selective overview of some important developments in music from the turn of the twentieth century to the present. As with the previous volumes in this series, our main concern will be with composers who saw themselves as building on, remaking, or rejecting the traditions of Western art music. But a main theme in the story of music in the twentieth and twenty-first centuries is the gradual breakdown of such borders, as musicians, ideas, technologies, and audiences increasingly have moved among very different cultural and geographic locales. Similarly, we will trace a dramatic transformation in composers' ideas of their audiences, just as the "we" who are reading this book includes a richness and diversity of backgrounds and perspectives that would have been unimaginable a hundred years ago.

Of course, composers and their works can be understood only in interaction with the people and institutions that will also figure centrally in this book, including performers, concertgoers, critics, publishers, patrons, scholars, schools, concert halls, instrument makers, and the media. All aspects of musical cultural are shaped by interactions with other art forms, with science and technology, and with economic, social, and political transformations and disruptions. By approaching Western music "in context," we can also consider how composers and their works have helped to define ideas of nation, race, and gender, and thus shaped our experiences and our world in both positive and negative ways.

Chapter 1 explores the origins and implications of what we will label a "sense of possibility." Over the fourteen chapters that follow we will observe composers, musicians, and audiences responding in very different ways to this notion that music could, or should, be quite "otherwise" than it had been customarily conceived. This has resulted in accelerating cycles of reaction and counter-reaction, as people challenge previous questions and solutions, sometimes ones that they themselves have proposed. Many of the ideas, styles, and techniques we will consider continue to be important possibilities for musical expression. Thus, while the book is organized chronologically, we will also be dealing with present-day concerns and issues throughout.

Chapters 2–4 trace the remarkable creative and cultural transformations that took place from the turn of the century through World War I (1914–1918), as many modernist artists felt the only way forward was to rework radically or simply jettison the past. Chapters 5–8 focus on the tumultuous period between the world wars and efforts to establish new foundations by reimagining or inventing musical languages and traditions. The years following the end of World War II in 1945, considered in Chapters 9–11, were marked by another phase of exploration. Driven by both the necessity of rebuilding and a desire to break with both old and new traditions, many composers were inspired by technological developments and scientific models of experimentation and research. Chapters 12–15 trace the diverse musical trends from the 1960s to the present, as all the musical possibilities of past and present seemed increasingly to coexist and intermingle.

The central themes of each chapter determine which composers and pieces are featured. As a result, many important figures are not included, and those who are included are not necessarily represented by their most well-known or characteristic pieces. Most chapters focus on one or two works that introduce central questions and that thus reappear as an organizing thread at several points throughout the discussion. For those who want to delve deeper into these and related works, twenty-six musical scores, each with detailed commentary, are included in the accompanying *Anthology for Music in the Twentieth and Twenty-First Centuries*. Links to recordings of anthology repertoire are available on StudySpace, Norton's online resource for students.

This book and the commentary in the accompanying anthology draw extensively on the flourishing body of scholarship on twentieth- and twenty-first-century music and broader cultural and social developments. To facilitate readability, endnotes are provided for direct quotations only; the selected readings at the end of each chapter identify key sources and useful starting points for further reading. An expanded bibliography is available on StudySpace. Frequent quotations from primary sources, many drawn from *Strunk's Source Readings in Music History*, offer vivid insights into the lived experience of the composers, musicians, and artists we discuss. For readers who wish to explore these sources in more detail, page references to both the single-volume and seven-volume editions of *Strunk* appear in parentheses after quotations drawn from this text. The glossary, which provides brief definitions of musical terminology, is intended for readers who may not have had previous coursework or training in music.

ACKNOWLEDGMENTS

This book is possible only thanks to the writings of all those scholars whose work informs the pages that follow. I am particularly grateful to the many colleagues who answered queries or offered feedback on portions on the text: T. J. Anderson, Lisa Barg, Elizabeth Bergman, Donald Berman, Jane Bernstein, Peter Burkholder, Joy Calico, Alessandra Campana, Theo Cateforis, Mark DeVoto, Barry Drummond, Jeremy Eichler, Joshua Fineberg, Alain Frogley, Sarah Fuller, David Gable, Gérard Gasarian, Perry Goldstein, Jason Hanley, Kassandra Hartford, Boris Hasselblatt, Deborah Heckert, Carol Hess, Stephen Hinton, Sonya Hofer, Kathleen Hulley, Miki Kaneda, Katherine Kaiser, Brian Kane, Elizabeth Keathley, Jamie Kirsch, Klaus Kropfinger, Sherry Lee, Paul Lehrman, Brian Locke, David Locke, Judy Lochhead, Tod Machover, Gayle Sherwood Magee, Marc Mandel, Margaret Martin, Drew Massey, Marilyn McCoy, John McDonald, Carol Oja, Thomas Peattie, Stephan Pennington, Alexander Rehding, Sindhumathi Revuluri, Joshua Rifkin, Gil Rose, Alex Ross, Kareem Roustom, Philip Rupprecht, Erica Scheinberg, Janet Schmalfeldt, Jennifer Shaw, Anne Shreffler, Joel Smith, Joseph Straus, Jane Sugarman, Judith Tick, Michael Ullman, Daniel Weymouth, Lloyd Whitesell, Peter Winkler, and Kirsten Yri. I owe special thanks to my prepublication reviewers—Sabine Feisst, Tamara Levitz, David Metzer, W. Anthony Sheppard, and an anonymous reviewer—for their encouraging words, for catching many errors, and for challenging me to figure out what I was trying to say. My deepest gratitude goes to Robert Morgan, whose seminars and writings first motivated me to focus on twentieth- and twenty-first-century music; his influence and inspiration is evident throughout this book.

Several current and former graduate and undergraduate students offered much useful feedback and assisted with the music examples and the preparation of the manuscript: Monica Chieffo, Eugene Clayton, Daniel Cooperman, Mike D'Errico, Stephanie Gunst, Brendan Higgins, Emily Hoyler, Kevin Laba, and David Stallings. I am grateful to the students in my Fall 2010 music history survey for their reactions to portions of the book, in particular Craig Flaster, Rachel Taranta, Sebastian Urrea, and Michael Zigismund. I am grateful to Tufts University for supporting this project through a research leave, a Faculty Research and Creative Activity Award; thanks also to the Ruth Lilly Music Library under the direction of Michael Rogan, and to the wonderful staff of the Department of Music.

This series has been a team effort from the start; I have benefited enormously from the opportunity to work with my fellow authors Margot Fassler, Richard Freedman, Wendy Heller, John Rice, and our ever-patient and visionary captain Walter Frisch. Just as crucial have been the contributions of the outstanding Norton team: Jack Borrebach, Ariella Foss, Harry Haskell, Courtney Hirschey, Justin Hoffman, Steve Hoge, Imogen Howes, Jane Miller, Graham Norwood, Stephanie Romeo, and the remarkable and inspirational Maribeth Payne.

Above all, I am grateful to my son and daughter Eric and Mary for introducing me to a lot of new music, and to my wife Edie for her many helpful comments on the text, musical insights, and constant support and encouragement all along the way.

MUSIC IN THE TWENTIETH AND TWENTY-FIRST CENTURIES

CHAPTER ONE

A Sense of Possibility

Debates about the attractions and dangers of the "new" have always been a factor in musical life. Writing 2,300 years ago, Plato warned of the political and social disruptions that would ensue if the "modes of music" were disturbed. In order to champion the new "sweetness" of the early-fifteenth-century works of Dunstable, Dufay, and Binchois, the composer and theorist Johannes Tinctoris dismissed all music written prior to 1430 as unworthy of performance. Johannes Brahms, who had been praised in 1853 by Robert Schumann for showing the way to "new paths," added his signature in 1860 to a declaration aimed at Franz Liszt and Richard Wagner that branded the works and theories of their New German School as "contrary to the most fundamental essence of music."

But beginning at the turn of the twentieth century and continuing to the present, it has become increasingly difficult for composers, performers, and audiences to avoid asking what it means for music to be "new," how and if we should preserve connections to the past, and where our musical cultures are headed. This chapter lays a foundation for understanding the diverse and often contradictory answers that have been proposed, as well as why such questions and answers might matter to us today.

TANGLED CHAOS AND THE BLANK PAGE

In the early decades of the twentieth century, some claimed that the only way forward for music and the other arts was to leave the past behind. Writing in 1931, the Hungarian composer Béla Bartók described a "turning point in the history of modern music" around 1900: "The excesses of the Romanticists began to be unbearable for many. There were composers who felt: 'this road does not lead us anywhere; there is no other solution but a complete break with the nineteenth century'" (SR 198:1438; 7/29:168). The Austrian-born Arnold Schoenberg proclaimed in 1910 that he had broken through all past artistic restrictions; three years later the Italian Futurist Luigi Russolo urgently sought to renovate music as an "art of noises." In an appeal for "new instruments and new music," the French-born American composer Edgard Varèse wrote in 1936: "We cannot, even if we would, live much longer by tradition. The world is changing, and we change with it" (SR 179:1340; 7/10:70).

Of course, many vehemently rejected such demands for change and the works that accompanied them. Audiences greeted the premieres of some of the most significant pieces in this book with riots and noisy opposition. A Berlin critic wrote in 1912 of Schoenberg's *Pierrot lunaire*, "if this is music of the future, then I pray my Creator not to let me live to hear it again." The Russian composer Sergei Rachmaninoff, famous for writing in a style that would have been at home in the nineteenth century, declared his refusal in 1939 "to cast out my musical gods in a moment and bend the knee to new ones."

Even among those who believed that something had to change, there was little agreement about how to move forward. Despite numerous attempts to identify new pathways, a defining characteristic of music since 1900 has been the lack of any single, unifying mainstream. This is evident in the maze of "isms" that figure in the pages ahead: Impressionism, Symbolism, Exoticism, Primitivism, Futurism, Expressionism, Neoclassicism, Serialism, New Romanticism, Modernism, Postmodernism, Minimalism, and Postminimalism. The same splintering exists in many styles of music today. At the time of this writing, for example, Wikipedia lists over 200 genres of electronic dance music. Under the heading "Psychedelic trance/Goa trance" (one of the subgenres of Trance), styles include Dark psytrance, Full on, Psyprog, Psybient, and many others.

Composition has never been easy, but for a surprising number of composers we will encounter in this book, it has at times seemed almost impossible. Bartók wrote in a letter to his wife in 1926 about his doubts of ever being "able to write anything new anymore":

> All the tangled chaos that the musical periodicals vomit thick and fast about the music of today has come to weigh heavily on me: the watchwords linear, horizontal, vertical, objective, impersonal, polyphonic, homopho-

nic, tonal, polytonal, atonal, and the rest; even if one does not concern
one's self with all of it, one still becomes quite dazed when they shout it in
our ears so much.

Just as all the colors of the prism can blend into a blinding white, this cacoph-
ony of choices threatened to result in a deafening silence. Igor Stravinsky
wrote in the 1940s of his need for self-imposed limits in the face of an "abyss
of freedom":

> As for myself, I experience a sort of terror when, at the moment of set-
> ting to work and finding myself before the infinitude of possibilities
> that present themselves, I have the feeling that everything is permissi-
> ble to me. If everything is permissible, the best and the worst; if nothing
> offers me any resistance, then any effort is inconceivable, and I cannot
> use anything as a basis, and consequently every undertaking becomes
> futile.

It is difficult to imagine any major composer before the twentieth century
having to confront so blank a page. And as we shall see, the range of choices
open to someone embarking on the journey of composition has continued to
expand far beyond anything Stravinsky could have contemplated. Yet while
some have reacted to this situation with despair, Bartók, Stravinsky, and all
those who figure in the chapters that follow managed to find their own solutions
to the challenges and opportunities in the tangled chaos of possibilities and the
blank page. Indeed, tangled chaos and blank pages have themselves become significant resources for reimagining what music might be.

MODERN, MODERNISM, MODERNITY

A major factor in the musical developments we will explore is the multifaceted
concept of Modernism. In its most common usage, Modernism refers to the
self-conscious search for new means of artistic expression that first emerged
in the decades around the turn of the twentieth century. The term *Modernism*
is thus distinct from the less-historically-specific label of "modern," which
has been applied to many musical trends throughout history. The notion of
modernity, discussed in greater depth in Chapter 2, concerns the broad transformations of culture and society associated with industrialization, science,
and technology. Trends associated with modernity date back to the end of the
Middle Ages, but in the years around 1900 there was a widespread sense in the

developed world that categorical changes were occurring in many aspects of daily life.

Modernism in the arts can thus be understood as one facet of the experience of modernity. Just as the world around them was changing, a number of painters turned away from realism, representation, and the finished surface to embrace abstraction and the free play of color and line. Many writers sought to liberate words from naturalistic narratives, as well as from conventional grammar and syntax, to allow a more immediate and powerful expression of inner truths. Music, with its inherent abstraction and its seeming ability to communicate independently of conventional languages, came to be regarded as the art form best suited to lead the way. As the English critic Walter Pater declared in 1873, "all art constantly aspires toward the condition of music." Many writers, painters, architects, and choreographers followed suit by seeking to develop analogs to music in their own art forms.

Ironically, of all the arts music was the most resistant to Modernist innovations, due to its highly codified theory, its conservatories, a firmly established canon of masterworks, and its social roles as entertainment and a means for display and cultivation. The composers we consider in Chapters 2–4 faced both external and internal opposition as they challenged long-held notions about the limits of artistic expression, ideals of beauty, and the meaning and purpose of art. Nevertheless, they and many others charted musical Modernism by questioning the system of functional tonality—the foundation of the common practice harmonic system that had governed classical music for centuries—and by opening up the boundaries between musical sound and noise, between disparate musical cultures, and between music and the other arts.

The many different meanings and connotations associated with the idea of Modernism limit its usefulness as an explanatory category. Thus, while Modernism is often linked to the avant-garde (originally a French military term for the troops who lead the charge), artistic developments usually labeled as Modernist have just as often been marked by a turn sideways or even in reverse, as is evident in the various "back to" or "neo" movements that we will encounter in this book. As we will see in Part II, for some the real beginnings of Modernism are to be found in the years between the world wars, typified by the emergence of Neoclassical trends, the rejection of Romanticism and Expressionism, and the renunciation of the radical styles from before World War I. Parts III and IV, which bring us from the end of World War II to the present, are marked by a multiplicity of "high," "anti-," and "post-" Modernist styles, with some proclaiming the end of Modernism, while others chart the continuation of the Modernist project under different guises.

As with all the "isms" in this book, it is better to think of Modernism not as an answer or an explanation, but as a starting point for discussion. Just as important, we should bear in mind that many significant musical developments in our period have little to do with Modernism as it is generally conceived.

BECOMING A "POSSIBILIST"

Another way to think about the destabilizing yet energizing condition of the blank page and the tangled chaos of unlimited choices is offered by the Austrian writer Robert Musil (1880–1942) in *Der Mann ohne Eigenschaften* (The Man Without Qualities), a novel he began in the 1920s and left unfinished at his death. Musil says very little directly about music or the other arts, focusing instead on politics, psychology, and ethics, but his insights are broadly applicable. The novel is set in Vienna, just before World War I swept away the Austro-Hungarian Empire and the tenuous stability it represented. Its central theme is the opposition between those who possess a sense of reality and an unquestioned belief that things are as they should be, and those who have what Musil calls "a sense of possibility." The protagonist of the book becomes a "man without qualities"— the word *Eigenschaften* in the title could also be translated as "particularities," "characteristics," or "properties"—through the realization that nothing *has* to be the way it is. Musil writes of this sense of possibility:

> Whoever has it does not say, for instance: Here this or that has happened, will happen, must happen; but he invents: Here this or that might, could, or ought to happen. If he is told that something is the way it is, he will think: Well, it could probably just as well be otherwise. So the sense of possibility could be defined outright as the ability to conceive of everything that there *might be* just as well, and to attach no more importance to what is than to what is not. The consequences of so creative a disposition can be remarkable, and may, regrettably, often make what people admire seem wrong, and what is taboo permissible, or, also, make both a matter of indifference. Such possibilists are said to inhabit a more delicate medium, a hazy medium of mist, fantasy, daydreams, and the subjunctive mood. Children who show this tendency are dealt with firmly and warned that such people are cranks, dreamers, weaklings, know-it-alls, or troublemakers.

Musil's ironic tone makes it difficult to tell whether he views the "creative" disposition of the "possibilist" as a positive or a negative trait. Writing in the shadow of two world wars, Musil was well aware of the seductions and perils of utopian thinking, the desire for change, and the quest for stability. Indeed, another central character in *The Man Without Qualities* is a psychotic murderer who has been driven mad by the same realization that everything might be completely different. It is precisely this ambivalence that makes the sense of possibility a helpful starting point for discussing the multiple trajectories and constant metamorphoses in music and musical life in the twentieth and twenty-first centuries. Indeed, at no other time would so many significant figures fall into one or more of Musil's categories of possibilists. One of the main themes in this book is that it is often those who were regarded as cranks, dreamers, weaklings, know-it-alls, and troublemakers who have had the most interesting things to say.

NEW POSSIBILITIES AND PERSPECTIVES

In borrowing the intentionally idiosyncratic concept of a sense of possibility from Musil, our goal is not to replace a problematic term like Modernism with one that is even more diffuse. The point is rather to broaden our perspective by alerting us to some of the surprising commonalities and contradictions that have emerged from composers thinking that music "could probably just as well be otherwise." This approach clarifies relationships between composers, works, and ideas that are usually kept separate by showing how they were responding in various ways to the same questions and problems. Thus in Chapter 4 we consider four quite different manifestations of the same possibility of making something new by delving deeply into ideas of the folk and the nation; for the composers in Chapter 8 the challenge was to create a sense of tradition and familiarity through original syntheses of diverse elements. We will see that an unexpected result of efforts between the world wars to create new musical systems of order and balance, discussed in Chapter 7, was that composers considered in Chapter 10 were led to explore the limits of systemization and thus to open up very different ways of hearing and thinking about sound.

COMPOSITIONAL TECHNIQUES AND THE URGE TO EXPLAIN

Starting with the notion of a sense of possibility can illuminate important aspects of musical Modernism while also showing points of contact between composers typically regarded as Modernist and those who continued to work in more traditional idioms. Modernism has been characterized in part by a disdain for an uncomprehending and intolerant public. While Musil's sense of possibility includes a strong component of the desire to break taboos and provoke, it also points to an underlying belief that others can be persuaded and ultimately won over. Many pieces in every style we will be considering made their way in the world accompanied by manifestos, theoretical treatises, and less formal publicity and propaganda. As with any historical documents, we need to consider such explanations, whether written by the composers themselves or by others in their circles, as part of the story and not as the final word. Like the rest of us, composers can be self-deluding, untrustworthy, and prone to changing their minds. Our goal is to understand why they felt the need to express themselves as they did in music and in words.

The urge to explain also reflects the fact that as compositional possibilities have expanded, the list of musical characteristics that can be taken for granted has shrunk. Correspondingly, composers have had to make conscious choices about how to proceed, resulting in blurred boundaries between the work, compositional techniques, and general theories about how music can be organized.

More than ever before, compositional practice for many Modernist composers since the early years of the twentieth century has been intimately intertwined with newly created and explicitly articulated compositional systems. Composing in this way is rarely as simple as following a formula, and the unintended consequences have often been just as important as the original intent. Yet such precompositional systems are crucial when every aspect of a work is the product of a deliberate choice. Determining the relevance of these systems to the experience of performers or audiences is another of the challenges we face in the chapters that follow. There have always been distinctions made between knowledgeable and naïve listeners, but composers in many styles assume some audience familiarity not only with features of the compositional technique but with specific precursor works.

Questions of compositional technique are just as significant for those working in more traditional styles as for those whose music was associated with Modernist developments. Many important composers do not fit well into the narratives of progress and stylistic experimentation that loom so large in music since 1900. In the broadest sense, only a tiny percentage of our culture's overall musical production could ever have been viewed as Modernist. From the perspective of the development of new compositional techniques, such "conservative," "traditionalist," or "moderate" composers stand outside what some historians have viewed as the mainstream of musical developments. From other perspectives, such as concert programming or recording sales, these composers might be seen as the real mainstream.

Yet, as we will see, the music and ideas of many of those who seem to have little to do with Modernism are inevitably shaped to some degree by the sense of possibility. While composers and artists can use any styles, materials, tools, and methods they choose, every choice—including the choice to compose in traditional styles—reflects the reality that it could have been otherwise. Decisions not to follow certain directions or use certain techniques can be just as strongly marked as decisions to do so. Even the refusal to take part in the crafting of narratives and "let the music speak for itself" reflects a judgment about the path music should take.

Composers who seem to have succeeded in escaping such self-consciousness still have to put their works before musicians and listeners—in the concert hall, on the radio, or on the Internet—who have themselves been exposed to a vast range of styles and possibilities. As noted earlier, many kinds of music have been characterized by the coexistence of multiple styles and "isms." In contrast to earlier understandings of history as a single trajectory or a long corridor moving forward in one direction, our experience of the past has been compared to exploring a mansion of countless rooms, each one leading to every other chamber. We can enter any room, make use of what is there, and leave. Thanks to smartphones and similar devices, millions now carry their musical mansions with them wherever they go.

POLITICAL AND SOCIAL CONTEXTS AND RAMIFICATIONS

As is the case with our own ways of thinking and hearing, composers' works and writings reflect their cultural and historical contexts as well as the inevitable limitations and prejudices that shaped their development. Yet there is no easy equation that determines the connections among conservative, radical, progressive, and reactionary political beliefs and artistic styles. Along with the language of emancipation and catharsis, artists have called for violent revolution, destruction, and purging. Untangling the ways in which music and art have opposed and supported authoritarian regimes and repressive ideologies is an important facet of the chapters that follow.

The hazy lack of consequence that might be implied by Musil's playful tone in his formulation of the sense of possibility should not distract us from how much is at stake. We will see many examples of the complex relationship between compositional developments and ideas with both constructive and destructive implications outside of the concert hall, conservatory, and classroom. It will also become clear that composers are no more or less generous, visionary, inspiring, opportunistic, or self-serving than others, though their status as artists sometimes gave their ideas greater impact or made them more prominent targets.

It is crucial to keep in mind that even the possibility of a sense of possibility was by no means available to all. Writing in her diary in 1899, 19-year-old Alma Schindler, who would go on to marry Gustav Mahler, despaired of becoming a composer after being disappointed by a concert of works by the French composer Cécile Chaminade: "I said to myself: rarely do you hear of female composers, but here's an exception to support me. . . . Now, after *this* concert, I know that a woman can achieve nothing, never ever." While, as we will see in Chapter 2, Alma Schindler did go on to considerable compositional achievements while overcoming great obstacles, there have no doubt been countless others whose circumstances meant that they never had a chance.

THE SENSE OF POSSIBILITY AND ITS LIMITS

Writing in 1968, the Italian composer Luciano Berio argued that "every meaningful work can be considered an expression of doubt." Throughout this book we will consider many composers whose works seem to embody a questioning sense of possibility and the idea that things could be otherwise. But their expressions of doubt inevitably leave unexamined many other assumptions about the nature of art, the human experience, and the world. As with everyone else, the ways composers, musicians, and listeners think and hear, and their conceptions of what is possible or impossible, are shaped and constrained by their social, economic, and cultural contexts.

For an example of how a composer can write a piece that offers a very different sense of what music might be, while at the same time illustrating blind spots and prejudices, let us consider *Golliwogg's Cake-Walk* from *Children's Corner* (1908), a set of piano pieces by Claude Debussy (1862–1918). After a lighthearted ragtime-style opening, the middle section of the piece features a satirical reworking of the instrumental Prelude to the opera *Tristan und Isolde* (Tristan and Isolde, 1859) by Richard Wagner (1813–1883). Debussy sabotages the original work's ponderous emotionality and seriousness with sudden intrusions of irreverent clowning.

This juxtaposition can be interpreted most literally as the fiercely nationalistic French composer's rejection of Wagner's music, and German music in general. At the same time, *Golliwogg's Cake-Walk* tells a more ambivalent story about Debussy's relationship to Wagner. At first glance, the opening measures appear to evoke ragtime's standard introductory flourish, which typically launches a steady left-hand pattern and a characteristic syncopated right-hand figure (Ex. 1.1). But on closer inspection we can hear that both the playfully diving arpeggio and the chordal accompaniment in measures 10–11 are permeated by the famous "Tristan" chord that opens Wagner's Prelude; indeed, they use precisely the same pitches as the original (Ex. 1.2). Such references to Wagner are found in many of Debussy's works and underscore the powerful attraction Wagner's music exerted on him—and why he felt the need to assert his independence so strongly.

Example 1.1: *Claude Debussy,* Golliwogg's Cake-Walk, *from* Children's Corner, *mm. 1–4*

Example 1.2: (a) *Claude Debussy,* Golliwogg's Cake-Walk, *m. 3;* (b) *"Tristan" chord from Richard Wagner,* Tristan und Isolde, *m. 2*

In a similar way, Debussy's allusion to the popular genre of ragtime has sharply contrasting connotations. When he wrote this piece, ragtime was extremely fashionable: the sheet music of *Maple Leaf Rag* (1899) by the African-American composer Scott Joplin had quickly sold more than a million copies. Debussy could have heard ragtime in minstrel shows and other popular entertainments in Paris, and through John Philip Sousa's band arrangements performed at the 1900 Universal Exposition. The "Golliwogg" of the title was a trendy rag doll caricaturing a blackface minstrel performer. The dolls had been around since the 1890s, but were first mass-produced in 1908, and no doubt strongly desired by Debussy's three-year-old daughter, for whom *Children's Corner* was written. The cakewalk, also then very much in vogue in Paris, was an African-American dance form that involved elaborate costumes with fancy dresses and white ties and tails. The cakewalk's intentionally exaggerated and comic movements, which Debussy depicts with sharp syncopations and abrupt breaks in continuity, appear to have originated on southern plantations as a way of mocking the behavior of genteel white society.

At a time when the cultures of classical and popular music were diverging ever more sharply, Debussy used the rhythmic vitality and syncopated energy of the African-American dance to poke fun at Wagner's solemnity. Yet though *Golliwogg's Cake-Walk* is clearly on one level a celebration of ragtime and the lightheartedness and novelty it represented for the French public, the humor and implied critique it embodies depend on an acceptance of both the essential incompatibility and the incommensurability of the two styles. Even as it challenges Wagner's vision for music, *Golliwogg's Cake-Walk* leaves many other racial, national, and class distinctions unquestioned.

Through its musical entanglements of constructions of French and German, European and American, high art and low art, fun and serious, and white and black, *Golliwogg's Cake-Walk* has a lot to say about both Debussy's world and our own. The depth and complexity of this little piece make clear that music's ability to raise questions and express doubts is more than just a *reflection* of what is going on in the "real world." Artistic representations and formulations have often helped shape the world, providing models and prototypes for racial, gender, national, and generational identities, and new forms of consciousness and "subjectivity"—in other words, for our most basic sense of self.

The cover of this book, from Tod Machover's *Death and the Powers: The Robots' Opera* (2011), offers an extreme present-day manifestation of this phenomenon. With a libretto by the American poet Robert Pinsky, the opera imagines a future world populated by robots that carry the downloaded personalities and memories of their human creators. The prologue begins with a Chorus of Operabots that enact a graceful mechanical ballet as they attempt to unravel the meaning of the word *death*. As we will see in Chapter 15, the work asks us to consider the exciting and chilling possibilities of our increasing interdependence with technology, only one of the many musical border crossings that define our lives today.

Coming to terms with even the small cross-section of musical developments we will be exploring offers considerable challenges. We must start from the realization that there is not just one story to be told, that the questions we ask will shape the answers we get, and that there will always be those possibilists saying, "It could probably just as well be otherwise." It is precisely this openness and uncertainty that make the music of the twentieth and twenty-first centuries so intriguing, while awakening us to the exciting and alarming potential that is in all of us to become possibilists as well. As Musil writes of the sense of possibility, "There is something quite divine about it, a fire, a soaring, a readiness to build, and conscious utopianism that does not shrink from reality but sees it as a project, something yet to be invented."

FOR FURTHER READING

Cook, Nicholas, and Anthony Pople, eds., *The Cambridge History of Twentieth-Century Music* (Cambridge: Cambridge University Press, 2004)

Dahlhaus, Carl, "'New Music' as Historical Category," in *Schoenberg and the New Music: Essays by Carl Dahlhaus*, translated by Derrick Puffett and Alfred Clayton, 1–13 (Cambridge: Cambridge University Press, 1987)

Fink, Robert, "Teaching Music History (After the End of History): 'History Games' for the Twentieth-Century Survey," in *Teaching Music History*, edited by Mary Natvig, 43–68 (Burlington, VT: Ashgate, 2002)

Morgan, Robert P., "Tradition, Anxiety, and the Current Music Scene," in *Authenticity and Early Music*, edited by Nicholas Kenyon, 57–82 (Oxford: Oxford University Press, 1996)

Morgan, Robert P., *Twentieth-Century Music* (New York: W. W. Norton, 1991)

Ross, Alex, *The Rest Is Noise: Listening to the Twentieth Century* (New York: Farrar, Straus, and Giroux, 2007)

Taruskin, Richard, *The Oxford History of Western Music*, vol. 4: *The Early Twentieth Century* and vol. 5: *The Late Twentieth Century* (Oxford: Oxford University Press, 2005)

Whittall, Arnold, *Exploring Twentieth-Century Music: Tradition and Innovation* (Cambridge: Cambridge University Press, 2003)

PART I

From the Turn of the Twentieth Century through World War I

Most of the composers considered in the first part of this book were born between 1857 and 1885, and thus initially took their bearings from cultural landscapes that had coalesced in nineteenth-century Europe, Russia, and the United States. As a result, their works and ideas are often understood as a continuation of well-established trends rather than a new beginning. Some historians speak similarly of a "long nineteenth century," beginning with the French Revolution in 1789 and extending to the outbreak of the "Great War" (1914–18), which precipitated so many of the momentous changes that we will consider in Part II.

The idea that the arts in the decades around 1900 could be seen as marking the close of an epoch is also implied by the frequently used French term *fin de siècle* (end of the century), which conveys a sense of things coming to a close, of decadence and overripeness. Many influential writings from the time contribute to this view, such as Max Nordau's book *Degeneration* (1892), which diagnosed a systemic decline in culture and society marked by what he regarded as the epidemic spread of the morbid tastes of a small elite. Oswald Spengler's widely read *The Decline of the West* (1918) argued that Western civilization had experienced an historically inevitable cycle of flourishing and decay.

Yet while there were many aspects of continuity with the nineteenth century in the music we will be considering, just as significant was the widespread feeling at the turn of the twentieth century that the world was changing and that artists had to respond, whether by striking out in new directions, defending all that seemed to be in danger of being swept away, or, most frequently, finding some common ground between the past and future. The cultural, social, and technological transformations of modernity, and the way these transformations unraveled established ways of living and thinking, brought not only anxiety and uncertainty but also the sense of rebirth, renewal, and new possibilities that marked the emergence of musical Modernism.

As we will see in Chapter 2, the gradual dissolution of centuries-old monarchies in many parts of Europe and in Russia in the years before World War I allowed for the formation of new national, ethnic, gender, and class identities. As the dominance of Austro-German music was challenged, there was a new openness to exciting and disruptive sounds from other cultures, popular styles, the folk, and even the noises of the city. Scientific breakthroughs also influenced composers: though the prospect was daunting, they grappled with new understandings of the immense spans of time and space through which we navigate in our daily lives, as well as the vast and mysterious expanses within our psyches.

Musical Modernism in these years can thus be understood not only as a response to and a manifestation of the disruptive experience of modernity, but as a multifaceted attempt to establish new forms of artistic expression that would make sense of a changing world. Chapter 3 deals with wide-ranging attempts by Schoenberg and his pupils Berg and Webern, Busoni, Strauss, Skryabin, and the Italian Futurists to unleash music's ability to express unconscious emotional sensations, rethink the theoretical bases of music, and align art with the new age of machines and technology. In Chapter 4 we will see composers seeking new inspirations and new foundations for their work by drawing on music of the folk, ideas of national identity, and the energizing force of the "primitive."

CHAPTER TWO

Expanding Musical Worlds

We begin with two works that open windows onto the dramatically expanding musical worlds of the turn of the twentieth century: Gustav Mahler's massive Third Symphony (1896) and Claude Debussy's set of three short piano pieces, *Estampes* (Prints, 1903). Though close contemporaries—Mahler lived from 1860 to 1911, Debussy from 1862 to 1918—the two composers were separated by language, their Austrian and French nationalities, and the expressive character of their music. While their compositions could hardly be more divergent, the similar problems and possibilities they encountered in figuring out how, what, and why to compose can help us understand the profound social and cultural transformations that made these years so stimulating and unsettling.

Much connects the music of Mahler and Debussy to the nineteenth century. Both composers were products of, and built their careers within, the dominant cultural institutions of the day. Mahler studied under Anton Bruckner at the Vienna Conservatory and shared an apartment with Hugo Wolf. Though Debussy was a rebellious student, he successfully completed his studies at the Paris Conservatoire and won its highest prize for composition. One can easily draw a line from Mahler's Third Symphony back to such works as Franz Liszt's *Faust Symphony* (1861), Hector Berlioz's *Symphonie fantastique* (Fantastic Symphony, 1830), and ultimately Beethoven's Ninth Symphony (1824). Debussy's *Estampes* can likewise be heard in the tradition of short programmatic character pieces for the piano going back to Robert Schumann and Felix Mendelssohn.

Yet still more important are all those facets of their music and thought that point to the emergence of new potentialities. We can see this in the ways Mahler and Debussy engage with so many aspects of modernity and the cultural, political, scientific, and technological developments that were transforming daily life at the turn of the twentieth century. We can hear it in the ways their works embrace new understandings of the vast expanses of space and time that exist both around and within us.

NEW INNER AND OUTER LANDSCAPES

With much of each year occupied by his duties as a conductor, Mahler composed most of his Third Symphony during the summer months, working in a small hut on the edge of a mountain lake near Salzburg (Fig. 2.1). At first glance this would seem to be a quintessential Romantic image: the solitary artist communing with nature to produce a work of genius. But Mahler's lakeside hut was less an idyllic refuge than a focal point for many of the conflicts with which he wrestled. His compulsion to retreat to the small, isolated space of this hut, or the several others he had built over the coming years, can be seen in part as a reaction to the dramatic expansion of his works and his sense of composition as the act of channeling immense forces. He described his Third Symphony as "a work of such magnitude that it actually mirrors the whole world"; he wrote of being gripped with terror while composing, feeling like an instrument played on by the universe. "Some passages of it seem so uncanny to me that I can hardly recognize them as my own work."

A listener to Mahler's Third Symphony is forced repeatedly to confront the overwhelming and unknown, as at the beginning of the fourth movement (see Anthology 1). For the first ten measures, all we hear are two low notes in the cellos and basses, slowly and softly alternating in irregular groupings that obscure the meter. Finally, out of the darkness, an alto voice intones, "O Mensch! Gib Acht!" (O man! Take heed!), the opening words of Zarathustra's "Midnight

Figure 2.1: *Gustav Mahler's composing hut on the Attersee, where he composed his Second and Third Symphonies*

Song" from Friedrich Nietzsche's philosophical novel *Also Sprach Zarathustra* (Thus Spoke Zarathustra, 1885). Mahler builds the vocal melody from the most basic elements—first a single note, then two. The accompanying harmonies are simple major and minor triads, but they are untethered from any tonal moorings, bumping against each other in strange combinations in the huge registral expanse that opens up. Eventually these scattered elements coalesce into something more familiar: a pair of horns moving in thirds in a serene folklike melody. Yet rather than providing an anchor, the ordinariness of the tune in this unfamiliar environment suggests something barely remembered from a far-off place or time. The movement ultimately returns to more conventional harmonic and melodic ground, but by the end everything dissolves back into its component parts, leaving us where we started, adrift in a dark space.

Debussy's *Estampes* likewise opens up an immense terrain of space and time. The first movement, *Pagodes* (Pagodas; see Anthology 2), evokes the Javanese gamelan orchestra Debussy first heard at the 1889 Universal Exposition in Paris. Instead of using traditional themes and harmonies, he layers circling wisps of exotic melodies that seem to go nowhere. In the second movement, *La soirée dans Grenade* (Evening in Granada), we find ourselves suddenly transported to Spain, bustling through shifting street scenes including an overheard habanera, a passing festival, and finally a hastily interrupted serenade, as if someone playing a guitar had to make a quick getaway. Debussy returns home in the closing *Jardins sous la pluie* (Gardens in the Rain), which is based on two well-known French nursery songs, but it is as if after these foreign travels he wants us to experience familiar scenes in new ways. As the composer wrote, "I want to sing my interior landscape with the naive candor of a child. This will always shock those who prefer artifice and lies."

MODERNISM, MODERNITY, AND "SYSTEMS OF HAPPINESS AND BALANCE"

To understand such works and the expanding worlds of Modernism and modernity, we need to consider why so many at the turn of the twentieth century felt that art, human nature, and the world itself were changing. In a chapter subtitled "Systems of Happiness and Balance" in *The Man Without Qualities*, Robert Musil challenges the notion that revolutions result from conditions gradually becoming so intolerable that a breaking point is reached. Rather, he argues that fundamental change is precipitated by "the loss of cohesion that bolstered the society's artificial peace of mind." Musil was writing about turn-of-the-century Vienna and the fragmentation of the Austro-Hungarian Empire along multiple fault lines of national and ethnic identity, religion, class, and gender. But the loss of cohesion that concerned him goes much deeper to include all the developments that are bound up with the idea of modernity.

Modernity refers in part to the massive changes brought about by the centuries-long processes of industrialization, urbanization, and expansion of technological infrastructure. These developments in turn called for a broad range of new institutions and bureaucracies to educate, manage, and entertain the emerging modern workforce. As the German sociologist Georg Simmel wrote in "Metropolis and Mental Life" (1903), the concentration of populations in large cities contrasted deeply with "the slower, more habitual, more smoothly flowing rhythm of the sensory-mental phase of small-town and rural existence."

Simmel describes the intellectual shields city dwellers create to protect themselves from the chaotic urban experience "and the tempo and multiplicity of economic, occupational and social life." In this light, we might also regard Mahler's composing huts as escapes from the cities where he built his conducting career and spent most of his time. Yet the nature that Mahler experienced was often an artificially constructed refuge: Because of his extreme sensitivity to noise, his family members were tasked with chasing away the birds, discouraging the peasants from sharpening their scythes, and keeping the village children at a distance. Ironically, Mahler's hut outside Salzburg is now surrounded by an RV park, with sunbathers crowding around his former sanctuary.

Modernity also involves the scientific and philosophical ideas that were transforming every sphere of life around the turn of the century. The writings of Charles Darwin, Nietzsche, Karl Marx, Albert Einstein, and Sigmund Freud challenged biblical authority, the political and economic structure of society, and accepted notions of the origins of the human species, the workings of the universe, and the structures of our psyches. Even the ground beneath people's feet was made foreign as Marie and Pierre Curie's research on radioactive decay dramatically extended estimates of the age of the earth to the mind-boggling figure of billions of years.

In light of such developments, and others to be discussed later, it is no wonder that there were many who perceived that the world was indeed changing around and within them. Musil describes "the immense but wholly unconscious effort human beings make just to preserve their peace of mind" as our seemingly stable existence threatens to dissolve "both outward into the inhuman distances of cosmic space and downward into the inhuman microspace of the atom."

> Looked at closely, it does seem to be an extremely artificial state of mind that enables a man to walk upright among the circling constellations and permits him, surrounded as he is by an almost infinite unknown, to slip his hand with aplomb between the second and third buttons of his jacket.

The loss of cohesion Musil describes is thus deeply interconnected with the sense of possibility, which along with opening up a seemingly infinite range of choices can engender a sense of disintegration and collapse. The Austrian writer Hugo von Hofmannsthal articulated this feeling in terms of a crisis of language in his famous *Lord Chandos Letter*, written in 1902. Hofmannsthal portrays the despair of a young writer who has "lost completely the ability to think or to speak of anything coherently":

> For me everything disintegrated into parts, those parts again into parts; no longer would anything let itself be encompassed by one idea. Single words floated round me; they congealed into eyes which stared at me and into which I was forced to stare back—whirlpools which gave me vertigo and, reeling incessantly, led into the void.

For Mahler, Debussy, and many others associated with musical Modernism, the elements of music threatened to dissolve in similar fashion: melodies crumbled into fragments, harmonic progressions broke apart into isolated chords, traditional forms ruptured at the seams, and the familiar boundaries between genres and styles became increasingly porous.

The Austrian painter Gustav Klimt (1862–1918), a close contemporary of Debussy and Mahler, depicted a similarly unsettling void in the painting *Philosophy*, which he completed in 1900 in response to a commission for the University of Vienna (Fig. 2.2). Instead of a representation of rationality, ordered thought, and logic, as his patrons might have been expecting, Klimt's *Philosophy* depicts humanity moving from birth to the grave in a dark, mysterious cosmos. The alarming figure who stares out at us from the lower edge has been compared

Figure 2.2: *Gustav Klimt,* Philosophy *(1900)*

to the singer in Mahler's "O Mensch!" movement, demanding that we confront our dissolution. Not surprisingly, the painting was rejected by the faculty amid attacks from art critics, such as, "Herr Klimt's latest work of Genius, now I beg you to try and think of something sensible in front of this picture. I can't—the walls are turning, and my stomach too. Help, where's the emergency exit!"

It is easy to mock such critics as shortsighted, but Musil's larger point is that few of us would or could choose to live our lives constantly aware of those huge expanses of the cosmos around us and the subatomic spaces within us. Instead, we all rely to varying degrees on what he calls our "systems of happiness and balance," made up of all the convictions, prejudices, theories, hopes, and beliefs we use to maintain our equilibrium in an unstable and changing world.

While many Modernist composers were compelled to challenge boundaries, search for the new, and disparage conventionally minded audiences, they were equally compelled to formulate their own systems of happiness and balance. Indeed, as we will see below in the works of Mahler and Debussy, it is often the case that the more strongly artists experienced the loss of cohesion, the more crucial it became for them to establish new ways of holding things together, both for themselves and for their listeners. One might argue that it is their ability to confront and ultimately transcend a sense of fragmentation and collapse that has made their music of such enduring interest.

GUSTAV MAHLER AND THE SYMPHONY AS WORLD

Mahler made a heroic struggle with the loss of cohesion central to the structure and meaning of his works. Born in Bohemia (then part of the Austro-Hungarian Empire, now part of the Czech Republic), Mahler often expressed a feeling of alienation, describing himself as "thrice homeless, as a native of Bohemia in Austria, as an Austrian amongst Germans, and as a Jew throughout the world. Always an intruder, never welcomed." Mahler's response to this sense of alienation and fractured identity was not to run away from it but to attempt to bring all that he experienced into his works. As he wrote, "To me 'symphony' means constructing a world with all the technical means at one's disposal." Throughout his career Mahler endeavored to integrate his Bohemian, Austrian, German, and Jewish identities, and we can hear the resulting tension as he brings together elements from the Austro-German symphonic tradition, lieder and song cycles, folk song and dance, marches, opera, and even Asian music at the end of his life in *Das Lied von der Erde* (The Song of the Earth, 1909).

The Third Symphony, which lasts over an hour and a half, calls for a huge orchestra, a women's choir, a boys' choir, and an alto soloist. In this and other works, Mahler attempted to reconcile the traditional idea of the symphony with the new genres that had emerged in the nineteenth century, including the multi-movement program symphony, the one-movement programmatic tone

poem, and other hybrid forms that incorporated elements of the song cycle, oratorio, and cantata. Part of the intellectual scaffolding of the Third Symphony
was an ambitious literary program that encompassed ideas from Darwin, the
philosopher Arthur Schopenhauer, and Nietzsche. The six movements enact an
evolutionary progression, with life developing through ever-higher forms:

> Introduction: "Pan awakes."
>
> I   "Summer marches in." (Bacchic procession.)
>
> II   "What the flowers in the meadow tell me." (Menuett.)
>
> III   "What the animals in the forest tell me." (Rondeau.)
>
> IV   "What man tells me." (Alto solo.)
>
> V   "What the angels tell me." (Women's chorus with alto solo.)
>
> VI   (Finale.) "What love tells me." (Adagio.)

Following the model of Beethoven's Ninth, the first three movements are
purely instrumental; the introduction of the alto soloist in the fourth movement, discussed earlier and in the Anthology, coincides programmatically with
the appearance of humankind. With characteristic incongruity, Mahler follows this mysterious and perplexing setting of Nietzsche's esoteric text with a
fifth movement that features bright ringing bells, simple folklike melodies and
harmonies, and a rambunctious children's choir singing a song from the early-
nineteenth-century folk anthology *Des Knaben Wunderhorn* (The Youth's Magic
Horn). In the original plan, the symphony was to end with a seventh movement,
"What the child tells me," using a soprano soloist singing a text from the same
source, but Mahler ultimately saved that for the final movement of his Fourth
Symphony. His decision to conclude the Third Symphony not with words but with
an instrumental movement as the highest point in the evolutionary progression
reflects his ambivalence toward the long-standing debates about the relative
merits of absolute versus program or vocal music. While he prepared programs
and incorporated vocal movements in many of his symphonies, he also continued to write purely instrumental music throughout his life. Mahler often later
sought to downplay the significance of the programs, describing them as only a
necessary expedient to assist listeners still unfamiliar with his style.

BUILDING BLOCKS, POPULAR BORROWING, AND POLITICS

The invocation of childhood in the last two movements of the Third Symphony
links Mahler's experiences as a child to the eclecticism and modular construction of his music. He described composing as "like playing with building blocks,
where new buildings are created again and again, using the same blocks. Indeed
these blocks have been there, ready to be used since childhood, the only time
that is designed for gathering." As Mahler's analogy suggests, the Modernist loss

of cohesion in his music can be traced to this feeling of ironic distance in his allusions to the music he heard as a child. He often treats these folk songs and military marches as objects that could be recombined in various ways, just as a visual artist creates a collage from existing materials. Mahler's approach to harmony can be understood from the same perspective. Unlike his contemporaries Richard Strauss and Aleksandr Skryabin (see Chapter 3), or, as we will see, his wife Alma, who composed extremely chromatic music with unusual chords and progressions, Mahler often worked with the most basic tonal materials, though usually treated in very unorthodox ways.

Mahler often breaks apart his musical forms to insert blocks of music that seem to come from somewhere else. In the Third Symphony, for example, the haunting "O Mensch!" music appears more than an hour earlier in the introduction to the first movement, where it is awkwardly juxtaposed with an opening fanfare played by eight French horns. Mahler also layers blocks on top of each other, allowing for very different types of music to sound simultaneously. Just before the recapitulation in the sonata-form first movement, an offstage musician plays a snare drum in the new tempo; Mahler explicitly directs the drummer to disregard the tempo of the basses and cellos, who are still finishing up the business of the development section.

Childhood memories also figure in Freud's account of his famous consultation with Mahler in 1910, which sheds light on what Mahler saw as the tendency for the most moving and emotional passages in his music to be interrupted "by the intrusion of some commonplace melody":

> His father, apparently a brutal person, treated his wife very badly, and when Mahler was a young boy there was a specially painful scene between them. It became quite unbearable to the boy, who rushed away from the house. At that moment, however, a hurdy-gurdy in the street was grinding out the popular Viennese air, *Ach, du lieber Augustin*. In Mahler's opinion the conjunction of high tragedy and light amusement was from then on inextricably fixed in his mind, and the one mood inevitably brought the other with it.

In the writings of Freud and others, discussed further in Chapters 3 and 4, we see the mind reimagined during these years as a mysterious and ultimately unknowable space within us, swirling with memories of past traumas and uncertainties and driven by uncontrollable forces.

The reference to the hurdy-gurdy also underscores the feeling, shared by Mahler and his audiences, that there was something transgressive about bringing music from the street and countryside into the concert hall. While he was working on the Third Symphony in 1896, Mahler wrote a letter to a friend that incorporated passages from bad reviews that he had received: "Everyone knows by now that some triviality always has to occur in my work. But this time it goes beyond all bounds. 'At times one cannot help believing one is in a low tavern or a stable.'"

There were also strong political implications in Mahler's borrowings at a time when mass movements were destabilizing the social equilibrium across Europe. Richard Strauss, for example, heard the exuberant marches in the Third Symphony as the rabble-rousing he associated with the socialist parades that displayed the growing power of the workers. In Mahler's Vienna there were increasingly noisy and occasionally violent movements across the political spectrum and among the various national identities that made up the empire. The Viennese novelist Stefan Zweig described in his memoir *The World of Yesterday* the shattering of a sense of security and order in all aspects of life, reaching even into the university, as "nationalistic rowdies" armed with heavy clubs drove "the Jewish, the Slavic, the Catholic, and the Italian students" out into the street.

We can see the complications of national, ethnic, and linguistic politics in Vienna in the fact that during his student years Mahler was part of a group that advocated German nationalism and admired Wagner, Nietzsche, and the politician Georg Ritter von Schönerer, who later founded the anti-Semitic Pan-German Party. Mahler's use of German folk songs and the poetry of *Des Knaben Wunderhorn* in his first four symphonies has been interpreted as a way of making explicit the national roots of his music while countering his feelings of alienation noted earlier. But his many hostile critics during these years rejected in explicitly nationalistic and anti-Semitic terms the "bizarre" and "grotesque" disjunctions between the "simple" and "naive" folk materials, and what they regarded as Mahler's overly intellectual technique and "nervous idiosyncrasies."

ALMA MAHLER AND THE NEW WOMAN

Mahler's eclectic borrowings and collage-like form seemed strange even to those sympathetic to his music. His future wife Alma wrote the following about the First Symphony in her diary not long before they were married: "An unbelievable jumble of styles—and an ear-splitting, nerve-shattering din. I've never heard anything like it. It was exhilarating all right, but no less irritating." Gustav Mahler met Alma Schindler (1879–1964) at a dinner party in 1901, and they were married a year later. She was instrumental in Gustav developing a close relationship with the composer Alexander von Zemlinsky, who had been her composition teacher, and with Zemlinsky's brother-in-law, Arnold Schoenberg. Alma also helped strengthen Gustav's links to the Modernist artists of the Viennese Secession; she was the stepdaughter of the painter Carl Moll and had been romantically involved with Gustav Klimt.

Gustav Mahler's relationship with Alma, like that between Robert and Clara Schumann in the mid-nineteenth century, shows how systems of happiness and balance often served to preserve the status quo. Mahler's retreat to his composing huts was also a withdrawal from the domestic sphere of his wife and children, and, before his marriage, from his sisters who had always managed his household.

A major destabilizing force at the turn of the century was the women's movement in Europe and the United States, which included campaigns for the right to vote, for economic, political, and sexual equality, and for an idea of the New Woman. Feminist writers such as Rosa Mayreder in *Toward a Critique of Femininity* (1905) argued for greatly expanded possibilities for women's life and work. Reactions against feminist movements were widespread and virulent, led by such famous misogynists as Otto Weininger, who in his influential *Sex and Character* (1903) wrote, "Away with the whole 'woman's movement' with its unnaturalness and artificiality and its fundamental errors."

Alma pursued her studies of composition and theory intensively and with considerable ambition; in a diary entry from 1900 she described the integration of song, recitation, and chorale in two recently completed works as "an entirely unique art-form." Yet the challenges faced even by a woman like Alma Schindler, who came from a privileged, well-connected background, with access to teachers and opportunities to compose, are clear from a note she wrote the year before:

> Why are boys *taught* to use their brains, but not girls? I can see it in my own case. My mind has not been schooled, which is why I have such frightful difficulty with everything. Sometimes I really try, force myself to think, but my thoughts vanish into thin air. And I really want to use my mind. I really do. Why do they make everything so terribly difficult for girls? That would be a goal for women: women's emancipation will never be possible, unless their minds are systematically trained, *drilled*. . . . Dear God, is there a place for me on this earth?

Her strongest challenge came from Gustav, who in a letter from December 1901 made it a condition of their marriage that she stop composing. Arguing that Alma lacked the "inherent and powerfully developed disposition" crucial for a creative artist, he described the idea of them both being composers as "ridiculous" and "degrading." He offered her instead the more familiar role of muse: "Would it mean the destruction of your life and would you feel you were having to forgo an indispensable highlight of your existence if you were to give up your music entirely in order to possess and also to be mine instead?"

Against the advice of her mother, who wanted her to break off the engagement, Alma agreed to give up composing. It was not until 1910 that Gustav realized the mistake he had made and encouraged her to publish the first of several sets of songs she had written much earlier. Alma's song "Die stille Stadt" (The Quiet Town) shows the sophistication of her harmonic thinking (Ex. 2.1).

Example 2.1: *Alma Mahler, "Die stille Stadt" mm. 1–3*

A town lies in the valley

Through its ambiguous opening chords, a half-diminished "Tristan" chord, and a secondary dominant on D♭, she sets up a tension between the main tonal center of D minor and keys a third higher and lower. Based on a text by the Modernist poet Richard Dehmel, who was also a favorite of Schoenberg and Anton Webern, "Die stille Stadt" uses the movement from tonal obscurity to bright clarity to depict a town closed in by an evening fog that grows increasingly threatening, until it is illuminated by a child's voice singing a hymn of praise.

DEBUSSY, SYMBOLISM, EXOTICISM, AND THE CENTURY OF AEROPLANES

Claude Debussy is one of the most interesting composers to consider from the perspective of Musil's notion of the systems of happiness and balance we use to deal with, or to avoid dealing with, the disruptions and loss of cohesion in our world. Though not given to over-dramatization, Debussy was remarkably attuned to the ways in which music and the world were changing, and he was driven by a strong nationalistic desire to nurture a specifically French music that he saw under fire from all sides. In a letter written in the fall of 1915, profoundly shaken by the savagery of World War I, in poor health, and just recovering from a year in which he had lost his "ability to think in music," he wrote: "One asks oneself at the moment whose arms music might be falling into. The young Russian school is extending hers, but, as I see it, they've become as un-Russian as could be. Stravinsky himself is leaning dangerously close to Schoenberg, though he remains the most wonderful orchestral technician of his age."

Like Mahler, Debussy responded to the multiplicity of choices by attempting to incorporate and synthesize an astonishing range of influences: eighteenth-century French composers like François Couperin and Jean-Philippe Rameau, avant-garde contemporaries like Erik Satie (see Chapter 6), new popular styles such as ragtime, music from around the world, ideas from Impressionist paint-ing and Symbolist literature, and the emerging technologies of sound recording and film.

SYMBOLIST POETRY AND IMPRESSIONIST PAINTING

Ideas from the other arts offered Debussy important strategies for reimagining a musical language that, as in Hofmannsthal's *Lord Chandos Letter*, was always on the verge of disintegrating into parts that could be configured in new ways. Debussy's focus on the sound and expressive effect of melody and harmony can be compared to the approach to words taken by Symbolist poets like Stéphane Mallarmé (1842–1898). Mallarmé saw in the crisis of language the potential of divorcing a word "from the direct and the palpable, and so conjure up its *essence* in all purity." In his poem "L'après-midi d'un faune" (The Afternoon of a Faun, 1876), literal sense is often secondary to the deeper resonances of the sounds of the words:

> . . . par l'immobile et lasse pâmoison
> Suffoquant de chaleurs le matin frais s'il lutte,
> Ne murmure point d'eau que ne verse ma flûte
> Au bosquet arrosé d'accords; . . .

> *This enervating swoon*
> *Of heat, which stifles all fresh dawn's resistance*
> *Allows no splash of water but that which my flute*
> *Pours into chord-besprinkled thickets . . .*

Mallarmé's use of musical imagery throughout the poem reflects his conviction that "the obscurity and ecstasy of sound" in music brought him closest to the true origins of poetry. When Debussy wrote his tone poem *Prélude à "L'après-midi d'un faune"* (Prelude to "The Afternoon of a Faun," 1894), he in turn created not a line-by-line account of the poem, but rather a "very free illustration" of the successive scenes of the text through which pass "the desires and dreams of the faun in the heat of this afternoon."

Debussy employs many techniques to separate his musical materials from their conventional meanings and allow us to experience music in new ways. His approach to harmony, in contrast to common-practice tonality, tends to treat chords as individual sounds rather than as components of a func-tional progression. Thus, for instance, in *Nuages* (Clouds) from his orchestral *Nocturnes* (1899), he writes chains of dominant seventh chords moving in par-allel motion, without the implication that the dissonances need to resolve. It follows that once chords are divorced from their role in functional progres-sions there is less incentive for harmonies to change. Many of Debussy's works feature extended passages that are harmonically static due to the use of pedal points and ostinato figures, including the first 14 measures of *Pagodas* and most of *Evening in Granada*.

Debussy's melodies, as in *Pagodas* or the opening of *Prelude to "The Afternoon of a Faun,"* tend to be short and static, often circling back to where they began rather than creating the directional sense of tension and repose associated with traditional thematic phrase structure. His avoidance of strongly goal-directed melodies stems from his interest in pitch collections that lack the clear hierarchies and functional implications of major and minor scales. The extended pentatonic passages in *Pagodas*, and his many pieces that use the various modes, convey this preference for scales that lack the leading tone so central to traditional harmonic relationships.

Debussy also worked with whole-tone scales (which can be reduced to two collections: C–D–E–F♯–G♯–A♯; and C♯–D♯–E♯–G–A–B), and octatonic scales (with their alternating whole steps and half steps; the three basic forms are: C–C♯–D♯–E–F♯–G–A–B♭; C♯–D–E–F–G–A♭–B♭–B; and C–D–E♭–F–F♯–G♯–A–B). With the whole-tone scale, the absence of a leading tone means that any one of the six pitches can be made the focus simply through emphasis or repetition. With the octatonic scale, the possibility of building triads and seventh chords at four different points allows multiple pitches to be established as central poles of attraction. (The octatonic scale is discussed further in Chapter 4.) In all but a few cases, Debussy showed little interest in remaining within any one scale, preferring instead a subtle interchange among diatonic, whole-tone, and octatonic elements.

Debussy also downplayed conventional modulation to different keys as a way of creating form and direction. Major and minor scales have the very significant property of producing a different set of pitches at every level of transposition, which underlies our sense of closely and distantly related keys. For example, transposing a C-major scale up a perfect fifth to G major preserves six pitches; only the F is changed to F♯. Transposing C major up a half step to D♭ major results in only two pitches in common. In contrast, whole-tone and octatonic scales offer greatly reduced possibilities for modulation. A whole-tone scale transposed by a whole step produces exactly the same set of pitches, as is the case with a transposition by a major third. The only place to modulate is to the other whole-tone scale. Whole-tone and octatonic scales in the nineteenth century were generally reserved for special harmonic effects or depictions of the supernatural or strange, in particular in the music of Russian composers such as Nikolay Rimsky-Korsakov (see Chapter 4). But for Debussy, Stravinsky, and others, the unusual characteristics of these and other collections greatly stimulated the formation of new sounds and structures.

Instead of relying on melodic development, harmonic progression, and modulation to build large-scale forms, Debussy explored several alternative techniques inspired by other art forms, including the paintings of French

Impressionists such as Claude Monet (1840–1926) and related artists such as the American-born James MacNeil Whistler (1834–1903). Like the Symbolist poets, the Impressionist painters aspired to musical effects; Whistler, for example, evoked music in the titles of paintings such as *Symphony in Gray* and *Nocturne in Blue and Green*. Though Debussy rejected the label of Impressionism, which art critics coined to deride the "unfinished" quality of Monet's paintings, he often described his music in visual terms that recall the techniques of the Impressionists. Thus he characterized his *Nocturnes* as designating "all the various impressions and the special effects of the light that the word suggests."

Impressionist painters were concerned less with the specific object depicted than with the temporal and spatial dimensions of the act of viewing, and the play of light, shadow, and color. Monet examined these phenomena by painting similar scenes at different times of day, such as his remarkable series of over twenty paintings of haystacks from around 1890 (Fig. 2.3). The point is not that these were particularly interesting or attractive haystacks; on the contrary, the goal was to reveal the depth of experience accessible through close attention to the most mundane objects. In a similar way, Debussy's approach to melody and harmony allows us to hear familiar intervals and chords as if for the very first time.

In a kind of musical analogy to Monet's representations of the same haystack in changing atmospheric conditions, Debussy presents his melodies in various harmonic, textural, and timbral settings. The *Prelude to "The Afternoon of a Faun,"* for example, starts with three statements of a flute melody in different harmonic contexts, so that we hear the same sequence of pitches in new ways each time. The idea of building up a piece not by harmonic or melodic development but rather through contrasts in rhythm, texture, dynamics, and register becomes even more fundamental in *Pagodas*. While echoing the static pitch content of gamelan music, Debussy sheds new light on the same simple repeating pentatonic melodies by presenting them in an astonishing range of figurations (see Anthology 2). Whereas Monet's art form required a separate painting for each moment of the day, Debussy's music can make us experience the changes in real time. As he wrote: "collect impressions . . . that's something music can do better than painting: it can centralize variations of colour and light within a single picture."

EXOTIC BORROWINGS

The evocations of Asia in Debussy's *Pagodas* mirrored the Parisian vogue for Oriental art in the late 1800s. Debussy was an avid collector of the Japanese prints and engravings that gave *Estampes* its title; his 1905 orchestral work *La mer* (The Sea) was inspired by a woodblock print by the great Japanese artist Hokusai (1760–1849). When he published *Estampes*, he took great care with the colors and fonts for the title page to make it a luxury object comparable to the Japanese-inspired clothing, chic cuisine, and artworks by Édouard Manet, Whistler, and others sought after by fashionable Parisians.

Figure 2.3: *Claude Monet,* Haystacks *(1890–1891)*

The widespread interest in exotic cultures exemplifies Musil's systems of happiness and balance, in this case as a way of coming to terms with and rationalizing the implications of imperialist expansion at the turn of the century. Between 1880 and 1914, technological and scientific advances allowed the European powers, the United States, and Japan to colonize vast areas of Africa,

Asia, the Middle East, and the Indian subcontinent in order to gain access to raw materials and open new markets. These cultural and material riches were showcased in world's fairs such as the 1889 Universal Exposition, which featured replicas of villages from Vietnam, Tunisia, Algeria, and other French colonies. Such ethnographic exhibits helped propagate the racist theories of cultural evolution that underpinned and justified the processes of colonization. The inhabitants of less technologically developed nations were regarded as representing earlier stages in the development of the human species from savagery to barbarism to civilization. Thus while modernity was experienced most directly by people in the urban environments of the developed world, through colonialization it had a direct or indirect impact on virtually everyone.

The history of Western music is full of encounters with exotic styles, but a new attitude toward these musics is a defining characteristic of Modernism and modernity at the turn of the twentieth century. For many of Debussy's contemporaries, music of non-Western cultures was primarily of anthropological interest, better suited to a museum of natural history than the concert hall. But Debussy treated other traditions as art forms in their own right, as well as resources for his own musical thinking. He observed of the Javanese music he heard at the 1889 Universal Exposition that it "obeys laws of counterpoint that make Palestrina seem like child's play. And if one listens to it without being prejudiced by one's European ears, one will find a percussive charm that forces one to admit that our own music is not much more than a barbarous kind of noise more fit for a traveling circus" (SR 197:1435; 7/28:165).

In some ways *Pagodas* is comparable to other Exoticist works from the turn of the century, such as Maurice Ravel's orchestral song cycle *Shéhérazade,* also composed in 1903. The text of Ravel's first movement, *Asia,* based on a poem by Tristan Klingsor, brings together fantasies of a vaguely defined "Orient" with references to Persia, China, and India. Ravel simulates exotic musical travels by incorporating clichéd "Asian" pentatonic melodies and "Middle-Eastern" augmented seconds like unusual spices added to a familiar tonal harmonic language.

Yet in *Pagodas* we hear Debussy's willingness to engage more substantively with other traditions in order to expand and transform his own musical language in profound ways. Inspired by the percussive sounds and stratified layers of Javanese gamelan music, he explores techniques for using textural contrasts to create form and movement in a context with limited melodic and harmonic development. And while he does not abandon tonality entirely, most of his melodies and the elaborate accompanimental figurations are based on the characteristic five- and seven-note Javanese scales. Debussy's productive encounter with gamelan music, here and in works such as the piano piece *Cloches à travers les feuilles* (Bells through the Leaves) from *Images* (1907), set the stage for many other composers we will be considering throughout the century, including Ravel, Colin McPhee, Benjamin Britten, György Ligeti, and Steve Reich.

TECHNOLOGY AND THE GENIUS OF ENGINEERS

Alongside displays of non-Western cultures, the 1889 Universal Exposition featured some of the latest technological marvels of modernity, including the newly completed Eiffel Tower. Debussy, writing in 1913, saw in technology both a challenge and an opportunity for art:

> Is it not our duty . . . to try and find the symphonic formulae best suited to the audacious discoveries of our modern times, so committed to prog-ress? The century of aeroplanes has a right to a music of its own. Let those who support our art not be left to waste away in the lowest ranks of our army of inventors, let them not be outdone by the genius of engineers! (SR 197:1433; 7/28:163)

The genius of engineers was evident everywhere in the mind-boggling achievements of these years. The telephone was patented by Alexander Graham Bell in 1876; the 1889 Universal Exposition included a pavilion of telephones transmitting live musical performances from the Opéra Comique, with visi-tors paying 50 centimes for ten minutes of listening. By 1902 wireless telegraph messages had been sent thousands of miles across the Atlantic. Thomas Edison demonstrated the first incandescent light bulb in 1879; a decade later small, cen-tralized power systems could be found across the United States. Debussy's "cen-tury of aeroplanes" was launched with the Wright brothers' successful flight of a heavier-than-air, self-powered aircraft in 1903, and the Brazilian pilot Alberto Santos-Dumont became a celebrity with a flight in Paris in 1906.

Automobile manufacturing firms were established in Europe in the 1890s, with the first mass-produced automobiles rolling off the assembly lines in 1901. Similar techniques of mass production had transformed the piano into an essential feature of a cultivated household by the middle of the nineteenth century. A still more fundamental transformation occurred in the early years of the twentieth century as increasingly sophisticated player pianos accounted for a major share of the market. Among the many composers who tried out the technologically advanced Welte-Mignon Reproducing Piano were Debussy and Mahler, whose meticulously preserved performances can still be heard today.

The technology that made the greatest impact on music was recording. Edison started mass-producing phonographs in 1888, and by 1902 a recording of the great opera singer Enrico Caruso sold a million copies. Marches and opera excerpts dominated early releases, but other repertories were explored as well, includ-ing non-Western musics, such as the recordings of Chinese music that Mahler reportedly received when he was composing *Das Lied von der Erde* in 1908–09.

Yet just as some were troubled by the implications of the player piano that one could "play" without any special training or discipline, recorded music's easy accessibility was also viewed as a threat; Debussy wrote in 1913 about shops in

Paris where for a small fee one could listen through ear tubes "to famous pieces of music as easily as one can buy a glass of beer." While he again praised the genius of engineers in making such technology possible, he worried about what would be lost with "this domestication of sound, this magic preserved in a disc" that anyone could "awaken at will." "Will it not mean a diminution of the secret forces of art, which until now have been considered indestructible?"

Another innovation of special import to Debussy was film, a technology pioneered in France. As the composer wrote in 1913, "There remains but one way of reviving the taste for symphonic music among our contemporaries: to apply to pure music the techniques of cinematography" (SR 197:1434; 7/28:164). A new aspect of film (that we now take for granted even though it was particularly perplexing for early viewers) was the rapid shift in perspective produced by splicing together film shot from different angles. In a vivid example of the destabilizing aspects of modernity, audiences who had experienced only the here and now suddenly found themselves seemingly moved without transition to a different point in space and time. We can hear an example of a "cinematic" edit in the middle section of *Golliwogg's Cake-Walk*, where Debussy mimics the effect of splicing together a film of Wagner's *Tristan* with scenes from a minstrel show. Such filmic editing effects can also be heard in the kaleidoscopic form of works like *Evening in Granada*, with its sudden alternations of very different types of music.

That Mahler would experience a sense of terror in his tiny hut as he struggled to wrestle the universe onto the blank pages of his score, or that Debussy would feel the need for a new art form like film to show composers the way out of the "disquieting labyrinth" in which they were trapped, says much about the challenges composers faced in representing and reconciling themselves with both modernity and their rapidly expanding musical worlds. Their success in integrating this multiplicity of influences, ideas, and sounds from the past and present into works that have spoken to a century of listeners is evident in the central place both eventually gained in the concert repertoire, while their distinctive techniques and approaches have continued to inspire composers in many styles down to the present day. Yet as we will see in Chapters 3 and 4, there were other composers in the early years of the twentieth century who responded to the same loss of cohesion and sense of possibility by calling into question the basic premises of music in ways that have proven more resistant to broad acceptance.

FOR FURTHER READING

Botstein, Leon, "Gustav Mahler's Vienna," in *The Mahler Companion*, edited by Donald Mitchell and Andrew Nicholson, 6–38 (Oxford: Oxford University Press, 1999)

Fauser, Annagret, *Musical Encounters at the 1889 Paris World's Fair* (Rochester: University of Rochester Press, 2005)

Frisch, Walter, *German Modernism: Music and the Arts* (Berkeley: University of California Press, 2005)

Fulcher, Jane, *French Cultural Politics and Music from the Dreyfus Affair to the First World War* (Oxford: Oxford University Press, 1999)

Hobsbawm, Eric, *The Age of Empire: 1875–1914* (New York: Vintage Books, 1989)

Kandel, Eric R., *The Age of Insight: The Quest to Understand the Unconscious in Art, Mind, and Brain from Vienna 1900 to the Present* (New York: Random House, 2012)

Kern, Stephen, *The Culture of Time and Space: 1880–1918* (Cambridge, MA: Harvard University Press, 1983)

Knapp, Raymond, *Symphonic Metamorphoses: Subjectivity and Alienation in Mahler's Re-Cycled Songs* (Middletown, CT: Wesleyan University Press, 2003)

Leydon, Rebecca, "Debussy's Late Style and the Devices of the Early Silent Cinema," *Music Theory Spectrum* 23 (2001): 217–241

Morgan, Robert P., "Secret Languages: The Roots of Musical Modernism," *Critical Inquiry* 10, no. 3 (1984): 442–461

Mueller, Richard, "Javanese Influence on Debussy's *Fantasie* and Beyond," 19th-Century Music 10, no. 2 (1986): 157–186

Painter, Karen, ed., *Mahler and His World* (Princeton: Princeton University Press, 2002)

Schorske, Carl E., *Fin-de-siècle Vienna: Politics and Culture* (New York: Vintage, 1981)

CHAPTER THREE

Making New Musical Languages

For many in the early years of the twentieth century, the concert hall and opera house were sanctuaries from the destabilizing forces of modernity. Yet even there it was hard to escape a feeling that traditional structures were threatened as Modernist artists pushed ever harder against established ideas of beauty and the limits of artistic expression. Composers extended and rethought existing techniques in innovative ways, while exploring the possibilities of creating new musical languages. Motivated by ideologies of progress and evolution, skepticism toward traditional rules and boundaries, and a conviction that their efforts were vitally important, they opened up their works to a vast emotional territory, ranging from ecstasy and spiritual apotheosis to uncertainty, pain, and even violence.

While some listeners were stimulated and inspired by this music, it was not uncommon for premieres in the years around 1910 to provoke vociferous and occasionally violent opposition from audiences and critics. Even composers sympathetic to the newest trends sometimes regarded each other's music as wrong-headed or incomprehensible. Gustav Mahler, who had come close to a physical altercation in attempting to silence dissenters at a performance of Arnold Schoenberg's music, confessed that he was unable to read the score of his First String Quartet, Op. 7 (1905). Richard Strauss, who had also shown interest in Schoenberg's early music, remarked in 1911 that the Austrian would be better off shoveling snow than scribbling on music paper. Alma Mahler, who would later become one of Schoenberg's strongest supporters, referred to him in her diary in 1900 as an "aberration," describing his Two Songs, Op. 1 (1898) as "unbelievably showy but without the slightest concession to an ear accustomed to melody. Flabbergasting, mind-boggling. Not a crescendo reaches its peak smoothly. By no means uninteresting—but beautiful . . . ?"

Many listeners today no doubt share their perplexity when faced with the works we will be discussing here and in Chapter 4. Our purpose is to understand why a significant number of composers working in quite different traditions and locales during these years came to feel that the existing musical languages were inadequate, and how they found new solutions for moving forward that have energized musical developments ever since.

ATONALITY, POST-TONALITY, AND THE EMANCIPATION OF THE DISSONANCE

In a 1910 review of Schoenberg's Three Piano Pieces, Op. 11 (1909), one critic declared that a line had been crossed: "Debussy only threatens; Schoenberg carries out the threat." The reviewer went on to describe the work as "a methodical negation of all heretofore accepted musical rules, [a] negation of syntax, of a conception of tonality, of all valid tonal systems." It may come as a surprise that the critic was essentially restating Schoenberg's own remarks about his music in the concert program: "Now that I have set out along this path once and for all, I am conscious of having broken through every restriction of a bygone aesthetic."

Far from simply "negating" the rules as we shall see, Schoenberg endeavored to refine his musical language in order to express the most profound truths. Yet while the first two movements of the Three Piano Pieces preserve many traditional thematic and formal features, the critic's remarks were accurate about the degree to which the third movement of Op. 11 jettisons traditional assumptions of how music should work (Fig. 3.1). Lasting just over two and a half minutes, the piece moves without transition between fierce outbursts and moments of sudden calm. There are no themes or melodies in the usual sense, and indeed very little repetition of any sort that listeners might use to orient themselves.

Most unsettling is Schoenberg's highly dissonant harmonic language, which dispenses with a tonal center and any sense of resolution. Not only does the piece exclude the functional harmonic progressions of tonality, but the individual harmonies have little to do with familiar triads or seventh chords. Schoenberg himself struggled to explain jarring sonorities like the ten-note chord that appears in measure 4: Bb–Db–E–F♯–A–C–F–Ab–B–D. "Laws apparently prevail

Figure 3.1: *Arnold Schoenberg, autograph manuscript of Op. 11, No. 3*

here," he wrote in his treatise *Harmonielehre* (Theory of Harmony, 1911), but "what they are, I do not know."

As we will see in Chapter 7, Schoenberg spent more than a decade developing his twelve-tone method, which was finally introduced in 1923. He later described the method as an attempt to "know *consciously* the laws and rules which govern the forms" that he had conceived "as in a dream." But the twelve-tone method operated according to very different principles than works like the Three Piano Pieces, in which the mystery and spontaneity of Schoenberg's musical language were essential facets of its meaning. In the 1902 *Lord Chandos Letter* discussed in Chapter 2, Hugo von Hofmannsthal's character sees a mysterious new tongue as the solution to the crisis of the dissolution of language. His only hope for a language that would once again allow him to write and think is one in which "not a single word is known to me, a language in which mute objects speak to me and in which perhaps one day, in the grave, I will have to give an account of myself before an unknown judge." That such a language by definition could not be understood in conventional ways was precisely the point.

Although many attempts have been made to explain the new conceptions of melody and harmony that emerged in the early twentieth century, composers and scholars have failed to agree about how even to label such music. Along with *free atonality* and *contextual atonality*, the term most frequently used today is *post-tonal*, which suggests that something has changed without attempting to specify what it is. Schoenberg disliked the term *atonality* because it emphasized what the music was not, rather than what it was. He preferred to speak of an all-inclusive *pantonality* and often used the phrase "the emancipation of the dissonance," believing that the richness of the harmonic series shows that dissonances are only more remote consonances and not something categorically different.

There is also still no consensus as to whether we should regard the music discussed in this chapter and the next as representing a break with tonality, a breakdown of the tonal system in general, an extension of tonal practice, or merely a temporary detour taken by a few misguided composers. As we will see throughout this book, the debate itself has been enormously stimulating for compositional developments down to the present.

The issue is further complicated by the different meanings attached to the word *tonality*. It is no coincidence that this questioning of basic assumptions about how music worked in the early twentieth century was paralleled by the creation of the most ambitious theories of tonal music by such figures as Hugo Riemann (1849–1919), Heinrich Schenker (1868–1935), and Schoenberg himself. For some theorists the presence of any pitch-centricity that creates the effect of a tonic is enough to make music tonal; for others, tonality requires common-practice functional harmonic progressions, along with traditional voice-leading and dissonance treatment. Similarly, some scholars of post-tonal music have advocated analyzing works like Schoenberg's Three Piano Pieces in terms of a completely autonomous system of contextually defined intervallic relationships, known as pitch-class set theory, while others have developed hybrid approaches that consider the continuing influence of elements of tonality. For our purposes, it is important to recognize the diversity of harmonic practice as composers pursued their own paths toward a music that seemed to keep pace with their rapidly changing inner and outer worlds.

BUSONI'S NEW AESTHETIC OF MUSIC

The Italian-born composer and pianist Ferruccio Busoni (1866–1924) inspired many composers to establish new starting points for their works. Entering the Vienna Conservatory at the age of nine, Busoni quickly came to the attention of such nineteenth-century luminaries as Johannes Brahms and Eduard Hanslick, laying the groundwork for a distinguished career. Busoni produced a substantial body of works defined by a remarkable pluralism and a creative engagement with the past, including his massive Piano Concerto (1904) and his solo piano piece *Fantasia contrappuntistica* (Contrapuntal Fantasia, 1910), inspired by J. S. Bach's *The Art of Fugue*. But his 1907 treatise *Entwurf einer neuen*

Ästhetik der Tonkunst (Sketch of a New Aesthetic of Music) also showed the way to a more radical break with tradition. He begins the treatise by challenging the idea that composers should be governed by eternal truths and principles, arguing instead that music was a very young art, "perhaps in the earliest stage of a yet unforeseeable development" (SR 176:1321; 7/7:51).

In his critique of conventional understandings of the tonal system, Busoni derided the strict differentiation between consonance and dissonance, and advocated replacing the system of 24 major and minor keys with 113 ways of dividing the octave into seven-note scales. Going still further, Busoni predicted that increasingly smaller microtonal divisions would replace the 12 pitches of the chromatic scale. As evidence that this was not a fantasy of the future, he pointed to the Dynamophone, or Telharmonium, a path-breaking electrical instrument that could precisely produce an "infinite gradation of the octave."

Invented by the American Thaddeus Cahill and first put on public display in New York City in 1906, the massive 200-ton device used large rotating magnets to produce sounds that could be controlled by keyboards and transmitted by phone lines. In 1911 the instrument was installed in New York's Telharmonic Hall with the intention of creating a subscription service that would bring music into businesses and homes via a wire, thus anticipating by a half-century the development of cable television and associated technologies. (Technological and financing problems caused Cahill's plan to fizzle within a few years.) But just as Busoni chose not to pursue microtonal possibilities in his own music, the Telharmonium was employed primarily to transmit well-known tonal works.

FUTURISM AND *THE ART OF NOISES*

The idea that technology could help remake the language of music became the focus of a group of artists known as the Italian Futurists. In his 1913 manifesto *L'arte dei rumori* (The Art of Noises), the Futurist composer Luigi Russolo (1885–1947) argued that music had to adapt to the modern world. Writing that listeners were satiated with having their hearts wrung by Beethoven symphonies and Wagner operas, he claimed that greater pleasure could be derived from "combining the noises of street-cars, internal-combustion engines, automobiles, and busy crowds than from re-hearing, for example, the 'Eroica' or the 'Pastorale'" (SR 177:1330; 7/8:60).

Futurism, which originated in Italy before World War I, with related movements springing up shortly afterward in Russia and elsewhere, involved all the arts: Russolo started out as a painter; Filippo Tommaso Marinetti (1876–1944) was a poet; along with Russolo, the most active composer in the group was

Francesco Balilla Pratella (1880–1955). The writings of the Futurists illustrate how the search for newness in art could be bound up with destructive and even pathological ideas. Marinetti's *Futurist Manifesto* (1909) explicitly endorsed war, violence, and misogyny: "We will destroy the museums, libraries, academies of every kind, will fight moralism, feminism, every opportunistic or utilitarian cowardice." After World War I, he and other Futurists became active supporters of Mussolini and the Fascists.

While the Futurists were ultimately limited in their achievements, their vision of an "art of noises" has had lasting impact. The Futurists' conception of noise is one consequence of the radical expansion of the limits of harmony during these years: If any combination of pitches could have musical potential, then any sound or noise could also be considered music. Percussion instruments with indeterminate pitch had been used throughout history, and the sounds of the environment had already made their way into opera houses through such "special effects" as wind and thunder machines, anvils, and church bells. But for Russolo and the Futurists, the noises of the modern world should become the primary material of music: "We shall amuse ourselves by orchestrating in our minds the noise of metal shutters of store windows, the slamming of doors, the bustle and shuffle of crowds, the multitudinous uproar of railroad stations, forges, mills, printing presses, power stations, and underground railways" (SR 177:1331; 7/8:61).

The Art of Noises divides the universe of sound into six categories based on the sound's mode of production: explosions and roars; hisses and whistles; whispers and bustling; screeches and friction; percussive impacts; and the voices of humans and animals. The Futurists constructed a corresponding set of noise machines, or *intonarumori*, including the *Gracidatore* (Croaker), the *Ululatore* (Howler), and the *Sibilatore* (Whistler), which produced sounds mechanically powered by the turning of cranks or the pumping of levers. Replicas of the instruments can be seen in operation, though not heard, in the 1993 music video for the song *Blume* (Flower) by Einstürzende Neubauten (Collapsing New Buildings), a German band that was part of the Futurist-inspired industrial music scene of the 1980s.

Although the Futurists presented their works in a series of concerts in Italy and London in 1914, the movement splintered with the outbreak of war. Little Futurist music survives today; the original instruments were destroyed and only a handful of recordings give a sense of their sounds. Yet a fragment of the score for Russolo's *La città che sale* (The City Rises, 1914; Fig. 3.2) shows the Futurists anticipating compositional techniques that would be fully developed only after World War II. Particularly striking is the graphic notation that Russolo used to indicate a continuum of pitches, echoing Busoni's call for a liberation from equal temperament. (For more on graphic notation, see Chapter 10.)

Figure 3.2: *Luigi Russolo,* The City Rises *(1914)*

STRAUSS AND REFERENTIAL TONALITY

While Busoni and the Futurists explored ways of fundamentally rethinking the basic assumptions of music, Richard Strauss (1864–1949) followed the more usual path of developing new approaches incrementally. One of the most prominent German composers of his time, Strauss built on the legacy of Wagner and Liszt in a series of symphonic tone poems and operas. He completed the tone poem *Also sprach Zarathustra*, based on Nietzsche's philosophical novel, in 1896, the same year as Mahler's Third Symphony. But whereas Mahler used only a brief excerpt from the novel as vocal text for his fourth movement, Strauss distilled the entire book into a purely orchestral work of about 30 minutes, formed as a prelude and eight sections titled after some of Nietzsche's chapters. As Strauss indicated in a program, his tone poem traced the evolution of the human race "through the various phases of its development, religious as well as scientific, up to Nietzsche's idea of the *Übermensch*" (usually translated as "Higher Man" or "Superman").

Written for a large orchestra of over 100 musicians, including a pipe organ, *Also sprach Zarathustra* begins with a musical representation of the sunrise and Zarathustra's revelation of a new path for mankind. The opening music, familiar from films such as *2001: A Space Odyssey* and *WALL-E*, introduces the rising C–G–C motive that is developed throughout the work in accordance with the program. With the technique of thematic transformation, Strauss uses the pitches and contour of the motive to create themes that illustrate the main point of each section of the narrative. Thus in the *Dance Song* the motive becomes a waltz tune, while in *On Science* Strauss turns it into a lugubrious and intricately worked fugue.

Strauss's concept of program music in this and other symphonic poems, such as *Tod und Verklärung* (Death and Transfiguration, 1889) and *Ein Heldenleben* (A Hero's Life, 1898), was shaped by the New German School stance that music was elevated by having specific content and meaning. Strauss's quite literal translation of ideas into music can be heard in the second and third sections of *Also sprach Zarathustra*, *The Backwoodsmen* and *Of the Great Longing*, which depict Zarathustra's encounter with a religious hermit (Ex. 3.1). Rejecting the hermit's call to join him in praising God, in Nietzsche's text Zarathustra goes away saying to himself, "Could it be possible? This old saint in the forest has not yet heard anything of this, that *God is dead!*" In Strauss's score, the hermit is depicted by a pipe organ playing the opening phrase of the sacred hymn the Magnificat, followed by the French horns intoning a line of the Credo from the Mass. In stark opposition to the hermit's music, Zarathustra's rising C–G–C motive sounds out piercingly in the oboe and English horn.

Strauss's presentation of the two musical ideas in jarringly different keys (the hermit's music starts in B major, while Zarathustra's motive is in C) is characteristic of his treatment of tonality in many pieces more as a referential device to communicate the program than as an overarching structure for the

Example 3.1: *Richard Strauss,* Also sprach Zarathustra, *mm. 83–90*

entire work. He signals this strategy of working *with* tonality rather than *within* it in the opening measures of the work with the surprising alternation between C-major and C-minor triads in the sunrise music. Throughout the piece, Strauss uses opposing keys to depict the destabilizing force of Zarathustra's message. Even in the closing measures, the low C in the basses undercuts the shimmering cadential B-major triad in the flutes and strings.

Strauss extended this referential treatment of tonality still further in his opera *Salome* (1905), which also demonstrated his commitment to Wagnerian techniques, including the use of leitmotives. To capture the lurid stage action of Oscar Wilde's scandalous play—including the *Dance of the Seven Veils*, in which Salome dances seductively for her stepfather, Herod, so that he will give her the head of John the Baptist—Strauss wrote long sections of extremely chromatic music that dispense with any clear tonal center. These passages contrast with episodes of functional tonality and strong arrivals on a C♯ tonic for Salome's moments of ecstatic exaltation. Yet in every case Strauss quickly moves away from these areas of tonal stability, and the opera closes abruptly in C minor when Herod orders Salome killed.

SKRYABIN'S NEW HARMONIC STRUCTURES

The mystically inclined Russian Aleksandr Skryabin (1872–1915) was a fervent believer in the idea that a new music could usher in a new world. He was willing to accept in this process great upheaval and suffering through "cataclysms, catastrophes, wars, revolutions," as he indicated in a letter he wrote in response to the outbreak of World War I: "At certain times the masses urgently need to be shaken up, in order to purify the human organization and fit it for the reception of more delicate vibrations than those to which it has hitherto responded."

Skryabin began performing on the piano and composing at a young age, graduating from the Moscow Conservatory in 1892. He then took several teaching positions interspersed with periods of travel, including an extended stay in Paris, where he came into contact with the Symbolist poets who influenced Debussy (see Chapter 2). His lifelong interest in new harmonic structures is foreshadowed in his early music. In the Prelude in E Minor for piano, Op. 11, No. 4 (1888), for example, Skryabin downplays both tonic and dominant; not until the closing measures do we hear a conventional chord progression and root-position tonic (Ex. 3.2). In place of the tonic and dominant, the Prelude focuses on augmented triads that combine elements of both I and V; thus the G–B–D♯ chord in measure 1 shares two pitches with both the E-minor and B-major triads. Skryabin treats these augmented triads almost as if they were consonances, foregrounded through duration and metric placement on strong beats, while similarly de-emphasizing major and minor triads.

Skryabin became increasingly interested in basing pieces on sonorities that combine aspects of a tonic and dominant. The most famous of these sonorities is the so-called mystic chord (C–F♯–B♭–E–A–D), which appears in his symphonic poem *Prométhée, le poème du feu* (Prometheus: The Poem of Fire, 1910) and other works. A 1912 article that appeared in *The Blue Rider Almanac* (see p. 50) by his friend, the Russian composer and critic Leonid Sabaneyev, describes how Skryabin treated the dissonant chord as a consonance from which both harmonies and melodies could be generated. As the harmonic content of his music became more static, he focused on contrasts in rhythm, dynamics, texture, and register to create form and direction. Like Debussy and Stravinsky

Example 3.2: *Aleksandr Skryabin, Prelude, Op. 11, No. 4, mm. 1–5*

(see Chapters 2 and 4), Skryabin embraced whole-tone and octatonic scales, frequently integrating them with diatonic features. This practice is prefigured in the mystic chord, which when presented in scalar form (C–D–E–F♯–A–B♭) can be seen to combine features of a whole-tone scale (C–D–E–F♯–G♯–B♭) and an octatonic scale (C–C♯–D♯–E–F♯–G–A–B♭).

Prométhée includes a part for a "color organ" that projects lights corresponding to each pitch: red for C, yellow for D, whitish-blue for E, and so on. Skryabin was one of many composers and artists around 1910 who were motivated by Symbolism and the mystical religion of Theosophy to explore the possibilities of synesthesia, a condition in which boundaries between the senses are blurred so that, for example, sound is perceived as color or color as taste. Founded in 1875 as a combination of science, religion, and philosophy, Theosophy included a belief that synesthesia was a manifestation of higher levels of spiritual development. The Russian painter Wassily Kandinsky created a series of abstract synesthetic stage works such as *The Yellow Sound* (1909) that combined color, dance, and music. In his opera *Die glückliche hand* (The Fortunate [or Fateful] Hand, 1913), Schoenberg similarly developed techniques for integrating gesture, color, music, and staging. (See p. 47 for a discussion of Schoenberg's related idea of tone-color melody.)

Skryabin devoted much of the final years of his life to his unfinished *Mysteriya* (Mysterium), to be performed on land he had purchased in India so that the Himalayas could provide a natural temple for this vast synesthetic symphony. Scored for an ensemble of solo piano, chorus, solo voices, and orchestra, augmented by dance, colored lights, perfume, and "bells suspended from the clouds," the work was intended to transport all the participants to spiritual enlightenment. Though Skryabin ultimately abandoned these plans, he continued work on a related and also unfinished piece called the *Acte préalable* (Preparatory Act), which Sabaneyev described as a "sonic dream." Upon hearing the composer perform from his sketches on the piano, he wrote: "It seemed to me that I'd descended into an ocean of new sounds. . . . I felt that I'd descended into an enchanted, holy kingdom, where sounds and colors merged into one fragile and fantastic chord."

SCHOENBERG, BERG, AND WEBERN

Born into a Jewish family of modest means in Vienna, Arnold Schoenberg (1874–1951) was forced by the death of his father to leave school at 16 and work as a bank clerk. Though he had little formal musical training beyond some lessons with his friend Alexander Zemlinsky, he managed to quit the bank when he was 20 and support himself by orchestrating operettas, conducting amateur choruses, and even for a time composing and arranging for a Berlin cabaret. It is one of many paradoxes concerning Schoenberg that a composer who was largely self-taught became one of the most active teachers in music history. Over a life that spanned turn-of-the-century Vienna, Berlin between the world wars, and Los Angeles, where he lived from the early 1930s until his death in 1951, he taught hundreds of students, including Alban Berg, Anton Webern, and several composers we will encounter in later chapters, such as Hanns Eisler and John Cage.

Both Berg (1885–1935) and Webern (1883–1945) started their lessons with Schoenberg in 1904. At age 30, Schoenberg was still in the beginning stages of his career and not much older than his pupils. Of the three, Webern alone had extensive formal training, having received a doctorate from the University of Vienna with a thesis on the Renaissance composer Heinrich Isaac. Berg heard about Schoenberg's lessons through a newspaper announcement; his only previous training was piano lessons from his governess. Very early on, the three composers became linked in the public eye through their writings and events such as what became known as the *Skandalkonzert* in 1913, when a performance of their works, together with pieces by Mahler and Zemlinsky, was disrupted by hecklers. The brawling got so out of hand that the concert organizer struck a member of the audience and was forced to appear in court and pay a fine.

THE EMANCIPATION OF THE DISSONANCE

Schoenberg justified the revolutionary elements of his music in part by arguing that he was driven by historical necessity to synthesize the two paths in nineteenth-century music represented by Brahms and Wagner, and thus to bring about the next stage in the Austro-German tradition. He identified the Brahmsian features in works like his String Quartet No. 2 in F♯ Minor, Op. 10 (1908) as the use of traditional forms and an emphasis on polyphony and contrapuntal devices. Most important was the technique he called "developing variation," which implies a logical process by which the components of a theme or motive are elaborated to produce both unity and variety, with each transformation building on the previous stage.

All three composers viewed the emancipation of the dissonance as a byproduct of pursuing these Brahmsian ideas to their logical conclusion. As Schoenberg wrote of his String Quartet No. 2, "There are many sections in which the individual parts proceed regardless of whether or not their meeting results in codified harmonies." While the quartet returns to a clear tonal center at decisive points, in subsequent works such as the Three Piano Pieces, Op. 11 (1909) and *Pierrot lunaire*, Op. 21 (Moonstruck Pierrot, 1912; see Anthology 3), melodies and harmonies are organized not by functional progressions but rather by motives, contextually established collections of pitches, and elaborate processes of developing variation. As noted earlier, several theoretical systems have been developed in recent decades to analyze these path-breaking works by Schoenberg and his pupils, but the composers themselves formulated no systematic theories, and evidence from their sketches suggests that they worked largely by ear.

Schoenberg also traced the emancipation of the dissonance to the impact of Wagner, Liszt, and Strauss. In his programmatic string sextet *Verklärte Nacht*, Op. 4 (Transfigured Night, 1899), which, like Alma Mahler's "Die stille Stadt," was based on a poem by Richard Dehmel, Schoenberg incorporated many techniques characteristic of the New German School and its successors, including expressive chromatic harmony, leitmotifs, thematic transformation, striking timbral effects, and the technique of building up form by sequencing an idea at various levels of transposition. Schoenberg's approach to each of these elements, taken separately, did not mark a radical departure from the music of his predecessors. But in bringing all of them together simultaneously, he crossed the boundary of what many considered good taste. When the Vienna Composers' Society rejected *Verklärte Nacht* for performance, the selection committee complained that the work "sounds as if someone had smeared the score of *Tristan* while it was still wet."

Wagner's influence is particularly explicit in *Gurre-Lieder* (Songs of Gurre, referring to a castle in Denmark), which calls for a massive orchestra, vocal soloists, three male choruses, and an eight-part mixed chorus—more than 400 musicians in all. Schoenberg composed most of *Gurre-Lieder* in 1900–01 and completed it in 1911; the premiere in 1913 was one of his great successes. The text, by the Danish writer Jens Peter Jacobsen, retells legends of the illicit passion of King Waldemar for his mistress Tove. When she is killed by the jealous queen, Waldemar curses God and is condemned after death to lead his ghostly army in a wild hunt each night. Long passages of the beautiful and chilling *Song of the Wood Dove*, which recounts the death of Tove, are based exclusively on the "Tristan" chord (Ex. 3.3). As Skryabin does with the mystic chord, Schoenberg treats the dissonant half-diminished seventh chord as a stable sonority, using upper and lower neighbor notes that resolve back to it. In contrast to Debussy's playfully irreverent allusions to Wagner's *Tristan und Isolde* in *Golliwogg's Cake-Walk* (discussed in Chapter 1), which emphasized differences between the two composers, Schoenberg's incorporation of the "Tristan" chord here and in other works served to demonstrate his connections to the Wagnerian tradition.

TONE-COLOR MELODY

Schoenberg's technique here and elsewhere of building an extended passage from a single sonority had profound ramifications for his treatment of all the other elements of music. The emancipation of the dissonance is closely connected to the tendency we have noted in the music of Debussy and Skryabin to foreground the formerly secondary characteristics of timbre, register, rhythm, dynamics, and texture. In the *Song of the Wood Dove*, Schoenberg uses the

Example 3.3: *Arnold Schoenberg,* Song of the Wood Dove, *from* Gurrelieder, *mm. 3–8*

Doves of Gurre! Troubles have tormented me all across the Island!

resources of his huge orchestra to give each statement of the "Tristan" chord a strikingly different timbre as it appears in various registers.

Schoenberg ends his *Theory of Harmony* with a discussion of what he called *Klangfarbenmelodie,* or tone-color melody. The most literal manifestation of this idea is a succession of different timbres on a single chord or pitch. A famous example is the third of Schoenberg's Five Pieces for Orchestra, Op. 16 (1909), originally titled *Farben* (Colors). The four-minute piece is based on a five-note collection, now referred to as the "Farben" chord (C–G♯–B–E–A), which slowly evolves with constantly changing timbres. (At his publisher's request, Schoenberg later renamed the movement with the more literally programmatic title *Summer Morning by a Lake.*)

Berg and Webern developed the idea of tone-color melody in distinctive ways in their own compositions. Webern, who was also influenced by Mahler's delicately nuanced orchestrations, made timbre the primary focus of many works during these years, including his own Five Pieces for Orchestra, Op. 10 (1913). Written for a small orchestra of 17 solo instruments and percussion, the first movement starts off very softly with a simple two-note motive, B–C–B with each pitch played by a very different combination of instruments:

B	C	B
Trumpet, muted	Celeste	Flute, flutter tongue
Harp	Harp, harmonic	Harp
	Viola, muted, harmonic	

This series of three different timbres is then contrasted with three notes—Eb–G–D—played by a single instrument, the glockenspiel. The movement ends with a "pure" *Klangfarbenmelodie* consisting of four statements of the note F in rapid succession, each time with a different scoring: flute, flute and muted trumpet, muted trumpet, celeste. As we will see when we return to Webern's Symphony, Op. 21 (1927–28) in Chapter 7, tone-color melodies continued to play an important role in his twelve-tone music.

In the third act of Berg's opera *Wozzeck* (1922), there is a chilling passage in the transition between scenes 2 and 3 that is based on a single note, B♮ (Anthology 4 and Opera Sampler; also discussed further in Chapter 7). This note had already been emphasized throughout scene 2, which Berg identified as an "Invention on a Note," with B♮ representing Wozzeck's obsession with the murder he is about to commit. In one of the most remarkable examples of *Klangfarbenmelodie*, the scene change presents two enormous crescendos, the first based on different instruments entering in succession on B in a single octave, the second spreading the note in various registers across the whole orchestra. Anticipating by several decades the texture music that we will discuss in Chapter 12, Berg creates a powerful effect using only timbre, dynamics, and register.

THE ELIMINATION OF THE CONSCIOUS WILL IN ART

Another source for the emancipation of the dissonance was Schoenberg's compulsion to extend the Romantic view of art as subjective expression of emotion to its most extreme conclusion. Schoenberg proposed in a letter to Busoni from 1909 that instead of its syntactic, "architectural" function, harmony must serve purely expressive ends: "Away with harmony as cement or bricks of a building. Harmony is *expression* and nothing else" (SR 170:1283; 7/1:13). In a series of works written in the summer of 1909, Schoenberg created a radically new style by pursuing an ideal that he called "the elimination of the conscious will in art." In his letter to Busoni, he described his vision of a music that would dispense with "conscious logic":

> It is *impossible* for a person to have only *one* sensation at a time.
>
> One has *thousands* simultaneously. And these thousands can no more readily be added together than an apple and a pear. They go their own ways.
>
> And this variegation, this multifariousness, this *illogicality* which our senses demonstrate, the illogicality presented by their interactions, set forth by some mounting rush of blood, by some reactions of the senses or the nerves, this I should like to have in my music.

We can see how seriously Schoenberg took this expressive ideal in every aspect of his works during the period 1909–12. Although he had always composed quickly, he now completed many movements in a matter of days. Schoenberg came to regard sketching and revision as signs of insufficient inspiration, honesty, or genius. Music history is full of amazing feats of rapid composition, but Schoenberg's achievement is particularly astonishing because it coincided with his attempt to downplay the techniques and tools that composers had long relied on when they set pen to paper: tonality, motivic and thematic development, counterpoint, repetition, and traditional forms.

While at first glance such an approach would seem to make composition easy, it in fact posed enormous difficulties, as can be seen from the manuscript of the third of the Op. 11 Piano Pieces (see Fig. 3.1, p. 37). All that survives is the two-page autograph; most of the piece was written down in something very close to its final form. Yet Schoenberg was always on the lookout for "the disturbing intervention of the constantly worried frightened intellect." His struggle to live up to the paradoxical goal he described to Busoni of "intending to have no intentions" is apparent in the crossed-out passages in the first three systems. The deleted measures depart from the character of the rest of the piece in a number of ways: in contrast to the constant change elsewhere in the movement, the passage is highly repetitive and clearly motivic; the toccata-like, more characteristically pianistic writing stands out against the otherwise unconventional polyphonic textures; and the emphasis on F♮ creates a tonal center that starts to anchor the harmonies. In other words, Schoenberg felt compelled to remove the one passage in the piece that worked the way most music was expected to operate. For Schoenberg and other creative artists, eliminating "the conscious will" was easier said than done. (See, for example, the discussion of John Cage's *4' 33"* in Chapter 10.)

It is no coincidence that a number of artists who were trying to free themselves from inherited technique turned to other art forms. Just as the painter Kandinsky wrote works for the stage, Schoenberg became active as a painter, creating a series of increasingly abstract self-portraits. Kandinsky, who created his luminous *Impression III* in response to a 1911 performance of Schoenberg's Three Piano Pieces and Second String Quartet, invited the composer to show his paintings in his *Blue Rider Exhibition* that year. Kandinsky's *Blue Rider Almanac* (1912) featured one of Schoenberg's self-portraits, his essay "The Relationship to the Text," and short pieces by Schoenberg, Berg, and Webern. Kandinsky's letters to Schoenberg from 1911 offer vivid testimony to the startling impact of the composer's music: "In your works, you have realized what I, albeit in uncertain form, have so greatly longed for in music. The independent progress through their own destinies, the independent life of the individual voices in your compositions, is exactly what I am trying to find in my paintings."

Another manifestation of how seriously Berg, Webern, and Schoenberg pursued this rejection of traditional technique is the radical compression of their works in these years. Schoenberg's best-known miniatures are the Six Little

Piano Pieces, Op. 19 (1911), which range in length from 20 seconds to a minute and a half. Berg's *Fünf Orchesterlieder nach Ansichtkartentexten von Peter Altenberg*, Op. 4 (Five Songs on Picture Postcard Texts by Peter Altenberg, 1912) and Four Pieces for Clarinet and Piano, Op. 5 (1913) are equally terse. Webern pursued his penchant for compression the most rigorously, focusing for the rest of his life on songs, orchestral pieces, and chamber music that sought to reduce music to its most essential elements. The first of his Four Pieces for Violin and Piano, Op. 7 (1910) is only nine measures long and takes less than a minute to perform; as we will see, the Variations movement of his Symphony, Op. 21 lasts just three minutes (see Anthology 11).

Such extreme brevity can be understood as the product of an ideal of composition as the unmediated transcription of unconscious sensations—a process that naturally tends to prohibit the repetition and development of ideas. But it also resulted from Schoenberg's goal of synthesizing Brahmsian and Wagnerian styles into "musical prose," which he defined as "a direct and straightforward presentation of ideas, without any patchwork, without mere padding and empty repetitions." Thus, Webern's Op. 7, No. 1 contains no literal repetition, themes, or motives in the traditional sense (Ex. 3.4). Rather, it presents four contrasting phrases related only by subtle associations of emphasized pitch classes (Eb is prominent in all four), similar melodic gestures, and nontriadic harmonies

Example 3.4: *Anton Webern, Four Pieces for Violin and Piano, Op. 7, No. 1*

featuring half steps linked to perfect fourths and fifths. The concluding E♭ $^6_4$ triad in the piano, heard against the sustained E♮ in the left hand, sounds more like a memory of tonality than any sort of resolution.

EXPRESSIONISM AND "THE ART OF THE REPRESENTATION OF INNER PROCESSES"

Many of Schoenberg's Viennese contemporaries were interested in breaking through to the unconscious forces that shape our behavior, most famously the psychoanalyst Sigmund Freud, but also the painter Gustav Klimt and the physician Marie Pappenheim, who wrote the libretto for Schoenberg's half-hour-long monodrama *Erwartung* (Expectation, 1909). Schoenberg, Berg, and Webern had many points of contact with the wide-ranging artistic movement in Austria and Germany known as Expressionism, which subordinated naturalistic representation to the goal of depicting inner forces and the irrational, often with a focus on extreme and violent emotions. The painter Oskar Kokoschka (1886–1980), a member of Schoenberg's circle who had a tempestuous relationship with Alma Mahler after Gustav's death, also sought to submerge traditional artistic techniques in an effort to capture elemental and instinctual emotional experience. The self-portrait Kokoschka created in 1910 for the cover of the Expressionist periodical *Der Sturm* (The Storm) seems to lay bare his nerves and emotions, opening up his inner life to the viewer with a Christ-like wound in his chest (Fig. 3.3).

Schoenberg, however, suggested that Expressionism was a problematic category for his music, proposing instead "the art of the representation of *inner* processes," which better captured the broad emotional range of his works. We

Figure 3.3: *Oskar Kokoschka,* Self-Portrait *(1910)*

can certainly hear connections to Expressionism in parts of Schoenberg's *Pierrot lunaire*, such as the *Red Mass* (No. 11), where Pierrot pulls out his own heart to serve as the communion wafer; or *Night* (No. 8), which depicts giant black butterflies drifting down on the hearts of men. In Schoenberg's setting, the moonstruck Pierrot—poet, prophet, and madman—is a metaphor for the liberated and fractured psyche of the modern artist. Berg's *Wozzeck* similarly exposes a painful and hostile world through the protagonist's disturbed psyche as he descends from hallucinations to murder and suicide. Webern's music includes such terrifying passages as the nightmarish funeral march in his Six Pieces for Orchestra, Op. 6 (1909). In works like these, dissonance creates its traditional tension and instability, while the distortion or absence of conventional musical genres, forms, and techniques evokes madness.

Yet analogies between Expressionism and the music of Schoenberg, Berg, and Webern can also obscure the emotional diversity of their works. The opening measures of Schoenberg's Piano Piece Op. 11, No. 3 burst out in pounding chords that leap erratically up and down the keyboard like a disturbed character. As the piece goes on, however, such outbursts alternate with passages marked by a gentle, nostalgic, and even lyrical tone. Through the close interaction of text and music, Schoenberg's *Pierrot lunaire* likewise covers a vast expressive range, including satire, irony, nostalgia, broad humor, and moments of grotesque horror, as we experience the world and the other characters through Pierrot's disordered and heightened senses. The first of Webern's Four Pieces for Violin and Piano, Op. 7 is extraordinarily refined and restrained; typical of Webern, the dynamics range only from *ppp* to *pp*. The goal for Schoenberg, Berg, and Webern, as for many other artists associated with Expressionism, was not to unleash inner demons, but to capture as directly and honestly as possible the full range of emotions in the stream of unconscious sensations.

After an initial sense of liberation that led to a period of remarkable productivity in 1909, Schoenberg failed to complete a single piece in 1910. His attempt to break through "every restriction of a bygone aesthetic" posed extreme challenges, and he began expressing doubts about his creative abilities and compositional direction. Only as he began, painfully and reluctantly, to relax the extreme strictures of "the elimination of the conscious will in art" did he regain the capacity to compose with his former fluency.

Pierrot lunaire, completed in 1912, marks the beginning of a new stage that anticipated many features of Schoenberg's later music and musical developments in general after World War I. Tonal allusions appear only sporadically, with nostalgic or ironic connections, but we see more conventional approaches to form, a range of historical references (waltz, chorale, barcarolle), and the use of imitative counterpoint and contrapuntal devices. Schoenberg referred to the individual movements as melodramas, a genre dating back to the eighteenth century that combined spoken text with musical accompaniment. The vocal part uses the technique of Sprechstimme (literarily, speaking voice), a nineteenth-century style of recitation between speech and song that was modeled on the expressive declamation of actors.

With *Pierrot* Schoenberg began constructing a musical language to replace tonality, a process that would occupy him intensively over the next decade leading up to the introduction of the twelve-tone method in 1923. As we will see in Chapter 7, Berg and Webern charted their own paths, working systematically with the total chromatic collection and exploring how to reconcile the new world of harmony with traditional forms and genres.

Strauss, too, turned away from the dissonance, tonal instability, and extreme emotions of *Salome* and its sequel, *Elektra* (1909). His opera *Der Rosenkavalier* (The Knight of the Rose, 1911) signals a reconciliation with the expressive idioms of the nineteenth-century Austro-German tradition, a project that he would pursue for the remaining 38 years of his life (we return to Strauss in Chapter 9). For his part, Busoni became increasingly interested in forging connections between eighteenth-century models and Modernism, coining the phrase *Die junge Klassizität* (Young Classicism) to describe works like his Mozartian opera *Arlecchino, oder Die Fenster* (Harlequin, or The Windows, 1916), thus anticipating trends we will discuss in Chapter 6.

Accounts of music before World War I often depict the period as a time of transition or crisis. After the war, there was a general feeling that composers needed to create larger forms, develop more systematic ways of rethinking tonality or doing without it, and continue the search for a new music that would communicate with a broader audience. But we should not lose sight of what this group of audacious composers attempted and achieved during these years through works and writings that have continued to move, challenge, and shock.

FOR FURTHER READING

Boehmer, Konrad, ed., *Schönberg and Kandinsky: An Historic Encounter* (Amsterdam: Harwood Academic, 1997)

Frisch, Walter, *The Early Works of Arnold Schoenberg: 1893–1908* (Berkeley: University of California Press, 1993)

Gilliam, Bryan, ed., *Richard Strauss and His World* (Princeton: Princeton University Press, 1992)

Hall, Patricia, *Berg's Wozzeck* (Oxford: Oxford University Press, 2011)

Keathley, Elizabeth, "'*Die Frauenfrage*' in *Erwartung*: Schoenberg's Collaboration with Marie Pappenheim," in *Schoenberg and Words: The Modernist Years*, edited by Charlotte Cross and Russell Berman, 139–178 (New York: Garland, 2000)

Levitz, Tamara, *Teaching New Classicality: Ferruccio Busoni's Master Class in Composition* (Frankfurt am Main: Peter Lang, 1996)

Morgan, Robert P., "A New Musical Reality: Futurism, Modernism, and 'The Art of Noises,'" *Modernism/Modernity* 1, no. 3 (1994): 129–151

Shaw, Jennifer and Joseph Auner, eds., *The Cambridge Companion to Schoenberg* (Cambridge: Cambridge University Press, 2010)

Simms, Bryan, ed., *A Companion to the Second Viennese School* (Westport, CT: Greenwood Press, 1999)

Straus, Joseph, *Introduction to Post-Tonal Theory* (Upper Saddle River, NJ: Prentice-Hall, 2004)

CHAPTER FOUR

Folk Sources, the Primitive, and the Search for Authenticity

I t is one of the central paradoxes of Modernism and modernity that folk music, whether heard in remote corners of the contemporary countryside or summoned up from distant regions of the past, seemed to provide a catalyst for music that was truly new while at the same time offering a sense of authenticity and rootedness in a national tradition. Composers have drawn on folk music throughout history, but in the early twentieth century the idea of "the folk" took on new significance for those seeking responses to the increasing multiplicity of possibilities and the rapid destabilization of their inner and outer worlds.

In this chapter we will examine four composers whose engagement with folk sources was a defining factor of their music: Jean Sibelius (Finland), Charles Ives (United States), Béla Bartók (Hungary), and Igor Stravinsky (Russia). In keeping with the breadth of the term as it was understood in the early years of the twentieth century, we will be using the category of folk music to cover a wide range of influences outside of the art-music tradition. By exploring these composers' very different strategies for defining and using these materials, we can also shed light on how specific cultural, racial, and political contexts have shaped conceptions of what folk music is, and who should be regarded as "the folk."

LOCATING THE FOLK

Defining folk music, or drawing clear boundaries between it and other forms of music-making, is surprisingly problematic. Readers of this book may have very different understandings of folk music, depending on where they grew up and their own backgrounds and family traditions. A newspaper blurb for a recent folk festival in Lowell, Massachusetts, plays upon such preconceptions, while also showing how issues of race, class, and ethnicity shape debates about who gets counted among the folk in today's multicultural United States: "What does the Lowell Folk Festival make you think of? A line-up larded with alfalfa-fortified singer-strummers bleating out wispy ballads? Think again—this year's program is awash in Tuvan throat singers, klezmer, zydeco, Senegalese akonting, Brazilian capoeira, and Punjabi dance."

This passage also illustrates how any definition of the folk contests previous formulations. Here we see a globalized, multiracial music displacing a presumably white folk style meant to evoke the U.S. folk revival of the 1950s and 1960s. Yet that revival itself redefined the folk in the service of political and social goals, as is clear in the landmark *Anthology of American Folk Music*, released on Folkways Records in 1952. Harry Smith, who assembled the collection from recordings made in the 1920s and 1930s of "old-time" music from the rural southern and eastern United States, was a musician and filmmaker associated with the Beat poets and 1950s San Francisco counterculture. Accompanied by a booklet featuring an avant-garde design and playfully irreverent notes, the *Anthology of American Folk Music* emphasized the strangeness of the music and lyrics as an alternative to what Smith and his colleagues saw as the increasing homogenization of American consumer culture. The West Coast artist Bruce Connor described how exciting the anthology seemed to a boy growing up in the American heartland. Coming across the recordings in his local public library in Wichita, Kansas, he wrote, was like "a confrontation with another culture, or another view of the world, that might include arcane, or unknown, or unfamiliar views of the world, hidden within these words, melodies, and harmonies—it was like field recordings from the Amazon, or Africa, but it's here, in the United States!"

Sibelius, Ives, Bartók, and Stravinsky similarly sought to differentiate their uses of folk material from those of their nineteenth-century predecessors. Many listeners then (as now) were perplexed by Ives's idiosyncratic vision of American music, just as Bartók met considerable resistance in his homeland to his version of what was truly Hungarian. Here we see another paradox of the new folk-inspired music: Many composers initially received the most favorable responses from cosmopolitan audiences abroad. Thus Stravinsky first achieved major celebrity in Paris, and it was international success that enabled Bartók and Sibelius to gain respect back home.

All four composers show the continuing influence of ideas that emerged one hundred years earlier as part of the interdependent developments of nationalism and Romanticism. The writings of Johann Gottfried Herder (1744–1803), for example, identified the folk as people who lived and worked on the land, sharing a common language, religion, and set of customs. Just as important to this formulation were expressions of a cultural heritage through a body of lore, music, dance, and costume, which together formed the basis for more-abstract commonalities of character and beliefs.

The flipside to Herder's definition is an implicit or explicit exclusionary principle. National boundaries frequently embrace various ethnicities, so that elevating one to the status of "true" folk means placing others in a subordinate position. The idea of a pure rural folk song has often been pitted against the "corrupted" music of cities and towns, associated with new social hierarchies, immigration, industrialization, and commercialization. Such a formulation explains why conceptions of the folk sometimes included elements of racism and xenophobia, as well as how often debates about the folk have been implicated in violent conflicts within and between nations.

For Sibelius, Ives, Bartók, and Stravinsky, notions of the folk similarly involved processes of exclusion. As we will see, the most significant musical "other" from which they sought to differentiate their music was the Austro-German tradition. Although it was just as bound up with a national identity as any other musical tradition, over the course of the nineteenth century Austro-German music acquired connotations of being "universal." The ubiquity of Beethoven's Ninth Symphony as a global symbol of brotherhood and freedom is a vivid illustration of this continuing legacy.

SIBELIUS: CREATING FINNISHNESS

The career of the Finnish composer Jean Sibelius (1865–1957) shows how newly composed music could have a national character even when specific folk melodies are not in evidence. Sibelius came of age during a period of strong nationalistic movements in Finland, though the country gained its independence from Russia only in 1917. As was the case for many emerging nations in the nineteenth century, the idea of a national music was a central concern, leading to the establishment of specifically Finnish cultural and musical institutions in the 1880s, including orchestras, choruses, and a music school that would be renamed the Sibelius Academy in 1939.

Sibelius's status as Finland's national composer, later enshrined through the use of his portrait on the 100-mark note, was established quite early in his career. Yet what came to be regarded as the Finnish character of his music was shaped as much by the reception of his works as by his compositional techniques.

Sibelius studied in Berlin and Vienna, and his early works reflect the influence of Wagner, Liszt, and Tchaikovsky. From these and other elements, including ideas adapted from Finnish folk materials, he forged a distinctive style. Indeed, critics argued that the essence of his music's Finnishness lay in its originality. Thus the Finnish composer Oskar Merikanto wrote on the day of the premiere of *Kullervo* (1892), Sibelius's symphonic poem for orchestra and chorus: "We recognize these [tones] as ours, even if we have not heard them as such." Even abstract instrumental sounds, such as in his tone poem *The Swan of Tuonela* (1900), vividly reminded listeners of the dark pine forests of the north and the contours of the rugged Finnish coast.

Sibelius did have some involvement with folk music; in 1891, when he was composing *Kullervo*, he heard a singer from the region of Karelia, which had become the focus of nationalistic efforts in Finland. He was also inspired around the same time by a newly composed song by his compatriot Ilmari Krohn that sought to capture the rhythmic characteristics of the Finnish language. In an 1896 lecture he noted that the oldest Finnish folk tunes lacked the effect of tonic and dominant. But for Sibelius, literary sources were more influential than musical ones. Most significant was the *Kalevala*, a collection of thousands of verses of poetry, first published in 1835 and soon regarded as the Finnish national epic. Like the nineteenth-century German collection *The Youth's Magic Horn*, which was so important to Mahler (see Chapter 2), the *Kalevala* was a mixture of folk poetry and newly written material. Sibelius drew on it for characters and subjects in such works as *Kullervo* (named for the hero of the epic), *The Swan of Tuonela*, and *Pohjola's Daughter* (1906).

As part of his creation of Finnishness, Sibelius deliberately isolated himself from the Modernist musical language of Schoenberg and Stravinsky. In a letter of 1911 he spoke of his "unconquerable distaste for the 'modern tendency,'" claiming that his works were succeeding abroad despite having "no 'modernity' in them." But recent scholarship has painted a more complex picture, focusing on the many Modernist elements of Sibelius's style, including the harmonic complexity and tonal ambiguity of his Fourth Symphony (1911) along with his innovative manipulations of traditional symphonic forms. Indeed, some composers now count Sibelius among the most innovative in his treatment of timbre and texture, and there are clear relationships between his works and the striking sonorities of the Spectralists (see Chapter 12), as well as the slowly accumulating forms of Minimalism (see Chapter 14).

As with Schoenberg and his tone-color melody (see Chapter 3), for Sibelius the identity of a sonority was determined as much by orchestration as by pitch content and spacing. In the Fifth Symphony (1919) he creates a dynamic sense of motion through the gradual addition of layers of material, rather than through harmonic progressions. The richly enveloping musical motto from the opening of the symphony uses the French horns and woodwinds over a soft timpani tremolo (Ex. 4.1). Sibelius produces a sense of stasis by avoiding root-position

Example 4.1: *Jean Sibelius, Symphony No. 5, movement 1, mm. 1–8, reduction*

triads and strongly defined dominant-to-tonic progressions, thus allowing the gently coalescing ostinato figures to float freely.

For Sibelius, writing music that embodied the Finnish culture and natural landscape allowed him to connect to the deepest levels of human experience. In a diary entry from 1915, he associated the soaring trumpet theme of the finale of the Fifth Symphony with a flock of swans returning to their home in the spring:

> They circled over me for a long time. Disappeared into the solar haze like a gleaming silver ribbon. Their call the same woodwind type as that of the cranes, but without tremolo. The swan-call closer to the trumpet, although it's obviously a sarrusophone [a double-reed band instrument] sound. A low [-pitched] refrain reminiscent of a small child crying. Nature's mysticism and life's *Angst*!

IVES'S AMERICA

The music of Charles Ives (1874–1954) offers a vivid example of the self-conscious construction of a sense of identity and place through the use of folk tunes and other borrowings from his sonic environments. Born in Danbury, Connecticut, Ives studied music at Yale University and for many years led a double life in New York City as an insurance agency executive by day and a composer by night. Ives distanced himself from the musical establishment and composed much of his music in isolation. Without the pressures or opportunities of performance, he often continued revising and recomposing pieces over many decades, making the precise chronology of his works notoriously hard to pin down.

Ives's programmatic works evoke the experiences and landscapes of his life, such as *Yale-Princeton Football Game* (ca. 1911), *Central Park in the Dark* (ca. 1909), and *Three Places in New England* (ca. 1917). By using spatially separated ensembles and unusual orchestrations that suggest music heard from a distance, he attempted to capture the psychological experience of hearing sounds in specific locales. In a note on the use of space in the Fourth Symphony (ca. 1917), Ives cited Henry David Thoreau's comment in *Walden* that he found "a deeper import even in the symphonies of the Concord [Massachusetts] church bell when its sounds were rarified through the distant air" (SR 178:1335; 7/9:65). Ives drew most of his song texts and programs from American writers, in particular the New England Transcendentalists. Ralph Waldo Emerson, Nathaniel Hawthorne, the Alcott family, and Thoreau are all depicted in his massive Piano Sonata No. 2 (ca. 1919), subtitled *Concord, Mass., 1840–60*.

Ives's idealized vision of the folk convinced him that if he succeeded in capturing something true and authentic about his own experiences, it would be universally expressive. In differentiating his music from the evocations of African-American spirituals and Native American music in works like Antonín Dvořák's Symphony No. 9, *From the New World* (1893), he wrote:

> If the Yankee can reflect the fervency with which "his gospels" were sung . . . , he may find there a local color that will do the world good. If his music can but catch that spirit by being a part with itself, it will come somewhere near his ideal—and it will be American, too—perhaps nearer so than that of the devotee of Indian or negro melody. In other words, if local color, national color, any color, is a true pigment of the universal color, it is a divine quality, it is part of substance in art—not of manner.

Ives's music is infused with quotations, paraphrases, and allusions to the soundscape that surrounded him. Like Mahler, Ives believed that a musical work resembled a world, with space in it for music ranging from the most esoteric to the most commonplace. He frequently juxtaposed passages of conventional harmony and well-known tunes with others marked by extreme dissonance, tonal ambiguity, and modernist innovations such as quarter tones. "Why tonality as such should be thrown out for good, I can't see," he wrote. "Why it should always be present, I can't see. It depends, it seems to me, a good deal—as clothes depend on the thermometer—on what one is trying to do, and on the state of mind, the time of day or accidents of life."

Ives credited his father, a band musician and music teacher, with inspiring his enthusiasm for the popular music of the day, including ragtime, marches, and the music of Tin Pan Alley. Such music sometimes figures in Ives's works with a sense of nostalgia and longing for childhood, as in the song "The Things Our Fathers Loved" (1917; Ex. 4.2), which is patched together from quotations like a quilt. Set to a melody based on the song "My Old Kentucky Home," in a dreamy polytonal harmonization, the text by Ives begins: "I think there must be a place in the soul all made of tunes, of tunes of long ago."

As a young man, Ives worked for many years as a professional church organist, and the Protestant hymn tunes he internalized are among the most important musical elements in his style. In the first movement of the Fourth Symphony, the hymn *Watchman* is sung in its entirety by a chorus, with small but significant textual emendations in the final stanza (see Anthology 5). More typical of his borrowings is the short excerpt from the tune of "Sweet By and By" played by a solo violin or the distorted fragment from "Nearer, My God, to Thee" that a distant ensemble of strings and harp plays throughout the movement, drifting in and out of audibility.

A surprising note in the score of the first movement indicates that Ives preferred a performance without the chorus. The notion that he thought it was unnecessary for the words to be sung points to his hope for likeminded listeners

Example 4.2: *Quotations in Charles Ives, "The Things Our Fathers Loved," mm. 1–7, as identified by J. Peter Burkholder*

who would have known all the same tunes and thus be able to fill in the words for themselves. Thus the music can be heard as a way of summoning up an imagined community of people who shared Ives's experiences and convictions, while also implicitly excluding those who did not.

Ives's use of folk tunes, hymns, and popular styles was shaped by his deep ambivalence toward the more proper established styles of art music of the day. But Ives was a product of the art-music tradition, having studied at Yale with the German-trained composer Horatio Parker (1863–1919). Some of his student music actually survives in the third movement of the Fourth Symphony, a scholastic fugue based on the hymn "From Greenland's Icy Mountains." Despite his claims of independence, many of Ives's works show a European influence; his First Symphony (1902), for example, was modeled on Dvořák's *New World* Symphony.

Ives often expressed his criticism of art music in explicitly gendered terms. Complaining about the criticism he had received from a "routine-minded professor" for using hymn tunes, he wrote:

> Well, I'll say two things here: 1) That nice professor of music is a musical lily pad. He never took a chance at himself, or took one coming and going. 2) His opinion is based on something he'd probably never heard, seen, or experienced. He knows little of how these things sounded when they came "blam" off a real man's chest. It was the *way* this music was sung that made them big or little—and I had the chance of hearing them big. And it wasn't the music that did it, and it wasn't the sounds (whatever they were—transcendent, peculiar, bad, some beautifully unmusical)—but they were sung "like the rocks were grown." The singers weren't singers, but they knew what they were doing—it all came from something felt, way down and way up—a man's experience of men!

For Ives, borrowings from folk and vernacular music offered a masculine authenticity rooted in the soil as a way to differentiate his works from what he saw as an art-music tradition that had become feminized and cosmopolitan.

As we have seen in the case of the Italian Futurists, the idea of new musical innovations as somehow more "masculine" was shared by a number of composers throughout the twentieth century, just as it has been in many other forms of music-making including jazz, rock, and hip hop. This way of thinking has depreciated and suppressed styles that were regarded as "feminine," along with the contributions of women composers, musicians, and patrons.

It also may have been a factor in Ives's decision to pursue a more typically "masculine" career in insurance, while keeping his musical interests on the side. As a result, many of his works were left unfinished and unpublished. Most of his songs were unavailable until 1922, when he published the collection *114 Songs* at his own expense. The Fourth Symphony is an extreme case; though much of the composition was done between 1912 and 1917, it incorporated music composed much earlier and Ives continued to work on it in later years. The symphony was finally published and first performed in 1965, thanks to the efforts of Henry Cowell (see Chapter 7).

PRIMITIVISM AND THE FOLK

Ives's characterization of the hymn performances he preferred—transcendently peculiar and beautifully unmusical, sung "like the rocks were grown," by singers who weren't singers—can also alert us to important links between conceptions of folk music and the idea of Primitivism. For all four composers we are considering here, the folk element included connotations of something primal, strange, and transgressive. The musicologist Cecil Gray wrote approvingly in 1924 of Sibelius's "essentially primitive mentality." Bartók's piano piece *Allegro barbaro* (1911) featured pounding chords, relentless repetition, and melodies stripped down to basics. Around 1912 Stravinsky was affiliated in Paris with "Les Apaches" (the Apaches), a loosely formed group that included Maurice Ravel (see Chapter 6) and others attracted to the exotic, decadent, and primitive.

Primitivism was a wide-ranging movement in all the arts in the early decades of the twentieth century. Unlike Exoticism and Orientalism, which centered on borrowings from Asia and the Middle East, Primitivism reflected a new interest in the so-called tribal cultures of Africa, Polynesia, and South America. Thus from the racially charged perspective of theories of cultural evolution, there was a shift away from traditions like Javanese gamelan, which Debussy described as being much *more* sophisticated and refined than the music of Palestrina, to musical and artistic influences that were perceived as primal, rough, and vital, unencumbered by the constraints of civilization. Primitivism, like Exoticism and Orientalism, was bound up with racism, colonialist expansion, and ignorance of the cultures whose traditions were being appropriated. Nevertheless, it has been a major force in many artistic movements since the early decades of the twentieth century.

Freud popularized the notion that present-day primitive peoples offered a window onto the earliest stages of mankind. In *The Interpretation of Dreams* (1900) he compared the task of psychoanalysis to an archaeologist digging down through the soil to find hidden truths from the past. For Freud, dreaming was not only a regression to the dreamer's earliest childhood when instinctual impulses dominated; it also offered "a picture of the development of the human race, of which the individual's development is in fact an abbreviated recapitulation."

Motivated by such conceptions, Modernist artists like Pablo Picasso, Paul Gauguin, and Henri Matisse studied and collected tribal masks, statues, and ritual objects as tools for exploring our instinctual inner life. It is no coincidence that collage emerged as an important technique in Picasso's work at this time, inspired in part by the miscellaneous nails, feathers, and beads used in the construction of tribal fetishes. In what Picasso referred to as a kind of exorcism, his Cubist painting *Les Demoiselles d'Avignon* (The Young Ladies of Avignon, 1907) depicts a group of French prostitutes with two of their faces replaced by African masks (Fig. 4.1). In addition to signifying a rejection of traditional artistic values of polish and refinement, the juxtaposition of tribal art and naked bodies was intended to evoke a frightening yet seductive mixture of sexuality, power, illness, fear, and death.

Because Modernist artists projected their own theories and fantasies onto these tribal artifacts and typically knew or cared little about their original function, it was easy for the idea of the primitive to become attached to a wide

Figure 4.1: *Pablo Picasso,* Les Demoiselles d'Avignon *(1907)*

range of cultural phenomena that had little to do with tribal cultures, including folk art, drawings by children, and the art of the insane. This jumble of ideas also influenced the reception of Primitivist music like Stravinsky's ballet *Le sacre du printemps* (The Rite of Spring), as is clear in a 1929 review of the *Rite* that transports it from pagan Russia to the jungle:

> Stravinsky . . . is entirely unable to formulate a musical idea of his own. As a member of a savage orchestra he might perhaps be allowed to play a recurrent rhythm upon a drum—as the only evidence of real form in his work is that kind of primitive repetition which birds and babies also do very well.

We have already seen a similar Primitivist response to the *Anthology of American Folk Music*, in the characterization of the "arcane" and "unfamiliar" music as sounding like "field recordings from the Amazon, or Africa."

Rather than any sort of accurate representation of "tribal" cultures, Primitivism was above all a manifestation of Modernism and modernity, as can be seen in Debussy's quip about the *Rite* as "an extraordinarily savage affair. . . . If you like, it's primitive music with every modern convenience." As we will see throughout this book, the fusion of the modern and the primitive has been a recurring theme of music history ever since, from the metaphors of "skyscrapers in the jungle" that shaped the early reception of jazz to the exotic samples used in psychedelic electronic trance music.

BARTÓK AND THE SEARCH FOR A MOTHER TONGUE

Like Sibelius in Finland, Béla Bartók (1881–1945) came to be regarded as *the* Hungarian national composer. A precociously talented pianist and composer, he studied at the Budapest Academy of Music before traveling abroad to perform in Vienna, Berlin, and Paris. He returned to the academy in 1906 to teach piano, a position he held until 1934. Concerned by Hungary's growing alliance with Nazi Germany, he immigrated to the United States in 1940, where he spent the last difficult years of his life (see Chapter 7).

Profoundly engaged with folk music as both composer and ethnomusicologist, Bartók believed it offered the basis for a style that was both modern and deeply rooted in his native soil. As he wrote, "A German musician will be able to find in Bach and Beethoven what we had to search for in our villages: the continuity of a national musical tradition." Bartók criticized previous attempts by Hungarian composers to create an authentic national style, dismissing those who in his view simply wedged Gypsy-style tunes or Hungarian dances into works that were otherwise based on Western European models. Yet his early tone poem *Kossuth* (1903), about the national hero who led the nineteenth-century resistance against Austria, is strongly indebted to Wagner, Liszt, and especially Strauss. While the music contains some markers of a national style, as with Sibelius's *Kullervo* it was primarily the piece's programmatic aspects that led listeners to hear it as Hungarian.

The major turning point in Bartók's career came in 1906, when he decided—together with fellow Hungarian composer Zoltán Kodály (1882–1967)—to create a comprehensive collection of Eastern European folk songs. Their goal was to preserve a tradition they viewed as threatened by not only the encroachment of cosmopolitan European styles, but also the commercialized Gypsy music popular in urban cafes and restaurants. This research, which occupied them until the outbreak of World War I, involved numerous tours throughout Hungary and surrounding regions, and as far afield as North Africa. Bartók, who is regarded as one of the founding figures of ethnomusicology, eventually collected nearly 10,000 folk melodies, which he transcribed and annotated in a series of scholarly books and articles. He also published many sets of folk song arrangements, which run the gamut from simple settings to elaborate reinterpretations. Bartók took special interest in tunes that he believed were very old, with roots dating back a thousand years to the Asiatic tribes that became the Hungarian Magyar people.

The political ramifications of any construction of the folk can be seen in the strong opposition Bartók faced because of his decision to study the music of many ethnic groups. He found significant inspiration in the additive rhythms of Bulgarian folk music, with meters made up of groupings of two and three beats, as reflected in the 4+2+3 over 8 time signature in his Fifth String Quartet (1934; Ex. 4.3). For his scholarly claims of the interrelations between Hungarian folk music and other national styles, as well as the bridging of traditions in his own works, Bartók was attacked by those who insisted on notions of national purity. In response he wrote in 1931 of his commitment to "the brotherhood of peoples, brotherhood in spite of all wars and conflicts. . . . Therefore I don't reject any influence, be it Slovakian, Rumanian, Arabic, or from any other source."

In contrast to earlier approaches to folk song that tended to regularize it within the parameters of tonal harmony, Bartók sought to make his transcriptions as accurate as possible. Recognizing the limitations of notation, he was an early advocate for the use of the phonograph in fieldwork. By preserving musical features that resist transcription, including timbre and nuances of rhythm and intonation, recording captured the sound of folk music in all its strangeness. Such recordings also destabilized traditional conceptions of melody and harmony. Writing in 1916, the German music theorist Hugo Riemann identified the use of the phonograph by ethnomusicologists to document other cultures as potentially dangerous, capturing as it did "indications of individual intervals that contradicted our habitual intonations. . . . The annoying result of this research of comparative musicology was, first and foremost, to shake up the very foundations of music theory."

In *Improvisations on Hungarian Peasant Songs*, Op. 20 (1920), Bartók demonstrates his conviction that the value of folk music was not just to preserve a

Example 4.3: *Béla Bartók, String Quartet No. 5, movement 3, Scherzo, mm. 1–4*

vanishing past, but to provide the seed of a new style. The short first movement consists of four increasingly complex variations on a four-measure folk tune. In keeping with his scholarly orientation, Bartók provided information in a preface about this and the other tunes he incorporated in the score, including the texts, and when and where they were collected. Example 4.4 provides the first two measures of each variation.

The drone-like accompaniment of the first variation is built on the first two notes of the Dorian theme. In the second variation, Bartók creates a rough-hewn effect by harmonizing the folk tune with block major and minor triads that lack a functional harmonic context. The more expressive third variation combines the theme with increasingly chromatic and dissonant harmonies, ending with a half-diminished "Tristan" chord. As if to conclude an overview of the development of harmony from modes to the emancipation of the dissonance, the final

Example 4.4: *Béla Bartók*, Improvisations on Hungarian Peasant Songs, *Op. 20, No. 1.*

variation abandons triadic harmonies while preserving only fragments of the tune.

The remarkable emotional trajectory of this short piece, from its simple bucolic beginning to the introspective ruminations of the final section, underscores Bartók's belief that folk materials were the key to the deepest layers of experience. This unlocking is dramatized in his Modernist opera *Duke Bluebeard's Castle* (1911), in which the duke's new bride forces him to open a series of symbolic doors. The focus here, as in many of Bartók's works, is not on specific borrowed tunes, but on creating what he described as a pervasive "atmosphere of peasant music." In the opera's speechlike melodies, modal harmonies, drones, and simple ostinato figures, we can hear what Bartók had in mind when he wrote in his 1931 essay "The Influence of Peasant Music on Modern Music" of a composer's ability to absorb "the idiom of peasant music which has become his musical mother tongue" (SR 198:1440–1441; 7/29:170–171). This implication that a mother tongue is not something you are born with but something you have to master is a stark reminder of the challenges composers faced during these years in forging a sense of identity and wholeness.

STRAVINSKY, RUSSIANNESS, AND THE FOLK ESTRANGED

The composer who figures most prominently in Bartók's essay "The Influence of Peasant Music on Modern Music" is Igor Stravinsky (1882–1971). Stravinsky's *Rite of Spring*, composed in 1913, is a stunningly powerful work that, more than any other, established the link between Modernism, Primitivism, and the folk. Bartók wrote that Stravinsky had increased "a hundredfold" the "air of strange feverish excitement" produced in folk music by "the steady repetition of primitive motives" (SR 198:1440; 7/29:170). In response to Stravinsky's silence about the origins of his themes, Bartók wondered if he used actual folk songs in his ballet or created convincing imitations.

In later years, Stravinsky maintained that, with the exception of the opening of the Introduction, there were no authentic folk melodies in *The Rite of Spring*—but this was part of the composer's attempt in the 1930s to downplay the Russian element in his music (see Chapter 6). In his ghostwritten *Autobiography* (1936), Stravinsky distanced himself from the "ethnographic, nationalistic aesthetic" and dismissed interest in folklore as "a sterile tendency and an evil from which many artists suffer." Stravinsky was then living in France as a French citizen, having left Russia 25 years earlier. The vehemence of his language reflects both the emergence of a new aesthetic in his music after World War I and his conviction that the folklorist tendency had been implicated with Bolshevism and the destructive forces that led to the Russian Revolution.

In attacking the folklorists, however, Stravinsky was disavowing his own past. Born near St. Petersburg into an upper-class and musical family—his father was a singer in the imperial opera—Stravinsky was intended for a legal career. But his musical interests led him in 1903 to composition lessons with Nikolay Rimsky-Korsakov (1844–1908), one of the so-called Mighty Handful of composers who had worked to create a distinctive Russian style in the second half of the nineteenth century. Rimsky-Korsakov's influence, as well as that of Mikhail Glinka (1804–1857) and, especially, Modest Musorgsky (1839–1881), is clear in many aspects of Stravinsky's "Russian Period" works, most famously the three ballets *L'oiseau de feu* (The Firebird, 1910), *Petrushka* (1911), and *The Rite of Spring*. These characteristics include the use of modal, whole-tone, and octatonic collections; an emphasis on unusual orchestral effects; subject matter drawn from characteristically Russian settings and scenarios; and the central role of Russian folk tunes.

The final section of *The Firebird* illustrates how much Stravinsky learned from his predecessors, starting with the theme, which is based on a folk tune that had appeared in a collection published by Rimsky-Korsakov in 1878 (Ex. 4.5). Modeled closely on the techniques of Glinka and Musorgsky, the entire finale consists of repetitions of the melody over changing accompaniments. Thus, rather than the characteristically Germanic techniques of development through harmonic motion or developing variation, the focus is on shifting timbres, textures, dynamics, and register.

The "Russianness" of Stravinsky's music from these years was also a product of his close involvement with the Ballets Russes (Russian Ballet), founded in 1909 by Serge Diaghilev (1872–1929), who commissioned him to write the music for the three ballets mentioned earlier and several other pieces. The Ballets Russes did not restrict itself to Russian-themed works; one of the company's most famous ballets was based on Debussy's *Prelude to "The Afternoon of a Faun"* (see Chapter 2), and Stravinsky's next major work for Diaghilev after the *Rite* was the "musical fairy tale" *Le rossignol* (The Nightingale, 1914), set in ancient China and based on a story by the Danish writer Hans Christian Andersen. But a col-

Example 4.5: *Igor Stravinsky*, The Firebird, *Finale, Rehearsal 197. Piano transcription by Stravinsky*

orful and exotic Russianness was a major part of the attraction of the Ballets Russes for the Parisian public. Thus *The Firebird* was based on well-known Russian folktales, *Petrushka* captured the characteristic sounds of a street fair in St. Petersburg at Carnival time, while *The Rite of Spring* reimagined rituals of prehistoric Russian tribes.

The idea of Russia that shaped these and other productions was a product of the strong nationalist movement that developed in Russia at the end of the nineteenth century. Associated with the influential journal *The World of Art*, Diaghilev and his fellow nationalists believed that the only way to create an authentic Russian art was by integrating ancient and uncorrupted folk art and music with Modernist techniques. In the words of the artist Ivan Bilibin from 1904: "Nationalist artists are faced with a task of colossal difficulty: using this rich and ancient heritage, they must create something new and serious that logically follows from what has survived. . . . There may even be created, at last, a new, completely individual Russian style with nothing of tawdriness about it."

The Rite of Spring pushed this idea further than any previous work, further indeed than the audiences who had made the previous ballets so successful were willing to go. To the end of his life Stravinsky smarted from the famous scandal incited by the Paris premiere of the *Rite*. Beyond the extremely dissonant music, the choreography by Vaslav Nijinsky was unorthodox and intentionally ungainly, while the scenario by the painter, writer, and amateur anthropologist Nicholas Roerich was obscure and violent. Subtitled *Scenes of Pagan Russia*, the ballet depicts a prehistoric Slavonic tribe celebrating the arrival of spring and ensuring the fertility of their land by offering a human sacrifice.

The work is in two parts. The first, *The Adoration of the Earth*, is made up of short, contrasting sections depicting ritualistic games of abduction and mock battles of rival tribes. Central to Stravinsky's and Roerich's conception of these rituals was an association between the awakening of the earth in spring and the sexual awakening of adolescence. In his article "What I Wished to Express in *The Rite of Spring*," published the day of the premiere in Paris on May 29, 1913, the composer wrote of the Introduction as representing the "vague and profound uneasiness of a universal puberty." Part 2 narrows the focus ominously to the selection of the "Chosen One," building relentlessly to the brutal *Sacrificial Dance*, in which the maiden chosen for the sacrifice repeatedly attempts to leap off the ground until she dies from exhaustion.

Great care was taken in the creation of the scenario, costumes, and scenery. Roerich sought ethnographic authenticity by drawing on sixteenth-century accounts of surviving pagan rituals. Stravinsky selected melodies that were connected with sun worship and springtime celebrations, and sought out folk material in the most accurate transcriptions. Yet the overall conception of *The Rite of Spring*, and the folk who appear within it, was shaped just as much by Modernist fantasies of the primitive. That we are not dealing with actual people

is evident in Stravinsky's description of the "very old woman" in the first section of the ballet, "whose age, and even whose century is unknown, who knows
the secrets of nature, and teaches her sons Prediction. She runs, bent over the
earth, half-woman, half-beast." The adolescent girls who then appear are "not
entirely formed beings; their sex is single and double like that of the tree."
Nijinsky wrote in even stronger terms of his intention to prevent the emergence
of any sense of individuality or subjectivity among the dancers: "It is the life
of the stones and the trees. There are no human beings in it. . . . It is a thing of
concrete masses, not of individual effects."

Stravinsky created musical counterpoints to these representations of the folk
as strange and even inhuman. In the opening measures of the Introduction, the
folk melody undergoes an unsettling transformation, starting with the peculiar
timbre of the bassoon at the top of its range (see Anthology 6). By dissolving the
original meter and adding a dissonant harmonization, Stravinsky detaches the
pitches of the melody from any sense of hierarchy or direction. He thus inverts
the Russian musical tradition of using folk melodies and diatonic harmonies
to depict the human sphere and scenes of folk life, while reserving octatonic
and whole-tone scales for the foreign, supernatural, or monstrous. In a striking
example of the Primitivist impulse, the rhythmic manipulation and dissonant
harmonization transform the folk tune into something uncanny and "other."
Over the course of the Introduction this feeling intensifies as layers upon layers
of similarly fragmented material pile up, capturing what Stravinsky described
as "the fear of nature before the arising of beauty, a sacred terror at the midday
sun, a sort of pagan cry."

The first scene of the ballet, *Augurs of Spring: Dances of the Young Girls,* takes
the idea of harmonic stasis to an extreme; this is made manifest in the notation
Stravinsky used in his sketchbook for the famous "Augurs" chord, which appears
in the middle of the page (Fig. 4.2). Because the harmony does not change for
eight measures, he indicates only the pounding quarter notes and shifting
accents. Stravinsky notates the chord as an F♭-major triad combined with a
first-inversion dominant seventh on E♭. Unlike the equally famous "Petrushka"
chord, made up of C-major and F♯-major triads, which is strictly octatonic, the
"Augurs" chord reflects Stravinsky's more typical practice of integrating octatonic and diatonic elements. In this case only one pitch, the E♭, would need to be
changed to D to fit within the octatonic collection C♯–D–E–F–G–A♭–B♭–B. But
the E♭ is crucial to the ostinato figure D♭–B♭–E♭–B♭ that is used throughout the
passage, as can be seen in many of the sketches on the page.

From this drastically reduced material Stravinsky builds up an extended passage, starting with eight measures of the "Augurs" chord, in which the violent
stomping of the dancers is accompanied by jarringly syncopated accents that dis-
rupt the duple meter established by the ostinato. As the section goes on, Stravinsky
creates contrast not through harmonic changes but by shifting textures. As can
be seen in the last two measures of the central sketch in Figure 4.2, he replaces

Figure 4.2: *Igor Stravinsky, sketchbook page for* The Rite of Spring

vertical statements of the "Augurs" chord with arpeggiations of the component harmonies (with the addition of C), while the ostinato provides the top notes of the chord. The sketch also shows how important timbre was in Stravinsky's basic conception of the material; from the earliest stages of the compositional process he indicates instrumentation and effects like pizzicato and the use of mutes.

The collage-like approach to form here and throughout the *Rite*, in which Stravinsky juxtaposes blocks of music rather than making smooth transitions between sections, further contributes to the Primitivist effect. Just as Nijinsky described choreographing the dancers in terms of masses rather than individuals, Stravinsky conceived of his musical material as if he were manipulating objects, including the isolated blocks of music scattered across his sketch page for the *Rite*.

Experiencing *The Rite of Spring* as a ballet or, as is more frequently the case today, in concert performance is a shattering experience. Rather than inviting us to identify with the Chosen One or hope that she will somehow escape her fate (as in most nineteenth-century operas and ballets), the *Rite* joins us to the tribe, whose welfare depends on the protagonist's death. This escape from individuality into a communal experience offered by the folk and the primitive is both seductive and alarming.

Some have viewed *The Rite of Spring*, with its struggles between rival tribes and its dance of death, as a prelude to the wholesale sacrifice of youth that would soon take place on the battlefields of Europe. Many works from these years are concerned with premonitions of cataclysm and apocalypse. Some artists prophesied destruction and collapse, while others envisioned catharsis and regeneration for mankind, but there was a widespread sense of possibility that the world could and should change profoundly. When World War I broke out in the summer of 1914, many intellectuals and artists in Europe and the United States responded with enthusiasm and even joy. They viewed the war as an opportunity to right old wrongs, to sweep away the encrusted traditions of the past, and to realize the transformative potential of avant-garde art. Yet by the time the war ended in 1918, it was clear that the world had changed far more profoundly than anyone could have anticipated.

The war and its vast ramifications also added new layers of meaning and complexity to the search for stability, authenticity, and national identity in folk music, while making explicit all that was at stake in determining what folk music is and who should be regarded as the folk. By the time the war began, Stravinsky had already moved with his family to Switzerland, an important step in the long process of severing ties with his homeland that accelerated after the Russian Revolution in 1917. As we will see in Chapter 6, his Neoclassical works after the war took inspiration from very different sources.

Bartók's Hungary was also dramatically changed by the war; the loss of more than two-thirds of its territory provoked a strongly xenophobic nationalism that made Bartók's openness to other traditions and Modernist ideas increasingly out of step. Like Stravinsky, his postwar music (see Chapter 7) introduced new solutions to the challenge of creating order within the increasingly "tangled chaos" of possibilities. The Russian Revolution also resulted in Finland gaining its independence, but the country soon plunged into a civil war; Sibelius's own house was occupied for a time by forces attempting to expand the Bolshevik Revolution. His later symphonies represent a turning inward in response to what he saw as the impending collapse of his musical world. Despite his international fame, there was a marked slowdown in his compositional output in the 1920s; he wrote his final work in 1931, then fell silent for the last 26 years of his life.

For many in the United States the war and revolutions overseas seemed at first to be very far away. But a German submarine's 1915 sinking of the *Lusitania*, a British passenger ship en route from New York to Liverpool with many Americans among the lost, shattered the sense of safe isolation. Ives gave musical expression to the nationalistic feelings the attack provoked in the last movement of his Second Orchestral Set, *From Hannover Square North, at the end of a Tragic Day, the Voice of the People Again Arose* (started shortly after the attack and completed in 1919). His inspiration was a diverse crowd of New Yorkers on an elevated train platform he heard responding to the shocking news of the attack by spontaneously joining together to sing "Sweet By and By." He describes the tone poem as depicting, amid the multitudinous bustle of the city, "the sense of many people living, working, and occasionally going through the same deep experience together."

FOR FURTHER READING

Bayley, Amanda, ed., *The Cambridge Companion to Bartók* (Cambridge: Cambridge University Press, 2001)

Bohlman, Philip, *The Study of Folk Music in the Modern World* (Bloomington: Indiana University Press, 1988)

Brooks, William, "Unity and Diversity in Ives's Fourth Symphony," *Yearbook of Inter-American Research* 10 (1974): 5–49

Grimley, Daniel, ed., *The Cambridge Companion to Sibelius* (Cambridge: Cambridge University Press, 2004)

Magee, Gayle Sherwood, *Charles Ives Reconsidered* (Urbana: University of Illinois Press, 2008)

Smith, Catherine Parsons, "'A Distinguishing Virility': Feminism and Modernism in American Art Music," in *Cecilia Reclaimed: Feminist Perspectives on Gender and Music*, edited by Susan C. Cook and Judy S. Tsou, 90–106 (Urbana: University of Illinois Press, 1994)

Taruskin, Richard, "Nationalism," in *Grove Music Online; Oxford Music Online*

Watkins, Glenn, *Pyramids at the Louvre: Music, Culture, and Collage from Stravinsky to the Postmodernists* (Cambridge, MA: Harvard University Press, 1994)

PART II

The Interwar Years

The years immediately after World War I marked a major turning point in music history, as composers, performers, and audiences confronted the exhilarating and disorienting realities of the Roaring Twenties. Much that defines our world today would be unthinkable without the new freedoms that resulted from the collapse of the old social and political orders. And yet the redrawing of both real and metaphorical maps that people used to give direction to their lives created profound uncertainties. At the same time a dramatic cycle of economic boom and bust led to the Great Depression, which began in the United States in 1929 and had global repercussions. These disruptions, together with the rise of increasingly repressive and totalitarian Fascist and Communist regimes around the world, helped set the stage for the outbreak of World War II in 1939.

Part I focused on efforts in the first two decades of the century to open up new musical worlds by pushing established techniques to extremes, developing new languages, and integrating elements from folk music and other traditions. In the interwar years such solutions no longer seemed adequate; creative artists in many fields rejected both the legacy of nineteenth-century Romanticism and what they came to view as a self-indulgent and solipsistic Modernism. But musicians disagreed about how musical Modernism might be reconfigured, as we will see in the "tangled chaos" of slogans, movements, and styles that characterized the "New Music" of the twenties and thirties.

For the younger composers who came of age after World War I, it was a time of bold proclamations and iconoclasm, but several members of the previous generation also sought to separate themselves from past practices, including their own. The writer Jean Cocteau (see Chapter 6), who had gained notoriety through his attacks on Impressionism, Exoticism, Expressionism, and Primitivism, and "the spells exerted by *Le sacre du printemps*," admitted that "in self-rejection Stravinsky was to outdo us all." Stravinsky was one of many, including Bartók and Schoenberg, whose music changed dramatically after the war. As we have already noted in the case of Sibelius, there were some who found it difficult simply to keep composing as the world around them was transformed.

Chapter 5 surveys the political, cultural, and social transformations that shaped musical developments in the interwar period. Technological innovations, including the radio, phonograph, and player piano, opened up a host of possibilities for reaching audiences in new ways, while also challenging long-held assumptions about who the audience was and what they needed or wanted. Many questioned the whole meaning and purpose of art, the role of emotional expression, and the notion of artists as geniuses composing only for themselves. In response, composers sought inspiration and relevance in many quarters, ranging from jazz to the sounds of the Machine Age and new electronic instruments.

Chapter 6 focuses on the diverse and politically charged musical scene in Paris, which brought together artists from around the world in an environment that encouraged new cultural fusions. An eclectic Neoclassical impulse combined the historical and contemporary in new ways by resurrecting elements from the classical world of ancient Greece and Rome, as well as the styles and forms of Baroque and Classical music from the eighteenth century. Many turned as well to popular music and "everyday" art as a source for new sounds and modes of expression.

In Chapter 7 we see how composers in many locales responded to the unsettled situation by undertaking a self-conscious search for order and stability in their work. Whether they created alternative theoretical models for tonality, innovative techniques for working with rhythm and other elements of music, or bold new methods like Schoenberg's "composition with 12 tones related only to one other," these efforts reflected a conviction that music required a new foundation to survive.

Chapter 8 turns to a different set of responses to the postwar situation that involved rebuilding or inventing national musical traditions. Starting with the ways in which diverse elements were brought together to create a sense of musical "Brazilianness" and "Englishness," we conclude by considering the challenges composers faced in defining and representing the heterogeneous American musical landscape.

CHAPTER FIVE

New Music Taking Flight

In the wake of World War I, heated debates arose concerning not just musical style, but the most basic assumptions about the purpose of art and the role of the artist. The musical scene was a maze of competing movements and slogans, many of them claiming to be "new" in one way or another. Radio and recording expanded rapidly, giving composers access to larger audiences than ever before, even as they struggled for attention and relevance as jazz and other styles surged in popularity. The creation of new-music societies throughout Europe and the United States spawned a raft of festivals that provided a context for contemporary composition, while helping shape musical developments by focusing on such topics as music for amateurs and new technologies.

The tremendous diversity of styles and trends that could be heard at these events is represented by the Third Chamber Music Festival of the International Society of Contemporary Music, held in Venice in September 1925 (Fig. 5.1). Selected by a panel of composers from nine countries, the programs included works by many composers who figure in this book, along with some whose names are largely forgotten. In a commentary published shortly after the event, the Czech composer Leoš Janáček (1854–1928) wrote: "I like these festivals of modern music. Twenty-eight composers of as many works and not one resembled another." Janáček, who was represented by his String Quartet No. 1 (1923), approvingly noted works that continued in the Romantic vein, those with echoes of Classicism, and those infused with a "healthy cheekiness." But even the open-minded Janáček reached his limit

PROGRAMMI DEI CONCERTI

Ore 21

I. — 3 Settembre.

a) Quartetto d'archi . . . . ERWIN SCHULHOFF
b) "L'horizon chimérique" (canto) . . . . GABRIEL FAURÉ
c) Duo per violino e violoncello . . . . HANS EISLER
d) Impressioni di Pekino (orchestra da camera) . . . . HENRY EICHEIM
    1. - Notturno.
    2. - Schizzo coreano.
e) Jazzband per violino e piano . . . . WILHELM GROSZ
f) 1. Quattro epigrammi ironici e sentimentali . . . }HEITOR DE VILLA-LOBOS
   2. Historieta (canto) . . . . }
g) Concerto per piano e orchestra da camera . . . . . PAUL HINDEMITH

Ore 21

II. — 4 Settembre.

a) Sonata per piano e violoncello . . . . GASPAR CASSADÒ
b) Tre preludi per pianoforte . . . . SAMUEL FEINBERG
c) Sonata per violino solo . . . . ZOLTAN SZEKELY
d) Cinque pezzi per quartetto d'archi . . . . MAX BUTTING
e) Tre lieder per canto . . . . LADISLAV VYCPÁLEK
f) Quartetto d'archi . . . . LEOŠ JANÁČEK

Ore 21

III. — 5 Settembre.

a) Quartetto d'archi - op. 16 . . . . ERICH W. KORNGOLD
b) Due tempi per due flauti, clarinetto e fagotto . . . . JACQUES IBERT
c) Sonata per violoncello e piano . . . . ARTHUR HONEGGER
d) Joueurs de flûte (quattro pezzi per flauto e pianoforte). ALBERT ROUSSEL
e) Tzigane (per violino e pianoforte) . . . . MAURICE RAVEL
f) Sonata per piano, flauto, oboe e fagotto . . . . . VITTORIO RIETI

Ore 21

IV. — 7 Settembre.

a) Quartetto d'archi . . . . MARIO LABROCA
b) Sonata per pianoforte . . . . ARTHUR SCHNABEL
c) Merciless beauty (canto) . . . . . . , ... R. VAUGHAN WILLIAMS
d) Serenata per orchestra da camera . . . . ARNOLD SCHÖNBERG

Ore 21

V. — 8 Settembre.

a) Quartetto d'archi . . . . KAROL SZYMANOWSKY
b) Le stagioni italiche (canto) . . . . G. FRANCESCO MALIPIERO
c) Angels (per sei trombe sole) . . . . CARL RUGGLES
d) Sonata per pianoforte . . . . IGOR STRAWINSKI
e) The Daniel Jazz (canto e orchestra da camera) . . . LOUIS GRUENBERG

Figure 5.1: *Program, Third Chamber Music Festival of the International Society of Contemporary Music, Venice, 1925*

with some pieces, expressing reservations about Schoenberg's proto-twelve-tone Serenade, Op. 24 (see Chapter 7), and the jazz-inspired piece *The Daniel Jazz* (1925) by the American Louis Gruenberg: their works, he wrote, "reeked only of the tavern, and their gaiety was dying away."

We can see how quickly the world and music were changing by considering a piece that premiered four years later at a German new-music festival, one of the themes of which was composition for the radio. *Der Lindberghflug* (Lindbergh's Flight, 1929) was jointly composed by Kurt Weill (1900–1950) and Paul Hindemith (1895–1963). Written specifically for the radio to a text by Bertolt Brecht, the cantata employs soloists, chorus, and orchestra to tell the story of the pioneering transatlantic flight in 1927 by the American pilot Charles Lindbergh.

Lindbergh took off from Roosevelt Field on Long Island, New York, and flew over 33 hours before landing in Paris, a feat that earned him a $25,000 prize. The 40-minute-long piece depicts the excited crowds at each end of the journey and his battles en route against fog, snow, and weariness. In the song "Introduction of the Pilot" (see Anthology 7), composed by Weill, Lindbergh describes his preparations in the terse, objective language of a news report:

> My name is Charles Lindbergh. I am twenty-five years old. My grandfather was Swedish. I am an American. I selected my airplane myself. It flies two hundred ten kilometers per hour. It's called the "Spirit of St. Louis." The Ryan airplane factory in San Diego built it in sixty days. I was there for sixty days, and I spent sixty days charting my course on my maps. I fly alone. Instead of a person, I am bringing along more fuel.

As we saw in Chapter 2, Debussy spoke of the need for a music suited to the "century of aeroplanes." Here we have a cantata in which an airplane is one of the main characters; at one point Lindbergh even talks encouragingly to the motor and asks if it has enough gas and oil.

In terms of subject matter, *Lindbergh's Flight* has points of contact with the Italian Futurists' fascination with technology, while the incorporation of popular materials can be linked to Mahler, Debussy, and Ives (see Chapters 2, 3, and 4). But the overall effect is sharply different in both musical style and subject matter from the pieces we considered earlier. In contrast to the mysterious and exotic musical worlds of Stravinsky's *Rite of Spring*, Schoenberg's *Pierrot lunaire*, and Debussy's *Pagodas*, the strangest aspect of *Lindbergh's Flight* is just how commonplace both the music and the words seem on first acquaintance.

Weill's early works, such as the Expressionist opera *Der Protagonist* (The Protagonist, 1920) and the Violin Concerto (1924), show the influence of his teacher Busoni, as well as of Stravinsky and Schoenberg, with whom he had also hoped to study. But in contrast to the acerbic dissonances and tonal ambiguity of his earlier harmonic language, "Introduction of the Pilot" features a simple declamatory vocal melody, tonal progressions, and jazz-inflected harmonies.

Weill also evokes the world of jazz with prominent wind solos and dancelike syncopated rhythms above a steady chordal accompaniment in a moderate "Blues-Tempo."

And yet there is much about the piece that is likely to strike listeners today as peculiar. If we listen to the 1930 Berlin broadcast recording of *Lindbergh's Flight*, we hear the song through a haze of static and noise that underscores our distance from a very different time and place. While "Introduction of the Pilot" strikes a note of emotional intensity when Lindbergh decides to take off despite the threat of bad weather, the prevailing tone is coolly detached. Just as Brecht goes out of his way to avoid effusive personal expression in the text, Weill's music also keeps us at arm's length. Although Weill would demonstrate his mastery of popular idioms in his successful Broadway career after moving to the United States in 1933, it is clear that "Introduction of the Pilot" was intended to be something other than a hit song.

To better understand both the familiar and foreign elements of *Lindbergh's Flight*, and the diverse and contradictory cultural developments of the 1920s and 1930s, we need to step back and consider some of the social and political factors that shaped musical life during the interwar years.

EUROPE AND AMERICA AFTER THE WAR

The most immediate impact of the war that was supposed to "end all wars" was the tremendous human loss. Of the 74 million soldiers mobilized by all the nations involved in the conflict, almost 10 million died; the total number of military and civilian casualties (the latter mostly due to famine) was about 37.5 million. The resulting collapse of faith in the institutions that had destroyed so many lives contributed to the breakdown of centuries-old political structures. In Germany, Kaiser Wilhelm's abdication in 1918 led to a period of revolution and civil war. The founding of the Weimar Republic in 1919 was marked by a proliferation of parties across the political spectrum, which managed to govern only through complex and shifting alliances. Weill aligned himself for a time with a group of Socialist and Communist artists in Berlin called the November Group, named in honor of the month when the German revolution was launched.

Russia had already experienced its own revolution with the abdication of the tsar in 1917 and the emergence of Vladimir Lenin and the Bolsheviks at the head of the world's first Communist government. Equally dramatic was the breakup of the vast Austro-Hungarian Empire after the death in 1916 of Emperor Franz Joseph, who had reigned since 1848 as a member of the Habsburg dynasty, which in turn dated back to the eleventh century. As the novelist Stefan Zweig, whom we met in Chapter 2, wrote in *The World of Yesterday*: "I was born in 1881 in a great and mighty empire, in the monarchy of the Habsburgs. But do not look for it on any map; it has been swept away without a trace." In its place arose a collection of newly independent states—Hungary, Czechoslovakia, and Yugoslavia—while Austria was greatly reduced in size and influence. Although the United States entered the war belatedly in 1917, it too was profoundly changed, emerging as a world power and a symbol of capitalist affluence.

As Zweig's elegiac tone suggests, World War I and the ensuing political and economic disruptions also destabilized individuals' lives and psyches. As the first modern conflict involving submarines, poison gas, and airplanes, the war dealt severe blows to the idea of progress and the belief that science and technology would solve all problems. In his classic antiwar novel *All Quiet on the Western Front* (1928), Erich Maria Remarque described a young German soldier on leave from the front at home in his room painfully revisiting his cherished collection of books that had meant so much to him before the start of the war:

> I take out one of the books, intending to read, and turn over the leaves. But I put it away and take out another. There are passages in it that have been marked. I look, turn over the pages, take fresh books. Already they are piled up beside me. Speedily more join the heap, papers, magazines, letters.
>
> I stand there dumb. As before a judge.
> Dejected.
> Words, Words, Words—they do not reach me.
> Slowly I place the books back in the shelves.
> Nevermore.
> Quietly, I go out of the room.

Much has been written about the trauma of trench warfare. Here we see how the war severed a soldier completely from his old life and the world of ideas that had given it meaning.

Some of the most extreme manifestations of this sense of disillusionment were associated with the Dada anti-art movement, which sprang up in Switzerland and soon spread to many countries. The Romanian-born poet Tristan Tzara, one of the movement's leading figures, viewed art as a pretentious irrelevance in a civilization capable of such stupidity and wanton violence. In the "Dada manifesto," published in 1918, he wrote: "There is great destructive, negative work to be done. To sweep, to clean. The cleanliness of the individual materializes after we've gone through folly, the aggressive, complete folly of a world left in the hands of bandits who have demolished and destroyed the centuries."

Dada rejected established forms of expression in all the arts; Tzara, for example, wrote a poem that called for musicians to smash their instruments. The Dadaists emphasized instead new forms of confrontational, and sometimes nonsensical, performance, or gave new meaning to existing works and objects through collage and other forms of repurposing. In 1917 the French artist Marcel Duchamp famously scandalized the art world by presenting a urinal as a sculpture sardonically entitled *Fountain*.

THE NEW MORALITY OF THE ROARING TWENTIES

This sense of rupture from traditional values and beliefs permeated many aspects of life. Hyperinflation in Germany, which made the currency practically worthless, turned Weimar society on its head by punishing those who had scrimped and saved while rewarding those who lived for the moment. Widespread food shortages and the collapse of normal channels of distribution forced even law-abiding citizens to trade on the black market. In the United States, the enactment of Prohibition in 1919 led illegal speakeasies to flourish. Social and moral structures were further undermined by the unrestrained speculation, corruption, and get-rich-quick schemes that fueled the precipitous economic growth of the Roaring Twenties, and then led to its collapse in the devastating worldwide depression of the 1930s.

No musical genre commented more effectively on the new morality, or lack of it, than the mordantly satirical songs popularized in the cabarets of Berlin and other German cities. "Alles Schwindel" (It's All a Swindle, 1931), by the cabaret and film composer Mischa Spoliansky and lyricist Marcellus Schiffer, made light of the country's pervasive criminality. Not only do "Papa" and "Mama" swindle, the song claims, but so does "Grandmama" and even the family dog: "Nowadays the world is rotten / honesty has been forgotten / Fall in love but after kissing / check your purse to see what's missing."

As "Alles Schwindel" suggests, the postwar years also saw significant changes in the relationship between the sexes. Despite a decline in organized women's movements compared to the first decade of the century, the 1920s and 1930s were the heyday of the New Woman, as women shifted in the workforce from farm and domestic employment to urban industry and the service sector. Women also played a larger role in politics; the constitution of the Weimar Republic gave them the right to vote in 1919, and the United States followed suit the next year. Increasing mobility and visibility brought a range of new images of and by women, from the representations of the urban poor by female artists such as Käthe Kollwitz and Hannah Höch to the "modern" young woman with short bobbed hair in the photograph *Secretary at West German Radio in Cologne* (1931) by August Sander (Fig. 5.2).

THE NEW OBJECTIVITY

The "New Objectivity" (*Neue Sachlichkeit*) that developed between the wars in music, painting, architecture, and literature was defined by a rejection of the intense emotions and subjectivity that characterized both Romanticism

Figure 5.2: *August Sander,* Secretary at West German Radio in Cologne *(1931)*

and Expressionism (see Chapter 3). In his essay "Women and the New Objectivity" (1929), the Czech literary critic Max Brod wrote of the "hard, cold, masculine tone" that characterized recent literature and music. He attributed it to the disillusionment of the younger generation, who as a result of the war had "justifiably learned to mistrust everything that partook of the passions of the heart."

The new fashion was for irony, sarcasm, parody, or simply no emotion at all. The American composer George Antheil, discussed further later, wrote in his memoir *Bad Boy of Music* (1945) that living in Berlin after World War I had served "to house-clean out of me all the remaining old poesy, false sentimentalism, and overjuicy overidyllicism. I now found, for instance, that I could no longer bear the mountainous sentiment of Richard Strauss or even what now seemed to be the fluid diaphanous lechery of the recent French impressionists." The music Antheil liked best was Stravinsky's, which he described as "hard, cold, unsentimental, enormously brilliant and virtuous." As we will see in Chapter 6, Stravinsky became a standard bearer for the idea that music was "essentially powerless to *express* anything at all, whether a feeling, an attitude of mind, a psychological mood, or a phenomenon of nature."

Brecht's dispassionately factual text for *Lindbergh's Flight* illustrates the new desire for clarity, simplicity, and objectivity. The pilot's description of the plane and the preparations for his flight are hardly the stuff of great poetry, and that is precisely the point. In this and other works, Brecht sought to elicit a detached response from the audience so that the artwork became less an entertainment than a "lesson" (*Lehrstück*). Indeed, the subtitle of *Lindbergh's Flight* was *Radiolehrstück*, underscoring Brecht's goal of encouraging listeners to learn from the performance by reflecting on their own situations.

One of the most famous products of the anti-Romantic reaction is *Die Dreigroschenoper* (The Threepenny Opera, 1928), which attracted crowds in thousands of performances across Europe and the United States. In this satirical theater piece, Weill and Brecht skewer all sectors of society; the main character, Mack the Knife, is a murderous criminal who develops a strong attraction to Polly Peachum, the daughter of a couple who make their living running a racket of fake beggars. Instead of celebrating love, the opera's songs mock sentimental romance.

The Threepenny Opera is modeled on a work written exactly two centuries earlier, *The Beggar's Opera* (1728) by the British composer John Gay (1685–1732). Gay was satirizing the dominant opera composer of his time, George Frideric Handel, whose work enjoyed a major revival during the Weimar Republic. In the postwar years, the clarity and logic of Handel's music (and even more significantly of J. S. Bach's) offered a welcome escape from subjectivity and emotion. We will return in Chapter 6 to the revival of Baroque and Classical forms and genres that was central to the Neoclassicism of the 1920s and 1930s.

The New Objectivity also influenced performance by fostering a rejection of what came to be regarded as overly effusive Romantic interpretations, marked above all by the constant use of rubato. The new fashion was for strict metronomic tempos, particularly in the performance of Baroque music. Stravinsky and others left no doubt that these practices, as well as the move away from the large orchestras of the nineteenth century, were intended to repudiate the expressivity of Romanticism. "Now, I go back to Bach," he wrote, "not Bach as we know him today, but Bach as he really is. You know now they play Bach with a Wagner orchestra and make him sound very pleasant, so people will like him."

An equally important influence on the performance of both early and modern music was the steady time kept by the rhythm sections of jazz and dance bands. We can also see the influence of the New Objectivity in the appeal to many composers of the player piano, which accounted for more than half of total piano sales in the early 1920s, both because of its precision and because it removed the element of interpretation from performance. Stravinsky prepared definitive versions of many of his works for the mechanized instrument, and Antheil brought player pianos on stage as an integral part of his *Ballet mécanique* (see p. 94).

RADIO, RECORDING, AND FILM

Novel technologies also had a far-reaching impact on musical composition, performance, and reception between the wars. By the time of the broadcast of *Lindbergh's Flight* in 1930 there were over three million radio receivers in Germany. The gramophone, which used flat lacquer discs rather than the cylinders of Edison's phonograph, experienced equally explosive growth; in the United States in 1927 alone nearly one million phonograph players were sold, along with more than one hundred million discs. In contrast to the state-controlled radio stations in Europe, radio in the United States was developed by what soon became major media corporations, including RCA (Radio Corporation of America) and NBC (National Broadcasting Company), founded in 1919 and 1926, respectively. After many years of experimentation and competing technologies, film with a synchronized sound track hit the mainstream in 1927 with *The Jazz Singer,* starring the popular blackface performer Al Jolson. Many of the composers we will discuss in the following chapters wrote film scores; for some it even became an important focus of their work.

Weill was involved with radio from early in his career, starting in 1925 as chief critic for a weekly radio magazine. He and many others viewed radio as an important tool for creating new music and reaching new audiences; works like *Lindbergh's Flight,* Weill believed, represented "an independent and valid art form." He wrote in 1926:

> We can see the artistic significance of radio only in the development of this specifically radio art, not at all in the continuation of the existing concert life. . . . For only radio can replace those more superficial formal concerts, which have become superfluous, by a worthwhile and really fruitful mass art: it alone can guarantee that widest dissemination which will produce the artistic public of the future.

Seeking to make their music accessible to radio's mass audience, composers like Weill rejected the complexities of prewar Modernism. In an essay titled *Shifts in Musical Production* (1927), Weill wrote that what was required in the new music was "clarity of language," "precision of expression," and "simplicity of emotion" (SR 186:1395; 7/17:125).

Weill's interest in small ensembles, simple textures, sharply defined rhythms, and clear melodies can be attributed in part to the sonic characteristics of early radio technology. Radio's limited frequency range produced a weak bass register, and the obtrusive background noise rendered soft dynamics inaudible. High voices sounded better than low voices, while instruments like the trumpet, clarinet, and saxophone came across better than strings. The phonograph presented its own technological constraints to which composers likewise had to adapt. Thus when Stravinsky wrote his Serenade in A for piano (1925), he made sure that each movement fit the three-minute maximum of a disc turning at the then-standard rate of 78 revolutions per minute, just as rock bands in the 1950s and 1960s would tailor their songs to the length of the 45-rpm single and today's pop stars keep in mind the 10- to 30-second duration of successful ringtones.

Radio and phonograph technologies allowed a musical performance to travel through space and time to reach listeners wherever they happened to be. Hermann Hesse's novel *Steppenwolf* (1927) features a character who appears sometimes as Mozart and other times as a "Spanish or South American" jazz saxophone player. In a climactic scene involving a radio broadcast of a Handel concerto grosso, the character exclaims:

> Observe how this crazy funnel apparently does the most stupid, the most useless and the most damnable thing in the world. It takes hold of some music played where you please, without distinction, stupid and coarse, lamentably distorted, to boot, and chucks it into space to land where it has no business to be; and yet after all this it cannot destroy the original spirit of the music; it can only demonstrate its own senseless mechanism.

In contrast to this unfavorable view, the German critic and philosopher Walter Benjamin argued in his influential essay *The Work of Art in the Age of Mechanical Reproduction* (1936) that such technologies represented a fundamental change in the nature of art, the artist, and the audience. Benjamin noted that Western art had traditionally served cult or ritual purposes for the wealthy and powerful, depending on unique objects of great age and value being kept locked away in museums, palaces, or churches. Technologies of reproduction and transmission shattered that tradition by bringing an unlimited number of copies up close to the new mass audience.

For Benjamin this development was both destructive and cathartic: destructive in that all the old Romantic ideas of art such as genius, eternal value, and mystery were lost, together with the inherent value of the unique, original work of art; cathartic in that this painful but necessary process made it possible for art to serve a vastly expanded audience, while reaching each listener in his or her own particular situation. Writing after Hitler's Third Reich had replaced the Weimar Republic—when it seemed that democracy had failed, fascism would triumph, and communism was the only hope—Benjamin believed that art had to engage with the new world:

> For the first time in world history, mechanical reproduction emancipates the work of art from its parasitical dependence on ritual. To an ever greater degree the work of art reproduced becomes the work of art designed for reproducibility. From a photographic negative, for example, one can make any number of prints; to ask for the "authentic" print makes no sense. But the instant the criterion of authenticity ceases to be applicable to artistic production, the total function of art is reversed. Instead of being based on ritual, it begins to be based on another practice—politics.

Radio was of special interest to left-wing artists and intellectuals like Benjamin, Brecht, and Weill because it could reach an audience that was not circumscribed by national boundaries. This is underscored in the 1930 broadcast of *Lindbergh's Flight*, which featured introductions to each scene in German, English, and French. Those on the political right saw the potential of radio as well; Hitler remarked that without it the Nazi Party never would have been able to gain control of Germany.

MUSIC FOR USE

Weill's call for a "specifically radio art" marked a major shift away from the Romantic ideology of "art for art's sake," which insisted on art's freedom from a function or purpose other than aesthetic contemplation. The new slogan "music for use" (*Gebrauchsmusik*) required composers to create works tailored to the intended audience's needs and preferences, as well as to the specific medium used (we return to *Gebrauchsmusik* in Chapter 7). In contrast to the Romantic ideal of the divinely inspired and unconstrained artist, composers were once again drawn to the image of the musician as craftsman, with Bach as their favorite model. That Weill and Hindemith originally shared the composing duties for *Lindbergh's Flight* similarly reflects an attempt to move away from individualistic approaches to art. The challenges of actually living up to this ideal are evident in Weill's replacement of all of Hindemith's movements with his own versions shortly after the premiere.

Rather than writing works mainly for the concert hall or the private salon, many composers became involved in music for children and the expanding youth movement, music for workers, and music with specific didactic purposes. Brecht and Weill adapted *Lindbergh's Flight* for use in schools by replacing the solo sections with simplified settings for children's chorus. In subsequent versions, Brecht also sought to downplay the "individualistic" aspects of Lindbergh's feat by portraying it instead as a collective triumph of humanity over adversity. Later, appalled by the aviator's Nazi sympathies, Brecht expunged Lindbergh entirely and changed the title of the cantata to *Der Ozeanflug* (The Ocean Flight).

NEW INSTRUMENTS, THE SOUNDS OF THE CITY, AND MACHINE ART

In the preface to his *1922* Suite, with its popular dance-inspired movements, Hindemith advised pianists to "play this piece very ferociously, but keep strictly in rhythm like a machine. Regard the piano here as an interesting kind of percussion instrument and treat it accordingly." The notion of playing "like a machine" points to another distinctive feature of much new music between the wars: the widespread interest in capturing the sights, sounds, and experiences of the modern urban world. *Lindbergh's Flight*, with its emphasis on the airplane and its representations of the crowds on Long Island and Paris who greeted the takeoff and landing, makes a striking contrast to the images of untamed mountain peaks and deep-forested chasms in nineteenth-century Romantic music, as well as to the mysterious foreign climes of twentieth-century Exoticism and Primitivism.

Eager to create new sounds and experiences, and following the lead of the Italian Futurists, composers and engineers intensified their efforts to develop electronic instruments that would be more practical than the massive Telharmonium (see Chapter 3). The theremin was invented in 1919 by the Russian Lev Termen. Players activated it by changing the proximity of their hands to the magnetic fields generated by two antennae, one controlling pitch, the other dynamics. The theremin was capable of extremely subtle expression in performances of traditional repertoire, but it also could produce a continuous glissando over many octaves and other unusual sounds that later lent themselves to supernatural sound effects for radio and film.

Another early electronic instrument was the Trautonium, introduced in 1930 by the German inventor Friedrich Trautwein, which used a wire controller that similarly gave the player great flexibility in pitch control. Hindemith wrote several pieces for it, including a Concertina for Trautonium and Strings (1931). The Ondes Martenot ("Martenot waves"), invented in 1928 by the Frenchman Maurice Martenot, could produce minute gradations of pitch, but it also had a keyboard that made it easier for composers like Olivier Messiaen to integrate it into traditional musical practice (see Chapter 10). It is not surprising that the most successful new invention of these years was also the one most closely related to existing instruments: the Hammond organ, first marketed in 1935, used a system of drawbars that mimicked the stops of a pipe organ. But the Hammond organ allowed precise control of the balance between the overtones, giving the player great flexibility in shaping timbres. (The development of electronic music will be explored further in Chapter 11.)

VARÈSE'S ART-SCIENCE

The music of Edgard Varèse (1883–1965) was closely connected with the interwar trends we are considering here. From early in his career he was attracted to new sounds and employed both the theremin and the Ondes Martenot in his works. He wrote in 1917 of his "dream of instruments obedient to my thought and which, with their contribution of a whole new world of unsuspected sounds, will lend themselves to the exigencies of my inner rhythm" (SR 179:1339; 7/10:69). But his music also shows how such technologies were only one facet of a whole new conception of art. Born in France, Varèse was trained as an engineer before turning to music. Moving to the United States in 1915, he soon gained celebrity through a series of works that evoked science, the city, and the modern world; the American critic Paul Rosenfeld described him in 1929 as "the poet of tall New Yorks." Varèse used the language of the New Objectivity to characterize his 1924 chamber work *Octandre* as "hard of surface and machine-sharp of edge."

The first work that brought Varèse wide attention was the short but intense *Hyperprism* (1923), which, in keeping with his concept of music as an "Art-Science," took its name from the multidimensional geometric form. The music is scored for a massive battery of percussion, including a siren and lion's roar (a kind of drum played by a cord pulled through the head), combined with brass and woodwinds; Varèse pointedly omitted string instruments as too expressive and sentimental (Ex. 5.1). In the opening measures, he dramatically reduces the roles of melody and harmony in favor of what he described as a counterpoint of sound masses differentiated by textures and timbres: "When these sound masses collide, the phenomenon of penetration or repulsion will seem to occur. Certain transmutations taking place on certain planes will seem to be projected onto other planes, moving at different speeds and at different angles" (SR 179:1340; 7/10:70).

One plane is an 11-measure tone-color melody centered on C♯ and moving between trombone and French horns, which animate it through constantly shifting rhythms, dynamics, and special performance effects. The other plane consists of a complex constellation of brief rhythmic gestures in the percussion. Some later passages include more extended melodies and blocklike harmonies, but rather than emerging as the focus of attention, melody and harmony serve to define the contrasting sound masses along with different rhythms, textures, and instrumental configurations. Varèse relied even less on pitch in his *Ionisation* for percussion ensemble (1931), which anticipated the textural approaches we will discuss in Chapter 12, and after World War II he became a pioneer of electronic music (see Chapter 11).

ANTHEIL'S *BALLET MÉCANIQUE*

One of the most famous works of machine art was George Antheil's *Ballet mécanique* (Mechanical Ballet), which premiered in Paris in 1926; its scandalous U.S. premiere at Carnegie Hall followed a year later (Ex. 5.2). Antheil described the work as the first piece of music on Earth "that has been composed OUT OF and FOR MACHINES." With its 16 player pianos, large percussion section, siren, electric bells, and stage-mounted airplane propellers, this raucous "ballet" of mechanical instruments was one of several works from these years designed to capture the sounds of trains, automobiles, and factories. Indeed, the Carnegie

Hall concert was preceded the day before by a performance of *Pacific 231* (1923), by the Swiss composer Arthur Honegger (1892–1955), which vividly captures the sonic effect of a train lurching into motion. At nearby Steinway Hall was the influential Machine Age Exposition that brought together artworks and industrial objects. Antheil's piece was conceived together with an experimental film by the French artist Fernand Léger (see Chapter 6), also called *Ballet mécanique*, that featured looping mechanized images of technology, abstract shapes, people, and animals. Other related Machine Age compositions from the time include *Iron Foundry* (1927), from the ballet *Steel* by the Soviet composer Alexander Mosolov and Sergey Prokofiev's ballet *Le pas d'acier* (The Steel Step), performed that same year by the Ballets Russes (see Chapter 6).

The *Ballet mécanique* exemplifies a set of musical markers for the Machine Age, common to all these pieces, including the layering of ostinatos, a high level of dissonance, the juxtaposition of incongruous materials, and the use of "noise" and sounds with indeterminate pitch. More surprising is Antheil's incorporation of the popular music of the city: amid the agitated evocation of industrial pistons, belts, and wheels, the ragtime tune "Oh My Baby" suddenly emerges, first interrupting and then absorbed into the chaotic mechanical dance. Antheil heard connections between machine art and urban African-American music, which he highlighted by featuring his *Jazz Symphony* (1925), performed by an all-black orchestra, on the first half of the Carnegie Hall concert with the premiere of the *Ballet mécanique*.

The architect Le Corbusier's remark that "Manhattan is hot jazz in stone and steel" reflected the increasing racial heterogeneity of city life in the United States, a consequence of the massive northward migration of blacks in the 1920s. These racialized connotations of the Machine Age underlie the ballet *Skyscrapers* (1926) by the American composer John Alden Carpenter, a musical representation of the New York skyline's transformation in the years leading up to the completion of the Empire State Building in 1931. The manic opening closely resembles Antheil's work, while later sections include interludes of jazzlike music as well as an extended banjo solo.

JAZZ, RACE, AND THE NEW MUSIC

Jazz, whose rich history and legacy lie outside the scope of this book, was an important influence on many of the composers we will study. The Original Dixieland Jazz Band began releasing records in 1917 and toured widely in the United States and England. Bix Beiderbecke, Louis Armstrong, Duke Ellington, Paul Whiteman, and other accomplished jazz musicians, both black and white, developed a range of popular styles, often in association with new dance forms (for example, the Lindy Hop, named in honor of Charles Lindbergh, featured acrobatic moves and aerial effects).

Example 5.1: *Edgard Varèse,* Hyperprism, *mm. 1–5*

Example 5.2: *George Antheil,* Ballet mécanique, *mm. 6–10*

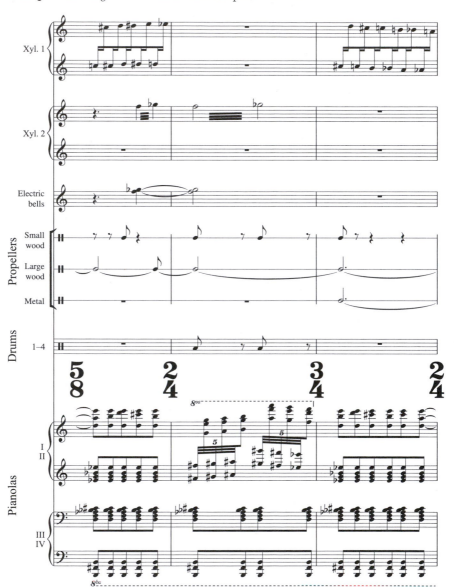

American jazz quickly made its way to Europe through recordings and live performances. A popular dance band called the Harlem Hellfighters was formed by a group of African-American soldiers stationed in France after the war. The French composer Darius Milhaud, who had traveled to London eager to hear a jazz band "straight from New York," was impressed by its innovative sound:

> The new music was extremely subtle in its use of timbre; the saxophone breaking in, squeezing out the juice of dreams, or the trumpet, dramatic or languorous by turns, the clarinet, frequently playing in its upper register, the lyrical use of the trombone, glancing with its slide over quarter-tones in crescendos of volume and pitch, thus intensifying the feeling; and the whole, so various yet not disparate, held together by the piano and subtly punctuated by the complex rhythms of the percussion, a kind of inner beat, the vital pulse of the rhythmic life of the music.

European musicians soon got into the act by forming their own jazz ensembles, such as Stanley Weintraub and the Syncopators, featured in the Marlene Dietrich film *The Blue Angel* (1930). Jazz solved many of the challenges composers faced in the period between the wars: In addition to speaking to a broader public than "classical" music, it provided a rich repertory of up-to-date rhythms, melodies, harmonies, and timbres that could be incorporated into other musical genres.

Opera, regarded by many as a vestige of a bygone era and threatened with obsolescence by the arrival of sound film, seemed particularly in need of resuscitation through jazz. The title character of *Jonny spielt auf* (Jonny Strikes Up, 1925), by the Austrian composer Ernst Krenek (1900–1991), is an African-American jazz musician (originally performed by a singer in blackface) who inspires an ineffectual white Modernist composer named Max. Along with such symbols of modernity as trains, taxis, and radio loudspeakers, Krenek's score includes allusions to jazz and popular dance forms such as shimmy, blues, and tango. Other composers similarly incorporated modern subject matter and sounds into the new genre of the *Zeitoper* (opera of the time).

As we will discuss further in Chapter 6, composers and artists often conflated contemporary African-American culture with stereotypical images of "primitive" Africa. In 1934 Antheil published a racially charged essay arguing that music since the time of Wagner had been energized by two "gigantic blood transfusions—first the Slavic, and, in recent times, the Negroid." In his view Negro music, "hard and as beautiful as a diamond," was the only path to the future. Like machine art, jazz represented the possibility of a new music that was relevant and popular but also masculine and unsentimental. Krenek described the meaning of all the modern technologies that were featured in *Jonny spielt auf* in language that vividly demonstrates how these disparate ideas of the new music, the New Objectivity, machine art, jazz, race, Primitivism, and the modern world could be jumbled together:

Showing these completely soulless machines is the shortest way of demonstrating the antithesis which inspires the piece—the antithesis between man as a "vital" animal and man as a "spiritual" animal—as incarnated in the diametrically opposed figures of Jonny and Max. In this sense Jonny is actually a part of the technical-mechanical side of the world; he reacts as easily, as gratifyingly exactly and amorally as a well-constructed machine. His kingdom is of this world, and as a matter of course he is the one who gains mastery over life here below, over the visible globe. He is in direct contrast to Max, who, starting out from spirituality, never comes to grips with problems he is set by external life, which is so attuned to vitality today.

In this deeply problematic formulation, which depends on racist assumptions widespread at the time, we can see some of the limitations and prejudices that shaped responses by composers, performers, and audiences to the challenges they faced in the radically transformed cultural, social, and political terrain after World War I.

Krenek's opera ends with Jonny standing on top of a globe while a dancing mob below sings, "The radiant New World comes across the sea to take over old Europe through dance." The image strikingly anticipates the conclusion of *Lindbergh's Flight*, which celebrated another hopeful arrival of the New World, bringing new kinds of art for new kinds of people. But just as the sight of a plane flying overhead can arouse for us today both optimism and anxiety, Jonny's moment of triumph also brings to mind the familiar metaphor for these years of "dancing on a volcano." For all their excitement and vitality, the 1920s and 1930s were also marked by many ominous developments that set the stage for the Second World War and its Cold War aftermath.

FOR FURTHER READING

Auner, Joseph, "Soulless Machines and Steppenwolves: Renegotiating Masculinity in Krenek's *Jonny spielt auf*," in *Siren Songs*, edited by Mary Ann Smart, 222–236 (Princeton: Princeton University Press, 2000)

Cook, Susan C., *Opera for a New Republic: The Zeitopern of Krenek, Waill, and Hindemith* (Ann Arbor: UMI Research Press, 1988)

Hailey, Christopher, "Rethinking Radio: Music and Radio in Weimar Germany," in *Music and Performance during the Weimar Republic*, edited by Bryan Gilliam, 13–36 (Cambridge: Cambridge University Press, 1994)

Kemp, Ian, "Harmony in Weill: Some Observations," *Tempo* 104 (1973): 11–15

Meyer, Felix, and Heidy Zimmermann, eds., *Edgar Varèse: Composer, Sound Sculptor, Visionary* (Woodbridge, UK: The Boydell Press, 2006)

Von Ankum, Katharina, *Women in the Metropolis: Gender and Modernity in Weimar Culture* (Berkeley and Los Angeles: University of California Press, 1997)

Watkins, Glenn, *Proof through the Night: Music and the Great War* (Berkeley: University of California Press, 2003)

CHAPTER SIX

Paris, Neoclassicism, and the Art of the Everyday

Many significant developments in music between the wars took root in the fertile artistic soil of Paris. Some of the composers drawn to the city, such as Igor Stravinsky and Sergey Prokofiev, already had international reputations. But among those who became the most prominent were lesser-known figures including Erik Satie (1866–1925), whose scandalously successful ballet *Parade* (1917), with its peculiar combination of materials and nonchalant tone, pointed to many of the divergent paths composers would explore in the 1920s and 1930s.

Like Stravinsky's *Rite of Spring*, *Parade* was written for Serge Diaghilev and the Ballets Russes, but it would be difficult to imagine two more dissimilar works. With a scenario by Jean Cocteau, choreography by Léonide Massine, and sets and costumes by Pablo Picasso, Satie's ballet is a cross between a music hall variety show and a traveling circus. The motley cast of characters includes acrobats, a Chinese magician, and an American girl who seems to have stepped out of a silent movie. Instead of a linear narrative, the plot consists of each of these acts trying unsuccessfully to lure the audience from the fairground into the theater where the actual performance is to take place. Overseeing their increasingly frenetic activities are three "managers," one played by two men in a horse costume, the others wearing large contraptions that make them look like walking cubist collages (Fig. 6.1).

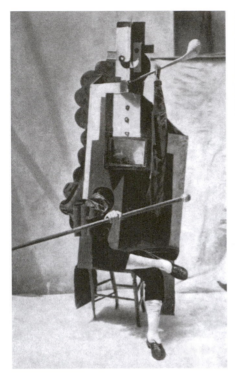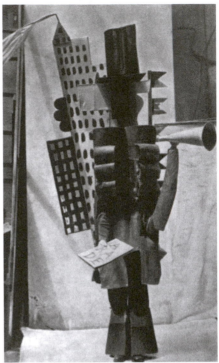

Figure 6.1: *Pablo Picasso's costumes for the French and American managers in Erik Satie's* Parade. *The American manager features skyscrapers and flags waving, while the French manager was reportedly modeled on Diaghilev's fashionable Parisian attire.*

The wartime premiere of *Parade* managed to offend almost everyone. Many viewed its flippant insouciance as unpatriotic at a time when battles were still raging at the front. Along with allusions to jazz and other "low" forms of entertainment, the choreography, costumes, and above all the music, with its simplistically repetitive melodies and juxtapositions of wildly contrasting sections, came across as flagrantly amateurish. But just as perplexing were the moments of seriousness and refinement, as in the opening, where, after a mock-grandiose introduction, Satie launches into a very proper four-voice fugue (Ex. 6.1). Despite or perhaps because of this heterogeneity, many experienced *Parade* as something new and important. The poet Guillaume Apollinaire was so inspired that he coined the term *Surrealism* to capture the heightened perception of reality—literally, super-realism—produced by the work's collisions of incongruous elements.

In this chapter we will unravel the various artistic, cultural, and political strands that Satie and his contemporaries brought together in their works.

Example 6.1: *Erik Satie,* Prelude of the Red Curtain, *from* Parade, *mm. 1–9. Reduction for two pianos*

Taking *Parade* as a starting point, we will examine the nature of Neoclassicism and the many opportunities for artistic cross-fertilization that Paris provided. We will then turn to the diverse sources composers drew upon in their works, ranging from the classicisms of the ancient world and the eighteenth century to the latest jazz and the sounds of the city.

NEOCLASSICISM

The many slogans proclaiming the "new" that emerged in Paris during these years, such as the New Simplicity and *l'esprit nouveau* (the New Spirit), reflect both a strong desire for change and a lack of consensus about what the new music should be and do. As a result, even the most widely used term, *Neoclassicism*, turns out to be quite difficult to define. Although the label is most closely associated with the postwar music of Stravinsky and the young generation of French composers, Neoclassical elements can be found in the works of composers from several national traditions and widely divergent aesthetic orientations, as we will discuss in Chapters 7 and 8. In the interwar years, the term generally denoted the use of eighteenth-century styles, genres, and techniques; new ways of incorporating elements of tonal harmony; and an emphasis on simplicity and clarity. But Neoclassicism also embraced allusions to the sounds of the music hall, the newest dance styles, jazz, machine art, and subject matter ranging from the classicism of ancient Greece to scenes of everyday life in the city.

Rather than attempting to pin down a single definition of Neoclassicism, we will explore how composers moved freely among these incongruous possibilities, sometimes, as in *Parade*, combining them in a single work. As we shall see, the broad category of Neoclassicism encompassed more than just a return to the past through historical allusions or the attempt to cash in on the latest styles through borrowings from popular music. It also represented composers' search for a music that was truly up-to-date and relevant to their experience of modernity, while also offering alternatives to those qualities that had been so important to music before the war: subjectivity, emotion, mystery, and individuality.

As with *Lindbergh's Flight* (see Chapter 5), there is much that initially may seem familiar in *Parade* and other compositions discussed later. But in most cases the conventional elements of style, harmony, and form, whether borrowed from the eighteenth century or taken from contemporary popular styles, are distorted and defamiliarized by their combination with musical materials from other traditions, or by their reappearance in very different sonic contexts. Indeed, *Parade* is subtitled *Ballet réaliste* (Realist ballet) and features the sounds of a typewriter, pistol shots, and a roulette wheel. Cocteau originally intended to include even more noises, and in a preface to the score the composer Georges Auric refers to Satie's contribution as a "musical background for percussion instruments and onstage sounds." As in the work of the Italian Futurists (see Chapter 3), these realistic elements were intended to inoculate the score against the sentimentality of Romanticism. Satie's music, Auric writes, "very humbly yields to the same reality that drowns the nightingale's song under the rumble of streetcars." We can see Satie already at work demolishing such Romantic notions as artistic inspiration in an essay titled "The Musician's Day" (1913):

An artist must organize his life.

Here is the exact timetable of my daily activities:

Get up: 7:18 a.m.; be inspired: 10:34 to 11:45 a.m. I take lunch at 12:11 p.m. and leave the table at 12:14 p.m.

Healthy horse-riding, out in my grounds: 1:19 to 2:53 p.m. More inspiration 3:12 to 4:07 p.m.

Various activities (fencing, reflection, immobility, visits, contemplation, swimming, etc. . . . .): 4:21 to 6:47 p.m.

Dinner is served at 7:16 and ends at 7:20 p.m. Then come symphonic readings, out loud: 8:09 to 9:59. (SR 208:1486; 7/39:216)

MUSICAL HIGH LIFE AND LOW LIFE

The older generation of French composers continued to exert a strong influence on musical life in the capital. Foremost among them were Gabriel Fauré (1845–1924), who in 1904 became director of the Paris Conservatoire, and Vincent d'Indy (1851–1931), who in 1894 helped found a rival school known as the Schola Cantorum. Both institutions played a role in thwarting Satie's early efforts to establish himself as a composer in Paris. He was dismissed three years after entering the Conservatoire in 1879, and even after he gained readmission in 1885 his piano teacher evaluated his performance as "worthless. Three months just to learn the piece. Can't sight-read properly."

Through his father's music publishing firm, Satie did manage to promote some of his early piano pieces, including the *Gymnopédies* (1888), whose extreme simplicity and emotional restraint were utterly antithetical to the Romantic spirit of the age. He was equally out of step with the mode of instruction at the Schola Cantorum, where he studied counterpoint with d'Indy from 1905 to 1908. "Boredom disguises itself behind wicked harmonies" was how Debussy described a fugue that Satie wrote for d'Indy, seeing it as evidence of the stultifying influence of the Schola's conservative curriculum.

Turning his back on the musical establishment, Satie found a more congenial home in Paris's thriving subculture of nightclubs and music halls. Stylish hotspots like Moulin Rouge (Red Mill) and Le Boeuf sur le Toit (The Ox on the Roof), named after a piece by Darius Milhaud (see p. 118), attracted artists, aristocrats, tourists, and poseurs eager to see and be seen. In the city's many clubs and salons, composers and musicians rubbed shoulders with writers, artists, and designers associated with Dada, Surrealism, Cubism, and the latest trends. In this wide-open milieu Satie supported himself for many years as a pianist, composing songs and dances in popular styles while living a flamboyantly bohemian existence on the edge of poverty.

The worlds of upper-class entertainment and the artistic avant-garde converged in Satie's *Sports et divertissements* (Sports and Diversions), a set of piano pieces that gently mocked the pastimes of the fashionable urban elite. Composed in 1914, the work was published in 1923 in a deluxe edition featuring drawings by the noted fashion illustrator Charles Martin (Fig. 6.2). Instead of the poetic titles and evocative performance indications Debussy used in his programmatic piano music, Satie's 21 miniatures are interspersed with playful narratives, intended for the pianist's eyes only. *Le Yachting*, for instance, depicts a pleasure cruise that is disrupted by rough weather; Satie captures the image of the little boat dancing on the waves with rolling ostinato patterns

Figure 6.2: *Erik Satie, "Le Yachting," from* Sports et divertissements. *"What weather! The wind is bellowing like a seal. The yacht is dancing. It's acting like a little fool. The sea is coming undone. Let's hope it won't break on a rock. No one can put it back together. I don't want to stay here, says the pretty passenger. This place is not amusing. I'd prefer something else. Call me a cab".*

based on static, nonfunctional harmonies overlaid with skittering scalar passages. When the unhappy passenger calls for a cab at the end of the piece, it is clear that we are in a very different world from any we have explored so far in this book. As with the Surrealism Apollinaire experienced in *Parade*, the moment is so surprising precisely because it reconnects us in new and vivid ways with the everyday.

FRENCHMEN, FOREIGNERS, AND EXPATRIATES

In the 1920s and 1930s, Paris became home to an extraordinary concentration of talented musicians. Maurice Ravel (1875–1937) emerged as the most famous French composer after Debussy. A student of Fauré at the Conservatoire from 1897 to 1903, Ravel exhibited remarkable technical facility as well as openness to a wide range of musical and literary influences. When the war broke out, Ravel rushed to enlist; after being turned down as a pilot, he served for several months driving a military transport. Ravel lost many friends in the war; in his symphonic poem *La valse* (The Waltz, 1920), he expressed his feeling that the world had spun into catastrophe; he described the piece as "a sort of apotheosis of the Viennese waltz" that culminates in a "fantastic, fatal whirling." Ravel's Piano Concerto in G (1931), to which we will return later, illustrates the heterogeneous mix of elements that he was able to incorporate in a single work, including Classical forms, the retrospective genre of the concerto, the harmonies and timbres of jazz, and a sharp-edged, Machine Age style. In 1933 he published an essay called "Finding Tunes in Factories," in which he wrote about the appeal of the sounds of modern life, traffic, and industry.

Igor Stravinsky, who spent the war years in Switzerland, settled with his family in Paris in 1920. The works he composed for the Ballets Russes continued to include folkloristic pieces, such as *Les noces* (The Wedding, 1923). But he also composed pieces like the ballet *Pulcinella* (discussed further later), distancing himself from his Russian past. At the same time, popular styles played an increasingly important role in Stravinsky's music, as evidenced by *Ragtime for Eleven Instruments* and *L'histoire du soldat* (The Soldier's Tale), both from 1918. A theater piece based on a Russian folk tale, *The Soldier's Tale* incorporates a tango and ragtime, and uses a small group of instruments that Stravinsky claimed was inspired by his discovery of jazz. He described the stripped-down ensemble, which includes a prominent and virtuosic percussion part, as marking his "final break" with the Russian orchestral sound of his prewar ballets.

Stravinsky's fellow Russian émigré Sergey Prokofiev (1891–1953) also settled in Paris in 1920, having launched an international career as a virtuoso pianist upon leaving Russia in 1918. In Paris he enjoyed considerable success with works ranging from the Machine Age ballet *Le pas d'acier* (The Steel Step, 1927), written for the Ballets Russes, to his Neoclassical Piano Concerto No. 3 (1921) and Violin Concerto No. 2 (1935). While Stravinsky severed his ties with Russia and ended up moving to the United States in 1939, Prokofiev felt the pull of his homeland intensify during his Parisian years. Returning to the Soviet Union in 1936, he made his way through its complex and dangerous cultural politics (see Chapter 9).

Paris attracted a group of young American composers clustered around the renowned teacher Nadia Boulanger (1887–1979). Boulanger had studied at the Conservatoire along with her sister Lili (1893–1918), a child prodigy whose promising career as a composer was cut short by an early death. Nadia Boulanger started out teaching harmony at the American Conservatory in Fontainebleau, eventually becoming its director in 1948. Her students, including Aaron Copland, Virgil Thomson, Roy Harris, Elliott Carter, and other members of the "Boulangerie" (meaning bakery, a play on her name) went on to have an enormous impact on musical life in the United States (see Chapter 8). Among the other significant composers who spent time in Paris during these years are Colin McPhee, Heitor Villa-Lobos, and the celebrated popular composer George Gershwin, whose colorfully exuberant symphonic poem *An American in Paris* (1928) depicted his impressions of France (see Chapter 8).

In this rich and diverse artistic environment Satie made his mark among composers and writers seeking a new direction for French music, thanks to the efforts of the poet, writer, and filmmaker Jean Cocteau (1889–1963). In his influential manifesto *Cock and Harlequin* (1918), Cocteau lauded Satie for offering composers an alternative to the "fogs" of Wagner, Romanticism, and Expressionism, the "sauce" of Russian music, and the sensuous imagery of Impressionism: "Enough of clouds, waves, aquariums, watersprites, and nocturnal scents; what we need is a music of the earth, every day music." (SR 171:1292; 7/2:22). Rejecting the ideal of "art for art's sake," Cocteau saw in Satie's works the possibility of a "music on which one walks." Satie took these words to heart in his *Musique d'ameublement* (Furniture Music, 1918), intended to be played during the intermission of a concert as background music to other activities. Despite Satie's plea to "go on talking! Walk about! Don't listen!," the audience insisted on giving the music its full attention.

In *Cock and Harlequin* Cocteau praised Satie's radical reduction of music to its basic elements: "Satie teaches what, in our age, is the greatest audacity, simplicity. Has he not proved that he could refine better than anyone? But he clears, simplifies, and strips rhythm naked." Clarity and simplicity were the watchwords of a circle of young French composers loosely formed under Satie's tutelage. Dubbed Les Six (The Six), by analogy to Russia's Mighty Handful, they included Darius Milhaud (1892–1974), Francis Poulenc (1899–1963), Arthur Honegger (1892–1955), Georges Auric (1899–1983), Louis Durey (1888–1979), and Germaine Tailleferre (1892–1983). Although Les Six functioned as a group for scarcely more than a year, joint publications, concerts, and the ballet *Les mariés de la tour Eiffel* (The Wedding on the Eiffel Tower, 1921), which featured movements by five of the composers and a tongue-in-cheek scenario by Cocteau, brought them considerable notoriety.

MUSIC AND CULTURAL POLITICS

Politics are always a factor in musical developments, but for composers in Paris after World War I, virtually every element of musical style was interpreted as making some sort of statement about political and national allegiances. We have seen in Chapter 4 how the folk were often defined against some "other"; those seeking to define a distinctive French musical identity in the postwar years encountered many "others," including long-dominant German music, Russian influences, and the growing presence of American jazz and other popular styles. Debates about the nature of French music were public and noisy; for example, the National League for the Defense of French Music, founded in 1916 by Camille Saint-Saëns and d'Indy, had advocated a wartime ban on the performance of German and Austrian music. They were countered by the Independent Musical Society, established by Ravel and Fauré in 1909, which continued to encourage openness to new music regardless of national origin.

The opposition of French and German came to be defined by a set of values mapped onto ideas of "Classic" versus "Romantic." Thus French music was marked by such virtues as charm, clarity, sobriety, lightness, grace, purity, and objectivity, while German music was associated with the opposite qualities. Such national imaginings led to some surprising conclusions: Bach, for example, was often claimed as part of the French heritage. By the same token, national origin did not prevent honorary "French" status being granted to Stravinsky, Prokofiev, and many of the expatriate Americans. Nadia Boulanger's enthusiastic description of the "constructivist . . . geometry" of Stravinsky's Octet for wind instruments (1923) shows how this constellation of aesthetic and national ideas coalesced:

> All of his thought is translated into precise, simple, and classic lines; and the sovereign certainty of his writing, always renewed, here takes on in its dryness and precision an authority without artifice. . . . The score of the Octet is among those which furnish the satisfaction of the spirit and the eyes which recognize the passions of counterpoint, for those who love to reread the old masters of the Renaissance and Johann Sebastian Bach.

In postwar Paris, as today, conservative and progressive elements in politics, culture, and personal morality mixed in complicated ways, so that specific musical and stylistic elements could carry wide-ranging and often contradictory political implications. Appeals to the eighteenth century, for example, were associated for some with a longing for the days before the royal families were deposed from the thrones of Europe and Russia. Aristocrats in Paris patronized the arts, and much of the music from these years is directed at a stylish upper-class audience capable of appreciating its ironies and allusions. Stravinsky and Diaghilev sported monocles and put on aristocratic airs to distance themselves from the Bolshevik rabble. Stravinsky tellingly described the last movement of his Serenade in A for piano (1925) as representing the ostentatious autograph of a nobleman, "tantamount to a signature with numerous calligraphic flourishes."

Anticommunist tendencies encouraged Stravinsky, Antheil, and others to sympathize with the growing fascist movements in France, Germany, and Italy. Neoclassical forms, clear textures, and the use of fugue could be interpreted as expressing a commitment to order, discipline, and subjugation of the individual will. An article published in Germany in 1935, two years after the Nazis seized power, described the celebrations of the 250th anniversary of Handel's birth and the revival of his music with its "steadfast architecture" as "protests" against Impressionism and atonality: "The clarity and simplicity of his musical language, which raises itself to heroic sublimity, is so much an expression of the German people that one must let its rejoicing song of triumph ring forth as the echo of the awakening Germany in order to let the whole people take part in this expression of the German spirit."

In Italy, Benito Mussolini revived the style of classical Roman art and architecture, with marble columns and statuary symbolizing the Fascist regime's purported links to the Roman Empire. Yet the iconography of classical architecture was also used during these years in the Soviet Union to represent the ideals of the new classless society and communism. And in Washington, D.C., elements of Greek and Roman architecture had long been used to evoke democracy and the unity of the American nation, as with the Lincoln Memorial, built in 1922.

In a similar fashion, musical evocations of eighteenth-century Classicism and the ideas of simplicity and clarity could also convey a wide range of political meanings. Writing in Paris at the time of his Violin Concerto No. 2 in 1935, Prokofiev described his search for a musical language suited to the new mass audience of the Soviet people:

> It is by no means easy to find the right idiom for such music. It should be primarily melodious, and the melody should be clear and simple without, however, becoming repetitive or trivial. . . . The same applies to the technique, the form—it too must be clear and simple, but not stereotyped. It is not the old simplicity that is needed but a new kind of simplicity.

It is important to remember, moreover, that composers' personal politics did not necessarily determine how their works were interpreted. Although Satie's works were promoted by the reactionary Cocteau for the fashionable elite, Satie himself was involved with both Socialist and Communist groups. And despite Cocteau's strong nationalistic convictions, *Parade* was viewed by many as anti-French. Recognizing the multivalent implications of such works does not devalue the music's significant political impact or meaning. Rather, the point is that such connotations can only be understood in reference to how they were constructed and understood in specific contexts.

ANTIQUITY AND RITUAL

While artists such as Pablo Picasso could model their drawings on Greek sculpture or depict well-known mythic images in their works, Neoclassical composers had few musical sources from antiquity to draw upon. Instead they focused on elements of staging, scenarios from history and myth, and the pursuit of a generic "classical" sensibility marked by simplicity, purity, and restraint. Stravinsky's opera *Oedipus Rex* (1927) used a Latin text adapted by Cocteau from the Greek drama by Sophocles, while his ballet *Apollo* (1928) featured a toga-wearing lead dancer and three Muses in tutus on their way to Parnassus. Satie's first major work after *Parade* was the "symphonic drama" *Socrate* (1918), a severely simple setting of texts by Plato featuring three episodes in the life of Socrates. Milhaud wrote three operas based on reworkings of Aeschylus's *Oresteia* by Paul Claudel, and Honegger collaborated with Cocteau on an operatic treatment of Sophocles's *Antigone*.

A major attraction of such classical sources was a sense of depersonalized ritual. As we saw in Chapter 4, Stravinsky and Roerich incorporated ritualistic elements in *The Rite of Spring* as a way of minimizing individuality and subjectivity. The staging of *Oedipus Rex* was intended to make the singers resemble living statues, while the use of a narrator in modern attire to introduce each scene in the language of the audience underscored the sense of formality and distance created by the Latin text. Further minimizing emotional expression was the deliberate eclecticism of Stravinsky's score, which he described as having been "put together from whatever came to hand," with allusions to Handel, Verdi, Musorgsky, Wagner, Mendelssohn, and dance-hall tunes of the Folies Bergère.

In his *Symphonie de psaumes* (Symphony of Psalms, 1930; see Anthology 8), Stravinsky also specified Latin as the language of performance. Thanks to his friendship with the conductor Serge Koussevitzky, he had received a commission for the *Symphony of Psalms* from the Boston Symphony Orchestra in celebration of its fiftieth anniversary. Dedicated to "the Glory of God," the *Symphony of Psalms* is the first of several works that Stravinsky composed to sacred texts. The three movements are based on the Latin Vulgate versions of verses from three Psalms. Stravinsky explained that he used the Latin texts precisely because modern audiences would not understand the words:

> What a joy it is to compose music to a language of convention, almost of ritual, the very nature of which imposes a lofty dignity. One no longer feels dominated by the phrase, the literal meaning of the words. . . . The text thus becomes purely phonetic material for the composer. . . . This, too, has for centuries been the Church's attitude towards music and has prevented it from falling into sentimentalism, and consequently into individualism.

Much of the *Symphony of Psalms* has an intentionally severe and stark tone characteristic of the New Objectivity. The score calls for a mixed chorus and an orchestra with the violins and violas replaced by an expanded (and, in Stravinsky's view, less emotive) wind section. He often further obscures the meanings of the Latin words by displacing the accents to weak syllables. With its impersonal and objective approach to religion, focusing on ritual rather than personal expression, the *Symphony of Psalms* pointed the way to the austerity of Stravinsky's late works, including his Mass (1948) and *Requiem Canticles* (1966).

EIGHTEENTH-CENTURY SOURCES

The most common connotation of Neoclassicism in music was a renewed interest in the music of the eighteenth century, in particular the works of Bach and Handel. French composers also sought forefathers in Rameau and Couperin; Ravel's *Le tombeau de Couperin* (Memorial to Couperin, 1917) is a suite of Baroque-inspired dance movements commemorating friends who died during the war. Ravel's resurrection of stylized dances such as the forlane, rigaudon, and minuet contrasted sharply with the rejection of conventional forms, genres, and techniques that characterized many works written before World War I. Composers also resurrected earlier genres, like the concerto grosso, and traditional forms including sonata form, rondo, and theme and variations.

The fugal passage at the beginning of Satie's *Parade* is another important marker of Neoclassicism. Before the war, composers often used imitative counterpoint to connote academicism and artificiality, as in the abstruse fugue representing misguided science in Strauss's *Also sprach Zarathustra* (see Chapter 3). But after the war fugues were everywhere, sometimes treated ironically, but often used as a sign of high seriousness and craftsmanship. The Neoclassicists' catchphrase "Back to Bach" is reflected in the second movement of the *Symphony of Psalms*, an elaborate double fugue whose theme recalls Bach's *Musical Offering*. With the strict contrapuntal organization of the movement, Stravinsky made clear that the order he created in the work was a symbol of the divine order: "I'm an advocate of architecture in art, since architecture is the embodiment of order: creative work is a protest against anarchy and nonexistence."

In works like Prokofiev's Symphony No. 1 (*Classical*, 1917), Neoclassicism involved a general stylistic modeling on the scoring, forms, and treatment of melody and harmony in Haydn's symphonies. The second movement of Prokofiev's Violin Concerto No. 2 evokes Bach's "Air on the G String," with a long, singing melody over a stately, steady bass line. Ravel remarked that in composing the Piano Concerto in G he had in mind the "old notion that a concerto should be a divertissement," referring to the seventeenth- and eighteenth-century genre of light entertainment music. More specifically, he drew inspiration from Mozart's Clarinet Quintet for the serenely flowing melody of the Concerto's second movement. Other composers actually borrowed material from earlier pieces, reworking it to various degrees. Ottorino Respighi created an orchestral suite, *Rossiniana* (1925), by arranging keyboard works by Rossini; Schoenberg wrote a Concerto for String Quartet and Orchestra (1933) that dramatically transforms Handel's Concerto Grosso, Op. 6, No. 7.

The most famous of these Neoclassical recompositions is Stravinsky's *Pulcinella* (1919–20), based on instrumental music then attributed to Giovanni Battista Pergolesi (1710–1736). The ballet, commissioned by Diaghilev for the Ballets Russes, featured characters from the Italian commedia dell'arte theatrical tradition that had influenced so many other early-twentieth-century works, including Schoenberg's *Pierrot lunaire* and Stravinsky's *Petrushka*. Stravinsky composed directly on the manuscript copies of the music that Diaghilev provided, "as though I were correcting an old work of my own."

> I began without preconceptions or aesthetic attitudes, and I could not have predicted anything about the result. I knew that I could not produce a "forgery" of Pergolesi because my motor habits are so different; at best, I could repeat him in my own accent. That the result was to some extent a satire was probably inevitable—who could have treated that material in 1919 without satire?—but even this observation is hindsight; I did not set out to compose a satire, and, of course, Diaghilev hadn't considered the possibility of such a thing. A stylish orchestration was what Diaghilev wanted and nothing more, and my music so shocked him that he went about for a long time with a look that suggested "The Offended Eighteenth Century."

Although his orchestration sometimes evokes the sound of a Classical symphony, it also includes modern effects such as trombone glissandi. But it was Stravinsky's reworking of eighteenth-century tonality that had the most profound long-term impact; he went on to describe *Pulcinella* as "the epiphany through which the whole of my late work became possible."

TONALITY DEFAMILIARIZED

With its dominant-to-tonic progressions, diatonic surfaces, and contrapuntal textures with clear voice-leading, *Pulcinella* marks a departure from the extreme chromaticism and dissonance of many works from before the war. Yet in most cases Stravinsky and others were not trying to reestablish the conventions of common-practice tonality, but rather to use those conventions in new ways. Even when common-practice tonality was employed, it functioned as a kind of quotation, always marked by the possibility of its absence. Prokofiev, for example, was famous for interspersing more or less traditionally tonal passages with sudden dissonances and distortions, as in the second movement of his Violin Concerto No. 2, when the serene opening section is interrupted by a tonally unstable passage that sounds as if the music were suddenly overcome by vertigo.

In *Pulcinella* Stravinsky generally retains the Baroque melodies and bass lines, while altering the harmonizations to subvert functional progressions. *Pulcinella*'s opening movement, based on a trio sonata now known to be by the eighteenth-century Italian composer Domenico Gallo, is only two measures longer than the original. But the small changes have significant ramifications, as with the repetition of a melodic figure and the addition of a beat in a formulaic cadential passage that concludes the first thematic statement (Ex. 6.2). By delaying the tonic so that it arrives

Example 6.2: (a) *Domenico Gallo, Trio Sonata in G Major, movement 1, mm. 10–12;* (b) *Igor Stravinsky,* Pulcinella, *movement 1: Sinfonia, mm. 10–13, reduction*

on what is heard as a weak beat, Stravinsky upsets the correlation of harmony and meter that is fundamental to our perceptions of tonal music. Such manipulations also serve to bring Gallo's music more in line with the sound of Stravinsky's "Russian" works by creating an ostinato passage where none existed before.

Likewise, Satie's *Parade* is full of passages that reinterpret the scales and triads of tonal music through relentless repetitions that turn the melodies and harmonies into static, immobile loops. As a result, the music seems able to move forward only by means of abrupt shifts to contrasting passages. This is evident early in the piece when the opening fugue suddenly gives way to a chain of seventh chords descending in parallel motion that effectively eradicates the sense of tonality by subverting the expected harmonic functions. This is no doubt the kind of passage Virgil Thomson had in mind when he wrote that Satie is the only composer "whose works can be enjoyed and appreciated without any knowledge of the history of music. . . . They are as simple, as devastating as the remarks of a child."

This playfully detached treatment of tonality is also found in Milhaud's technique of polytonality, which results from the superimposition of two or more chords or melodies in different keys. In an essay from 1923 he described a variety of approaches to polytonality that range from an ornamental coloration of tonal harmony to the "domain of atonality." Ravel also often employed polytonal effects, as in the opening theme of the Piano Concerto in G, where the pianist plays arpeggios in G major in the right hand and in F♯ major with an added sixth in the left hand. The orchestral part, with its syncopated clusters, is derived from the pitches of the combined sonority. The second theme, discussed further on p. 118, can be heard as an F♯ Phrygian melody on top of an F♯-major accompaniment (see Anthology 9).

One of the most striking examples of this defamiliarization of tonality is the E-minor triad that opens Stravinsky's *Symphony of Psalms*. In *Petrushka* and *The Rite of Spring*, Stravinsky had used dissonant combinations of two familiar chords to create memorable sonorities. Here he achieves something still more remarkable: making a minor triad sound unique and new through unusual doubling, spacing, and scoring. As the piece unfolds, the E-minor triad is sometimes heard within an octatonic context (E–F–G–A♭–B♭–B–C♯–D) and sometimes within an E Phrygian context (E–F–G–A–B–C–D), but it always retains its strange, monolithic quality (Ex. 6.3). In the finale of *Pulcinella*, Stravinsky further estranges us from the elements of tonality by obsessively repeating a dominant-to-tonic cadential formula to the point that, like a word uttered over and over again, it sounds like nonsense.

This breakdown of functional tonality and its implications of direction, tension, and release is closely related to the anti-Romantic, anti-Expressionist turn to objectivity and emotional restraint discussed in Chapter 5. In *Parade*, although there is a certain sense of melancholy in the failed efforts of the performers to attract an audience, individual psychology and expression play no role. The work keeps us at a distance from characters like the American Girl. Her actions in the *Steamship Ragtime* section—riding a horse, driving a Model T, playing Cowboys and Indians, all clichés of American life—are staged in rapid succession like a movie montage; indeed, at times she is instructed to shake as if she were an actual film image.

By transforming tonal harmonies, along with traditional forms, genres, and styles, into static symbols or quotations, Neoclassical composers intentionally subverted the central means of creating expression in music that had been used for centuries. Stravinsky called attention to the anti-expressive implications of this detachment from musical materials when he wrote in 1924 that his wind Octet was "not an 'emotive' work but a musical composition based on objective elements which are sufficient in themselves."

Example 6.3: *Igor Stravinsky,* Symphony of Psalms, *movement 1; (a) opening chord; (b) in octatonic context, (c) in Phrygian context.*

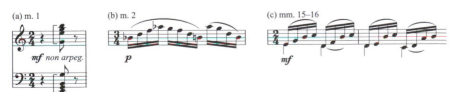

THE ART OF THE EVERYDAY

Stravinsky, Satie, Milhaud, and others employed elements of jazz and popular music in much the same way, manipulating them while at the same time holding them at arm's length. The intent was not to write actual jazz or popular music, but to incorporate "everyday" material to give their music greater relevance, vitality, and modernity. Here, too, *Parade* was seen as leading the way; Poulenc wrote of the work that for the first time the music hall had "invaded Art with a capital A." Satie evoked popular styles primarily through a collage of short fragments of simple tunes, familiar chord progressions, and dance rhythms. The only substantial quotation in *Parade* is from "That Mysterious Rag" by the American composer Irving Berlin. Appearing in the "Little American Girl" section, the quoted passage stands out sharply from the surrounding music due to the length of the song's melody, balanced phrase structure, and conventional harmonic motion.

In many cases, composers took the art of the everyday and set it even further apart by integrating it within the very different contexts of eighteenth-century styles and forms. The first movement of Ravel's Piano Concerto in G incorporates a Gershwinesque second theme, with blue notes and jazzy instrumentation, into a full-scale sonata form (see Anthology 9). This appears, in turn, as the first movement of a concerto in its "Classical" formulation, with three movements organized as fast, slow, fast and concluding with a rondo. Ravel had long been interested in jazz and had included a blues movement in his Sonata for Violin and Piano (1927). In 1928 he undertook a four-month concert tour of the United States that included a visit to New York, where he published an article titled "Take Jazz Seriously!" He also had an opportunity to meet Gershwin, and shortly after his return to Paris he heard the American's *Rhapsody in Blue* (1924) for piano and orchestra, an important early effort to create a "highbrow" jazz suitable for the concert hall.

One of the most striking fusions of jazz, eighteenth-century allusions, and Primitivism is Milhaud's ballet *La création du monde* (The Creation of the World, 1923). After a short introduction, a four-voice fugue based on a syncopated, bluesy theme is played first by a solo double bass, then by trombone, saxophone, and trumpet. Milhaud creates a polymetric effect similar to his technique of polytonality by superimposing the melody in four beats per measure on top of an accompaniment played by piano and percussion in triple meter (Ex. 6.4). The fugal passage ends up sounding something like an improvisatory Dixieland band, and this is precisely the point, as is clear from Milhaud's description of a performance by Jean Wiéner and the banjo and saxophone player Vance Lowry: "Without any transition these two would pass from fashionable ragtime and fox-trots to the most celebrated works of Bach. Besides syncopated music calls for a rhythm as inexorably regular as that of Bach himself."

Example 6.4: *Darius Milhaud,* The Creation of the World, *movement 1, mm. 1–10*

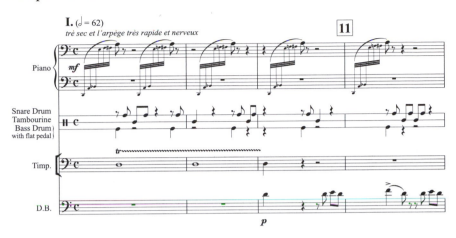

JAZZ AND "THE PRIMITIVE"

Cocteau's essay *Cock and Harlequin* points to more troubling implications of such stylistic fusions. In explicitly racist terms, Cocteau wrote:

> The music hall, the circus, and American negro bands, all these things fertilize an artist just as life does. To turn to one's own account the emotions aroused by this sort of entertainment is not to derive art from art. These entertainments are not art. They stimulate in the same way as machinery, animals, natural scenery or danger. (SR 171:1292; 7/2:22)

Milhaud's *Creation of the World* offers insight into the French fascination with what was then known as *l'art nègre* (black art). Like Primitivism and Exoticism before the war, *l'art nègre* was shaped by racial stereotypes and pervasive ideas of cultural evolution that placed Europeans at the culmination of human development and "primitives," governed by primal forces and sexual vitality, somewhere earlier along the continuum. Yet as we noted in connection with Krenek's opera *Jonny spielt auf* (see Chapter 5), the new element after the war was the peculiar fusion of African and Polynesian tribal art with an enthusiasm for African-American musical forms, including ragtime and jazz.

Thus it did not seem incongruous at the time for Milhaud in *The Creation of the World* to combine the melodies, harmonies, rhythms, and instrumentations of American jazz with a scenario based on African creation myths collected by the Swiss-French poet Blaise Cendrars. Cocteau proclaimed that Cendrars was the "one among us who best embodies the new exoticism. Mix of motorcars and black fetishes." The Cubist painter Fernand Léger drew on African sculpture for the ballet's backdrop, which showed three gods overseeing the act of creation, as well as for the props and costumes depicting the successive stages of creation: first plants, then animals, then a man and woman who enact a dance of desire (Fig. 6.3). The choreography was by Jean Börlin, who had made a name for himself performing African dances in ostensibly authentic costumes.

To varying degrees, all the collaborators were pursuing an ideal of ethnographic accuracy, while no doubt sincerely attempting to celebrate their African and African-American sources. Yet the ultimate effect of *The Creation of the World* was to perpetuate Primitivist myths and flatten out any sense of the dancers' individuality or humanity. Léger described the purpose of his stage design as making man "a mechanism like everything else: instead of being the end, as he formerly was, he becomes a means." A similar transformation takes place over the course of the jazz fugue, which mutates into an increasingly chaotic and dissonant mass of sound that evokes Stravinsky's *Rite of Spring*.

This Primitivist reimagining of jazz took place in spite of a considerable African-American presence in Paris, including groups like the Harlem Hellfighters (see Chapter 5). The extent to which jazz was viewed through the distorting prism of *l'art nègre* can be seen in the popular stage show *La revue*

Figure 6.3: *Fernand Léger's costumes and backdrop for Darius Milhaud's* The Creation of the World

nègre (The Black Revue, 1925), starring the St. Louis–born singer and dancer Josephine Baker. During rehearsals for the elaborate production, the French directors encouraged the African-American performers to dispense with their carefully choreographed swing dance routines in favor of "authentic" Primitivist numbers such as Baker's *Danse sauvage*, which she performed in a skirt made of bananas. Baker, who had previously performed in Ellington's "jungle" shows at New York's Cotton Club, capitalized on the vogue for *l'art nègre* by leading a pet leopard through the streets of Paris and appearing in successful films like *Princess Tam Tam* (1935), in which she played a Tunisian woman brought to Paris disguised as a princess from India.

Baker's strange conflation of identities in the film demonstrates how *l'art nègre* made little distinction between sources from Africa, Polynesia, and North and South America, and Parisian composers were no exception to its influence. Milhaud spent the years 1916–18 in Rio de Janeiro as secretary to the writer Paul Claudel, who was serving as a government official. His exposure to Brazilian popular music bore fruit in *Le boeuf sur le toit* (The Ox on the Roof, 1919), which quoted from and celebrated the works of a number of well-known Brazilian composers. Yet back in Paris Milhaud worked with Cocteau in 1920 to transform the orchestral work into a nonsensical ballet set in Prohibition-era America and featuring as its characters a "Boxer," a "Negro Dwarf," a "Lady of Fashion," and a "Red-headed Woman, dressed as a man."

Poulenc's *Rapsodie nègre* (Black Rhapsody, 1917) illustrates the eclectic imaginary space in which *l'art nègre* circulated and which makes such works so problematic today. Dedicated to Satie, the piece was first performed at a special event organized by the art dealer Paul Guillaume and the poet Guillaume Apollinaire that included an exhibition of African sculptures along with jazz performances. A five-movement work for chamber ensemble and voice, *Rapsodie nègre* brings together a host of idioms associated with the primitive and exotic, including octatonic passages in the finale that explicitly echo *The Rite of Spring*.

The central movement, *Honoloulou*, is a mixture of nonsense syllables and a few Japanese words (Ex. 6.5). The poet Marcel Ormoy, identified by a pen name in the score as "Makoko Kangourou," was imitating the so-called *poèmes nègres* of Dadaists like Hugo Ball, which used nonsense syllables in rhythmic patterns. (*L'art nègre* has a long trajectory: Ball's poem turned up in 1979 as part of the Talking Heads' song *I Zimbra* from the album *Fear of Music*, marking the beginning of the band's exploration of the rhythms and textures of African music.) The setting consists almost entirely of two alternating chords—E major with an added C, and D major seventh—accompanying a repetitive descending four-note diatonic melody. Poulenc underscores how the intentionally childlike and Primitivist music was intended as an escape from subjectivity and expression by indicating that the vocalist is to sing "without nuance."

In a passage that makes clear the highly charged cultural politics that characterized Paris between the wars, the 18-year-old Poulenc described the violent response he received when he showed *Rapsodie nègre* to the composer Paul Vidal in hopes of admission to the Conservatoire:

> He read it attentively, furrowed his brow and, upon seeing the dedication to Erik Satie, rolled his eyes furiously, got up and yelled these very words: "your work stinks, it is ridiculous, it is merely a load of balls. You are trying to make a fool of me with these parallel fifths everywhere. And what in the hell is this "Honoloulou?" Ah! I see that you are running with Stravinsky, Satie, and company. Well then, good day!" and he all but threw me out.

Example 6.5: *Francis Poulenc,* Honoloulou, *from* Rapsodie nègre, *mm. 4–8*

And yet, as with many composers, writers, and artists of these years, the works that Poulenc went on to compose over his long career demonstrate how stimulating the Parisian environment was, with its fusion of classic models from the eighteenth century and ancient Greece, everyday music from the jazz club to the circus, Primitivism, machine art, and many other elements. Poulenc's racy *Les biches* (The Does, 1924), written for the Ballets Russes, interleaves echoes of Mozart with contemporary dance styles, while the allusions in his Concerto for Two Pianos (1932) range from the eighteenth century to Balinese gamelan. Beginning in the 1930s, Poulenc, inspired by his rediscovery of Catholicism, wrote a series of sacred choral works, including *Gloria* (1960), that combine the classic and the popular, lightheartedness and seriousness, and simplicity and profundity in the free-ranging spirit of Neoclassicism.

FOR FURTHER READING

Albright, Daniel, *Untwisting the Serpent: Modernism in Music, Literature, and Other Art* (Chicago: University of Chicago Press, 2000)

Carr, Maureen, *Multiple Masks: Neoclassicism in Stravinsky's Works on Greek Subjects* (Lincoln: University of Nebraska Press, 2002)

Danuser, Hermann, "Rewriting the Past: Classicisms of the Inter-war Period," in *The Cambridge History of Twentieth Century Music*, edited by Nicholas Cook and Anthony Pople, 260–285 (Cambridge: Cambridge University Press, 2004)

Davis, Mary E., *Classic Chic: Music, Fashion, and Modernism* (Berkeley and Los Angeles: University of California Press, 2006)

Fulcher, Jane F., *The Composer as Intellectual: Music and Ideology in France 1914–1940* (Oxford and New York: Oxford University Press, 2005)

Mawer, Deborah, ed., *The Cambridge Companion to Ravel* (Cambridge: Cambridge University Press, 2000)

Messing, Scott, *Neoclassicism in Music, from the Genesis of the Concept through the Schoenberg-Stravinsky Polemic* (Ann Arbor: UMI Research Press, 1988)

Straus, Joseph, "Centricity and Some Important Referential Collections," in *Introduction to Post-Tonal Theory*, 112–35 (Upper Saddle River, NJ: Prentice Hall, 2004)

Walsh, Stephen, *Stravinsky: A Creative Spring: Russia and France, 1882–1934* (Berkeley: University of California Press, 1999)

Whiting, Steven Moore, *Satie the Bohemian: From Cabaret to Concert Hall* (Oxford: Oxford University Press, 1999)

CHAPTER SEVEN

The Search for Order and Balance

The clearest manifestation of the depths of personal and creative upheaval some composers experienced after World War I was their conviction that a search for new foundations for their music was not only possible but essential. As we saw in Part I, many before the war pursued individualistic and subjective approaches to music, often based on appeals to the unconscious, inspirations from far-off times and places, or the spirit of the folk. During the postwar period, conscious control and codified musical systems, such as the twelve-tone method developed by Arnold Schoenberg and his pupils, played a more central role. Equally important were the innovative techniques of working systematically with rhythm and other musical elements, introduced in the compositions and writings of Henry Cowell, Joseph Schillinger, and Ruth Crawford Seeger; and novel ways of creating music with a tonal center, explored by Béla Bartók and Paul Hindemith.

Robert Musil's formulation in *The Man Without Qualities* of systems of happiness and balance—all those theories, principles, and "faith in something or other" that we rely on to function in an unstable world (see Chapters 1 and 2)—is particularly pertinent to the developments we will consider in this chapter. In many cases composers not only relied on these new techniques for creating order and balance in the act of composition, but they also sought to make the techniques part of how their works were heard and understood by listeners. While all the new compositional strategies we will consider were regarded at first as idiosyncratic and marginal, they became to varying degrees important features of the intellectual and artistic landscape in which composers had to situate themselves in the interwar years, and even more so after World War II.

CULTURAL POLITICS OF THE SEARCH FOR ORDER

Despite personal, political, and aesthetic differences, there were significant points of contact between the composers we will discuss below and those we encountered in Chapters 5 and 6. Reflecting the broad impact of the New Objectivity, the search for order often de-emphasized emotional expression. As in the Parisian scene, composers in many locales saw no inconsistency in connecting their new techniques with evocations of eighteenth-century styles, genres, and forms, or with borrowings from popular music and jazz. For example, Schoenberg's twelve-tone Suite, Op. 29 (1926), first performed in Paris at Ravel's invitation, contains Neoclassical elements—including stripped-down instrumental forces (a septet of clarinets, strings, and piano), an overture in sonata form, and a concluding gigue in fugal style—along with a movement featuring a fox-trot and other "everyday" dance music, and a set of variations on a German folk song that plays with tonal allusions.

Mirroring the complex and contradictory cultural politics in Paris, the search for order and balance by composers in Germany, Hungary, and the United States could be aligned with, and rejected by, ideologies of every stripe. Just as Cocteau trumpeted the purportedly French virtues of clarity and simplicity, Schoenberg viewed his twelve-tone method in nationalistic terms as a tool for restoring the dominance of Austro-German music. He and his pupils justified their new techniques through appeals to Bach and other past masters. They made orchestral arrangements of Bach works, incorporated allusions or actual quotations of Bach in their own pieces, and even made his name part of their twelve-tone rows (in German music nomenclature, BACH translates to B♭–A–C–B♮).

Schoenberg experienced the collapse of the Austro-Hungarian Empire and the end of the Habsburg monarchy as "the overturning of everything one has believed in." His nostalgia for the old social order is clear in a letter to Prince Egon von Fürstenberg, the patron of a new-music festival in the German town of Donaueschingen, where his Neoclassical Serenade, Op. 24 was premiered in 1924. The festival, Schoenberg wrote, was "reminiscent of the fairest, alas bygone, days of art when a prince stood as a protector before an artist, showing the rabble that art, a matter for princes, is beyond the judgment of common people." And yet despite Schoenberg's strong political conservatism, national-ism, and opposition to both socialism and communism, he was often attacked as a symbol of the politically progressive factions of the Weimar Republic, through whose auspices he became professor at the Prussian Academy of Arts in Berlin from 1926 to 1933. During these years he composed not only traditional concert music but also music for workers' choral organizations and for amateurs.

Anton Webern, who had been active on behalf of Socialist workers' musical organizations in the 1920s and early 1930s, came to sympathize with the fer-vent nationalism of the Third Reich during World War II. In the 1940s he even succeeded in obtaining financial support from the Reich Music Chamber, the Nazi-controlled music bureau. Yet this did not prevent Webern's music, along with that of Schoenberg, Berg, Hindemith, Weill, Krenek, and Stravinsky, from being vilified and eventually banned by the Nazis. Their compositions, along with artworks by Kandinsky, Kokoschka, and hundreds of others, were mocked in the Nazis' widely publicized Degenerate Art (1938) and Degenerate Music (1939) exhibitions.

Shortly after fleeing Germany in 1933, when the Nazis came to power, Schoenberg drafted a statement titled "My Enemies" that summarized the con-tradictory ways in which his music had been interpreted in political terms:

I.   a) Nationalistic musicians regard me as *international*

    b) but abroad my music is regarded as too *German*

II.   a) National Socialists regard me as a *cultural-Bolshevik*

    b) but the communists reject me as bourgeois

III. a) Anti-Semites personify me as a Jew, my direction as Jewish

    b) but almost no Jews have followed my direction.

As Schoenberg's statement suggests, advocates of internationalism, com-munism, and socialism were divided in their stance toward the new composi-tional methods. Composers like Ruth Crawford Seeger employed complex and arcane techniques in works intended to promote social justice and progressive political causes. Hindemith, famous for engaging with every Modernist trend, worked closely with Socialist and Communist artists, including Kurt Weill and Bertolt Brecht, and during the Weimar Republic he composed *Gebrauchsmusik* (music for use) for children and the youth movement. Bartók wrote his *Mikrokosmos* (1926–39), a set of 153 graded piano pieces that take students from beginner to an advanced level—and although Bartók avoided aligning him-self with any political faction, a 1937 Budapest performance of some of the *Mikrokosmos* pieces and his folk-song arrangements for children was stridently attacked as a Modernist corruption of Hungarian youth. The Italian composer Luigi Dallapiccola (1904–1975) turned to the twelve-tone method in the 1930s as a way to protest against Mussolini and fascism in his choral work *Canti di pri-*

gionia (Songs of Imprisonment, 1941) and the opera *Il prigioniero* (The Prisoner, 1948). After immigrating to the United States, Schoenberg composed several twelve-tone works with overtly political themes, including the anti-Fascist *Ode to Napoleon* (1942) and *A Survivor from Warsaw* (1947), written in response to the Warsaw Ghetto Uprising in 1943.

Yet many on the left viewed any sort of Modernist music as inherently elitist and reactionary. The belief in the early days of the Soviet Union that a new political order should be open to new art soon gave way to extreme hostility toward Modernism and "formalism" (see Chapter 9). In Germany, Schoenberg's pupil Hanns Eisler (1898–1962) was one of the first to take up the twelve-tone method. As he became increasingly active in Communist politics in the mid-1920s, however, Eisler broke with Schoenberg and devoted himself to writing accessible music designed to combat fascism and rally the proletariat. The Communist-affiliated Composers' Collective in New York debated how best to compose politically engaged music (see Chapter 8). We will see that questions concerning the relationship between new compositional techniques and politics have continued to be an issue down to the present (see Chapter 13).

THE TWELVE-TONE METHOD

Of all the attempts after the war to create a new technical and theoretical foundation for music, Schoenberg's method of composing with 12 tones was the most ambitious. While his goal of providing a new common language to replace tonality was never realized, many composers from very different traditions explored the method, and it continues to play a significant role in composition and music theory. In keeping with his insistence that twelve-tone composition was a method and not a closed "system," Schoenberg and his students never stopped refining and reimagining the technique; composers after World War II took it still further, often in directions quite different from Schoenberg's initial formulation.

Schoenberg in his 1911 *Theory of Harmony* had already given examples of chords containing all 12 tones, and over the next decade he worked on a large number of pieces in which he explored composing with ordered and unordered rows of pitches of various lengths. In the second decade of the twentieth century, several other composers began to explore ways to work systematically with the 12 tones of the chromatic scale. Starting before the war, the Russian Nikolay Roslavets developed a method involving transpositions of chords of six or more tones, resulting in complete chromatic collections. Around 1920 the Viennese composer and theorist Josef Hauer published writings and works concerning his technique of organizing the 12 tones into two unordered six-note sets, or hexachords.

In 1923, anxious not to be upstaged by Hauer, Schoenberg called together his pupils to unveil the "method of composing with 12 tones related only to one another." That same year he published the Five Pieces for Piano, Op. 23, which included one twelve-tone movement, as did the Serenade, Op. 24, published the following year. The first fully twelve-tone piece with all the movements based on a single tone row was the Suite for Piano, Op. 25, completed in 1923 and published in 1925. Schoenberg's students at once began to integrate the twelve-tone method into their own works.

Although Schoenberg waited until 1950 to publish a detailed explanation of the method, he and his pupils began promulgating the techniques in the early 1930s through lectures, publications, and their own teaching. Countering charges that the method was arbitrary and artificial, they argued that twelve-tone composition was the product of historical necessity. They defended the method as the culmination of a progression that began with the fusion of the church modes into major and minor tonality, continued through Wagner's chromatic harmony, and followed as the necessary next step after the emancipation of the dissonance.

In styling themselves the "New" Viennese School (now often referred to as the Second Viennese School), Schoenberg, Berg, and Webern claimed to be the true successors of Mozart, Haydn, and Beethoven, and worked to integrate the twelve-tone method with the forms and genres of the Classical style. Their intent was both to situate their work within the Austro-German musical tradition and to make their music comprehensible to a broader audience by providing familiar formal, rhythmic, and textural elements. Although they did not use the term Neoclassicism for their own works, their music in the 1920s and 1930s employed these and other Neoclassical elements, such as traditional contrapuntal techniques of canon and fugue, and conventional rhythmic types like the waltz and march.

Beyond answering the harsh criticisms his claims about the twelve-tone method provoked, Schoenberg may have also felt the need to justify the method so vehemently because it represented a significant shift in his own thinking, away from his prewar emphasis on the intuitive "elimination of the conscious will in art" to the grudging acceptance of the need for conscious control. His essay *Composition with 12 Tones* (1941, published 1950) begins with a passage that suggests the sense of loss he felt in moving beyond his earlier commitment to the spontaneous expression of his emotions so central to works like the 1909 Three Piano Pieces, Op. 11: "In Divine Creation there were no details to be carried out later; 'There was Light' at once and its ultimate perfection. Alas human creators, if they be granted a vision, must travel the long path between vision and accomplishment; a hard road where, driven out of Paradise, even geniuses must reap their harvest in the sweat of their brows."

ELEMENTS OF TWELVE-TONE COMPOSITION

When Schoenberg composed his Piano Piece, Op. 33a (1929), he was at the height of his career as a professor of composition at the Prussian Academy of Arts. During this period he put a great deal of effort into informing the public about his new method of twelve-tone composition, including a 1931 radio lecture on his Variations for Orchestra, Op. 31 (1928). It seems likely that Op. 33a was intended as a kind of showcase for the method, and indeed the piece has become one of the most frequently analyzed and discussed twelve-tone works. (Figure 7.1 provides a facsimile of his first draft; the complete piece is discussed in Anthology 10.)

The most important principle of Schoenberg's method is that each piece is based on a single ordering of the 12 chromatic pitches, which he referred to as the "row," "basic set," or "theme"; later twelve-tone theory introduced the equivalent terms "prime form" and "series." Op. 33a is based on the row notated in the treble clef at the bottom left of the draft in Figure 7.1 (B♭–F–C–B–A–F♯–C♯–D♯–G–A♭–D–E). The emphasis on the fixed order of the row was a crucial innovation of Schoenberg's method and underlies the development of serial music after World War II (see Chapter 10). Not just a series of pitches, the ordering of the

Figure 7.1: *Arnold Schoenberg, Piano Piece, Op. 33a, autograph manuscript, first draft*

row also produces a series of intervals that gives each row a distinctive sound and compositional potential. The choice of an ordering of the chromatic collection from the nearly ten million unique possibilities has many ramifications for all aspects of a twelve-tone work, and, as we will see, Schoenberg, Berg, and Webern used very different types of rows.

The fixed series of intervals created by the order of the 12 pitches makes it possible to generate three transformations of the row: the retrograde (the row played in reverse order), the inversion (produced by reversing the direction of the intervals of the row), and the retrograde inversion (the inversion played in reverse order). In response to objections that such manipulations of the row were artificial or mathematical, Schoenberg pointed out that inversions and retrogrades had been part of contrapuntal technique since the Renaissance. The four forms of the row could be transposed to start on any one of the 12 chromatic pitches, thus giving the composer a total of 48 rows to use as the basis for a work.

It is customary today to identify the 12 transpositions of row forms by integers from 0 to 11. Some use a "fixed-do" system, where C always equals 0; we will follow the "movable-do" method and identify the first pitch of the main row as 0, which is closer to Schoenberg's approach of labeling row forms in terms of diatonic intervals as measured from the first note of the basic set. Thus in the row table on the lower right of the draft in Figure 7.1, the row labeled T^5 is the "theme" transposed up a perfect fifth from B♭ to F. The row labeled U_8 is the inversion (*Umkehrung*) transposed down an octave to start on B♭; in the table on the left U_5 is the inversion transposed down a perfect fifth to E♭. In present-day twelve-tone theory these would be labeled as P^0 (prime form starting on B♭), I^0 (inversion starting on B♭), and I^5 (inversion starting on E♭), with the 5 signifying the number of half steps from B♭ to E♭. When identifying the order number of pitches in a row, some count, as might be expected, from 1 to 12; in contemporary theory it is more common to use 0 to 11, which is more amenable to mathematical formalizations of the relationships between the pitches and order number.

Schoenberg developed many different ways of writing out the various forms of the row, including tables, card files, and the so-called "magic square," or 12-by-12 matrix (see Anthology 11). While for longer pieces he would use many of the 48 row forms, for shorter pieces, like Op. 33a, he often limited himself to a small group. Together with the two main forms of the row given on the bottom left of Figure 7.1, the row table on the right provides all the additional forms he used in this piece.

In a twelve-tone piece, the composer derives all the melodic and harmonic material of the work from the row, thus resulting in what Schoenberg described as "the unity of musical space." But this does not mean that he expected us to be able to hear the row as a linear succession of 12 pitches; indeed, in Op. 33a he states the row unambiguously from beginning to end only in measures 32–33. Thus he treats the row not as a theme or melody, but as a source of motives, as suggested by his division of the row tables in the draft into groups of four and six notes (tetrachords and hexachords). Schoenberg starts the piece in measures 1–2 by dividing up the original row and the U_5 inversion into three chords of four notes each. He then uses the retrograde of the U_5 inversion to create the material in the right hand of measures 3–5, while the left hand is based on the retrograde of the original row.

Schoenberg structured his rows to produce many different intervals between the pitches, which allowed him in turn to create a wide range of harmonies. This harmonic variety is audible in Op. 33a, with the distinctive stack of perfect fourths or fifths that starts the row appearing as a chord or melodic motive at the beginnings and ends of phrases throughout the piece. In contrast, the central tetrachord of the row (A–F♯–C♯–D♯) is a half-diminished seventh, while the final four pitches produce a dissonant cluster. What mattered most to Schoenberg was the richness and unity of the material that could be generated from the row in interaction with its various transformations— and this led him to deviate occasionally from what the row structure would dictate. The violist Eugene Lehner of the Kolisch Quartet, which championed Schoenberg's music, described the composer's fury when after a rehearsal they pointed out some "wrong notes" in the Third Quartet: "And Schoenberg gets mad—red in the face! . . . 'if I hear an F♯, I will write an F♯. If I hear an F♮, I will write an F♮. Just because of your stupid . . . theory, are you telling me what I should write?'"

Schoenberg always emphasized that the goal of the twelve-tone method was comprehensibility, by which he meant the ability of the mind to grasp the logic of the musical development. As noted earlier, he attempted to achieve this in Op. 33a and other twelve-tone works by combining the method with more familiar styles, forms, and genres. The most salient feature in this regard in Op. 33a is the Neoclassical allusion to sonata form, including two contrasting themes (the second with a more lyrical character), a clearly developmental central section, and a recapitulation that brings back the two themes from the exposition in a compressed form. Schoenberg defines these formal points of demarcation using elements of the row structure, but also through traditional means of contrasts in texture, rhythm, and tempo.

WEBERN'S PATH TO THE NEW MUSIC

In a series of lectures on twelve-tone composition called *The Path to the New Music* (1932–33), Webern said: "It's my belief that ever since music has been written, all the great composers have instinctively had this before them as a goal." Yet Webern's own path to becoming a twelve-tone composer was not without difficulties. Beginning in 1922 he spent several years working to reconcile the method with his own beliefs in a kind of mystical unity inspired by Johann Wolfgang von Goethe's early-nineteenth-century writings on organicism, as well as with his interest in working intensively with small motivic cells, as we saw in his Four Pieces for Violin and Piano, Op. 7 (see Chapter 3).

Webern's first published twelve-tone work was the String Trio, Op. 20 (1927); like his teacher, he consciously integrated the method with forms and genres of the Classical style. Arguably his most influential piece for later musical developments was his Symphony, Op. 21 (1928). The two-movement Symphony—he had originally intended to include a rondo movement as well—is written for an ensemble of nine instruments (the string parts can be played by a small section or by solo instruments). The score exemplifies the remarkable compression and intricate structures that made Webern's music as challenging for contemporary audiences as it would be revelatory for later composers.

In contrast to Schoenberg's preference for a variety of intervals, Webern's twelve-tone row for the Symphony is characteristically tightly unified and economical (Ex. 7.1). The ordering of the row produces, in the first hexachord, a minor third followed by two half steps (with octave displacements), then a major third (appearing as its inversion, a minor sixth) followed by another half step; the second hexachord is a retrograde of this pattern transposed a tritone. The resulting symmetrical row structure has many ramifications that Webern explores in the piece. For example, the palindromic structure of the row is developed in the second movement in the structure of the theme and in the overall form of the movement, which is itself a large-scale palindrome (see Anthology 11). Webern explicitly described such structural features as substituting for tonality:

> Considerations of symmetry, regularity now come to the fore, as against the emphasis formerly laid on the principal intervals—dominant, subdominant, mediant, etc. . . . The original form and pitch of the row occupy a position akin to that of the "main key" in earlier music, the recapitulation will naturally return to it. We end "in the same key." This analogy with earlier formal construction is quite consciously fostered; here we find the path that will lead us again to extended forms.

The second movement of the Symphony consists of a theme with seven variations and a coda. The use of theme-and-variations form became particularly important for all three composers because of its close association with the basic principle of twelve-tone composition: presenting the row and its transformations in changing contexts. Webern went the furthest in connecting twelve-tone techniques to rhythm and dynamics. The palindromic theme, for example, includes an exact retrograde of dynamics, rhythm, texture, and articulation. It was only with the post–World War II development of Integral Serialism that composers followed up on this idea of applying the twelve-tone method systematically to the other elements of music (see Chapter 10).

The first movement of the Symphony combines a double canon in contrary motion with sonata form. As is often the case in his music, however, Webern

Example 7.1: *Anton Webern, Symphony, Op. 21, movement 2, twelve-tone theme, mm. 1–11*

obscured these structural devices with constant overlapping of the voices and pointillistic textures. What we are more likely to hear is a slowly evolving constellation of shifting timbres and intervals that gradually coalesces and then dissolves. It is crucial to keep in mind that for Webern the symmetries, palindromes, and canons were not an end in themselves, but were intended to provide an analogy to the deep organic unity he saw in nature. The continuing influence of Romanticism is also evident in the frequent programmatic elements in his compositional sketches. For the Symphony he indicated programmatic associations with mountain landscapes, sun and moonlight, and meaningful locations from his life, including the gravesites of his mother and father. Webern's delicate tone-color melodies create subtle expressive effects, including moments of significant stillness and evocations of the crystalline atmospheres of alpine light.

BERG'S ALLUSIONS TO TONALITY

While the complex structures and abstract surfaces of Webern's music obscure his connections to Romanticism, the more familiar sounds and forms of Berg's atonal and twelve-tone works mask his obsession with elaborate and arcane compositional devices. Completed in 1922, Berg's three-act opera *Wozzeck* is not a twelve-tone work, but it anticipates his later interest in integrating tonal allusions, Neoclassical forms and genres, and complex structures. The first act is a set of five character pieces, including a Baroque-style suite, a march, and a passacaglia. Act 2 is a symphony in five movements. The third act, as discussed in Chapter 3, is a set of what he referred to as "inventions," no doubt intended to evoke Bach's famous contrapuntal keyboard inventions. In Berg's case, the inventions are closer to the idea of variations that explore different elements, including a theme, a note, and a rhythm.

Wozzeck demonstrates Berg's systematic approaches to structure. For example, the "invention on a rhythm" in Act 3, scene 3 of *Wozzeck* is based on a rhythmic ostinato, presented in both augmentation and diminution, that expresses Wozzeck's gnawing sense of guilt for his crime (see Anthology 4). While Berg at times de-emphasized the significance for the listener of the many intricate forms and technical devices in the opera, in 1924 he published a letter to a critic that singled out this scene for the audibility of the rhythm that permeates the vocal parts and orchestral accompaniment, "subjected to every conceivable combination, contrapuntal device (fugato, stretti) and variation (augmentation, diminution, displacement, etc.)."

Among Berg's earliest completed works using twelve-tone technique are his Chamber Concerto for Piano, Violin, and 13 Wind Instruments (1925), which includes themes based on the names Schoenberg, Webern, and Berg; and his second string quartet, the *Lyric Suite*, composed in 1925–26. Both pieces are full of intricate compositional devices and are connected to detailed programmatic elements, both public and private. The discovery years after Berg's death of his heavily annotated pocket score of the *Lyric Suite* revealed that many aspects of the row structure, the formal organization, and even the tempo markings contained coded messages concerning an extramarital affair. In the final movement he added a vocal line, based on a poem by Charles Baudelaire, that is sometimes now included in performances of the work.

When Schoenberg used the phrase "composing with 12 tones related only to one another," he was insisting that the method was intended to provide an alternative to tonality. Many features of the method, including the use of all 12 tones in regular circulation, the avoidance of octave doubling, and cautions regarding the use of tonal triads and scales, were designed to prevent any one pitch from inadvertently emerging as a tonic and thus subverting the emancipation of the dissonance. But this does not mean that Schoenberg and his students always avoided intentional allusions to tonality; on the contrary, their explorations into how the twelve-tone method could assimilate aspects of tonality turned out to be particularly productive.

Berg's Violin Concerto of 1935, his last completed work, provides an example of the effort to subsume tonality within twelve-tone composition. The second of the two movements concludes with a theme and two variations based on the Bach chorale "Es ist genug" (It Is Enough) from Cantata No. 60 (Ex. 7.2). The phrases of the chorale are presented first in a twelve-tone arrangement and then in Bach's original harmonization, with the winds emulating the sound of a pipe organ. Like most of Berg's works, the Violin Concerto has programmatic and autobiographical dimensions. Bach's chorale is about the peaceful acceptance of death; the concerto was dedicated to the memory of Manon Gropius, the daughter of Alma Mahler, who died of polio in 1935 at age 18. Other programmatic elements were discovered after Berg's death, including references to an illegitimate daughter he had fathered when he was 17. The dance-like Allegretto section in the first movement quotes a crude folk song about an illicit love affair. This passage, to be played "in a Viennese manner," is one of several examples of folk music, dance music, and jazz that Berg incorporated into his twelve-tone works.

Berg was able to integrate tonal music so seamlessly into twelve-tone composition by constructing rows that included diatonic scales and triads, something that Schoenberg did as well despite his warnings against it. The row of the Violin

Example 7.2: *Alban Berg, Violin Concerto, movement 2: Chorale, mm. 136–143*

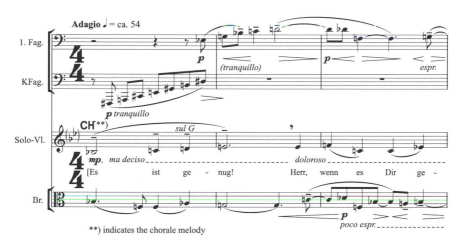

**) indicates the chorale melody

It is enough! Lord, if it please you, Unyoke me now at last! My Jesus comes: . . .

Example 7.3: *Alban Berg, Violin Concerto, movement 1, solo violin's twelve-tone theme, mm. 15–18*

Concerto (Ex. 7.3), for example, can be segmented into functionally related triads, as Berg makes explicit in measures 11–14, where we hear G minor and D major (i and V) and A minor and E major (ii and V/ii). It is a striking irony that the most "modern"-sounding segment of the row—the whole-tone tetrachord in the last four pitches—is based on the opening melody of the Bach chorale. In suggesting that Bach's music is so closely connected to his own, Berg underscores the insistence by the Second Viennese School that their music, as Schoenberg wrote, was a "truly new music which, being based on tradition, is destined to become tradition." Such a claim—just as controversial now as when Schoenberg made it in 1931—illustrates how strongly many composers felt the need for a new foundation for music, as well as their belief that a new musical language was in their reach.

NEW APPROACHES TO RHYTHM, TEXTURE, AND FORM

The twelve-tone method was primarily intended as a means for controlling melody and harmony. While Schoenberg and his pupils explored ways of extending it to other musical elements, for the most part they intentionally based rhythm, texture, form, dynamics, and phrase structure on traditional practices. Yet several composers between the wars did explore new ways of working systematically not only with pitch, but also with rhythm, texture, and form. While their impact was initially limited, their ideas became increasingly important for later efforts to open up new ways of hearing and thinking about musical sound.

COWELL'S NEW MUSICAL RESOURCES

The American composer Henry Cowell (1897–1965) was born near San Francisco in Menlo Park, California. At age 17 Cowell began to study at the University of California at Berkeley, including lessons with the composer and scholar

Charles Seeger. In the 1920s Cowell attracted attention touring Europe and the Soviet Union with his piano pieces featuring such unorthodox performance techniques as forearm clusters in *The Tides of Manaunaun* (1917) and plucking, strumming, and scraping the strings in *The Aeolian Harp* (1923) and *The Banshee* (1925). In addition to composing and teaching, Cowell promoted the music of Schoenberg, Varèse, Ives, and other contemporary composers. The New Music Society, which he founded in 1925, published the influential journal *New Music: A Quarterly of Modern Compositions*. Cowell was also an early advocate of integrating world and folk music into concert-hall works, supported by his studies of ethnomusicology, gamelan, Japanese and Indian music, and Theosophy (see Chapter 3).

In his book *New Musical Resources* (1930), Cowell proposed a "theory of musical relativity" based on the notion that the overtone series provided a way of integrating melody, harmony, and rhythm. As Schoenberg had done in his *Theory of Harmony*, Cowell argued that music had evolved to incorporate harmonies produced by the closely spaced upper overtones. But he went further in formulating a theory for the use of tone clusters consisting of major and minor seconds, thereby building on Seeger's work theorizing and promoting "dissonant counterpoint," which treats dissonant intervals as the foundation and consonances only as passing or auxiliary notes.

Anticipating an interest of many composers after World War II, Cowell also described ways of generating rhythm, meter, tempo, and texture from the ratios of the overtone series, thus applying to those elements the same constructive principles used for melody and harmony (Ex. 7.4). He argued that the same ratios that control the relationship between a fundamental frequency and its overtones—1:2:3:4:5—could be applied to rhythmic values. From the fundamental frequency of C we hear the harmonics G, C, E, created by the ratio of frequencies

Example 7.4: *Henry Cowell, example of a rhythmic harmony (a) based on time ratios of 3, 4, and 5 beats, derived from the frequency ratios of (b) a second-inversion major triad 3:4:5*

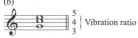

3:4:5—based on the perfect fourth between the second and third harmonic partials, and the major third between the third and fourth partials. According to
Cowell, this phenomenon can be expressed rhythmically as layered patterns of
three against four beats and four against five beats.

To avoid the normative assumptions of traditional musical notation, in
which such subdivisions require some form of "-tuplet," Cowell gave each
rhythmic type a different-shaped notehead: triangles for third notes, squares
for fifth notes, and so on. An excerpt from his piano piece *Fabric* (ca. 1917; Ex. 7.5)
shows the use of ninth and eighth notes in the lowest voice, fifth and third notes
in the middle voice, and seventh and third notes in the top voice. Building on
the idea of turning harmonic ratios into rhythmic patterns, Cowell worked
with Lev Termen (see Chapter 5) in the design of the Rhythmicon, a precursor
of the drum machine. Built in 1931 with funding from Charles Ives, the instrument made it possible to superimpose 16 different subdivisions of a basic
pulse. Cowell used the device in his Concerto for Rhythmicon and Orchestra
(1931).

THE SCHILLINGER SYSTEM

Cowell was not alone in his efforts to create new forms of order and balance by
working systematically with rhythm. Joseph Schillinger (1895–1943) was a Russian composer, conductor, and theorist who came to New York in 1928, where
he taught at the New School, Columbia Teachers College, and other institutions.
Schillinger had been a leader in introducing jazz to Russia, and he worked with
many important jazz musicians in New York, including George Gershwin, Benny
Goodman, Eubie Blake, and Glenn Miller. Trained in mathematics, Schillinger
designed a system that was presented in two massive volumes prepared by his
students after his death. He used graphic notation to show underlying commonalities of rhythm, melody, harmony, orchestration, and form. Schillinger
described these commonalities as controlling "not only music and the arts in
general, but also the proportions of the human body, as well as various forms of
growth in nature," like horns, shells, and leaves.

Example 7.5: *Henry Cowell,* Fabric, *mm. 7–9*

Schillinger's system offered tools for generating a vast range of material through systematic variation and combination of simple building blocks. Figure 7.2 shows rhythmic patterns, which he called "resultants," that could be generated by combining patterns of two, three, and five beats. With his techniques for generating rich and diverse surfaces from simple mathematical principles, Schillinger and his ideas have recently attracted the interest of scholars exploring the connections between music and the self-duplicating patterns of fractals, as well as of electronic composers seeking ways of creating complex textures resembling those of the natural world. (See also the discussion of sound art in Chapter 15.)

Figure 7.2: *An illustration, from* Schillinger's System of Musical Composition, *of how rhythmic patterns can be generated by a number series, such as 2, 3, 5. Schillinger first multiplies the numbers to find their common product (2 × 3 × 5 = 30), which he then subdivides into its factors (30, 15, 10, 6, 2, 3, 5). He then combines these subdivisions to create two resultant patterns, which he labels as theme (r) and countertheme (r'). Schillinger gives these resultant patterns in numeric form and in musical notation, with 1 = ♪.*

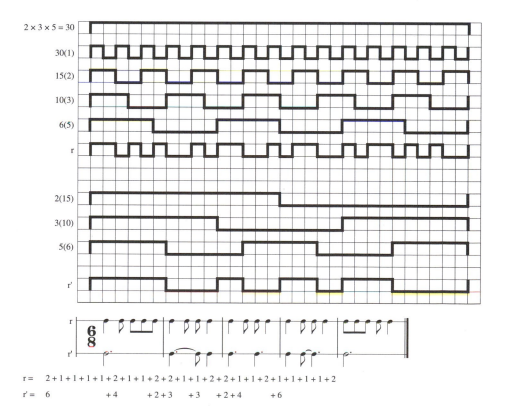

RUTH CRAWFORD SEEGER'S NEW COMPOSITIONAL SYSTEMS

The American composer Ruth Crawford Seeger (1901–1953) developed techniques for structuring pitch, rhythm, dynamics, and texture that anticipated both Integral Serialism and process-based Minimalism (see Chapters 10 and 14). Born in Florida, she studied at the American Conservatory in Chicago before moving to New York in the mid-1920s and establishing herself as a composer in what became known as the Ultra-Modernist group that included Carl Ruggles, Varèse, Cowell, and Charles Seeger, whom she married in 1932.

Crawford Seeger composed her String Quartet (1931) while in Berlin on a Guggenheim Fellowship, the first to be awarded to a woman. Each of the four movements explores different innovative possibilities for systematically organizing the elements of music. In an analysis prepared at Varèse's request, she described the third movement as "a heterophony of dynamics—a sort of counterpoint of crescendi and diminuendi." The final movement was a struggle between two voices in which the idea of dissonance is applied to dynamics and rhythm: "There is therefore a sort of dissonance within each voice between volume, in dynamics and number of tones, and also a sort of dissonance between the voices, in volume and number."

At the start of the fourth movement, the first violin plays a single emphatic note that grows, one note at a time, into a melody 20 notes long (Ex. 7.6). The other three instruments reverse the pattern, starting with a muted 20-note melody played in unison that with each statement becomes one note shorter until it is reduced to a single note. Crawford Seeger bases the lower voice on a 10-note row that is rotated with each statement to start on a new pitch. At the same time these processes unfold, the two voices exchange their dynamic character, the violin becoming softer as its statements are extended, and the lower instruments growing louder and more strident. In the second half of the movement all these processes are reversed, with both voices transposed up a half step, resulting in a large-scale palindrome.

These elaborate structural devices may have had programmatic significance for Crawford Seeger; for example, she characterized the relationship between the two voices in the String Quartet's finale as a struggle between two characters of contrasting mood and personality, pitting the initially forceful and uncomplicated top voice against the more subdued and unsettled lower voice. Scholars have read the movement as an expression of her own struggles to establish herself as a composer in a hostile, male-dominated environment. Shortly before she began work on the Quartet, she wrote in her diary: "I also vent my spleen today on the fact of being a woman, or rather on the fact that beastly men, not satisfied with their own freedom, encroach on that of women and produce in them a kind of necessitous fear which binds them about."

Though she later turned her attention to folk music and other more accessible musical forms, Crawford Seeger saw no contradiction in the early 1930s between new compositional systems and music with a political purpose. The song "Chinaman, Laundryman," the first of her *Two Ricercari* (1932), concerns

Example 7.6: *Ruth Crawford Seeger, String Quartet, movement 4, mm. 1–14. (Accidentals affect only the note before which they appear.)*

the exploitation of Chinese immigrants and explicitly calls for the workers of the world to unite against economic and social oppression. The text was originally published in the Communist newspaper *The Daily Worker*. The second *Ricercare* denounced the execution of the Italian-American anarchists Sacco and Vanzetti in 1919. "Chinaman, Laundryman" is based on systematic transformations of a nine-note row, while the rhythm in each measure explores all the possible permutations of three rhythmic patterns; against this rigid framework the *Sprechstimme* voice struggles to assert its independence. The *Two Ricercari* were presented for a mass audience in the First American Workers Music Olympiad in New York in 1933.

NEW TONALITIES

The new approaches to musical structure discussed above all assumed the need to move beyond traditional conceptions of tonality and functional harmony. But we can also see the search for new forms of order and balance in the works of composers who remained committed to writing tonal music. Bartók, Hindemith, and others experimented with the innovative techniques of manipulating tonal materials discussed in Chapter 6, including Milhaud's polytonality and Stravinsky's defamiliarization of tonal triads and cadential formulae. Yet in their compositions that we will consider here, we find a greater concern for systematization in the effort to provide a new foundation for composition.

BARTÓK'S SYMMETRICAL STRUCTURES

Bartók's music never stopped being, as he wrote, "pervaded by the atmosphere of peasant music" (SR 198:1440–1441; 7/29:170–171). But in the mid-1920s he began integrating Neoclassical elements into his compositions, including eighteenth-century forms and genres and imitative counterpoint. The fugal opening movement of the *Music for Strings, Percussion, and Celesta* (see Anthology 12), composed in 1936 for the Basel Chamber Orchestra, is a famous example. The second movement is a sonata form, while the third is a rondo (the concluding fourth movement evokes folk dances). Unlike Stravinsky, Bartók was little interested in ironic play with such historical allusions for their own sake; rather, he used them as a tool for creating clarity and order. Alongside works in sonata and other conventional forms, he composed pieces based on symmetrical structures such as ABCBA. Bartók used this "bridge form" both within individual movements (such as the rondo of the *Music for Strings, Percussion, and Celesta*) and to organize complete works. The five movements of the Fourth String Quartet (1928), for example, are arranged symmetrically around a central movement (which itself is in a symmetrical ABA form), with formal balance enhanced by the many similarities between the second and fourth movements and the first and fifth.

Bartók's interest in symmetrical patterns is also evident in the systematic pattern of transpositional levels governing the statements of the fugue theme in the *Music for Strings, Percussion, and Celesta*. After the initial presentation of the theme starting on A, subsequent versions trace a sequence of perfect fifths both above and below; once they reach the shared midpoint of E♭, Bartók retraces the sequence in reverse.

As we saw in Chapter 4, Bartók wrote voluminously about folk music. Yet he made his aversion to prescriptive compositional theory clear in his 1943 lectures at Harvard University: "I never created new theories in advance, I hated such ideas. I had, of course, a very definite feeling about certain directions to take, but at the time of the work I did not care about the designations which would apply to those directions or to their sources." In works like the Fourth String

Quartet, Bartók used dissonances based on tightly unified manipulations of chromatic and whole-tone tetrachords, but he never embraced either atonality or Schoenberg's twelve-tone method. Instead, he developed several techniques for creating a tonal center without resorting to functional harmonic progressions.

Bartók embraced a constant interchange between chromatic and diatonic elements, as well as fluid transitions among modal, whole-tone, and octatonic passages. One way he effected this synthetic approach was through a technique he described as compressing a motive into a chromatic version or expanding it into a diatonic form. Thus, for example, the chromatic theme of the first movement of the *Music for Strings, Percussion, and Celesta* returns in the last movement in a diatonic expansion (Ex. 7.7). He also developed what he called "polymodal chromaticism," which involved the layering of two distinct modes. In the first of his *Six Dances in Bulgarian Rhythm*, No. 148 from his piano set *Mikrokosmos*, the two hands exchange passages in E major and E Phrygian. While the idea is comparable to Milhaud's polytonality, Bartók insisted that his music was "always based on a single fundamental tone" and rejected the notion that two tonal centers could operate simultaneously.

Bartók was particularly interested in creating a tonal center by arraying inversionally symmetrical pitch structures around a central axis. Whole-tone and octatonic scales lend themselves to this approach, as both have the property of inversional symmetry between the two halves: (C–D–E/F♯–G♯–A♯) and (C–D–E♭–F/F♯–G♯–A–B). Bartók also used symmetrical collections such as C–C♯–F♯–G [represented in pitch-class set theory as (0167)], which can be generated by transposing a half step (01) up a tritone (67), or transposing a tritone (06) up a half step (17). As noted earlier, the fugal entries in the *Music for Strings, Percussion, and Celesta* move through cycles of perfect fifths upward and downward from the starting point on A to E♭. Bartók concludes the movement with a brief passage that, like a mathematical formula, encapsulates the thematic structure, the mirrored symmetries of the overall form, and the role of A as the fulcrum of balance (Ex. 7.8).

Example 7.7: *Béla Bartók,* Music for Strings, Percussion, and Celesta, *chromatic and diatonic versions of main theme;* (a) *first movement;* (b) *fourth movement*

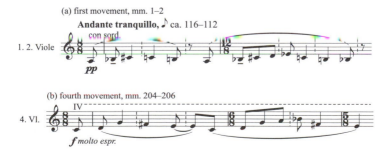

Example 7.8: *Béla Bartók,* Music for Strings, Percussion, and Celesta, *movement 1, mm. 86–88, violins 1 and 2*

HINDEMITH'S *CRAFT OF MUSICAL COMPOSITION*

Paul Hindemith (1895–1963), whom we encountered in Chapter 5, made one of the most ambitious attempts to systematize a new approach to music with a tonal center in his *Unterweisung im Tonsatz* (The Craft of Musical Composition, 1937). Hindemith was born in Frankfurt, where he attended the conservatory and established a career as a professional violinist and violist in orchestras and quartets. After World War I he emerged as one of Germany's leading composers and, through his involvement with music festivals, played a major role in setting the agenda for new music. First known for his intentionally scandalous Expressionist operas, such as his setting of Oskar Kokoschka's play *Murder: Hope of Women* (1919), he quickly became associated with virtually all the latest trends, from Neoclassicism to music for radio and film. In keeping with his interest in *Gebrauchsmusik*, he wrote functional music for amateurs as well as his famous series of solo sonatas for over 25 different instruments.

In his book *A Composer's World* (1952), Hindemith harshly criticized the twelve-tone method and other new approaches:

> This rule of construction is established arbitrarily and without any reference to basic musical facts. It ignores the validity of harmonic and melodic values derived from mathematical, physical, or psychological experience; it does not take into account the differences in intervallic tensions, the physical relationship of tones, the degree of ease in vocal production, and many other facts of either natural permanence or proven usefulness.

In *The Craft of Musical Composition*, Hindemith starts from the premise that tonality is a natural law or force, like gravity: "Music, as long as it exists, will always take its departure from the major triad and return to it." He proposes a hierarchical relationship in which every note of the chromatic scale is related to the tonic by virtue of its position in the overtone series, thus creating a strong tonal center around which the other pitches are arrayed like a "planetary system." Rather than the traditional approach of constructing chords by the superimposition of thirds, he thus creates a system of classification that allows for any combination of intervals.

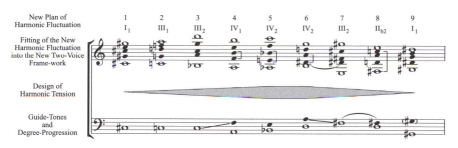

Figure 7.3: *Paul Hindemith,* The Craft of Musical Composition, *Example 119*

From these classifications, Hindemith sets up four categories of chords based on the number and types of dissonance they contain. In the example from *The Craft of Musical Composition* illustrated in Figure 7.3, he shows a series of nine chords with an indication of their category, roots, and degree of harmonic tension. Each level of structure, from a phrase to a complete movement, reflects motion through these categories, from consonance to ever-greater harmonic tension, concluding with a return to the initial consonance. Hindemith used this approach in the first movement of his Second Piano Sonata (1936). The first two phrases remain almost exclusively in a G Dorian collection; only in the cadential passage starting in measure 11 are other pitches introduced. After reaching a dissonant climax in measure 13 with a chord from category IV, he lowers the level of dissonance through categories III, II, and I to make the cadence back to a unison G in measure 17.

Like Schoenberg, Hindemith was a prominent teacher, taking his first position in 1927 at the Musikhochschule in Berlin. He stayed in Germany after the Nazis came to power but soon fell out of favor, and a complete ban on his works was imposed in 1936. The following year Hindemith immigrated to Switzerland and then to the United States, where he taught composition at Yale University. After returning to Switzerland in 1953, Hindemith increasingly distanced himself from contemporary musical developments. He compared "the sectarian character" of the twelve-tone method and other new systems to fascism and communism in that "the supreme condition for your participation is that you have no disbelief whatsoever in the perfection of the system." Ironically, Hindemith demonstrated a similarly rigid commitment to his own system in his later years by rewriting his earlier works to fit more closely with his theoretical formulations.

For all the composers we have considered in this chapter, the new systems of order and balance they endeavored to create testify to their conviction that their musical worlds were in need of repair and improvement, and that they were in a position to do the job. Their achievement in developing new ways of working with all the elements of music can be measured in the impact of their music and ideas on composers, performers, and audiences down to the present day. At the same time, they faced ongoing challenges in determining what and how to compose as the world around them continued to change dramatically in the years leading up to outbreak of World War II in 1939.

One of the last major works Hindemith wrote in Germany was the opera *Mathis der Maler* (Matthias the Painter, 1935). The story concerns the Renaissance painter Matthias Grünewald's disillusionment with political engagement and his decision to devote himself exclusively to his art. The opera has been interpreted as an allegory for Hindemith's "inner emigration" from German public and political life to an independent artistic sphere in the face of the Nazis' suppression of his music. Indeed, the opera had to be premiered in Zurich in 1938, a year before Hindemith was being attacked with other Modernists in the "Degenerate Music" exhibition. The term "inner emigration" is most often used to describe the situation of artists who stayed in Germany after the Nazis came to power and survived by turning inward. Although in fundamentally different contexts, the composers we will discuss in Chapter 8 made a similar attempt to emigrate from the world in which they found themselves after World War I by rebuilding and inventing musical traditions and homelands.

FOR FURTHER READING

Auner, Joseph, "Proclaiming a Mainstream," in *The Cambridge History of Twentieth-Century Music*, edited by Nicholas Cook and Anthony Pople, 228–259 (Cambridge: Cambridge University Press, 2004)

Cascone, Kim, "The Use of Density Groups in Electro-Acoustic Music," *Contemporary Music Review* 30, no. 2, Special Issue: Joseph Schillinger (2011), 143–153

Cohn, Richard, "Bartók's Octatonic Strategies," *Journal of the American Musicological Society* 44, no. 2 (1991): 263–300

Hicks, Michael, *Cowell the Bohemian* (Bloomington: University of Indiana Press, 2002)

Kaminsky, Peter, "Ravel's Late Music and the Problem of 'Polytonality,'" *Music Theory Spectrum* 26, no. 2 (2004): 237–264

Neumeyer, David, *The Music of Paul Hindemith* (New Haven: Yale University Press, 1986)

Schneider, David, *Bartók, Hungary, and the Renewal of Tradition: Case Studies in the Intersection of Modernity and Nationality* (Berkeley: University of California Press, 2006)

Straus, Joseph, *Remaking the Past: Musical Modernism and the Influence of the Tonal Tradition* (Cambridge, MA: Harvard University Press, 1990)

Whittall, Arnold, *The Cambridge Introduction to Serialism* (Cambridge: Cambridge University Press, 2008)

CHAPTER EIGHT

Inventing Traditions

The trends we have been considering up to now largely set the terms of the debate about where music should be heading after World War I. Yet for those unwilling or unable to be part of the New Music, it was easy to feel left behind. Sergei Rachmaninoff (1873–1943), one of several major figures who found it increasingly difficult to compose after the war, spoke for many when he wrote of feeling "like a ghost wandering in a world grown alien." Edward Elgar (1857–1934), whose last major work was the intensely melancholic Cello Concerto in E Minor (1919), lamented to a friend about all that had been destroyed by the war: "I have been thinking so much of our lost festivals—no more music. . . . Everything good & nice & clean & fresh & sweet is far way—never to return."

Yet many composers saw in the overturning of the old order the opportunity to create a place for themselves by constructing their own musical worlds. Among the most prominent was Leoš Janáček (1854–1928), who reconfigured the language, music, and lore of his Czech homeland in works like the operas *Kátá Kabanová* (1921) and *The Cunning Little Vixen* (1924). Carl Nielsen (1865–1931) came to be regarded as Denmark's national composer through his large body of folklike songs, six symphonies, and works like the cantata *Springtime on Funen* (1921), about life and the people on the island where he was born. Rachmaninoff, who left Russia at the end of 1917 never to return, managed over the course of a peripatetic life that included extended stays in the United States and Switzerland to re-create a Russian environment around himself and his family. His later years included such major works as the *Rhapsody on a Theme of Paganini* (1934) for piano and orchestra and his Third Symphony (1936), both indebted to the Romantic tradition in which he had been raised.

This chapter focuses on five composers from different cultures who created distinctive musical identities by synthesizing widely disparate musical elements. We begin with Heitor Villa-Lobos in Brazil, then turn to England and the music of Ralph Vaughan Williams; we conclude in the United States with Aaron Copland, William Grant Still, and Colin McPhee. Their music builds on developments considered in the preceding chapters, including the establishment of new musical languages, the Neoclassical manipulation of past forms and styles, and the reworking of folk materials. But much more so than figures like Schoenberg, Stravinsky, and Bartók, these composers succeeded in combining these and other modernist elements to invent styles that have been embraced by many listeners as offering a sense of tradition, wholeness, and stability. Indeed, the music of Villa-Lobos, Vaughan Williams, and Copland has become so synonymous with a Brazilian, British, and American sound that it can be difficult to see the recent origins and heterogeneity of their styles. While less well known, the music of McPhee and Still helped establish new hybrid cultural forms that have become central to our musical worlds today.

Given the broad familiarity of their music, due in part to their incorporation of tonality, folk, and other popular and traditional materials, these five composers may appear far removed from Modernism and modernity. But when considered in the wider context of the interwar years and the many different pathways that were open to them, their efforts to construct new musical homelands for themselves and others can be understood as among the most ambitious and far-reaching manifestations of Musil's "sense of possibility."

As historians have discussed, all traditions are invented to some degree, but the process accelerates during times like the interwar period, when rapid transformations of society render older structures inviable. Because the arts can speak so directly and powerfully to us, they play a vital social role in fostering a sense of group identity. For the same reason, the invented musical traditions discussed in this chapter often have a significant political dimension. In some cases national and political connotations were an explicit factor in the creative process; in other cases a composer's works or style were co-opted after the fact, sometimes for very different purposes than the composer may have intended.

VILLA-LOBOS AND *BRASILIDADE*

Heitor Villa-Lobos (1887–1959) devoted much of his life to inventing a Brazilian musical identity that integrated the cultural diversity of his vast homeland with the achievements of modern European music. Born in Rio de Janeiro a year before the abolition of slavery, he grew up in an environment shaped by Brazil's emergence from centuries of colonial rule by the Portuguese and debates about defining *Brasilidade*, or "Brazilianness." The son of an amateur musician, Villa-Lobos immersed himself in Rio's musical life as a cellist in cinema and theater orchestras, while also making his way as a guitarist in the city's popular music scene. From age 18 he traveled widely, exploring the music and cultures of Brazil's indigenous peoples.

The other major influence in Villa-Lobos's early musical life was the European salon, operatic, and orchestral music cultivated by Brazil's urban upper class. In 1913 he attended a performance by the touring Ballets Russes and saw Vaslav Nijinsky dance his version of Debussy's *Prelude to "The Afternoon of a Faun."* Villa-Lobos became friends with Darius Milhaud during the latter's Brazilian sojourn from 1916 to 1918, as well as with the pianist Arthur Rubinstein, who introduced him to Stravinsky's music and later performed Villa-Lobos's works around the world. Villa-Lobos became part of a group of musicians, painters, and poets who organized a modern art festival in 1922 dedicated to encouraging works that were simultaneously Modernist and Brazilian. Between 1923 and 1930 he spent much of his time in Paris, where he encountered many of the artists and composers we studied in Chapter 6.

As part of his search for a music that would encompass Brazil's rich heterogeneity, Villa-Lobos researched the country's music, folklore, and natural history. In the 1920s, he began to compose a series of pieces for various instruments and ensembles that he called *chôros*, after the Brazilian street bands known for their lively, improvisatory music. The style of these works ranges from the gently nostalgic *Chôros No. 1* for solo guitar (1920) to the eclectic *Chôros No. 10* for chorus and orchestra (1926), which incorporates Brazilian percussion, Indian chants, birdsong, and quotations from popular song (Ex. 8.1). In Villa-Lobos's words, the text for *Chôros No. 10* was "constituted of syllables and vocalises, without any literary sense or coordination of ideas, serving only as onomatopoetic effects, to form a phonetic atmosphere characteristic of the language of the aborigines." Like Milhaud's Primitivist ballet *The Creation of the World* (see Chapter 6), *Chôros No. 10* combines dissonant passages featuring bitonal progressions, layered ostinato patterns, and driving syncopated rhythms with sections that evoke popular idioms. In another series of works, titled *Bachianas Brasileiras* (1930–45), Villa-Lobos hybridizes Brazilian music and Bach, thus recalling the Neoclassical trends discussed in Chapters 6 and 7. *Bachianas Brasileiras No. 7* for orchestra (1942), for example, crosses a Brazilian country dance with a stylized Baroque gigue.

Villa-Lobos's career and works like the *Bachianas Brasileiras* were closely bound up with the regime of President Getúlio Vargas. Though initially populist, the Vargas government became increasingly authoritarian and repressive in response to Communist uprisings and other opposition, building connec-

Example 8.1: *Heitor Villa-Lobos,* Chôros No. 10, *mm. 217–218*

tions to domestic and European fascist groups and ultimately establishing the authoritarian Estado Novo (New State) that lasted from 1937 to 1945. Starting in the early 1930s, Vargas used music to unify Brazil, including promoting the samba from Rio de Janeiro as the national dance and centralizing Brazil's system of music education. As director of the Superintendency of Musical and Artistic Education, Villa-Lobos oversaw the activities of thousands of music teachers. In 1942 he founded the National Conservatory of Orpheonic Singing, connected to the very successful mass music festivals he had organized that involved up to 40,000 singers and musicians in a single performance. In his writings he argued that choral singing was the ideal way of weaving the individual into the social fabric of the nation:

> Through singing songs and commemorative hymns to our Country, in celebration of national heroes, the Brazilian child will become, in a very short space of time, impregnated with the spirit of *Brasilidade*, which, in the future, will mark all his ideas, actions, and thought, and allow him to acquire without doubt an authentic Brazilian musical conscience.

That Brazil ultimately sided with the Allies in World War II no doubt facilitated Villa-Lobos's international career, particularly in the United States, where he became known as one of the most prominent living composers. Many questions remain to be explored with regard to the political context of Villa-Lobos's music. That the issue concerned him as well is suggested by his attempt to draw a distinction between patriotism and nationalism in an interview that appeared in the *New York Times* in 1944, near the end of the Vargas regime:

> Patriotism in music and capitalizing upon it is very dangerous. You cannot produce great music in that way. You will have instead propaganda. But nationalism—power of the earth, the geographic and ethnographic influences that a composer cannot escape: the musical idioms and sentiment of a people and environment—these origins, in my opinion, are indispensable to a vital and genuine art.

As we have seen in previous chapters, any attempt to define "the musical idioms and sentiment of a people and environment," whether it be the idea of "the folk," a national tradition, or even more abstract notions like "the classic," can be both constructive and destructive. With the music discussed in this chapter that seeks to invent traditions, as with the works to be discussed in later chapters that seem to subvert any sense of tradition or history, we need to remain attuned to all that is involved in differentiating such notions as patriotism from nationalism, and propaganda from genuine art.

VAUGHAN WILLIAMS AND "ENGLISHNESS"

Defining a national tradition had been a central goal of England's musical life since the nineteenth century, when the nation established itself as a dominant economic and political power with an empire that stretched around the globe. Yet England's standing in the musical world was much less certain, as evidenced by the emergence around 1880 of the movement known as the English Musical Renaissance, associated with such figures as Charles Hubert Parry, Charles Villiers Stanford, Edward Elgar, Gustav Holst, and our focus here, Ralph Vaughan Williams (1872–1958).

Partly inspired by a desire to counter the changes wrought by industrialization and urbanization, the "renaissance" sparked a renewed interest in England's important Tudor and Elizabethan composers. A second goal of the movement was to differentiate English music from French and German influences, as well as from the more clearly established Scottish, Welsh, and Irish musical traditions in Great Britain. We can hear both processes at work in the early music of Vaughan Williams, such as his tone poem *The Lark Ascending* (1914), a paean to the English countryside, and the *Fantasia on a Theme by Thomas Tallis* for double string orchestra (1910, rev. 1919), based on a modal tune by the sixteenth-century English composer.

Born into a prosperous family, Vaughan Williams spent most of his life in London, where he showed early talent on the violin, viola, piano, and organ. Studies with Parry and other major figures at leading institutions provided an entrée to England's musical establishment. Like Villa-Lobos, Vaughan Williams devoted himself to defining and sustaining the country's musical life as a composer, teacher, conductor, author, and collector of folk songs. Many of his projects were intended for a broad public, including his work in film and radio and his editing of such landmark collections as *The English Hymnal* (1906) and *The Oxford Book of Carols* (1928).

The end of World War I engendered a widespread feeling of decline in Great Britain. There was a new sense of urgency in defining "Englishness" in the face of the huge loss of life, falling birthrate, and economic instability. Wilfred Owen's 1917 poem "Anthem for Doomed Youth," which Benjamin Britten later used to powerful effect in his *War Requiem* (see Chapter 9), vividly describes the horrors of trench warfare. A lieutenant in the British Army, Owen was killed in 1918, shortly before the end of the war; the first collection of his poetry was published posthumously in 1920.

At the same time, the destruction of the war also gave rise to the construction of new traditions and realities. J. R. R. Tolkien (1892–1973), a student of early English at Oxford who after his service returned to teach there in 1925, started while still a soldier to invent the languages and mythologies of Middle Earth that would become familiar to millions through *The Hobbit* (1937) and the *Lord of the Rings* trilogy (1954–55). Tolkien drew on the *Kalevala*, the Finnish epic that was so important to Sibelius (see Chapter 4), as well as on the German and Norse sources that Wagner used for his operatic cycle *The Ring of the Nibelungen*. His goal as a storyteller, he wrote in 1939, was to create a "Secondary World" into which the reader's "mind can enter. Inside it, what he relates is 'true': it accords with the laws of that world. You therefore believe it, while you are, as it were, inside."

For Vaughan Williams and Tolkien, who both had witnessed the trauma of mechanized warfare, inventing traditions was not escapism, but a resolute assertion of alternatives to the current state of the world. This is evident both in the enormous energies they expended in their creative work and in the fragility of their invented homelands. Even though Tolkien's bucolic Shire is eventually preserved, his Middle Earth is defined by the inevitable passing of the old world of elves, dwarves, and wizards. Vaughan Williams's *Pastoral Symphony* (1922) elicits a similar sense of a beloved homeland that is all the more precious for its vulnerability. For contemporary listeners, the symphony almost became the landscape itself. A reviewer for the *Times* of London described its themes as "the stuff of plainsong and folk-song, the blades of grass and tufts of moss, the primitive growth of musical nature. . . . The interlacing growth of these intervals brings a polyphony on which the ear rests, as one's foot does in the turf of the hillside."

Yet the reviewer also speaks of the fragmentary nature of the tunes and the sense of an "infinitely distant" horizon. Vaughan Williams said that the *Pastoral Symphony* was partly inspired by the desolate wartime landscape of France, where he served in an ambulance corps bringing in the wounded at night. The poignant trumpet call in the second movement echoes his experience of hearing a solitary bugler missing a note while practicing; the passage returns in the last movement, transfigured into a wordless vocalise. Instability pervades the end of the first movement, where, against an ethereal G-major triad in the strings, a folklike English horn melody heard earlier returns, now out of place and unable to resolve (Ex. 8.2). Just as its B Dorian pitch content with C♯ and F♯ obscures the tonality, the melody's shifting rhythms undermine any sense of metric stability.

Like Bartók in Hungary (see Chapter 4), Vaughan Williams expended considerable energies in the study of folk song and dance, collecting and publishing transcriptions and basing new works on folk tunes. As in Brazil and the United States, the English folk music revival was given government support and mandated for inclusion in school curricula. Folk songs contained "the spiritual life-blood of a people," Vaughan Williams wrote in his essay *National Music* (1934). "They have behind them not the imagination of one great poet, but the accumulated emotion, one might also say, of the many successive generations who have read and learned and themselves afresh re-created the old majesty and loveliness." Unlike Bartók, Ruth Crawford Seeger, and other folklorists, Vaughan Williams eschewed the use of phonograph recordings in his collecting work. He preferred instead to create an "ideal" version of the tune filtered through his own musical voice, just as he endeavored to capture the essence of English folk song in the newly composed melodies of the *Pastoral Symphony*.

Example 8.2: *Ralph Vaughan Williams,* Pastoral Symphony, *movement 1, mm 179–188*

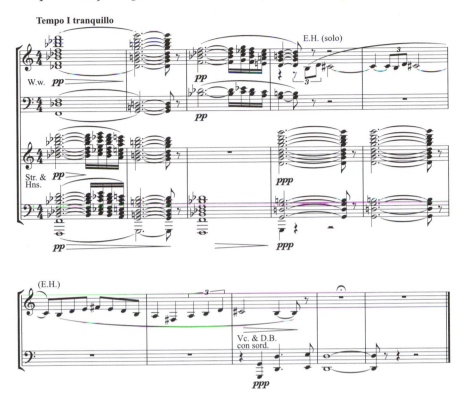

Yet the richness of Vaughan Williams's style also builds on many different musical elements, absorbed in his studies before the war with Max Bruch in Berlin and Ravel in Paris. Debussy's influence is apparent in his practice of harmonizing melodies with parallel triads, as in the cadential figure from the *Pastoral Symphony* shown in Example 8.2. Like Mahler, Bartók, Weill, and Ravel, Vaughan Williams wrote music that was largely triadic but minimized functional progressions. Nor did he shy away from higher levels of dissonance and tonal instability, as in his Fourth (1934) and Sixth Symphonies (1947). Other works employ Neoclassical elements, such as *Job,* subtitled *A Masque for Dancing* (1930), with its parodic use of old dance forms and references to the sixteenth- and seventeenth-century English masque tradition.

Although not all of Vaughan Williams's works were equally successful with the public, his musical language was embraced as intrinsically "English"; he was buried in Westminster Abbey near the seventeenth-century master Henry Purcell, known as the "British Orpheus." Indeed, so strong was his influence that it provoked a reaction by composers after World War II who rejected what they saw as Vaughan Williams's insularity and conservatism (for example,

Benjamin Britten and Peter Maxwell Davies; see Chapters 9 and 13). In the 1970s, however, his style would be an important source for British progressive rockers like Genesis; Emerson, Lake & Palmer; and King Crimson, whose "Lark's Tongue in Aspic" (1973) harked back to *The Lark Ascending*. Vaughan Williams's film scores, including *Scott of the Antarctic* (1948), also had a lasting impact, and it is no coincidence that Howard Shore's music for the film version of the *Lord of the Rings* (2001–03) includes many echoes of the *Pastoral Symphony*.

THE BORDERS OF AMERICAN MUSIC

In the United States, the interwar years generated a lively debate about what an "American" music should sound like. As we saw in Chapter 4, Charles Ives confronted the challenges of creating a style that captured the richness and diversity of American musical life. The difficulty of this effort multiplied dramatically after World War I, with the emergence of the United States as a major political and cultural power more determined than ever to cast off the dominance of European music in general, and German music in particular.

Yet composers seeking inspiration within the country's borders found an increasingly complex and conflicted terrain. In the same way that definitions of the folk depend on implicit or explicit ideas of an "other," with the establishment of an invented tradition comes the inevitable marginalization of other voices, identities, and possibilities. The Great Migration of the 1910s and 1920s substantially shifted the African-American population from the rural south to cities in the north. In 1917 Puerto Ricans were granted U.S. citizenship; two years later the first bill was introduced in Congress to make Hawaii a state (an effort that reached fruition only in 1959). A massive influx of immigrants brought the foreign-born share of the population to nearly 15 percent by 1910, provoking a strong nativist backlash. In 1924 Congress prohibited Japanese immigrants and set tight quotas on immigration from Eastern and southern Europe, in part to slow the growth of the Jewish population. The 1920s and 1930s also saw the Ku Klux Klan rise into a nationwide force that perpetrated acts of violence against African Americans, Catholics, and Jews.

As the ebullience of the Roaring Twenties collapsed in the economic debacle of the Great Depression, American composers, like their counterparts across the Atlantic, became increasingly interested in making their music broadly accessible and socially useful. In addition to sponsoring new works and musical performances, the Federal Music Project and Works Progress Administration (WPA), part of President Franklin Roosevelt's New Deal, provided funds for musical education and supported large-scale folk music preservation projects. As the folklorist Alan Lomax observed, the officials behind these government programs "hoped that the cultivation of folk music, and the spread of the feeling of cultural unity that lies somehow embedded in our big and crazy patchwork of folksong, would give Americans the feeling that they all belonged to the same kind of culture."

The collection of essays *American Composers on American Music*, published in 1933 by Henry Cowell, was likewise intended to encourage composers to develop a "national consciousness" and cut the "apron-strings of European tradition." Cowell's remarkably diverse roster of two dozen contributors included prominent figures like Roy Harris (1898–1979) and George Gershwin (1898–1937), Ultra-Modernists like Edgard Varèse and Ruth Crawford Seeger (see Chapters 5 and 7), and others who are comparatively little known today. It is thus striking that it was Aaron Copland—who was just beginning to establish himself, as can be seen in his rather lukewarm treatment in Cowell's book—whose music more than any other's would come to define musical Americana.

COPLAND AND THE AMERICAN LANDSCAPE

Like Villa-Lobos and Vaughan Williams, Aaron Copland (1900–1990) had a long and productive creative life, writing music for many audiences and venues, from the concert hall and opera house to schools and movie theaters. He was also enormously effective as a conductor, author, and organizer. In works like *Lincoln Portrait* (1942), *Fanfare for the Common Man* (1942), and the ballets *Billy the Kid* (1938), *Rodeo* (1942), and *Appalachian Spring* (1944), Copland compiled a lexicon of the American pastoral soundscape. Works by Copland, or imitations of his style, can now be heard in advertisements by the U.S. Army and the American beef industry, at political conventions and other patriotic events, and in countless film scores that seek to evoke the American landscape and spirit.

Copland composed *Billy the Kid* in 1938 for Ballet Caravan, a touring company that performed works linking American themes, Modernist styles, and progressive politics. The American dancer and actor Eugene Loring created the scenario and choreography, loosely based on the short life of the famous outlaw of the old west. From the very first measures, Copland evokes the stillness and timelessness of the prairie by means of a simple repeating melody harmonized in open fifths, careful control of dissonance, and avoidance of functional progressions. With gradually accumulating layers and modal harmonies, the passage builds to a massive climax that creates a sense of the solitude and grandeur of distant horizons.

In the next section, "Street in a Frontier Town" (see Anthology 13), Copland introduces several American folk songs, freely adapted from published anthologies of cowboy tunes. His treatment of the tunes shows the influence of the four years he spent in France, starting at age 21, when he made his way to Paris to study with Nadia Boulanger (see Chapter 6). We can hear the influence of Stravinsky and Milhaud in the frequent use of ostinati, the enlivening of static harmonic passages with sudden rhythmic disjunctions, and the polytonal layering of melodies in different keys and modes.

Yet Copland applies these techniques quite differently than his models. Each new idea is introduced separately and frequently repeated; more complicated passages are made comprehensible through close connections with the stage action. Copland explained that his style was aimed at the "entirely new public for music [that] had grown up around the radio and phonograph. It made no sense to ignore them and continue writing as if they did not exist. I felt it was worth the effort to see if I couldn't say what I had to say in the simplest possible terms."

What Copland called the "imposed simplicity" of Billy the Kid makes it easy to overlook the fact that the ballet is no simplistic Western; instead, it paints an ambivalent image of the outlaw as a lonely outsider who is ultimately destroyed. In a montage of scenes from his life, Billy is depicted as a nonconformist out of step not only with the townspeople, who drunkenly celebrate his capture, but also with the social norms enforced by Sherriff Pat Garret, who, after Billy's escape, hunts him down and kills him.

The broad popularity of Copland's music and his stature as one of America's leading composers has similarly obscured the many facets of his identity, including his homosexuality, leftist politics, and Jewishness. Copland was the child of immigrants from Lithuania who ran a successful department store in Brooklyn. He began studying the piano and composing when he was very young; his formal composition studies commenced when he was 17 with the Viennese-trained composer Rubin Goldmark. In his 1951 essay "The Composer in Industrial America," Copland described his discovery of "serious music" as "rather like coming upon an unexpected city—like discovering Paris or Rome if you had never heard of their existence." The main point of the essay was to document Copland's growing conviction while in Paris that "the two things that seemed always to be so separate in America—music and the life around me—must be made to touch." In his works we can see very different strategies for pursuing this goal, which in turn shows the complexities of defining what American music might be.

THE PLACE OF JAZZ

Copland's interest in jazz became the first manifestation of this impulse to connect his music to the life around him. Jazz's influence is reflected in several works written after Copland's return to New York, including Music for the Theater (1925), the Piano Concerto (1926), and the blues-inflected Nocturne for Violin and Piano (1926). We can hear the Parisian origins of his jazz enthusiasms in the "Dance" movement of Music for the Theater (1925). The piece alludes to jazz in its scoring and instrumental effects (Copland calls for the kind of "harsh" mute used in jazz bands), blue notes and bent pitches, and syncopated rhythms. But the sound of the music owes as much to the jazz-inspired works of Stravinsky and Milhaud as it does to actual jazz, and the influence of the racial stereotypes associated with *l'art nègre* can be felt in the disruptive, Primitivist intensity of the "Dance" movement and the languid sensuality of the *Nocturne*.

In *American Composers on American Music*, Gershwin described jazz as the "voice of the American soul" and acknowledged its African-American roots. Yet no black jazz musicians were featured in Cowell's book, despite the growing prominence of Duke Ellington and other black composers who were writing ever more ambitious and large-scale jazz works. Indeed, it was not long before Copland and other composers in the 1930s lost interest in jazz as the solution to the problem of defining an American music. As Copland later wrote, with striking condescension: "Jazz played a big role in the twenties. But I had been observing the scene around me and sensed it was about to change. Moreover, I realized that jazz might have its best treatment from those who had a talent for improvisation. I sensed its limitations, intended to make a change."

FOLK SONG AND PAN-AMERICANISM

A major factor in the development of American music during the Depression years was the goal of writing accessible music that served a progressive social function. Copland joined the Communist-affiliated Composers' Collective in New York, whose members energetically debated how to define politically engaged music. Some believed that revolutionary politics were best served by music that employed a revolutionary style, such as Crawford Seeger's "Chinaman, Laundryman" (see Chapter 7) or Copland's dissonant and challenging Piano Variations (1930). But by the mid-1930s there was a consensus that "experimental" and "revolutionary" techniques should be downplayed in favor of preserving "the best of the old traditions, harmonic and melodic," while "injecting new life into these old forms so that the most unsophisticated singer may be drawn into the singing." These words are taken from a text that accompanied the publication of Copland's song "Into the Streets May First" in the leftist journal *New Masses*; the piece was written for the International Workers' Day celebrations in 1934.

For Copland, Crawford Seeger, and other members of the Composers' Collective, folk music emerged as the most effective alternative to both jazz and Modernist styles. In 1934 and 1935 the Collective joined the Workers Music League in publishing the two-volume *Workers Song Book*. Throughout the 1930s Crawford Seeger collaborated with John and Alan Lomax on their Archive of American Folk Song, laying the foundation for the folk-music revival that blossomed in the following decades. The Kansas City–born composer Virgil Thomson (1896–1989) incorporated folk songs into many of his works, notably the score for *The Plow That Broke the Plains* (1936), a film sponsored by the New Deal government agency responsible for assisting and relocating destitute families. The many cowboy tunes in *Billy the Kid* similarly attest to Copland's reliance on folk song as part of his "imposed simplicity."

As we have seen, however, deciding who should be included among "the folk" is always complicated. In an essay titled "The Music of American Folk Song," Crawford Seeger grouped cowboy songs and Celtic fiddle tunes alongside African-American spirituals and music with Cajun and Caribbean origins. Composer Earl Robinson, a leading figure in the folk music revival, and lyricist John La Touche cast their net even wider in the cantata *Ballad for Americans* (1939), which the renowned African-American singer and actor Paul Robeson (1898–1976) performed on a nationwide radio broadcast. Originally written as part of a WPA-sponsored stage show, the cantata answers the question "Are you an American?" with: "I'm just an Irish, Negro, Jewish, Italian, French and English, Spanish, Russian, Chinese, Polish, Scotch, Hungarian, Litvak, Swedish, Finnish, Canadian, Greek and Turk and Czech and double Czech American."

Among the characters in *Billy the Kid*'s frontier town is a group of Mexican women who dance a traditional jarabe, a song form associated with left-wing resistance during the Mexican Revolution of the 1910s. Indeed, Copland's involvement with folk music started not with cowboy tunes but with the Mexican folk songs that appear in his symphonic poem *El salón México* (1936). Taking its name from a dance hall in Mexico City, the piece weaves well-known Mexican folk tunes and contemporary dance styles into an exuberant answer to the fragmentation of modern life. Like other leftists at the time, Copland viewed the countries of Central and South America as offering alternatives to American-style capitalism and industrialization.

The question of where to draw the borders of American music was also hotly debated during these years, with some advocating a definition that would include all of the Americas. The Pan-American Association of Composers, founded by Varèse in 1928, was dedicated to bringing together composers from North, Central, and South America to promote "wider mutual appreciation of the music of the different republics of America, and . . . stimulate composers to make still greater efforts toward creating a distinctive music of the Western Hemisphere." *American Composers on American Music* included a chapter by Copland on the Mexican composer and conductor Carlos Chávez who, like Villa-Lobos, integrated Modernist and indigenous elements in his works. It also contained several essays on music and composers in pre-revolution Cuba, then a popular destination for American travelers. Over the six years of its existence the Pan-American Association presented a large number of concerts in the United States, Cuba, and Europe, supported in part by donations from Charles Ives.

During World War II, pan-Americanism took on new life thanks to U.S. government support. Copland was appointed to the Committee for Inter-American Artistic and Intellectual Relations, a branch of the Council of National Defense, which sent him on a tour of Central and South America in 1941. His popular

Danzón cubano for two pianos (1942), based on a stately Cuban folk dance, was another outgrowth of his desire to foster a pan-American culture. As we will see in Chapter 9, however, the Cold War fundamentally changed attitudes toward these and other such efforts, with damaging ramifications for the careers of Copland, Robeson, and many others.

STILL AND THE AFRICAN-AMERICAN EXPERIENCE

The lone African-American composer represented in *American Composers on American Music* was William Grant Still (1895–1978), who contributed the essay "The Afro-American Composer's Point of View." At home in both the classical and jazz worlds, Still depicted various aspects of the African-American experience in such compositions as the song cycle *Levee Land* (1925), the cantata *And They Lynched Him on a Tree* (1941), and a trilogy of programmatic orchestral works: the *Afro-American Symphony* (1930), the Symphony in G Minor, subtitled *Song of a New Race* (1937), and the symphonic poem *Africa* (1928–35).

Born in Alabama into a musical family, Still spent his early years in Little Rock, Arkansas, where he learned to play the violin and oboe and aspired to become a composer. His studies at the Oberlin Conservatory of Music were interrupted by his service in the Navy during World War I. He then went to Memphis to play in the band of the noted blues composer W. C. Handy. Following Handy's band to New York, Still built a career writing orchestral arrangements for theater and radio, and later film and television. At the same time he pursued his interest in composition, influenced by both the traditional idioms of George Whitefield Chadwick, with whom he studied in Boston, and the Ultra-Modernist approach of Varèse, who gave him composition lessons in New York.

Still achieved his first major success with the *Afro-American Symphony*, which was performed by major orchestras in the United States, Europe, and Japan. He described the work's four movements as a narrative tracing the elevation of the "sons of the soil" from "Longing" and "Sorrow" to "Humor" and "Aspiration." His conception of the African-American experience was shaped in part by writers and artists associated with the Harlem Renaissance in the 1920s and 1930s, including Alain Locke and Langston Hughes. Still's attitude toward African-American musical materials, particularly the distinctive melodic and harmonic aspects of the blues that was so important to his works, also can be linked to the racialized frameworks of Exoticism and Primitivism discussed in previous chapters.

Though to very different ends than a figure like Cocteau (see Chapter 6), Still implies a Primitivist distinction between the "natural and deep-rooted feeling for music, for melody, harmony, and rhythm" he associated with African-American blues and jazz, and the more "intellectual" conventions and techniques of classical music: "Our music possesses exoticism without straining for strangeness. The natural practices in this music open up a new field which can be of value in larger musical works when constructed into organized form by a composer who, having the underlying feeling, develops it through his intellect." Still's approach to this synthesis can be seen in his use of standard forms in the *Afro-American Symphony*, such as sonata form in the first movement and a scherzo in the third. It is also illustrated by Still's combination of traditional developmental techniques and his richly chromatic, jazz-inflected harmonic language.

Still's notes on the three sections of *Africa—Land of Peace*, *Land of Romance*, and *Land of Superstition*—suggest the piece's links to the notion of invented traditions: "An American Negro has formed a concept of the land of his ancestors based largely on its folklore, and influenced by his contact with American civilization. He beholds in his mind's eye not the Africa of reality but an Africa mirrored in fancy, and radiantly ideal." As Still points out, there is little reference in the work to actual African music beyond the evocation of drumming at the beginning of the first movement, which owed more to the "jungle" style of jazz heard in Harlem's Cotton Club than to any specific African sources.

Land of Romance opens with a languorous blues theme accompanied by lightly strummed chords in the piano anchored by an open-fifth pedal in the low strings (see Anthology 14). The orchestration clarifies the complex texture as other layers are added to the melody in the solo bassoon, with each layer given its own distinctive sound, including interjections from a harp and a countermelody by a flute chorus. Still attributed his approach to instrumentation to jazz, which offered "an entirely new style of orchestration." As he wrote in 1939, "Jazz (as one black form) has given one important thing to American music as a whole: great variety and charm in instrumental effects that were unknown to classic composers." But as the *Land of Romance* continues Still also introduces elaborate developmental techniques, passages that evoke the orchestral scores of Debussy and Ravel, and progressions that fuse jazz harmonies with Wagner's "Tristan" chord, as if to overcome the assumptions of incompatibility and difference that defined Debussy's *Golliwogg's Cake-Walk* (see Chapter 1).

The first version of *Africa* was premiered by the Rochester Philharmonic in 1930, followed by other performances across the United States and in Europe. The coming years brought Still wide attention, awards, commissions from major orchestras, and many "firsts." Among other distinctions, he was the first African-American composer to have an opera produced by a major opera company. *Troubled Island*, presented by the New York City Opera in 1949, was based on a libretto by Langston Hughes about the 1791 revolution that ended slavery in Haiti. Despite the enthusiastic reception, however, the opera had only three performances; like many other African-American composers at the time, Still had difficulty getting his works performed and published. With the exception of the belated premiere in 1972 of *Treemonisha* (1910), by the ragtime composer-pianist Scott Joplin, it would be nearly 40 years before another opera by an African-American composer was staged by one of the major houses: Anthony Davis's *X: The Life and Times of Malcolm X*, which premiered in 1986 at the New York City Opera (see Chapter 13).

MCPHEE'S IMAGINARY HOMELAND IN BALI

The music of the Canadian composer Colin McPhee (1900–1964), also featured in *American Composers on American Music*, offers a very different model for creating a musical style in its fusion of classical techniques, Indonesian gamelan music, and the rhythms and harmonies of jazz. Along with Henry Cowell and Lou Harrison, McPhee helped invent a cross-cultural tradition that bore fruit in the Minimalism and Postminimalism of the late twentieth century (see Chapter 14); the World Beat and Afrobeat of pop musicians like Youssou N'Dour, Paul Simon, and Peter Gabriel; and the global border crossings by today's emerging generation of composers (see Chapter 15).

The gamelan, as we saw in Chapter 2, has inspired composers ever since the 1889 Universal Exposition in Paris. But for McPhee the music and culture of Bali played a more profound role as a kind of invented homeland offering both artistic and personal fulfillment. During World War II he reflected on the years he spent on the island: "Everyone carries within him his own private paradise, some beloved territory whose assault is an assault on the heart. Some felt this when Paris was taken, others when Britain was bombed. For me it was Bali, for I had lived there a long time and had been very happy." Yet the life of privilege that McPhee experienced in Bali was to some degree an artificial reality. Nor was the island paradise free of conflict: it had been forcibly colonized by the Dutch, whose arrival in 1906 was greeted by the mass suicide of members of the royal families.

McPhee devoted over half his life to gamelan music, as both scholar and composer. His book *Music in Bali* (1966) remains an important resource, and he is credited with not only reenergizing gamelan traditions in Bali, but also establishing the foundation for the now-thriving gamelan scene in many North American colleges and universities. Some of McPhee's gamelan-inspired works remain close to the original sources; his *Balinese Ceremonial Music* (1934), for example, is essentially a transcription for two pianos of well-known examples from the gamelan repertory. The piece illustrates his talent for evoking with Western instruments what he described as the "strange beauty of the sound" of the bronze gamelan percussion orchestra. But McPhee's most famous piece, *Tabuh-tabuhan: Toccata for Two Pianos and Orchestra* (1936), is remarkably eclectic, bringing together many of the elements discussed in this and previous chapters. According to his program note from the score:

Although *Tabuh-tabuhan* makes much use of Balinese musical material, I consider it a purely personal work in which Balinese and composed motifs, melodies and rhythms have been fused to make a symphonic work. Balinese music never rises to an emotional climax, but at the same time has a terrific rhythmic drive and symphonic surge, and this partly influenced me in planning the form of the work. Many of the syncopated rhythms of Balinese music have a close affinity with those of Latin-American popular music and American jazz—a history in itself—and these have formed the basic impulse of the work from start to finish.

The early trajectory of McPhee's career resembled that of many other North American composers. Born in Montreal, he studied piano and composition in Toronto and in Baltimore at the Peabody Conservatory. After graduating in 1921, he began to establish himself as a composer and performer, studying composition at the Schola Cantorum in Paris from 1924 to 1926. McPhee then settled in New York, where he studied with Varèse and became friends with Cowell, Copland, and others; along with Copland, he was one of the pianists in the Carnegie Hall premiere of Antheil's *Ballet mécanique* (see Chapter 5). He also joined the circle around the writer and critic Carl Van Vechten, who introduced McPhee to the leading figures of the Harlem Renaissance.

McPhee's works from these years offer a compendium of contemporary styles, including Neoclassical elements, folk materials, jazz, polytonality, and machine art. His career took a very different turn in 1929, when he heard some of the earliest recordings of Balinese music that friends had brought back from travels in Indonesia. He described the bright, percussive sounds of the bronze instruments as "like the stirrings of a thousand bells, delicate, confused, with a sensuous charm, a mystery that was quite overpowering." In 1931 McPhee set out on the long sea journey to Bali, first visiting for several months, and then moving there for most of the next eight years. He built a large house, adopted a Balinese lifestyle, and became involved with Balinese dancers and musicians. For McPhee, who had long been frustrated by the isolation of new music from the public, the integration of music-making into the rituals of daily life in Bali represented the ideal of a functional music.

Another part of the island's attraction for McPhee was an acceptance of homosexual relationships that had to be hidden in North America and Europe; Henry Cowell, for example, spent four years in the late 1930s in San Quentin Prison for having a consensual homosexual relationship with a 17-year-old. McPhee traveled to Bali with the anthropologist Jane Belo, whom he had married the year before, but for much of the time they lived separately. Scholars have discussed McPhee's role in helping to establish the sound of the gamelan as a marker of "queer" identity, for example in the operas of Benjamin Britten, who collaborated with McPhee on the premiere of *Balinese Ceremonial Music*. Such associations help explain Britten's evocations of gamelan in passages dealing

Example 8.3: *Colin McPhee,* Tabuh-tabuhan, *movement 1, mm. 1–6, reduction. Adapted from Carol Oja.*

with unusual and mysterious desires (see Chapter 9). A crackdown by the Dutch in 1938 on Westerners in general, and homosexuals in particular, may have been a factor in McPhee's decision to return to the United States early the following year.

McPhee wrote *Tabuh-tabuhan* in New York and Mexico City during an extended absence from Bali in 1935–36; it was premiered in Mexico City in 1936 under the baton of Carlos Chávez. The title refers to the Balinese word for a mallet, and the score features an extensive percussion section that includes two large Indonesian gongs. McPhee evokes the timbres and textures of Balinese music, with its static pentatonic pitch content, stratified layers, sudden interruptions, and dramatic contrasts. The opening movement, *Ostinatos*, is based on five layers, labeled A–E in Example 8.3, differentiated by rhythm, timbre, and register. As in gamelan music, there is a slowly moving melody, "B" (B–E–F♯–A), ornamented by "A" with high, fast figuration using the same four notes in shifting patterns.

All three movements of *Tabuh-tabuhan* include extended quotations of Balinese music, alongside which McPhee brings in references to Latin rhythms and Gershwin-style orchestral jazz—leading one critic at the time to label the piece "An American in Bali." Just as important are the work's many Neoclassical features, evident in the subtitle *Toccata*, in the use of the concerto genre, and in McPhee's characterization of the form as "more or less that of the classical symphony." McPhee's description of watching a group of men and boys in concentrated rehearsal also suggests that he heard the music in terms of both the New Objectivity and *l'art nègre*, as a way of escaping subjectivity and expression into a new world:

> I wondered at their natural ease, the almost casual way in which they played. This, I thought, is the way music was meant to be, blithe, transparent, rejoicing the soul with its eager rhythm and lovely sound. As I listened to the musicians, watched them, I could think only of a flock of birds wheeling in the sky, turning with one accord, now this way, now that, and finally descending to the trees.

McPhee struggled to reestablish himself as a composer after his return to the United States, and his life was marked by long periods of depression, self-doubt, and alcoholism. Many of his scores were lost or destroyed. His work, like much of the music discussed earlier in this chapter, soon came to be regarded as out of place in the very different cultural climate that emerged after World War II. As we will see in Chapter 9, although works by Villa-Lobos, Vaughan Williams, Copland, Still, and McPhee have continued to resonate with concertgoers, many composers of the next generation felt the need to distance themselves from styles that evoked a particular nation, folk, or tradition. When composers in the 1960s and 70s once again became interested in working with elements from the past and other styles, their efforts could seem less like an attempt to invent traditions than a demonstration that any sense of wholeness or stability is illusory. Only in recent decades have composers reconsidered the possibility of attempting without irony or anxiety the remarkable and persuasive musical syntheses achieved during the interwar years.

FOR FURTHER READING

Crist, Elizabeth B., *Music for the Common Man: Aaron Copland During the Depression and War* (New York: Oxford University Press, 2005)

Frogley, Alain, "Rewriting the Renaissance: History, Imperialism, and British Music since 1840," *Music and Letters* 84, no. 2 (2003): 241–256

Garrett, Charles Hiroshi, *Struggling to Define a Nation: American Music and the Twentieth Century* (Berkeley: University of California Press, 2008)

Hobsbawm, Eric, and Terence Ranger, eds., *The Invention of Tradition* (Cambridge: Cambridge University Press, 1983)

Hubbs, Nadine, *The Queer Composition of America's Sound: Gay Modernists, American Music, and National Identity* (Berkeley and Los Angeles: University of California Press, 2004)

Oja, Carol, and Judith Tick, eds., *Aaron Copland and His World* (Princeton: Princeton University Press, 2005)

Riley, Matthew, "Elgar the Escapist?" in *Edward Elgar and His World*, edited by Byron Adams (Princeton: Princeton University Press, 2007)

Starr, Larry, "Tonal Traditions in Art Music from 1920–1960," in *The Cambridge History of American Music*, edited by David Nicholls (Cambridge: Cambridge University Press, 1998)

PART III

World War II and Its Aftermath

In the eyes of many, the end of World War II in 1945 marked a fundamental rupture in human history. While the physical effects of the war varied widely around the world, the implications of its savagery and the profound restructurings of the social, cultural, and political orders that followed in its aftermath left few untouched. The German composer Karlheinz Stockhausen (1928–2007) wrote of becoming aware in his early twenties "that I was part of a new epoch; and that an epoch which had started hundreds of years ago, even 2,500 years ago with the way of thinking of the ancient Greeks, had finished during the last war."

This new epoch was born in the shadow of the atomic mushroom cloud, the horrors of the Holocaust, and the Cold War. Anchored in the ideological struggles between the Western powers and the Soviet Union, the Cold War became an axis around which many aspects of life, including music, were reconfigured. Yet the new epoch was also defined by a belief that it was possible to build a new and better world from the ground up through science, technology, and radically reimagined social and political structures. The French composer and conductor Pierre Boulez (b. 1925) described the sense of urgency and opportunity felt by many of his generation: "In 1945–1946 nothing was ready and everything remained to be done: it was our privilege to make the discoveries and also to find ourselves faced with nothing—which may have its difficulties but also has many advantages."

Boulez and others trumpeted their belief that composers between the wars had been on the wrong track. Most of the trends discussed in the previous four chapters—Neoclassicism, music for use, borrowings from popular styles and folk music, and the invention of traditions to unify far-flung communities—were viewed by composers in the postwar period as tainted by association with the forces that had led to such destruction. The search for order remained a central concern, with the twelve-tone method as the most important resource, but it was accompanied by a strident rejection of Schoenberg and his attempt to integrate the new technique with the forms and genres of the past.

Part III focuses on musical responses to the difficulties and potentialities of this situation from the end of the war though the 1960s, when a different set of cultural priorities began to emerge. Although the new epoch was driven by the younger generation, older composers who had established their careers before the war also had to come to terms with the experience of destruction and rebuilding. Chapter 9 focuses on Benjamin Britten and Dmitri Shostakovich, whose lives and works can help us understand the changing culture and politics in the early years of the Cold War, as well as the challenges of rebuilding a musical language in the ruins.

Chapters 10 and 11 concern efforts to create a new autonomous music inspired by models of scientific experimentation and the burgeoning technologies of the postwar period. Comparing the extension of the twelve-tone method through Integral Serialism to the incorporation of elements of chance and indeterminacy, Chapter 10 considers how the exploration of limits of control and freedom became a means for escaping from tradition and subjectivity. In the context of the atomic age and the space race, Chapter 11 focuses on the technological and aesthetic development of electronic music as a tool for reconstructing the basic elements of sound, composition, and performance.

Since contemporary debates both reflected and shaped musical trends, the structure of Chapters 9–11 is partly chronological, tracing the emergence of ideas as they were experienced and articulated at the time. But we will also consider the far-reaching ramifications of these ideas on many forms of music-making up to the present. Reflecting the notion of composition as research and experimentation, we will see composers who have worked in quite different areas and "isms," and who thus reappear in multiple chapters in both Parts III and IV. In keeping with the ever-increasing multiplicity of musical developments, our perspectives will also necessarily become broader as we move forward, with many more figures filling the stage.

CHAPTER NINE

Rebuilding amid the Ruins

In his famous "Iron Curtain" speech in March 1946, British prime minister Winston Churchill spoke of the "unestimated sum of human pain" that afflicted people around the globe after the war:

> The awful ruin of Europe, with all its vanished glories, and of large parts of Asia glares us in the eyes. When the designs of wicked men or the aggressive urge of mighty States dissolve over large areas the frame of civilized society, humble folk are confronted with difficulties with which they cannot cope. For them all is distorted, all is broken, all is even ground to pulp.

World War II was the deadliest and most destructive conflict in human history. In the six years between Nazi Germany's invasion of Poland in September 1939 and the surrender of Japan in August 1945, more than 20 million military personnel and at least twice as many civilians died. Hitler's "Final Solution" resulted in the systematic murder of 6 million Jews, along with many Roma, homosexuals, and political opponents. Stalin killed millions in the forced-labor camps of the Soviet Gulag. Whole cities across Europe, Asia, and the Middle East were reduced to rubble. As in the aftermath of World War I (see Chapter 5), the postwar years saw widespread economic deprivation, violent episodes of "ethnic cleansing," and cycles of reprisal and revenge.

The war's wanton destruction is memorialized in the remains of the magnificent Gothic cathedral in the English industrial city of Coventry, some two hours northwest of London (Fig. 9.1). Erected in the fourteenth century, Coventry Cathedral was virtually destroyed by a German bombing raid the night of November 14, 1940, that also killed several hundred civilians. When Debussy imagined the "century of aeroplanes," or Weill and Brecht celebrated

Figure 9.1. *The ruins of Coventry Cathedral, November 1940*

Lindbergh's flight across the Atlantic, they could not have envisioned the waves of 500 fighter planes that battered Coventry for more than ten hours that fateful night. Hundreds of other cities in the United Kingdom, Germany, the Soviet Union, Poland, Greece, and elsewhere were laid waste during the war by carpet bombing, incendiary rockets, and, in the case of Hiroshima and Nagasaki in Japan, the first use of atomic weapons. Unexploded bombs from World War II are still being found; one such discovery in a theater in Coventry in March 2008 shut down the center of the city for several days.

For everyone after the war, coming to terms with the horrific loss of life and physical destruction was made even more challenging by the necessity of punishing, forgiving, forgetting, or covering up the actions of war criminals and collaborators. A famous example is the case of Richard Strauss (see Chapter 3). Although he never joined the Nazi Party and privately criticized the Fascist regime, Strauss held important positions in the Third Reich and met personally with Hitler and other prominent Nazis. Writing in 1934 as president of the Reich Music Chamber, he enthusiastically described his hopes for the Nazis' musical reforms in "winning over the entire people to our music, saturating them with our music, and implanting within the heart of every individual fellow citizen a love for his German music." Despite the official support he enjoyed, Strauss's position remained uncertain due to his high-profile partnerships with Jewish librettists, including Stefan Zweig, and the constant threats directed toward his Jewish daughter-in-law and grandchildren. Strauss was deeply distressed by the war's devastation, but seems never to have acknowledged the horrors perpetrated by his Nazi patrons.

In the midst of his denazification trial in 1948, Strauss composed the songs for soprano and orchestra that were published after his death the following year as *Vier letzte Lieder* (Four Last Songs). In their soaring melodies and lush tonal harmonies, they seem to betoken the aged composer's longing for a world that he knows is gone forever. Indeed, after recovering from surgery in 1948, he wrote: "I ask myself why have they brought me back into an existence in which I have actually outlived myself." In the final song, "Im Abendrot" (In the Glow of the Evening), the text by the German Romantic poet Joseph Freiherr von Eichendorff describes a couple reaching the end of their path, hand in hand, walking into the sunset. At the words "Can this be death?" we hear a seamlessly integrated quotation in the horn from *Tod und Verklärung* (Death and Transfiguration), Strauss's tone poem of 60 years earlier.

But for most composers, however, there was no going back. This was literally the case for the many who fled Europe for North America, such as Weill and Schoenberg (who left when the Nazis came to power in 1933), Zemlinsky and Krenek (1938), Stravinsky (1939), and Bartók (1940). Some, like Erich Wolfgang Korngold and Ernst Toch, managed to build new lives in Hollywood as successful film composers. Others, like Stefan Wolpe (1902–1972), had a more unsettled existence. Wolpe, whose works incorporated twelve-tone technique, elements of Dada, and jazz, left Germany in 1933, then spent several years in Palestine before moving to New York City in 1938. He served as director of music at Black Mountain College in rural North Carolina from 1952 to 1956, finally ending up teaching at C.W. Post College on Long Island. As a result, Wolpe influenced a wide range of musicians and artists including Milton Babbitt, Morton Feldman, jazz composer George Russell, film composer Elmer Bernstein, and the avant-garde musician and artist Yoko Ono.

And, of course, huge numbers of composers, performers, artists, and writers did not survive the war. One whose works have since come to wide attention is Viktor Ullmann (1898–1944), a student of Schoenberg and Zemlinsky, who was building a career in Prague when he was sent to the Theresienstadt concentration camp in 1942. There he composed several works, including the opera *Der Kaiser von Atlantis* (The Emperor of Atlantis, 1943), before being sent to Auschwitz in 1944, were he was killed in the gas chambers. Scholars and musicians have been working to recover the works of many other composers whose lives were cut short, along with the remnants of the musical life of the concentration camps and ghettos.

SOCIAL TRANSFORMATIONS

World War II's aftermath restructured social, cultural, and political orders around the world. Ambitious new global institutions were created, including the International Monetary Fund (1944) and the United Nations (1945), with the goal of preventing future conflicts. Jean Paul Sartre, Simone de Beauvoir, and Albert Camus introduced the influential philosophy of Existentialism, which required each of us to determine our own path in an indifferent and amoral universe. With feelings of uncertainty and the lack of stable moorings came a sense of liberation; as de Beauvoir wrote, "To be twenty or twenty-five in September of '44 seemed the most fantastic piece of luck: all roads lay open. Journalists, writers, budding filmmakers, were all arguing, planning, passionately deciding, as if their future depended on no one but themselves."

As Western Europe's colonial empires disintegrated—in some cases peacefully, in others violently—new powers arose such as Egypt, Indonesia, Communist China, and Cuba. Meanwhile, the Soviet Union and the Eastern European states it controlled walled themselves off behind Churchill's Iron Curtain, often brutally attempting to repress and reshape its own populations, and setting the stage for nearly half a century of Cold War with the West.

Equally far-reaching transformations were taking place in the United States and other nations. In the decade after World War II the battle for civil rights intensified with the desegregation of the U.S. armed forces in 1948, the 1954 Supreme Court decision mandating desegregation of public schools, and new narratives of the African-American experience, including Ralph Ellison's *Invisible Man* (1952) and James Baldwin's *Go Tell It on the Mountain* (1953). At the same time, the creation of the interstate highway system helped to weave the nation together and make possible a new mobility, while also facilitating the rise of the suburbs. A distinctive youth culture emerged, signaled by the publication of J. D. Salinger's iconic coming-of-age novel *The Catcher in the Rye* (1951); the works of Beat poets and writers like Allen Ginsberg and Jack Kerouac; and the rise of rock and roll in the music of Chuck Berry, Elvis Presley, and many others.

England, too, changed profoundly in the 1950s. After the Conservatives were voted out of power in 1945, the Labour Party moved the country sharply to the left, nationalizing railways, health care, and other services. As the British Empire gradually devolved into a commonwealth of independent states, a new generation known as the "angry young men" assailed England's class-ridden social structure in plays and novels, much as the Beatles and the Rolling Stones would upend the country's staid pop music scene in the 1960s. Meanwhile, Benjamin Britten (1913–1976), on his way to becoming Britain's most honored living composer, celebrated the coronation of Queen Elizabeth II in 1953 in his opera *Gloriana*, linking the young monarch to her formidable sixteenth-century namesake.

BRITTEN'S *WAR REQUIEM*

Britten's career, and his monumental *War Requiem* in particular, illustrate the challenges of constructing a musical language out of the ruins of war. He dedicated the *War Requiem* to four of his friends, three of whom had been killed in combat; the fourth had recently committed suicide. Completed in 1961 and premiered a year later, the work was commissioned for the consecration of the new cathedral at Coventry that was built adjacent to the bombed-out shell of the old. The powerful symbolism of rebuilding while leaving the rubble in place as a commemoration and a warning also shaped other projects from these years, including the Pearl Harbor Memorial in Hawaii (1962), which was built over the sunken wreckage of the battleship *Arizona*, and the Kaiser Wilhelm Memorial Church in Berlin (1963), with its charred and broken spire.

Taking his cue from the new cathedral's stark architectural juxtaposition, Britten forged the *War Requiem* from deliberately incongruous elements that resist easy reconciliation. The six movements are based on the Latin Mass for the Dead, integrating nine poems in English by Wilfred Owen lamenting the death and destruction of World War I. A large mixed choir and orchestra together with a soprano soloist present the Mass sections, while the passages featuring Owen's texts are sung by tenor and baritone soloists, accompanied by a 12-member chamber orchestra with its own conductor. Placed in the distance and supported only by a portable organ, a boys' choir singing portions of the Latin text comprises a third musical layer.

Britten sharply differentiates the three layers in the opening movement of the *War Requiem* (see Anthology 15). The Requiem aeternam begins in a cold and unearthly realm, punctuated by slow, solemn bells, with the choir intoning the call for eternal peace over static dissonant harmonies based on an F♯–C tritone. When the boys enter with a song of praise, the harmony shifts to the more familiar sounds of bright, ringing triads, though the progressions are unusual and avoid any tonal resolution. In sharp contrast to these otherworldly layers, the tenor then sings Owen's "Anthem for Doomed Youth" in an unsettled B♭ minor, bitterly dismissing the false comfort of choirs, bells, flowers, and hymns of praise for "those who die as cattle."

Alongside these diverse ingredients, Britten alludes throughout the *War Requiem* to a host of historical styles and techniques, as well as to musical traditions from Indonesia and Japan. The impact of the work results from Britten's ability to meld these elements together without denying their distinctiveness and differences. We can hear this amalgamation of the three layers in his setting of the final line of the Owen poem in the Requiem aeternam, "And each slow dusk a drawing-down of blinds" (Ex. 9.1). The tenor's music suddenly softens as he echoes the melody first sung by the boys' choir; rather than a clear cadence, the passage ends with a collapse back to the tritonal harmony of the opening choral music. The grim resignation in this evocation of the suffering of those

Example 9.1: *Benjamin Britten, Requiem aeternam, from* War Requiem, *mm. 154–161*

left behind to mourn the dead undercuts a simple resolution, exposing the inadequacy of any consolation.

A commentary on the *War Requiem* that appeared a few days before the premiere observed, "It is not a *Requiem* to console the living, sometimes it does not even help the dead to sleep soundly. It can only disturb every living soul, for it denounces the barbarism more or less awake in mankind with all the authority that a great composer can muster." Yet the work does offer some glimpses of hope and momentary solace, as in the closing measures of the Requiem aeternam, which break out from the cold tritonal harmonies of the Kyrie eleison with a gentle shift to F major. In this and many other works, Britten managed to communicate painful truths about the plight of the individual and the state of the world in music of great empathy and moments of transcendent beauty. Indeed, the *War Requiem* spoke to people despite—and arguably because of—its difficulty, as can be seen in the fact that it was very well received at its premiere, which was soon followed by a recording that quickly became one of the best-selling classical releases of the time.

BRITTEN'S EARLY YEARS

After studying privately under the Modernist composer Frank Bridge, Britten entered the Royal College of Music in London in 1930, at age 17. Five years later he took a job writing music for a government agency that produced documentary films, which led to a long-term post with the British Broadcasting Corporation (BBC). As we have seen with many other composers in the interwar years, Britten's belief that music should serve a practical social function also led him to compose music for film and television, a series of pieces for children and amateurs, and a significant body of sacred and liturgical music, including one of his most famous works, *A Ceremony of Carols* (1942). The Aldeburgh Festival, which he founded in 1948 with his partner, Peter Pears, continues to be a major force in British musical life.

Yet the trajectory of Britten's career was also shaped by his feelings of not belonging, due to his pacifism, his leftist politics, and the open secret of his homosexuality (which was not decriminalized in the United Kingdom until 1967). Persecuted outsiders figure prominently in many of his works, notably his operas *Peter Grimes* (1945) and *Billy Budd* (1951). In 1939 Britten left England for the United States to escape military service; upon returning three years later, he requested status as a conscientious objector. In his application he wrote: "Since I believe that there is in every man the spirit of God, I cannot destroy, and feel it is my duty to avoid helping to destroy as far as I am able, human life, however strongly I may disapprove of the individual's actions or thoughts."

Britten made these sentiments explicit in the closing Libera me movement of the *War Requiem*, which includes a setting of Owen's poem "Strange

Meeting" that sympathetically depicts an encounter between two dead soldiers from opposing armies. As part of the intended message of "the universal desire for peace," the parts were sung at the premiere by representatives of the former warring parties, the English tenor Peter Pears and the German baritone Dietrich Fischer-Dieskau. Britten had also hoped to feature in other movements the Russian soprano Galina Vishnevskaya, but the Soviet government forbade her participation and she was replaced at the last minute by Irish-born Heather Harper.

AMBIVALENCE AND EMPATHY TOWARD
THE PAST AND PRESENT

Unlike many of his contemporaries after World War II, Britten felt little impulse to reject the past. Rather, like Gustav Mahler (see Chapter 2), whose music he admired, he assimilated a huge range of influences, both old and new. In 1969 he described the feeling of being guided by the examples of earlier composers: "I couldn't be alone. I couldn't work alone. I can only work really because of the tradition that I am conscious of behind me." He added that he felt as close to the Elizabethan composer John Dowland as to his youngest contemporary. Scholars have identified many historical allusions in the *War Requiem*, including melodies that sound like plainchant, organum-like parallel harmonies, and a resurrection of the medieval practice of troping, with the interpolation of the Owen poems into the liturgical texts of the Mass. There are also echoes of earlier Requiem settings, including those by Mozart, Berlioz, and especially Verdi.

On a deeper level, however, Britten felt a sense of detachment from both the past and the present. In his essay "England and the Folk-Art Problem," which appeared in the American periodical *Modern Music* in 1941, he critiqued what he regarded as the amateurishness and insularity of the English Musical Renaissance. Instead of a feeling of continuity with tradition, his own arrangements of folk songs and the music of his British predecessors often emphasize historical distance. For example, his figured-bass realization of Henry Purcell's *Music for a While* (1947) depicts the whip falling from the hand of the Fury Alecto with jarringly anachronistic dissonant chords syncopated against the steady bass. The *Serenade for Tenor, Horn, and Strings* (1943), with its unsettling depictions of the night, underscored by the eerie effects of natural harmonics in the horn, evokes a pastoral landscape that is shadowed and even diseased, as in the third-movement *Elegy* based on William Blake's poem "The Sick Rose." In contrast to his later statement claiming that he "couldn't be alone," Britten ends the "Folk-Art Problem" essay with a quote from the poet W. H. Auden that artists should "accept their loneliness and refuse all refuges, whether of tribal nationalism or airtight intellectual systems."

Britten's feeling of isolation was, to some extent, self-imposed; as suggested by his dismissive reference to "airtight intellectual systems," he sought to separate himself from composers who had adopted Schoenberg's twelve-tone method as well as from other modernist trends. As he wrote in 1964, "There are many dangers that hedge round the unfortunate composer: pressure groups that demand true proletarian music, snobs who demand the latest avant-garde tricks; critics who are already trying to document today for tomorrow, to be the first to find the correct pigeonhole definition."

Yet Britten's stance toward twelve-tone composition was characterized less by outright rejection than by an inventive rethinking of aspects of the method that he found useful. Unlike many composers after the war who turned to Webern's music because it seemed cut off from the past (see Chapter 10), Britten was drawn to Berg's attempt to synthesize tonality and twelve-tone technique. For example, the sequence of triads in the "Te decet hymnus" section of the Requiem aeternam moves systematically through all 12 scale degrees. The melody the boys sing in this section is also an extension of twelve-tone technique, with the second half (mm. 33–36) being a strict inversion of the first (mm. 29–32). Several other works by Britten show a similar assimilation of the twelve-tone method, most notably the opera *The Turn of the Screw* (1954), which uses a twelve-tone theme as the basis for variations between each of the scenes and to organize other aspects of the form and harmony.

Like his complex relationship with the twelve-tone method, Britten's engagement with tonality was characterized by an interest in reworking and rebuilding, while preserving a certain distance. Stravinsky's manipulation of tonal harmonies and traditional forms and genres in his Neoclassical works was a major influence. But in his rethinking of harmony Britten also drew on the music of Bali, to which he was introduced by Colin McPhee (see Chapter 8). Britten evokes gamelan in subtle ways in the *War Requiem*, with the bright percussion passages at the beginning of the Sanctus and the slowly tolling, harmonically static gong cycles in the Requiem aeternam. The sound of gamelan is more explicit in his operas, such as *Death in Venice* (1973, based on the novella by Thomas Mann), a work in which Britten dealt directly with homosexual desire.

Britten was adept at integrating functional tonality, nonfunctional triadic structures, chromatic and atonal passages, and serial principles. In Example 9.1 we see how he uses the F♯/G♭–C tritone to bridge the three layers of material in the Requiem aeternam; it simultaneously defines the boundary points for the chromatic vocal line from the boys' music, functions as part of a dominant ninth of the tenor's key of B♭ minor, and returns to its original function in the static harmonies of the opening choral passage. And yet the dissonant tritone can provide only a fractured foundation. In the *War Requiem*, the ultimate irreconcilability of the musical elements Britten has assembled—as if gathered from the ruins of the past and present—is just as significant as his untiring efforts to bring them together in some kind of whole. As the epigraph to the score from a poem by Owen states: "My subject is War, and the pity of War. / The Poetry is in the pity. / All a poet can do is warn."

In order to understand Britten's ambivalence toward the possibility of fully realizing a vision of peace, cooperation, and reconciliation in the *War Requiem*, as in many other works from those years, we need to examine conditions in the "real" world and the impact of the deeply entrenched enmities of the Cold War.

MUSICAL RAMIFICATIONS OF THE COLD WAR

The ideological struggle between communism and capitalism that became known as the Cold War had its roots in negotiations among the victorious Allies at the end of World War II. At the Yalta Conference in February 1945, American president Franklin Roosevelt, British prime minister Winston Churchill, and Soviet general secretary Joseph Stalin agreed to divide Germany and Austria into separate zones of occupation. During the ensuing Cold War, which dominated international politics until the dissolution of the Soviet Union in 1991, the world was organized into competing spheres of influence defined by the countries associated with the North Atlantic Treaty Organization (NATO, formed 1949) and those of the Warsaw Pact (1955). There were also nonaligned nations like India, Indonesia, and many nations of Africa that attempted to chart an independent course. At first metaphorical, the Iron Curtain between East and West became heavily fortified in many places, with the Berlin Wall, built in 1961 and demolished in 1989, as its most visible symbol.

The distinctive mushroom-shaped cloud created by the first successful atomic detonation in New Mexico in 1945, followed by the bombings of Hiroshima and Nagasaki, haunted these years as a constant threat (see Chapters 11 and 14). When the Soviets developed their own atomic weapon in 1949, and with both sides achieving the more powerful hydrogen bomb in 1952, nuclear annihilation became possible and, some thought, inevitable. Under the doctrine of "mutually assured destruction," the United States and the Soviet Union, joined soon by Communist China, replaced direct conflict with a series of proxy wars and provocative incursions, including the Korean War (1950–53), the Cuban missile crisis (1962), and the Vietnam War (1955–75). Entering the popular imagination through Ian Fleming's James Bond novels (the first appearing in 1953) and books like Graham Greene's *Our Man in Havana* (1958), the struggle was also conducted through espionage and covert activities, including assassinations, kidnappings and defections, and the installation of puppet regimes.

Beyond its military and tactical dimensions, the Cold War was a battle of ideas and competing visions for the future. Both sides made intensive efforts to enforce ideological conformity and root out internal dissent. Many aspects of the musical developments we will consider in the chapters that follow were shaped by these Cold War ideologies, including an emphasis on technological progress, a massive investment in universities and research, and the attraction of scientific models for creating and writing about music.

THE ARTS AS A TOOL OF POLITICS

Both the United States and the Soviet Union used the arts to show off the vitality of their cultures. The U.S. State Department, with support from the Central Intelligence Agency, sponsored world tours by jazz musicians like Louis Armstrong, who showcased distinctively American music while promoting the ideal of racial harmony. But there was also considerable official support for the newest avant-garde art and music, including Abstract Expressionist paintings by Mark Rothko and Jackson Pollock, and the complex Serialism and Indeterminacy that were the focus of influential summer music courses in Darmstadt, Germany (see Chapter 10). Modernist art and music were useful as a symbol of the West not only because they were seen to represent progress, rationality, and freedom, but also because they had been often singled out for repression by the Fascists in Germany and Italy, and by the Communist authorities in the Soviet Union.

Along with official support for the avant-garde came a growing suspicion of the populist, folk-based, and politically engaged art and music that had been so dominant before the war. The House Committee on Un-American Activities, in tandem with a Senate committee headed by Joseph McCarthy, conducted hearings starting in the 1940s to expose alleged Communists in government, Hollywood, and the arts. During the so-called McCarthy Era, thousands of Americans from all walks of life were blacklisted because of their actual or suspected political beliefs and activities, effectively rendering them unemployable. The African-American singer and actor Paul Robeson (see Chapter 8), who had come under suspicion for his outspoken support of progressive causes and the civil rights movement, as well as for a highly publicized trip to the Soviet Union in 1949, had his passport revoked between 1950 and 1958 to prevent him from traveling abroad. Also blacklisted for many years was Pete Seeger, Charles Seeger's son and the stepson of Ruth Crawford Seeger, who with the group the Weavers had used folk songs like "If I Had a Hammer" (1949) in support of trade and labor unions. Schoenberg's pupil Hanns Eisler was under constant surveillance by the Federal Bureau of Investigation as he built a successful career as a film composer in Hollywood starting in 1942. His FBI file includes detailed summaries of his collaborations with Bertolt Brecht (see Chapter 5); after both were called to testify before the House committee in 1947, Brecht left the country voluntarily, while Eisler was deported. Eisler went to East Germany, where he placed his talents at the service of the Communist regime, composing music for the new national anthem. Yet despite his many official successes and honors in East Germany, Eisler often fell under suspicion for being excessively Modernist—ironic evidence of the complex cultural politics of those years.

Some composers openly supported the anticommunist effort. Schoenberg, despite gaining U.S. citizenship, feared for his status because of his connections to Eisler and other prominent left-wing artists. In response to Aaron Copland's widely publicized appearance with Dmitri Shostakovich (1906–1975) at the Cultural and Scientific Congress for World Peace in New York in 1949, Schoenberg published remarks in the *New York Herald Tribune* linking Copland and Stalin:

> You cannot change the natural evolution of the arts by a command; you may make a New Year's resolution to write what everybody likes, but cannot force real artists to descend to the lowest possible standard, to give up morals, character, and sincerity, to avoid presentation of new ideas. Even Stalin can not succeed and Aaron Copland even less.

Copland was also attacked in *Life* magazine, which published a photo from the Congress captioned: "Dupes and fellow travelers dress up communist fronts." In a speech at the event Copland himself described the "mood of suspicion, ill-will, and dread that typifies the cold war attitude." In 1953 his *Lincoln Portrait*, once a paradigm of musical patriotism, was withdrawn from President Dwight D. Eisenhower's inauguration as being uncomfortably close to the tenets of Soviet Socialist Realism (discussed later). Although he consistently denied affiliation with the Communist Party, he was subpoenaed by Senator McCarthy and forced to testify in a closed hearing. Scholars have interpreted Copland's turn to twelve-tone composition in works like the Piano Quartet (1950) as an attempt to distance himself from the populist nationalism of pieces like *Billy the Kid* (see Chapter 8).

SHOSTAKOVICH'S STRING QUARTET NO. 8

Shostakovich's life, too, was deeply bound up with World War II and its Cold War aftermath. He wrote the Symphony No. 7 (*Leningrad*, 1941) during the Nazi siege of Leningrad, and composed works with Jewish themes in response to the Holocaust, including the Second Piano Trio (1944) and the Symphony No. 13 (*Babiy Yar*, 1962), with texts concerning the Nazi mass murder of Ukrainian Jews at Kiev. Other works, such as the String Quartet No. 8 (1960), written as he battled serious health troubles and thoughts of suicide, delve into the traumas of these years in more personal terms (see Anthology 16).

Shostakovich composed the Eighth Quartet in three days immediately after touring the ruins of Dresden. He had traveled there to compose music for a film about the advancing Soviet Army's attempts to remove artistic treasures before Allied bombers destroyed the city in the closing months of the war. On the title page, the quartet is dedicated "to the victims of Fascism and war," but in a letter to a friend Shostakovich described it as a requiem to himself: "I started thinking that if some day I die, nobody is likely to write a work in memory of me, so I had better write one myself. The title page could carry the dedication: 'To the memory of the composer of this quartet.'" He underscored this autobiographical dimension by using a motive based on his name, DSCH, which, using German note names, corresponds to D–E♭–C–B. The motive is introduced by the cello at the very beginning in a somber fugato that evokes Beethoven's late string Quartets Opp. 131 and 132 (Ex. 9.2). It then reappears in different contexts and moods throughout the five continuous movements that comprise the work.

In much the same way that Britten's *War Requiem* was an attempt to rebuild a musical language amid the rubble of the past, Shostakovich's quartet is built from allusions to earlier works by other composers and from fragments of his own pieces, enumerated in the same letter to his friend:

> The quartet also uses themes from some of my own compositions and the Revolutionary song *Tormented by Grievous Bondage*. The themes from my own works are as follows: from the First Symphony [1925], the Eighth Symphony [1943], the [Second Piano] Trio [1944], the Cello Concerto [1959] and *Lady Macbeth* [1932]. There are hints of Wagner (the Funeral March from *Götterdämmerung*) and Tchaikovsky (the second subject of the first movement of the Sixth Symphony). Oh yes, I forgot to mention that there is something else of mine as well, from the Tenth Symphony [1953]. Quite a nice little hodge-podge, really.

Throughout the work the quotations are distorted and broken off, just as each movement is interrupted by the unexpected beginning of the next. All five movements are in the minor mode, and three have a slow and mournful tone. The second and third movements are faster, but their character is darkly sardonic, violent, and—especially in the distorted waltz of the third-movement Scherzo—almost unhinged.

At the 1960 premiere of the String Quartet No. 8 in Leningrad the audience demanded an encore of the complete work, and the piece went on to become one of

Example 9.2: *Dmitri Shostakovich, String Quartet No. 8, movement 1, mm. 1–8*

the most frequently performed and recorded twentieth-century quartets. Yet to a far greater extent than Britten, who despite his success often felt like an outsider, Shostakovich veered between the highest official honors and fears of impending arrest as he made his way within the byzantine totalitarian system of the Soviet Union. Gauging the intent of his works as compliant with or defiant to his repressive environment is the subject of intense debate by musicians and scholars today, just as it was for those who were in charge of policing him during his life.

ACCLAIM AND NOTORIETY

Shostakovich was born into a well-off musical family in St. Petersburg (the city's changing names over the years—Petrograd from 1914–24, Leningrad from 1924–91, then back to St. Petersburg—mirror the disruptions and upheavals through which Shostakovich lived.) He started studying piano and composing when he was nine, soon demonstrating enormous musical talent and virtuosic performance abilities. In 1919 he was admitted to the Petrograd Conservatory, where he encountered the latest European new music, including works by Strauss, Bartók, Hindemith, and later Stravinsky and Prokofiev.

Shostakovich's First Symphony, composed in 1925 when he was 18, brought him international attention. The score foretells his lifelong openness to a broad range of influences; for example, the unsentimental tone of the New Objectivity and Neoclassical manipulation of styles and genres can be heard in his many off-kilter polkas, waltzes, and marches. The first quotation that appears in the Eighth Quartet after the opening fugato is the playful first theme of the symphony, now transformed into a brooding lament around which the other voices circulate nervously.

In addition to performing as a pianist, Shostakovich built his early career writing music for ballet, theater, and film. The formal disjunctions in the Eighth Quartet and other works have been compared to filmic editing technique, as has his use of dramatic quotations that function like flashbacks to earlier points in a narrative. Shostakovich's works from the 1920s and early 1930s reflect the official openness to Modernist art during the early Soviet period. His two early operas, *The Nose* (1928) and *Lady Macbeth of the Mtsensk District* (1932), were based on bizarre and lurid subject matter, while the music shows the influence of the Futurists' noise effects, the dissonant intensity of Berg's *Wozzeck* (which made an enormous impression on Shostakovich in 1927), and allusions to jazz and popular dance styles characteristic of the topical operas (*Zeitopern*) of Hindemith and Krenek.

These and other works brought Shostakovich considerable notoriety and performances throughout Europe and the United States, but they also attracted the attention of Stalin, who after Lenin's death in 1924 sought to suppress all external intellectual and artistic influences. Scholars have argued that *Lady Macbeth* was consistent with Soviet ideology in its depiction of the main character

Katerina's murders of her merchant husband and father-in-law, who symbolized the oppressive capitalist social order. Nevertheless, the opera was publicly criticized for its dissonance, vulgarity, and "petty-bourgeois 'innovations'" in 1936 in the Communist Party newspaper *Pravda* (SR 188:1398; 7/19:128). The attack, in an article entitled "Chaos Instead of Music," signaled not only that Shostakovich's works had fallen out of favor, but also that he faced the very real possibility of being arrested or killed, the fate of several of his acquaintances and family members during Stalin's purges.

The fourth movement of the String Quartet No. 8 contains a quotation from Katerina's lovesick aria in Act 4 of *Lady Macbeth*, where, among a group of convicts on their way to Siberia, she meets her lover Sergei, not realizing that he has taken up with another woman. This melody is prefaced by a grim quotation from the Revolutionary song "Tormented by Grievous Bondage" (see p. 188). The movement ends with a return of the terrifying music with which it begins, a strained stillness interrupted by sudden, sharp, repeated chords heard by some as the ominous pounding on the door in the middle of the night, when the Soviet authorities came to take someone away.

SOCIALIST REALISM

Shostakovich and other "formalist" composers were charged in the early 1930s with having "debased the lofty social role of music and narrowed its significance, limiting it to the gratification of the perverted tastes of esthetizing egocentrics." Such was the voice of Socialist Realism, which sought to counter Western Modernist experimentation with a healthy and optimistic art "for the people." In the terminology we used in Chapter 8, Socialist Realism can be seen as a different kind of "invented tradition," one all the more potent in that adhering to it could be a matter of life and death. Paradoxically, the power of the doctrine lay in its vagueness: as defined by Andrey Alexandrovich Zhdanov, the influential Party official who oversaw the arts, Socialist Realism represented "a creative method based on the truthful, historically concrete artistic reflection of reality in its revolutionary development."

Fearing for his life, Shostakovich withdrew a scheduled performance of his vast, Mahlerian Fourth Symphony (1936) and began composing a series of works, starting with the Fifth Symphony (1937), characterized by a simplified style and a more traditional approach to harmony, melody, and form—all ostensibly in the service of broad accessibility and a positive and uplifting message. Of the Fifth Symphony, another work alluded to in the Eighth Quartet, Shostakovich was quoted in official sources as saying: "I wanted to convey in the symphony how, through a series of tragic conflicts of great inner spiritual turmoil, optimism asserts itself as a world-view." Another sign of the times was his new interest in the more private world of chamber music; in 1938 he wrote the first of 15 string quartets that marked a split between his sometimes bombastic and overtly propagandistic public works, such as the later symphonies and choral music, and deeply personal works like the Eighth Quartet.

In the context of Socialist Realism, questions about tonality versus atonality and twelve-tone composition were extremely fraught. Whereas some of Shostakovich's earlier works featured passages of emancipated dissonances, most of his works after the Fifth Symphony were in a key. The five movements of the Eighth Quartet, for example, zigzag from C minor through G♯ minor, G minor, and C♯ minor before finally returning to C minor. Yet while triads and cadential progressions feature prominently in Shostakovich's music, tonality is constantly subverted by modality, octatonicism, and even twelve-tone passages in the works of his last decade. That his music remains so immediately effective despite the complexity of the harmonic language can be attributed to its sharply defined rhythms, its clear and regular phrase structure, and the composer's preference for homophonic textures with memorable melodies.

COLD WAR PARADOXES

In the early years of the Cold War Soviet authorities sharply intensified their efforts to insure orthodoxy and stamp out opposition. In 1948 Shostakovich, Prokofiev (see Chapter 6), and others were again attacked for "formalism" and their music pronounced unsuitable for the Soviet people. Though Shostakovich attempted to downplay the "tragic" elements of the Eighth Symphony (another work quoted in the Eighth Quartet) by describing it as "optimistic and life-affirming," this and other recent compositions were censured at a Communist Party conference. Shostakovich abjectly accepted the criticism, promising to "try again and again to create symphonic works that are comprehensible and access-ible to the people, from the standpoint of their ideological content, musical lan-guage, and form. I will work ever more diligently on the musical embodiment of images of the heroic Russian people." He lost his teaching post at the Leningrad Conservatory, took remedial instruction in Marxism-Leninism, and endured intense mockery and threats on his life. With performances of his earlier music essentially banned, he wrote a series of propagandistic works praising Stalin and the Russian victory in the "Great Patriotic War," such as the film score for *The Fall of Berlin* (1949) and the cantata *The Sun Shines over Our Motherland* (1952).

During the regime of Nikita Khruschev (1953–64), who came to power after the death of Stalin, official control relaxed, opening up artistic expression to develop-ments abroad. Gradually returning to official favor, Shostakovich was useful to the political authorities as the country's most important living composer and a symbol of the post-Stalin "thaw." Bans on his works were lifted and he was allowed to visit the United States and England for performances of his Cello Concerto No. 1 (1959), another piece quoted in the Eighth Quartet. Chain-smoking, drinking heavily, and often described as anxious and ill at ease, Shostakovich gave official speeches that had been written for him. While privately he showed considerable interest in the works of composers like Britten, Boulez, and Karlheinz Stockhausen, his public statements included denunciations of new musical developments in Europe, including the twelve-tone method.

In 1960 Shostakovich yielded to the incessant pressure and took the painful step of joining the Communist Party. In his Symphony No. 12 (*The Year 1917*, 1961), dedicated to the memory of Lenin, many listeners heard a ringing affirmation of Socialist Realism. Dissidents like Alexander Solzhenitsyn wrote Shostakovich off as a lost cause. Asked why he had not bothered to invite the composer to sign a petition criticizing the 1968 Soviet invasion of Czechoslovakia, the writer acidly explained, "The shackled genius Shostakovich would thrash about like a wounded thing, clasp himself with tightly folded arms so that his fingers could not hold a pen."

Shostakovich may have been passing a similar verdict on himself in the Eighth Quartet, with its extensive quotation in the fourth movement of "Tormented by Grievous Bondage," a patriotic song that was reputed to be a favorite of Stalin's. It opens with the words: "Tormented by grievous bondage / You died a glorious death / In the struggle for the people's cause / You laid down your life with honor." Yet through the multiple layers of irony, self-mockery, and fear, Shostakovich created a work that continues to speak to audiences about the challenges of the human condition. Describing the Eighth Quartet as an "ideologically depraved quartet which is of no use to anybody," he wrote to his friend: "It is a pseudo-tragic quartet, so much so that while I was composing it I shed the same amount of tears as I would have had to pee after half-a-dozen beers. When I got home, I tried a few times to play it through, but always ended up in tears."

In a commentary on Shostakovich's works written in 1976, the year after his death, the composer Alfred Schnittke (1934–1998) emphasized the strong individual voice underlying the diversity of his output over his long career. In a formulation that could be equally applied to Britten, who had died that year, Schnittke described how through the manifold borrowings and allusions in works like the Eighth Quartet "the past enters into new relations with the present, invades musical reality, like the ghost of Hamlet's father, and shapes it." In combining "the images of his own musical past . . . with images from the history of music," Schnittke claims that Shostakovich was able to join "the individual with the universal" and "to influence the world through confluence with the world."

As we will see in Chapters 10–12, for many younger composers the only adequate response to World War II and its aftermath was to banish such ghosts from the past and to question the possibility of meaningful connections to the history of music or to the music that had been embraced by the world around them.

FOR FURTHER READING

Brinkmann, Reinhold, and Christoph Wolff, eds., *Driven into Paradise: The Musical Migration from Nazi Germany to the United States* (Berkeley and Los Angeles: University of California Press, 1999)

Cooke, Mervyn, *Britten: War Requiem* (Cambridge: Cambridge University Press, 1996)

Crawford, Dorothy, *A Windfall of Musicians: Hitler's Émigrés and Exiles in Southern California* (New Haven: Yale University Press, 2009)

Davenport, Lise E., *Jazz Diplomacy: Promoting America in the Cold War Era* (Jackson: University Press of Mississippi, 2009)

DeLapp-Birkett, Jennifer, "Aaron Copland and the Politics of Twelve-Tone Composition in the Early Cold War United States," *Journal of Musicological Research* 27, no. 1 (2008): 31–62

Fairclough, Pauline, and David Fanning, eds., *The Cambridge Companion to Shostakovich* (Cambridge: Cambridge University Press, 2008)

Gilbert, Shirli, *Music in the Holocaust: Confronting Life in the Nazi Ghettos and Camps* (Oxford: Oxford University Press, 2005)

Judt, Tony, *Postwar: A History of Europe since 1945* (New York: Penguin, 2005)

Rupprecht, Phillip, *Britten's Musical Language* (Cambridge: Cambridge University Press, 2001)

Schmelz, Peter, ed., "Music in the Cold War," *Journal of Musicology* 26, nos. 1 and 2 (2009)

Whitesell, Lloyd, "Men with a Past: Music and the 'Anxiety of Influence,'" *19th-Century Music* 18, no. 2 (1994): 152–167

CHAPTER TEN

Trajectories of Order and Chance

In the ongoing search for a music that seemed true to their new world, composers after World War II headed in two seemingly opposite directions. Some extended the twelve-tone method in pursuit of rationality, control, and structure; others relinquished control, embracing chance procedures in composition and giving performers enormous freedom in deciding what to play.

This chapter explores the origins and implications of these trends, which we will identify respectively as Integral Serialism and Indeterminacy, by focusing on the interactions between Pierre Boulez (b. 1925) and John Cage (1912–1992). The letters they exchanged from 1949 to 1954, starting when Boulez was 24 and Cage 36, reveal significant temperamental and philosophical differences. Yet their paths converged on a central paradox of twentieth- and twenty-first-century music: On the one hand, the attempt to give up control of sounds required the strictest discipline; on the other, the pursuit of rigorous structure could emancipate music in unexpected ways. Just as paradoxical was their realization that the pieces produced by such contrary techniques could sometimes sound astonishingly similar. Although Boulez and Cage each ultimately followed a path that the other could not accept, their music and the ways of hearing and thinking they and others developed during these years have influenced composition ever since.

POST–WORLD WAR II CONTEXTS

Just as Boulez wrote of the general feeling after the war of "being faced with nothing," so Cage compared the situation of contemporary composers to being in "a bombed-out city," forced to build again from the ground up. Both rejected Neoclassicism, Schoenberg's integration of twelve-tone music with eighteenth-century forms, and the interwar engagement with popular music, jazz, and folk traditions. Instead of relying on personal taste, expression, and emotion, they and many of their contemporaries were attracted to abstract systems that minimized the role of the composer's individuality and subjectivity. Thus, while Cage and his circle were inspired by the ancient Chinese *I Ching*, Zen Buddhism, and new abstract styles of painting and dance, the Serialists turned to mathematics, psychoacoustics, and, as we will see in Chapter 11, new technologies.

This was the era of all-encompassing theories that sought to explain human actions in terms of systems. In a 1957 article entitled "Meaning in Music and Information Theory," the music theorist Leonard B. Meyer argued that systems of probability, expectation, and entropy could model "the seemingly disparate worlds of physical phenomena, bio-social behavior, and humanistic creation." As a result, he predicted that "the possibility of a statistical analysis of style" would soon lead to "the construction of devices for composing music on the basis of probabilities inherent in the style of western music." (For one recent realization of this idea in the development of artificial intelligence systems for composition, see Chapter 15.)

As part of composers' adoption of scientific models of experimentation, they felt compelled to explain what they were doing and why. Many connected their musical works to analytical and theoretical writings, publishing their explanations with the score or in specialized journals like *Die Reihe* (The Row, or The Series) in Austria or *Perspectives of New Music* in the United States. The notion of composition as research made it possible for a piece of music to have more impact through what was written about its compositional techniques than through actual performances. Reviving the model of the composer-theorist, mostly dormant since the eighteenth century, a number of composers established themselves as prominent music theorists, particularly in North American universities, which prized research and publication. In an essay that he called "The Composer as Specialist" (better known by the provocative title "Who Cares If You Listen?" under which it was published in the audiophile magazine *High Fidelity* in 1958), Milton Babbitt likened composition to scientific research, noting that "the time has passed when the normally well-educated man without special preparation could understand the most advanced work in, for example, mathematics, philosophy, and physics." Just as a layman could not be expected to appreciate the finer points of a mathematics lecture on "Pointwise Periodic Homeomorphisms," Babbitt argued that it was unrealistic to present highly specialized music in concerts aimed at the general public.

By embracing an experimental, scientific mindset, many composers distanced themselves from the interwar tendency to place music in the service of nationalism, propaganda, and mass culture. The German musicologist H. H. Stuckenschmidt, who had been forced from his journalistic position by the Nazis and then conscripted into the German Army as a translator, wrote in 1947: "For twelve years we have been raised to disrespect and reject the principles of *l'art pour l'art* [art for art's sake] to the point where many believed that art had no rules of its own." Babbitt, who taught at Princeton, described universities as "the mightiest of fortresses against the overwhelming, outnumbering forces, both within and without the university, of anti-intellectualism, cultural populism, and passing fashion." Artists, too, rejected the notion that their work should serve social or political functions. Writing in 1952, the influential art critic Harold Rosenberg described the paintings of the American Abstract Expressionist Jackson Pollock as "a gesture of liberation from Value—political, esthetic, moral . . . *the lone artist did not want the world to be different, he wanted the canvas to be his world.*"

Yet the cultural arms race set off by the Cold War made it harder than ever for composers and artists to avoid politics. As avant-garde music and art came to symbolize the Western liberal values of freedom and individuality (see Chapter 9), significant funding for new music came directly or indirectly from governments in both Europe and the United States. Part of the postwar denazification and reeducation efforts in West Germany included support from the U.S. State Department and military for a wide range of musical activities; Stuckenschmidt himself was hired by the State Department as a cultural ambassador between the United States and West Germany. Perhaps the most striking example is the State Department's support for the International Summer Courses for New Music that began in the West German town of Darmstadt in 1946, quickly having a substantial impact on musical developments. The State Department's music officer in charge of the region reported approvingly in 1948 of the emphasis on avant-garde music and the exclusion of older composers associated with nationalism or the folk. "Contemporary music *only* is taught and performed—and then only the more advanced varieties. R. Strauss and J. Sibelius do *not* come into consideration."

TWELVE-TONE COMPOSITION AFTER WORLD WAR II

Prior to the war, interest in the twelve-tone method in Europe had been limited to Schoenberg, his pupils, and a few others (see Chapter 7). Although Schoenberg continued to compose twelve-tone works after immigrating to the United States in 1933, he also wrote a number of tonal works, either in response to commissions or in the hope of getting performances. With some exceptions, including Wallingford Riegger and Ruth Crawford Seeger, few American composers were drawn to the method, in part because little information about it was available in English. This changed in the 1950s, when a number of prominent international figures as diverse as Babbitt, Boulez, Copland, Britten, and Shostakovich demonstrated that twelve-tone techniques could be used to very different stylistic ends than those represented by Schoenberg's music.

The most surprising case was Igor Stravinsky, who had come to be viewed as Schoenberg's antithesis in the interwar years. In a series of works written after Schoenberg's death, including *Canticum sacrum* (1955), the ballet *Agon* (1957), and *Movements* for piano and orchestra (1959), Stravinsky developed his own distinctive twelve-tone idiom. The pointillist texture and floating rhythms of *Movements* evoke Webern's aesthetic, which had a strong impact on many composers seeking alternatives to Schoenberg after the war. The second volume of *Die Reihe* in 1955, marking the tenth anniversary of Webern's accidental shooting death by an American soldier, was devoted to his music and included a foreword by Stravinsky. Illustrating the feeling many had of discovering a misunderstood genius—and thus downplaying the limited but still considerable recognition that Webern had received in the 1920s and 1930s—Stravinsky described him as "a real hero . . . doomed to a total failure in a deaf world of ignorance and indifference, he inexorably kept on cutting out his diamonds, his dazzling diamonds, the mines of which he had such a perfect knowledge."

INTEGRAL SERIALISM

Boulez took the lead in championing Webern over Schoenberg in a provocative essay titled "Schönberg est mort" (Schoenberg Is Dead, 1952), published a year after Schoenberg's death. Asserting that it was Webern rather than his teacher who had pointed the way to the future, he dismissed Schoenberg's attempt to combine twelve-tone technique with Neoclassical forms as so fundamentally wrong-headed "that it would be hard to find an equally mistaken perspective in the history of music." Instead, Boulez praised Webern for having sought in works like his Symphony, Op. 21 (see Chapter 7) to "derive the structure from the material" and for originating the idea of applying "the serial principle to the four sound-constituents: pitch, duration, intensity and attack, timbre."

Boulez was one of several postwar composers who extended twelve-tone technique beyond melody and harmony to rhythm, dynamics, timbre, articulation, and texture. This effort, referred to variously as Integral Serialism, Total Serialism, and General Serialism, took different forms depending on the composers' backgrounds and interests. The many problems, the very significant perceptual difficulties, and the unintended consequences that Boulez and others encountered in the attempt vividly illustrate the idea of composition as an experimental process.

MESSIAEN'S SYSTEMS, SPIRITUALITY, AND MAGIC

A major influence on Boulez, and on the development of Integral Serialism in general, was his teacher Olivier Messiaen (1908–1992). In contrast to those who grounded new compositional techniques in science and mathematics, Messiaen drew upon an extraordinary range of sources, including his fervent Catholicism, synesthesia, the music of India and Japan, and the sounds of birdsong. Messiaen's enormous musical talent gained him entrance to the Paris Conservatoire when he was only 11. Upon completing his studies at age 22, he became organist at La Trinité Church in Paris, a position he would hold for more than six decades. His output includes organ works on religious themes such as *La nativité du Seigneur* (The Nativity of the Lord, 1935), compositions for piano like the massive *Catalogue d'oiseaux* (Catalogue of Birds, 1958), and many orchestral works, in particular the exoticist *Turangalîla-symphonie* (1948), which features the electronic Ondes Martenot (see Chapter 5).

Messiaen's most famous piece, *Quatuor pour la fin du temps* (Quartet for the End of Time), was written in 1940–41 in a German prison camp, where he had been sent upon being captured shortly after beginning his military service. Written for the instruments available—violin, clarinet, cello, and piano—the quartet was first performed in the camp for an audience of prisoners and guards. Like many of Messiaen's compositions, the eight-movement work is programmatic, drawing on the New Testament Book of Revelation. In the preface to the score, Messiaen describes the first movement, *Liturgie de cristal* (Liturgy of Crystal): "Between three and four in the morning, the song of the birds, a blackbird and nightingale improvise, a halo of trills high in the trees, they are transported to a religious plane: you hear the silence of the heavens."

Messiaen nests the flamboyant violin and clarinet parts, each marked to sing "like a bird," upon a mysteriously timeless accompaniment in the cello and piano. Building on the medieval technique of isorhythm, the cello part is based on a series of 5 pitches and a rhythmic pattern of 15 durations:

Cello pitch series (5 pitches)

```
 *              *             *            *
 C   E   D   F♯  B♭ / C  E   D   F♯  B♭ / C  E   D   F♯  B♭ / C  E   D   F♯  B♭  etc.
 4   3   4   4    1   1   1   3   1   1    1   1   3   1   1   4 / 4  3   4   4    1   etc.
 *                                        *
```

Cello rhythm series (15 durations, given in eighth notes)

In the cello part, the pitches and rhythms realign after three statements of the 5-pitch series. The piano part, however, uses more-elaborate patterns, with a series of 29 chords combined with a rhythm that is 17 durations long; since these are prime numbers, the two series would realign only after 493 events.

Example 10.1: *Nonretrogradable rhythm from Olivier Messiaen's* Quartet for the End of Time, *preface, p. III*

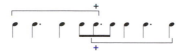

That this eventual meeting takes place far beyond the bounds of the actual movement is typical of Messiaen's use of structural devices to symbolize mystical and spiritual realms. Another example of this metaphysical dimension is his interest in symmetrical collections like the whole-tone and octatonic scales, which he described as "modes of limited transposition," and in "nonretrogradable rhythms," or palindromic rhythms that read the same backward as forward (Ex. 10.1). He heard these structures, with their "mathematical impossibilities"—by which he meant, for example, that there was only a single transposition of the whole-tone scale—as possessing a "strength of bewitchment, a magic strength, a *charm*." For Messiaen, such musical devices ultimately symbolized the eternity and boundlessness of God.

The most direct influence on composers of the younger generation involved with the development of Integral Serialism was Messiaen's short piano piece *Mode de valeurs et d'intensités* (Mode of Values and Intensities), one of a set of four études on rhythm written at Darmstadt in 1949. As Messiaen explains in a preface to the score, the piece uses a "mode of pitches (36 notes), of note-values (24 durations), of touches (12 touches), and of dynamics (7 levels)." As shown in Example 10.2, Messiaen divides the material into three overlapping registral layers, or divisions. Each division contains 12 different pitches, and each pitch is assigned a dynamic value and articulation that it preserves throughout the piece.

Messiaen's attraction to systems can be seen in the way he constructs the rhythms of each division by adding rhythmic values (a thirty-second note in Division I, a sixteenth note in Division II, and a quarter note in Division III). He then generates the piece's scintillating traceries of notes from an arrangement of these precisely predetermined elements. While he uses all 12 pitches in each layer, he intentionally diverges from the central tenet of twelve-tone composition by constantly varying the order of each of the divisions, treating them instead as unordered modes, as suggested by the work's title. The new sound world that resulted from Messiaen's techniques, liberated from traditional notions of harmony, meter, and texture, was a revelation for composers like Boulez and Stockhausen.

BOULEZ FROM *STRUCTURES TO MARTEAU*

Ever since he burst onto the scene as an *enfant terrible* around 1950 with his inflammatory writings and astonishing works, Boulez has been a major figure in contemporary music as a composer, conductor, author, and long-time director of

Example 10.2: *Olivier Messiaen,* Mode de valeurs et d'intensités, *analysis by the composer*

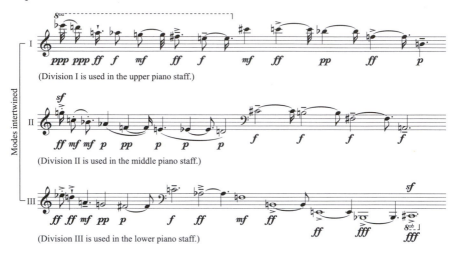

the musical research center IRCAM in Paris (see Chapter 11). Talented in mathematics and engineering as well as music, he studied harmony with Messiaen at the Paris Conservatoire, followed by private lessons on twelve-tone composition with Schoenberg's pupil René Leibowitz (Leibowitz's *Schoenberg and His School,* published in French in 1947 and in English two years later, was one of the first books to provide details on the twelve-tone method).

Boulez's Second Piano Sonata (1948) first brought him wide attention. Through what he described as an "anarchic" expansion of register, he challenged Neoclassical conceptions of melody, form, rhythm, and texture. His *Structures I* for two pianos (1952) was a milestone in the history of Integral Serialism. Boulez developed the basic twelve-tone row through the standard serial transformations of transposition, retrograde, inversion, and retrograde inversion, but he also constructed a series of 12 rhythmic values, based on the addition of thirty-second notes; a series of 12 dynamic values, from *pppp* to *ffff*; and 12 different types of articulation (Ex. 10.3). The connections to Messiaen's *Mode of Values and Intensities* are clear in his adoption of Messiaen's Division I (see Ex. 10.2) as the row for *Structures.* But whereas Messiaen treated the division as unordered mode, for Boulez the ordered "serial" treatment is fundamental.

Once these series were established, Boulez composed the piece by referring to two 12-by-12 matrices of order numbers. He selected pitches, rhythms, dynamics, and other parameters based on the various sequences of numbers, while making adjustments according to other, less formal criteria (Ex. 10.4). As we will see later, another inspiration for Boulez's use of these tables was his correspondence with John Cage, who precisely at this time was writing his *Music of*

Example 10.3: *Pierre Boulez,* Structures I, *series of pitches, rhythms, articulations, and dynamics. As presented by Robert P. Morgan.*

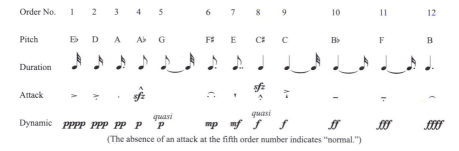

(The absence of an attack at the fifth order number indicates "normal.")

Changes, similarly based on charts for the individual musical elements (though to very different ends).

In an analysis of *Structures I* published in *Die Reihe*, the Hungarian-born composer György Ligeti (discussed further in Chapter 12) pointed out the inconsistencies in Boulez's method, as well as the illogicality of "transposing" a series of durations or dynamics: "What is inorganic is this pointless transplantation of a system; note qualities labeled with numbers, the dematerialised numbers organised into tables, and the tables finally used like a fetish." In noting that it would be impossible to reconstruct the compositional process from the sound of the music, Ligeti also raised the question of how Boulez's compositional techniques relate to the listener's perception of the piece. Yet he concluded by marveling at the "beauty in the erection of pure structures" that Boulez had achieved, using language that anticipated the mass effects and textures he would explore in his own music. Ligeti compared the kaleidoscopically shifting surface of *Structures I* to the patterns created by flashing neon lights on a city street: "the individual lights are indeed exactly controlled by a mechanism, but as the separate lights flash on and off, they combine to form a statistical complex."

Boulez's lifelong habit of reworking his older pieces, and his willingness to set techniques aside after he learned what he could from them, exemplify the postwar experimental mindset. He quickly turned away from the procedures used in *Structures I* to a more flexible approach that still built upon elaborate serial techniques. As he was composing his next major work, *Le marteau sans maître* (The Hammer without a Master, 1955), he wrote of feeling the need to constrain the sense of possibility: "The network of possibilities the system offers is not something simply to be presented as sufficient in itself to satisfy the needs of the composition. . . . [W]e might instead regard a piece of music as a series of rejections among many probabilities."

Based on three poems by the French Surrealist poet René Char, *Le marteau sans maître* (see Anthology 17) is a song cycle for contralto and a small ensemble

Example 10.4: *Pierre Boulez,* Structures I, *Part 1c, mm. 1–3*

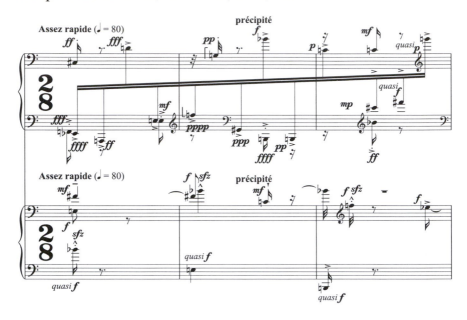

of flute, xylorimba, vibraphone, percussion, guitar, and viola, which Boulez uses to create what Ligeti described with approval as a "sensual feline world." The choice of timbres and the floating, static rhythmic quality, signal Boulez's growing interest in the music of Asia and Asian conceptions of time as an alternative to the linearity of Western temporality: "we are always ready to go from A to B and when we get there through a straight line, we are always very happy because we think that is the best solution. But I like to stop and listen to the sound only, although with a sense for logic and development."

In part an homage to Schoenberg's *Pierrot lunaire, Le marteau sans maître* features a singer employing a range of vocal techniques from speaking to singing, including Sprechstimme. As in *Pierrot,* each movement calls for a different collection of instruments; Boulez brings in the full ensemble only at the end of the work. Yet, in the context of his essay "Schoenberg Is Dead," it should come as no surprise that Boulez also intended *Le marteau* as a critique of Schoenberg. In his writings on the piece he contrasted the improvisatory freedom of Schoenberg's compositional techniques at the time of *Pierrot lunaire* and the emancipation of the dissonance, with what he viewed as the rigidity of Schoenberg's twelve-tone music. That Boulez was also in essence critiquing the rigidity and limitations of his own efforts to extend the twelve-tone method in *Structures I* is another manifestation of the idea of composition as a kind of research, with each experiment pointing the way to the next.

BABBITT'S EXTENSIONS OF TWELVE-TONE TECHNIQUE

Among the composers in Europe and the United States who explored aspects of Integral Serialism, Milton Babbitt (1916–2011) has had the greatest impact through his works, writing, and teaching. Babbitt developed his approach to extending the twelve-tone method in tandem with his theoretical investigations of Schoenberg's music. Both his compositional methods and his theoretical writings were influenced by a background in mathematics that was strong enough to earn his first teaching post at Princeton in the Department of Mathematics. Starting with the Three Compositions for Piano (1947), which used a twelve-tone row and a series of rhythmic values, with specific dynamics and registers associated with each row form, Babbitt focused on developing "a completely autonomous conception of the twelve-tone system . . . in which all components, in all dimensions, would be determined by the relations and operations of the system."

In "The Composer as Specialist," Babbitt described how each pitch in a work becomes an "'atomic' event . . . located in a five-dimensional musical space determined by pitch-class, register, dynamic, duration, and timbre," the accurate differentiation of which was crucial for intelligible communication. As we will see in Chapter 11, the quest for precision led Babbitt, Boulez, and others to electronic music synthesizers, which offered more precise and quantifiable control over each of the musical parameters than was possible for human performers.

In a series of works composed over six decades, including *All Set* for jazz ensemble (1957), the String Quartet No. 3 (1970), and *Danci* for solo guitar (1996), Babbitt explored ways of creating large-scale structure through arrays of simultaneously presented rows, and a technique for organizing rhythm using what he called a "time-point system," based on when events occur in a fixed metrical unit.

For some, Babbitt came to represent the epitome of the intellectual academic composer, but his music is often playful and mischievous, as suggested by the many irreverent puns in the titles he chose, such as *Whirled Series* for saxophone and piano (1987) and *The Joy of More Sextets* (1986) for piano and violin. In 2008, the jazz trio The Bad Plus recorded an arrangement of Babbitt's piano piece *Semi-Simple Variations* (1956) emphasizing elements of his style that allude to his background in jazz and musical theater. Indeed, among Babbitt's many students are the prominent jazz musician Stanley Jordan, as well as the noted stage composer and lyricist Stephen Sondheim.

CHANCE, INDETERMINACY, AND THE BLANK PAGE

Cage and Boulez discovered much common ground in their intensive correspondence of the early 1950s. But as Cage became increasingly interested in chance procedures in composition and Indeterminacy in performance, Boulez eventually reached a line that he refused to cross: "I do not admit—and I believe

I never will admit—chance as a component of a completed work of music," he declared in 1954. "I am widening the possibilities of strict or free music (constrained or not). But as for chance, the thought of it is unbearable!" Previously we have used the metaphors of tangled chaos and the blank page to represent the multiplicity of choices that faced composers in the twentieth century; Cage demonstrated how much more could be brought into the musical experience by erasing the pages of a score almost entirely.

4' 33"

One of the most influential works of art in the twentieth century, Cage's *4' 33"* was premiered in 1952 in a small open-air concert hall in the Catskills near Woodstock, New York. It was part of a recital of contemporary piano music that included Henry Cowell's *The Banshee* and works by Boulez and others. But nothing prepared the audience for the experience of Cage's piece: Each of the three movements consisted of the pianist David Tudor lowering the cover over the keyboard to begin the movement, then lifting it to signal the conclusion (Fig. 10.1). Throughout the performance of the three movements, which added up to 4 minutes and 33 seconds, he sat quietly, gazing at a stopwatch and occasionally turning pages of music paper on which no notes were written.

As Cage made clear in later accounts of the performance and the audience's perplexed response, the blankness of *4' 33"*, far from engendering silence, allowed the sounds of the world to rush in:

> What they thought was silence, because they didn't know how to listen, was full of accidental sounds. You could hear the wind stirring outside during the first movement. During the second, raindrops began pattering on the roof, and during the third the people themselves made all kinds of interesting sounds as they talked or walked out.

But the audience had not yet learned to listen in the way Cage had in mind, and the premiere of *4' 33"* cost him friends and supporters. Cage acknowledged that it had taken him many years to formulate the piece and work up the courage to present it. He experimented with several different forms of notation, including regular staff notation with empty staves, and time-scale notation, with each page representing a number of seconds. In the final version, he simply lists three movements, each marked "Tacet," the musical indication for silence.

CAGE'S PATH TO 4' 33"

Cage came to the idea of *4' 33"* by way of an extraordinary range of influences. Born in Los Angeles, he headed to New York at age 22, where he studied with Cowell and with Schoenberg's pupil Adolph Weiss. In 1935 he returned to Los

I

· TACET

II

TACET

III

TACET

Figure 10.1: *John Cage, 4' 33"*

Angeles to study harmony with Schoenberg. After a period in Seattle, where he began his lifelong personal and artistic relationship with the choreographer Merce Cunningham, Cage moved back to New York in 1942 and immersed himself in an artistic environment dominated by Beat writers and the Abstract Expressionist painters of the New York School. It is no coincidence that Cage's friend Robert Rauschenberg began his series of monochromatic *White Paintings* (Fig. 10.2) in 1951, a year before *4' 33"*. In Cage's eyes, Rauschenberg's seemingly empty canvases focused the viewer's attention on the play of light and shadows in the room, and even the particles of dust moving through the air.

In his early works, Cage explored the idea of measuring time in systematic ways and then allowing a wide range of sounds to inhabit those spans of time. In addition to tone rows, Cage used other elaborate precompositional techniques to determine form and rhythm. His *First Construction in Metal* (1939), for example, is based on a 16-measure unit symmetrically divided into groups of 4, 3, 2, 3, and 4, with 16 rhythmic motives and 16 instruments. Many aspects of the piece, including its overall form, are based on this numerical series. The work

Figure 10.2: *Robert Rauschenberg,* White Painting *(Three Panel) (1951)*

also illustrates Cage's interest in expanding the sound world through the use of percussion instruments and found objects, such as brake drums and lengths of metal piping.

A similar experimental impulse led Cage to invent the prepared piano, an outgrowth of the extended piano techniques that Cowell had pioneered before World War II. In *Bacchanale* (1940), Cage placed bolts, screws, and other materials between the strings to create richly clangorous sounds that evoked the percussion instruments of the Balinese gamelan. Cage also was drawn to electronic sounds, and in 1952 he worked with Louis and Bebe Barron (see Chapter 11) on *Williams Mix,* which consisted of minutely spliced fragments of recorded sounds of the city, the natural world, and electronics. A series of pieces titled *Imaginary Landscapes* (1939–52) featured turntables, radios, and other devices. The experience of manipulating lengths of magnetic recording tape profoundly shaped Cage's sense of the temporal dimension of music: In 1957 he wrote that since "so many inches or centimeters equal so many seconds," counting was no longer necessary: "magnetic tape music makes it clear that we are in time itself, not in measures of two, three, four, or any other number."

During these years, free jazz emerged in New York and elsewhere, embracing extended instrumental techniques and a new style of improvisation, while expanding the definition of meter, texture, melody, and harmony. The parallel with the development of Cage's thinking is clear in the words of jazz saxophonist James Moody: "Any sound makes sense to me. Any sound at all. You fall on the floor—it makes sense. You fell, didn't you? Music is supposed to represent a feeling." Yet in contrast to art forms like free jazz or the Abstract Expressionist paintings of Jackson Pollock, Cage sought to move away from music as a representation of the artist's psyche.

CHANCE PROCEDURES AND THE LIBERATION
FROM LIKES AND DISLIKES

Around 1950, inspired by his studies of Indian, Japanese, and Chinese philosophy, Cage began integrating elements of chance into composition and performance as a way of making music that was "free of individual taste and memory (psychology) and also of the literature and 'traditions' of the art." Drawing on the centuries-old Chinese book of divination, the *I Ching* (Book of Changes), he began composing through elaborate processes of tossing coins or throwing dice. (Aleatory music, another term for chance composition, comes from *alea*, the Latin word for "dice.") In *Music for Piano 21–36/37–52* (1955), Cage selected pitches by placing a sheet of transparent paper over the staves and marking notes where there were imperfections. Chance procedures also figured in his prose and lectures, such as a series of talks given at Harvard in 1988–89 in which he used the *I Ching* to extract excerpts from writings by Thoreau, Wittgenstein, and others.

The first major work that Cage composed in this way was the piano piece *Music of Changes* (1951; Ex. 10.5). In a painstaking year-long process, he first wrote out a set of charts containing pitch material, innovative piano sounds, dynamics, rhythms, tempos, and textures. Then he tossed coins to determine the selection of items from the charts, while basing the piece's form on a series of proportions similar to those he had used in *First Construction in Metal*. The result was a constantly changing music marked by irregular rhythms, abrupt dynamic changes, and a fractured, pointillistic texture that allowed the sounds to float freely.

As Cage explained to Boulez, who was then composing his rigorously serial *Structures I*, "By making moves on the charts I freed myself from what I had thought to be freedom, and which was only the accretion of habits and tastes." Up to this point, Cage had focused on readjusting only the composer's and listener's relationship to sounds; musicians were still asked to perform a score as written. Even *4' 33"* is prescriptive to a considerable degree: the performer can, in principle, do anything during the piece *except* make a sound. But Cage didn't stop there. Still more radical, and the ultimate cause of his break with Boulez, was his introduction of elements of Indeterminacy into performance.

Example 10.5: *John Cage,* Music of Changes, *Book I, mm. 1–4*

INDETERMINATE NOTATIONS IN CAGE'S AND FELDMAN'S MUSIC

As we have seen earlier in Boulez's agitated response, Cage's use of graphic and indeterminate notations to give the performer wide latitude in shaping the work was new and unsettling. The score of *TV Köln* (TV Cologne, 1958), for example, consists of four systems of equal length, indicating the relative place-ment of a set of sounds, with the position above or below a line to be inter-preted in terms of pitch, duration, or dynamics. As explained in the score, the symbols I and O in Figure 10.3 refer to sounds made on the inside or outside of the piano; K instructs the player to use the keyboard and shows the num-ber of keys to be depressed; and A is any kind of auxiliary noise. Cage left the meaning of P undefined, perhaps to demonstrate the limits of the composer's control. The duration of *TV Köln* varies depending on how long the performer makes each system last. While available recordings range from one and a half to four minutes, it is possible to make the piece much longer, as with the ongo-ing performance in a German church of Cage's *Organ²/ASLSP—As SLow aS Pos-sible* (1987), which is intended to last 639 years.

Boulez was troubled by Cage's abrogation of control in such scores, which illustrated what he called the "seduction of graphism alone." Composers, Boulez complained, "are musicians and not painters, and pictures are not made to be performed." Ironically, a large number of Cage's scores have been

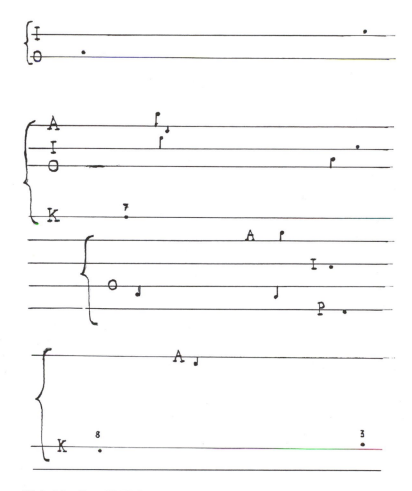

Figure 10.3: *John Cage*, TV Köln

valued as artworks in themselves and can be found in museum collections around the world. Many composers explored new forms of notation in the late 1950s and 1960s as ways to stimulate performers and themselves to reconceptualize the act of making music. In 1969 Cage edited *Notations*, a collection featuring excerpts from pieces by hundreds of composers, ranging from fairly traditional scores to maps, diagrams, charts, written directions, and completely abstract drawings.

Morton Feldman (1926–1987), a major figure in Cage's circle in New York, used indeterminate graphic notation in a series of works composed in the early 1950s. The score of *Intersection 3* (1953), for example, consists of three systems of boxes representing low, middle, and high registers, with each box equivalent to a metronome marking of 176; the numbers within the boxes indicate how many notes are to be played (Fig. 10.4). As Feldman's directions specify: "The player is free to choose any dynamic and to make any rhythmic entrances on or within a given situation." Feldman used graphic scores to give the performer leeway in realizing the details of the piece while maintaining control over its overall shape. Contrasting the varying degrees of Indeterminacy he and Cage allowed in their works, Feldman quipped that Cage "opened up the door and got pneumonia," while he "just opened up a window and got a cold."

Although Feldman returned to more conventional notation by the end of the 1950s, inspiration from the visual arts remained central to his works. One of Feldman's most famous works is *Rothko Chapel* (1971), composed for the dedication of a chapel in Houston that featured a series of dark-hued canvases by the American Abstract Expressionist painter Mark Rothko, completed shortly before his suicide. Written for chorus, soprano, alto, viola, celesta, and percussion, the half-hour work captures the experience of both the paintings and the remarkable skylit space that houses them. In the 1970s Feldman began developing musical analogs to the subtle repetitive patterns, symmetries, and progressions characteristic of Middle Eastern carpets and Jasper Johns's contemporary series of crosshatch paintings. *Why Patterns* (1978), for flute, piano, and glockenspiel, features shifting juxtapositions of the three instruments moving softly in unsynchronized layers through slowly evolving patterns. To Feldman, the organic, mathematical precision of Johns's art brought to mind Cage's dictum of "imitating nature in the manner of its operation."

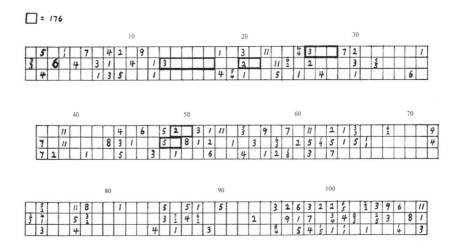

Figure 10.4: *Morton Feldman,* Intersection 3

CONTROLLING CHANCE

Obviously, a great deal is left to the performer's judgment in works such as *Intersection 3* and *TV Köln*. For example, the three notes on the keyboard that conclude *TV Köln* and the two groups of three pitches in the middle register that launch *Intersection 3* could both be C-major triads. In his "Experimental Music" essay, Cage indicated a certain openness to traditional musical sounds in his pieces: "It goes without saying that dissonances and noises are welcome in this new music. But so is the dominant seventh chord if it happens to put in an appearance" (SR 173:1304; 7/4:34). But in Cage's circle there was a clear preference for a performance practice that would exclude such recollections of "the literature and 'traditions' of the art." In David Tudor's recorded performance of *Intersection 3*, of which Cage was the dedicatee, there are no triads at any point.

There was, in fact, a surprisingly authoritarian element in Cage's thought. The kind of freedom that interested him depended on a strict renunciation of the self, and thus, to his way of thinking, was not for everybody:

> When this freedom is given to people who are not disciplined and who do not start—as I've said in many of my writings—from zero (by zero I mean the absence of likes and dislikes), who are not, in other words, changed individuals, but who remain with particular likes and dislikes, then of course, the giving of freedom is of no interest whatsoever.

Cage's complaint that the audience at the first performance of *4' 33"* "didn't know how to listen" suggests that he believed that there were correct and incorrect ways to hear the piece. Are there also correct and incorrect ways to perform it? It is not clear how Cage would feel about performances of *4' 33"* today that include the pattering sounds of people texting, the blare of stereos from passing cars, or the eruptions of cell phone ringtones. Indeed, Cage's earlier idea for a "Tacet" piece called *Silent Prayer* suggests that there was an element of actively silencing music and sounds that troubled him. In a surprising inversion of Satie's notion of Furniture Music (see Chapter 6), Cage imagined selling *Silent Prayer*, which was to be a silent piece the standard three- to four-minute length of a popular song, to the Muzak Corporation to interrupt the constant stream of music filling up elevators and public spaces.

The rich and contradictory legacy of *4' 33"* includes official and unofficial cover versions by musicians including Frank Zappa and John Lennon and Yoko Ono; the Cage estate has successfully pursued legal action against groups that have violated the copyright by placing silent tracks on their recordings. In 2010 a sanctioned recording of Cage's *4' 33"* by a group of pop all-stars (under the name Cage Against the Machine) reached number 21 on the British pop charts. Recalling Cage's censorious intent with his *Silent Prayer*, their unfilled goal was to seize away the number 1 spot from the winner of the *X-Factor* talent search.

<h2 style="text-align:center">BECOMING FLUENT WITH LIFE</h2>

Notwithstanding his attempt to control certain aspects of the musical experience, Cage espoused throughout his life a kind of apolitical passive resistance. This stance may have been linked to the Cold War and McCarthyism, wherein silence seemed the only way to make an alternative space for his anarchic political beliefs and homosexual identity. Works like *TV Köln* and *4'33"* emphasize the performers' and listeners' actions much more than the composer's intentions. Cage attributed his interest in breaking down the boundaries between art and life to Asian philosophy: "Our business in living is to become fluent with the life we are living, and art can help this." In a lecture from 1958, published the following year in *Die Reihe*, he took issue with the typical concert situation in which an audience member is put in the position of having to figure out what the composer is trying to say through music:

> I said that since the sounds were just sounds this gave people hearing them the chance to be people, centered within themselves where they actually are . . . I said that the purpose of this purposeless music would be achieved if people learned to listen; that when they listened they might discover they preferred the sounds of everyday life to the ones they would presently hear in the musical program; that that was alright as far as I was concerned.

Inspired by Cage, a number of composers, performers, and artists pursued the notion of merging art and life. Many were associated with the loosely organized interdisciplinary movement known as Fluxus, founded in 1962. Drawing on both Cage and the Dadaists (see Chapter 5), Fluxus emphasized communally produced "happenings" rather than individual works of art. An important figure in the New York scene was Yoko Ono (b. 1933), who created conceptual art and experimental films and also offered her loft as a Fluxus meeting place and performance space. Fluxus activities also flourished in Cologne, West Germany, thanks to the artist Mary Bauermeister (b. 1934), who brought Cage and his circle together with European and Asian avant-garde artists, including Stockhausen, whom Bauermeister would marry in 1967. After attending a performance at Bauermeister's house of *Poem for Chairs, Tables, and Benches* (1960) by the American composer La Monte Young (see Chapter 14), David Tudor described it to Cage as "a live friction sound piece" that used "1 piano stool, 1 scrub-brush on wall, 1 piece of rubber-tire on wet glass, 1 wooden stool in corridor, and 1 wooden chair upstairs."

The American composer Pauline Oliveros (b. 1932) has been a leader in the use of improvisation and Indeterminacy to connect music-making with meditative practices, ritual, and theater. Many of her scores, such as *Traveling Companions* for percussion ensemble and dancers (1980; see Anthology 18), include graphic elements that shape the sounds or indicate location and movements for the participants. The piece is designed to allow the performers, in close interaction with the audience, to model different possibilities for social interactions ranging from cooperation to conflict.

After her early involvement with the San Francisco Tape Music Center, Oliveros developed the idea of "deep listening" whereby musicians and listeners can focus on a profound experience of sound. She traces the idea back to her earliest childhood in Texas, where the noises of insects and animals "seemed to float in the air." Her participatory work *Sonic Meditations* (1971) consists solely of written directions for making, imagining, listening to, and remembering sound. The purely textual score of *Sonic Meditation I* indicates the connection of "deep listening" to the experience of our living and breathing bodies:

> Any number of persons sit in a circle facing the center. Illuminate the space with dim blue light. Begin by simply observing your own breathing. Always be an observer. Gradually allow your breathing to become audible. Then gradually introduce your voice. Allow your vocal cords to vibrate in any mode which occurs naturally. Allow the intensity to increase very slowly. Continue as long as possible naturally, and until all others are quiet, always observing your own breath cycle.

The performance artist and composer Meredith Monk (b. 1942) has similarly created a large number of works that combine extended vocal techniques with theater, dance, and multimedia. Monk has described works like *Turtle Dreams* (1983), for four voices and four organs, as offering liberating occasions for exploring different models of human interaction, "as a sort of microcosm of what could be possible. John Cage always used to say that what art can provide is a behavioral alternative in nonmanipulative situations." The way such performance art by Monk and others engages the whole person—their voice, body, gestures, and character—in the creation of a work is a powerful realization of Cage's vision of music-making as a way of becoming "fluent with life."

Given how strongly Boulez criticized Cage's exploration of chance procedures in the early 1950s, it may come as a surprise that by the end of the decade he,

Stockhausen, and other European serialist composers had come to embrace Indeterminacy as an important element of their work. After first meeting Boulez in Paris in 1949, Cage made several visits to Europe that brought him wide attention, including a course he taught at Darmstadt in the summer of 1958, filling in for Boulez on short notice. Although Boulez critiqued Cage in his 1957 essay *Alea*, he also admitted the limits of Integral Serialism and the impossibility of achieving complete control:

> One seeks desperately to dominate the material by arduous, sustained, vigilant effort, but chance desperately subsists, introducing itself through a thousand crevices that it is impossible to stop up. . . . "And it is good that way!" Nevertheless, will the composer's ultimate ruse be to *absorb* this chance? Why not tame this potential and force it to an account of itself, an accounting?

Ultimately, Boulez came to see his experiments in using Integral Serialism to control all the musical parameters as futile; they had merely proven his inability to control anything. He recognized that the "effects of chaos" he had created lasted "only for a limited time," because the listener's perception could not "be disoriented for too long without the interest collapsing completely." Boulez began to incorporate indeterminate elements in works like the Piano Sonata No. 3 (1957), which allows the performer to chart multiple pathways through its various sections. Likewise, Stockhausen's Piano Piece XI (1956) is structured like a mobile, with 19 sections arrayed on a large sheet of paper that the pianist can play in any order.

According to the Italian novelist and critic Umberto Eco, such "open" works charted a middle course between Serialism and Indeterminacy by inviting the performer to complete the composer's work within a "given *field of relations*." As Eco wrote in 1962, "The author is the one who proposed a number of possibilities that had already been rationally organized, oriented, and endowed with specifications for proper development" (SR 212:1503–1504; 7/43:233–234). As we will see, the question of how to work with the new possibilities of sound opened up by the trajectories of order and chance has occupied musicians working in many styles ever since.

FOR FURTHER READING

Boulez, Pierre, "Speaking, Playing, Singing: *Pierrot lunaire* and *Le marteau sans maître*," in *Orientations: Collected Writings*, edited by Jean-Jacques Nattiez, translated by Martin Cooper, 330–343 (Cambridge, MA: Harvard University Press, 1986)

Carroll, Mark, *Music and Ideology in Cold War Europe* (Cambridge: Cambridge University Press, 2003)

Kahn, Douglas, "John Cage: Silence and Silencing," *Musical Quarterly* 81, no. 4 (1997): 556–598

Katz, Jonathan D., "John Cage's Queer Silence; or, How to Avoid Making Matters Worse," in *Writings through John Cage's Music, Poetry, and Art*, edited by David Bernstein and Christopher Hatch, 41–61 (Chicago: University of Chicago Press, 2001)

Koblyakov, Lev, *Pierre Boulez: A World of Harmony* (Langhorne, PA: Harwood, 1993)

Lewis, George E., "Improvised Music After 1950: Afrological and Eurological Perspectives," in *Audio Culture: Readings in Modern Music*, edited by Christoph Cox and Daniel Warner, 272–284 (New York: Continuum, 2006)

Mockus, Martha, *Sounding Out: Pauline Oliveros and Lesbian Musicality* (New York: Routledge, 2008)

Morgan, Robert P., "On the Analysis of Recent Music," *Critical Inquiry* 4, no. 1 (1977): 33–53

Nicholls, David, ed., *The Cambridge Companion to Cage* (Cambridge: Cambridge University Press, 2002)

Strauss, Joseph, *Twelve-Tone Music in America* (Cambridge: Cambridge University Press, 2009)

CHAPTER ELEVEN

Electronic Music from the Cold War to the Computer Age

Music that is to some degree "electronic" is now everywhere around us. Many musical and technological innovations that we have come to take for granted, such as the sonic spatialization of home theater systems, music-making software on home computers and smartphones, and even the notion of sound as a separate category from pitch or rhythm, emerged in the decades after World War II. Indeed, we are so inundated with electronically produced music today that it can be surprising to consider the excitement and anxiety that first greeted the new technologies.

In the 1955 issue of *Die Reihe*, which was focused exclusively on electronic music, the German musicologist H. H. Stuckenschmidt proclaimed the dawn of a new musical epoch through which, "the natural is abolished. Vocal and instrumental forms are eliminated, tonality, functional harmony, simple polyphony and symmetrical rhythm are suspended." In aligning music with contemporary science and technology, he argued, composers had broken free from the constraints of nature and history: "We are astonished, and not without pride, to have before us an art totally controlled by the spirit of man, in a way not previously imaginable."

Stuckenschmidt might have had in mind works like *Electronic Study No. 2* (1954) by Karlheinz Stockhausen (1928–2007), which featured previously unheard timbres and an electronically generated scale of 81 pitches that had no octaves or other familiar intervals. The five sections of the piece are differentiated not by modulation or new themes but by the density of the textures and the dynamic contours, or "envelopes," of the individual sounds. To represent his music in the first electronic score to be published, Stockhausen developed an equally innovative system of notation (Fig. 11.1): the numbers on the center line indicate the precise durations of the sounds, measured on the magnetic recording tape, with 76.2 centimeters equaling 1 second. The lower system shows the dynamic range measured in decibels, while the upper system indicates the frequency range of the individual sonorities.

In 1958 Stockhausen described the necessity of breaking with music from the first half of the twentieth century not only in terms of harmonic and melodic structure, but even in regard to the sounds themselves: "We realized that the historical development of instruments was closely linked with a music which was no longer ours." Born near Cologne, Germany, Stockhausen was a 17-year-old orphan when World War II ended. Intending to become a teacher like his father, he studied music education, piano, and composition. In 1951 he attended a summer course at Darmstadt, followed by a year in Paris studying with Olivier Messiaen (see Chapter 10), where he first encountered new techniques for using electronic technology in composition. Returning to Cologne in 1953, he took a job at the recently established Studio for Electronic Music, sponsored by Radio Cologne, and quickly emerged as one of the leading composers and theorists of the European avant-garde.

The new technologies soon were heard in rock and jazz, as well as in film soundtracks, embedding electronic music in the popular imagination more

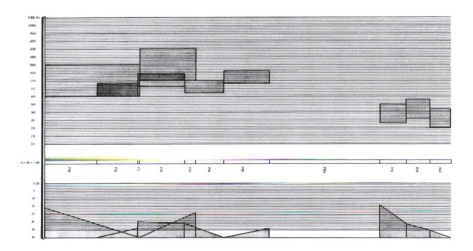

Figure 11.1: *Karlheinz Stockhausen,* Electronic Study No. 2, *p. 1*

deeply than any other contemporary form of composition. DJs and producers today cite Stockhausen and other figures discussed later as important influences, but Stockhausen was shaping popular music as early as 1967, when he appeared in the collage of figures on the cover of the Beatles' landmark album *Sgt. Pepper's Lonely Hearts Club Band* (see p. 221). Both the strangeness of his music and its cultural cachet are evident in an ironic passage from Thomas Pynchon's 1966 novel *The Crying of Lot 49* that takes place in a fictional bar in Los Angeles frequented by workers from a nearby electronics corporation:

> A sudden chorus of whoops and yibbles burst from a kind of juke box at the far end of the room. "That's by Stockhausen," the hip graybeard informed her, "the early crowd tends to dig your Radio Cologne sound. Later on we really swing. We're the only bar in the area, you know, that has a strictly electronic music policy. Come on around Saturdays, starting midnight we have your Sinewave Session, that's a live get-together, fellas come in just to jam from all over the state."

The profound newness of these forms of music-making, with their own tools, techniques, and even national characters, is evident in the range of terms that emerged to describe them. The term *Elektronische Musik* originally referred to developments centered in Germany that allowed sounds to be produced and modified by electronic devices. As we discuss later, composers in France developed a different approach, called *musique concrète* (concrete, tangible, or material music), based on manipulating preexisting sounds recorded on tape. Meanwhile, composers in the United States used the term *tape music* to refer to both recorded and electronically produced sounds. In the late 1950s musicians and sound engineers began developing programs and devices for digitally producing and manipulating sound under the general heading *computer music*. In this book we will use *electronic music* as an umbrella term, although some musicians prefer to describe any music that depends on electronics and loudspeakers for composition and performance as *electroacoustic music*.

MUSIC, SCIENCE, AND TECHNOLOGY
IN THE COLD WAR

During the Cold War music became increasingly bound up with science, technology, the drive to modernize and rebuild, and the fear of being left behind. *Die Reihe* featured so many articles couched in scientific and mathematical terminology that one commentator observed, "music has evidently become the province of mathematicians and engineers as well as of composers." Stuckenschmidt did, in fact, cite an essay by the Nobel Prize–winning physicist Werner Heisenberg that appeared in a collection titled *Arts in the Technical Age* (1954). In contrast to preceding epochs in which "mankind viewed itself in contrast to nature," Heisenberg argued that the modern world had been "so utterly transformed by mankind that everywhere—whether we are dealing with everyday appliances, consuming processed food or passing through landscapes transformed by human hands—we encounter time and again structures created by mankind; in a sense, we encounter only ourselves."

With the atomic bomb as the most vivid symbol of both the power and the danger that could result, the Cold War saw massive investments in scientific and technological research involving the military, industry, and universities. Heisenberg himself had played an important role in Nazi efforts to develop an atomic bomb, before being captured near the end of the war and put to work for the Allies. Heisenberg's moral qualms about the project, and whether he deliberately slowed down research on a bomb for the Nazis, is the subject of the play *Copenhagen* (1998) by Michael Frayn. In Chapter 14 we will discuss another physicist, J. Robert Oppenheimer, and issues connected to the origins of the bomb in the context of John Adams's opera *Doctor Atomic*.

Competition for technological supremacy took many forms. The Soviet Union activated its first nuclear power plant to provide electricity in 1953, with the United States following suit a year later. Building on the expertise of German rocket scientists, both sides developed intercontinental ballistic missiles by the late 1950s. The urgency of the "space race" was underscored when the Soviet Union launched the satellite *Sputnik* in 1957 and the first manned space flight in 1961. To assert American leadership in space, President John F. Kennedy in 1961 committed to put a man on the moon by the end of the decade, a goal that was realized with the success of the Apollo program in 1969.

Not coincidentally, music with space-age sounds and themes became popular in many different styles. Electronic music first reached the general public in such science-fiction films as *The Day the Earth Stood Still* (1951), with music by Bernard Herrmann featuring the Theremin, and *Forbidden Planet* (1956), with its path-breaking all-electronic score by Louis and Bebe Barron (discussed further later). In 1963 the British rock band The Tornados topped the charts with their song *Telstar* (1963), named for the recently launched communications satellite and featuring the distinctive vibrato of the clavioline (an electronic keyboard instrument and precursor to the synthesizer). Space travel was a theme of several albums from the 1950s and 1960s by the avant garde jazz musician Sun Ra, including *Sun Ra Visits Planet Earth*, *We Travel the Spaceways*, and *The Nubians of Plutonia*. Sun Ra even maintained that he had been transported to Saturn as a young man. This period also saw a rash of accounts of alien abductions, UFO sightings, and the alleged conspiracy to cover up a UFO crash at Roswell, New Mexico, in 1947. Electronic music composers embraced science-fiction and space elements in works like *Silver Apples of the Moon* (1967) by Morton Subotnick (b. 1933), *Alien Bog* (1967) by Pauline Oliveros (see Chapter 10), and Stockhausen's *Sternklang* (Star Sound, 1971) and *Sirius* (1977); Stockhausen claimed that the latter was the result of extraterrestrial inspiration.

Millions of listeners were introduced to electronic music by Edgard Varèse's *Poème électronique* (Electronic Poem) at the 1958 World's Fair in Brussels. The performances took place in a special pavilion built for the Philips Corporation (Fig. 11.2), with gleaming futuristic curves designed according to complex mathematical formulas by the architect Le Corbusier and composer Iannis Xenakis (see Chapter 12). After his early of productivity and notoriety (see Chapter 5), Varèse had gone through a compositional drought in the 1930s and 1940s, but he was reenergized after the war by the renewed openness to musical exploration and by the new technological tools for generating and manipulating sound. Performances of the *Poème électronique* included film images projected onto the soaring, asymmetrical walls inside the pavilion, while the "sound masses" of the music moved through the space along various "sound routes," distributed by

Figure 11.2: *Philips Pavilion, Expo 1958, Brussels*

hundreds of loudspeakers. The eight-minute piece, which combined electronically generated noises and the *musique concrète* sounds of recorded instruments and voices, loosely followed the film's episodic representation of the evolution of mankind.

Yet many were concerned that the increasing prominence of science and technology in musical life would come at the expense of expressivity, humanity, and authenticity. The cultural historian Jacques Barzun addressed these fears in a series of lectures preceding the first concerts of music created in the Columbia-Princeton Electronic Music Center at Columbia University in 1961. Anticipating a hostile response to the electronic works from the audience, he acknowledged the perception of a fundamental gap between the cultures of science and art: "Most people of artistic tastes share the widespread distrust and dislike of machinery and argue that anything pretending to be art cannot come out of a machine: art is the human product *par excellence,* and electronic music, born of intricate circuits and the oscillations of particles generated by Con Edison, is a contradiction in terms." Yet music and technology had always been closely interrelated, Barzun argued. "The moment man ceased to make music with his voice alone the art became machine-ridden. Orpheus's lyre was a machine, a symphony orchestra is a regular factory for making artificial sounds, and a piano is the most appalling contrivance of levers and wires this side of the steam engine."

The first concert in the United States to include electronic music took place in New York on October 28, 1952. The audience at the Museum of Modern Art heard two pieces for tape recorder by Vladimir Ussachevsky and Otto Luening "performed" on an empty stage, with the only sounds coming from loudspeakers. In his brief introductory remarks, the conductor Leopold Stokowski noted that "for centuries composers have been obliged to write down their ideas for music on paper, and it has always required living performers to bring these ideas to life." According to a report in *The New York Times*, Stokowski went on to predict that future composers would "work very much like painters, directly in the materials of sounds, with the assistance of devices like tape recorders."

MANIPULATING SOUND IN THE STUDIO

In earlier chapters we observed how recordings and radio influenced musical developments in the first half of the twentieth century. There were experiments in the 1920s manipulating optical film sound tracks; in the 1930s and 1940s Paul Hindemith, John Cage, Pierre Schaeffer, and others worked with phonograph records in unorthodox ways, thus anticipating DJ techniques a half-century later. Yet until the invention of magnetic recording tape in the

1930s, there were only limited possibilities for working with sounds during the recording process, and virtually none for altering the music once the recording was complete.

In the 1920s German engineers developed machines that recorded sounds magnetically on a spool of thin wire. These wire recorders were superseded in 1935 by the Magnetophone, which used a paper tape coated with magnetic particles that allowed for improved sound quality and longer recordings. This tape recorder was only one of several electronic devices originally developed for military applications that went on to be useful for music; for example, the Vocoder, which produces the machine-like voices used in pieces like the German techno band Kraftwerk's *The Robots* (1978) and much contemporary hip-hop, was developed by Bell Labs as a way of encoding secret telephone transmissions.

Several German tape recorders were brought back to the U.S. by soldiers after the war. One was given to Louis (1920–1989) and Bebe Barron (1925–2008) as a wedding gift in 1947; using it and other electronic devices, they set up a studio where, in addition to creating the *Forbidden Planet* film score, they worked closely with John Cage manipulating tape for several pieces (see Chapter 10). Another of the German recorders came into the hands of the popular singer/actor Bing Crosby, who quickly put it to use for high-fidelity rebroadcasts of his radio shows, thereby reaching different time zones without having to perform an entire show twice. Crosby provided financial backing to engineers working for Ampex, which introduced the first commercially produced tape recorder in 1948. More convenient and affordable tape formats followed in the mid-1960s, notably the eight-track tape and cassette. Magnetic tape remained the primary storage medium for analog and digital information until the 1980s; the last U.S. tape manufacturer ceased operations in 2005.

Musicians and technicians soon discovered the potential of tape recorders as versatile creative tools. In the early 1950s, for example, the guitarist Les Paul developed the first multitrack tape machine, allowing musicians to record one layer of music at a time. Dramatically improved audio and video technology also made their way into the home. After a period of competing formats, the long-playing (LP) record came to the fore in the late 1940s, and stereo LPs were common by the early 1960s. Television ownership became widespread in the United States in the 1950s, challenging the dominance of radio as a medium for musical performance; within a decade, color TVs could be found in homes across the country.

Electronic music required new spaces and institutions to bring people and technologies together. The earliest electronic music studios arose in Europe as branches of state-owned radio stations, which had long been exploring the creative use of sound in radio dramas. In 1948 Pierre Schaeffer (see p. 222) established the first electroacoustic music studio in Paris under the auspices of Radiodiffusion-Télévision Française. The 1950s saw the founding of the Studio for Electronic Music in Cologne (Fig. 11.3) and the BBC Radiophonic Workshop in London, which provided sound effects and music for radio and television programs. North American studios were supported primarily by research universities, contributing to the "hard science" connotations of the genre while connecting composers with computer science and engineering departments. The Tape Music Studio at Columbia University led the way in 1951, becoming the Columbia-Princeton Electronic Music Center in 1959.

Figure 11.3: *Stockhausen in the West German Radio Studio for Electronic Music in Cologne. Stockhausen began working in the studio in 1953 and became its director ten years later.*

LIVE ELECTRONIC MUSIC

Much early electronic music existed only on magnetic tape, produced through a painstaking process of creating and layering sounds that was not possible to re-create in real time. A performance could consist of broadcasting the tape on the radio or playing it over loudspeakers in a concert hall. As the medium evolved, however, composers reintroduced aspects of live performance by combining the tape part with musicians on stage or incorporating dancers, projections, or other multimedia content.

The San Francisco Tape Music Center, a private studio founded in 1962, had strong connections to the West Coast counterculture and presented performances accompanied by elaborate light shows, dances, and costumes, and in some cases for audiences under the influence of hallucinogenic drugs (see Chapter 14). In the mid-1960s a group of musicians in Rome known as Musica Elettronica Viva (Live Electronic Music) used improvisational electronics designed to allow participation by untrained members of the audience. In *Soundpool* (1969), the electronic sounds produced by the ensemble were supported by masses of people "singing, chanting, droning, drumming on chairs, tables, [and] walls." Stockhausen had also used live electronic manipulation of sounds produced by acoustic instruments and voices to create complex textural effects, as in his *Mikrophonie II* for chorus (1964) and *Mixtur* for orchestra (1964), which combined the live sounds with sine waves processed through the bell-like distortions of an electronic circuit called a ring modulator.

In addition to his compositions for traditional instruments and a few purely electronic works, Mario Davidovsky (b. 1934) is best known for his twelve *Synchronisms* for instruments and electronic sounds (1962–2006), including works for solo instruments, chamber ensembles, and orchestra. *Synchronisms No. 6* for piano and electronic sounds (1970; see Anthology 19) demonstrates the rich possibilities opened up by combining electronic sounds with acoustic music. Born in Argentina, Davidovsky studied violin and composition there until he made his first trip to the United States in the summer of 1958 to work with Aaron Copland and Milton Babbitt. His aptitude for electronic music led to his immigration in 1960, when he become associate director of the new Columbia-Princeton Electronic Music Center in New York. There Davidovsky assisted Varèse on his electronic works and collaborated with other electronic music pioneers. Davidovsky went on to become an important composer and teacher, spending many years at Columbia, Harvard, and several other universities and conservatories.

In the early years of electronic music, Davidovsky missed the intensity and variability that a live musician can bring to a performance on stage. But when he began composing his series of *Synchronisms*, few models were available to demonstrate practical or effective interactions between recorded electronic sounds and live instruments. While the earlier works in the series were characterized by a loose relationship between the acoustic and tape parts, with *Synchronisms No. 6* Davidovsky succeeded in creating what sounds like a new hybrid electroacoustic instrument, due to the intricate counterpoint between the synthesized sounds on tape and the live performance of the piano. In a program note included with the score, Davidovsky wrote: "the electronic sounds in many instances modulate the acoustical characteristics of the piano, by affecting its decay and attack characteristics. The electronic segment should perhaps not be viewed as an independent polyphonic line, but rather as if it were inlaid into the piano part." Some passages foreground sharp contrasts in timbre between the two media, while others remind us that the piano, too, is a technological device—in Barzun's words, a "contrivance of levers and wires."

Such tape-and-instrument pieces challenged live performers, who had to adapt to the precise and unchanging recorded part. As we will see, it was only with the advent of digital interfaces in the 1980s that truly interactive live electronic music became possible.

RECORDING STUDIOS

Paralleling the establishment of studios for avant-garde electronic music, record companies large and small began setting up studios and creating record labels, including the two Memphis studios, Sun (1953), which specialized in early rock and roll, and the rhythm-and-blues Stax (1957). Thanks to the efforts of producers, conductors, and performers like Mitch Miller, Les Baxter, and Les Paul, recordings in the 1950s began to reflect careful attention to the sounds of the instruments, and included the use of artificial reverberation and striking sound effects. In the decades that followed, recording techniques became crucial in defining styles like the "Nashville sound" and the "Motown sound." Rock music recordings began with the goal of capturing the energy and immediacy of live performances, but before long groups like the Beach Boys (with their 1966 *Pet Sounds*) reintroduced elaborate production techniques and the sounds of electronic music and *musique concrète*.

New technologies and new ways of thinking about sound were particularly important for *Sgt. Pepper's Lonely Hearts Club Band*, which the Beatles recorded in 1967. The album was the product of months of intensive work in the studio, with both the recording engineer and the producer integrally involved in the creative process. Certain elements of production, including the placement of sounds in the stereo field created by the left and right speakers, modifications to the timbres of the instruments and voices, and the use of reverberation and other effects, became central to the conception of the Beatles' songs.

Studio techniques became increasingly important for the Beatles after they stopped touring regularly in 1966. Two years earlier the Canadian pianist

Glenn Gould had likewise given up his concert career and devoted himself solely to recording the music of Bach and others. Gould—who edited multiple takes of each passage to produce his final recordings—created a furor when he predicted that "the public concert as we know it today would no longer exist," soon to be replaced entirely by recorded performances transmitted by electronic media.

MUSIQUE CONCRÈTE

The musician's ability to record and physically manipulate a sound on magnetic tape is fundamental to the idea of *musique concrète*. The term was coined in 1948 by Pierre Schaeffer (1910–1995), one of a group of French composers who discovered that, by using a razor blade and splicing tape, it was possible to isolate a segment of a sound from a magnetic tape or splice together a collage of different sounds. Other manipulations included adjusting the speed of the tape, playing it backward, passing the sound through filters and echo chambers, and creating tape loops by joining the ends of short segments of tape together, thus allowing a potentially endless series of repetitions. (Figure 11.3 on p. 219 shows Stockhausen working with two tape loops running on the recorders behind him.) We will return in Chapter 14 to the central importance of tape loops for the development of Minimalism, including works like Steve Reich's *Violin Phase*. Composers could also mix synthesized and *concrète* sounds, as in Varèse's *Poème électronique* and Stockhausen's *Gesang der Jünglinge* (Song of the Youths, 1956), which combined a boy's singing voice with electronically generated material.

Up to this point, with few exceptions (sound effects in opera, the experiments of the Futurists, and Satie's noise effects in *Parade*), composers differentiated between "musical" sounds produced by voices or instruments and the "noises" of the real world. Schaeffer rejected this distinction, explaining that "we have called our music 'concrète' because it is constituted from pre-existing elements taken from whatever sound material, be it noise or conventional music, and then composed by working directly with the material." Today it is common for digitally sampled natural or man-made sounds to be used in many forms of popular music, film scores, and advertising.

The earliest examples of *musique concrète* used turntables, mixers, microphones, filters, and other equipment widely available at radio stations in the late 1940s. Schaeffer's *Etude aux chemins de fer* (Railway Study, 1948) is created in its entirety from the sounds of a steam train—wheels on the track, whistles, pistons, and men shoveling coal. The first section of the piece can be diagrammed as shown in Figure 11.4.

Section 1

00:00	Whistle, squeak, toot
00:04	Chugging with crescendo;
	gradual addition of soft metallic squeal
00:16	Wheels on tracks: slow and unmeasured, with reverb
00:22	Ostinato 1: Rhythmic track noise
00:27	Ostinato 2: Lower-pitched rhythmic track noise
00:34	Ostinato 1
00:38	Ostinato 2 and 1 combined
00:45	Ostinato 3: Syncopated bangs
00:51	Silence

Figure 11.4: *Chart of the first section of Pierre Schaeffer's* Etude aux chemins de fer

NOTATING, ANALYZING, AND LISTENING TO ELECTRONIC MUSIC

This admittedly subjective attempt to chart the character and succession of the sounds in Schaeffer's piece highlights a challenge posed by much electronic music: how to represent and analyze works that lack notation. Of course, much of the music played around the world is not notated, but in most cases the sounds are based on systems of melody, harmony, and rhythm that can be represented, albeit imperfectly, in musical notation. For both *musique concrète* and synthesized music, however, traditional forms of notation cannot capture crucial elements of timbre, texture, and spatial location.

As we saw with Stockhausen's *Electronic Study No. 2*, some composers attempted to notate aspects of their electronic pieces, either as part of the compositional process or, as in the case of Davidovsky's *Synchronisms*, to aid a performer who is interacting with a recorded part. Analysts have also employed spectrograms and other forms of visualization to represent changing frequencies, amplitudes, and other features in great detail. Computer music programs such as Pro Tools, Logic, and Reason, and the new types of graphic interfaces that we will encounter in Chapter 12, provide visual representations of the sound waves and textures over the course of a piece that can be useful for both musicians and analysts.

The electronic music analyst, like any listener, must make sense of the music as it unfolds, noting areas of similarity and contrast, formal features, points of arrival, and expressive content and meaning. In listening to a piece like Pink Floyd's song "Money" (1973), with its ostinato of cash register noises, the words make clear that we are intended to think of coins and their role in society. Schaeffer, by contrast, described *musique concrète* as liberating sounds from their real-world associations. Repetition was the basic tool he used in transforming sounds into "sound objects," distinguished by texture and timbre. For Schaeffer, a work qualified as *musique concrète* only if the composer succeeded in extracting the "sound material" from its original "dramatic or musical context."

The attempt to divorce sounds from their traditional contexts or meanings recalls the strand of postwar Modernist thought that sought separation from artistic conventions, everyday life, mass culture, and commercial or political function (see Chapter 10). Schaeffer and his colleague Pierre Henry demonstrated that with enough editing it was possible to disguise the origins of a sound; however, the process of "extraction" is rarely complete. Although in *Etude aux chemins de fer* the sounds of the steam train do become increasingly abstract, the work preserves the overall narrative shape of a railway journey: starting off at the station, gaining speed, passing through different spaces, and heading off into the distance.

The constant tension between where a sound comes from and what has been done with it is a distinctive feature of *musique concrète*. This is especially true of pieces that include the singing or speaking voice, such as *Thema: Omaggio a Joyce* (Theme: Homage to Joyce, 1958) by Luciano Berio (1925–2003; we will discuss him further in Chapter 13). This work takes all of its sounds from the voice of Berio's wife at the time, the singer Cathy Berberian, reading an excerpt from James Joyce's novel *Ulysses*. Joyce himself treated the words musically; that is, he was less interested in their meanings than in the sounds and feelings they evoked. Berio's piece contains passages where Berberian's voice is nearly unchanged and the text is completely intelligible; in other sections it is so cut up and modified that words dissolve into phonemes and the sounds are hardly recognizable as a human voice. The rich assonances in Joyce's words "A husky fifenote blew. Blew. Blue bloom is on the Gold pinnacled hair" multiply through repetitions and manipulations into a trilling sound like birdsong. In contrast to this emphasis on processes of abstraction in early *musique concrète*, we will see in Chapter 13 a growing interest in reattaching recorded sounds to their origins and histories.

SYNTHESIZERS

While composers working in the tradition of *musique concrète* started with pre-existing sounds from the real world, synthesizers generated sounds electronically. The Canadian composer and engineer Hugh Le Caine is credited with creating the first programmable synthesizer, the Electronic Sackbut, in 1945. A decade later the Soviet inventor Yevgeniy Murzin developed a synthesizer that used photo-optic technology; he named it the ANS synthesizer in honor of the Russian composer Aleksandr Nikolayevich Skryabin (see Chapter 3). The Cold War context of the invention is clear in its characterization by a Soviet composer as "a revolutionary invention, worthy of its century, the century of Sputnik and flights to the cosmos." Another important early synthesizer was the RCA Mark I, developed in 1956 by RCA engineers as both a tool for acoustical research and a musical instrument. The device, the second version of which (the Mark II) became the basis of the Columbia-Princeton Center in 1959, allowed precise control over all aspects of a sound, though only through a laborious programming process that involved punching holes in a 15-inch-wide paper tape.

In its most basic form, a synthesizer is a collection of electronic modules that make it possible to create a sound from scratch. Figure 11.5 shows one version of the 100 Series synthesizers, produced starting in 1963 by the musician and engineer Donald Buchla. A modular synthesizer such as this is an assemblage of various electronic circuits, each with its own function: an oscillator produces a sound wave; filters modify the timbre by removing or emphasizing parts of the harmonic spectrum; an envelope generator controls the dynamic shape and duration; and amplifiers determine the overall volume and spatial location of the sounds produced by loudspeakers. In early synthesizers, these and other components were patched together by means of cords. To produce a single complex sound required considerable time and skill, as well as a web of patch cords. A composition had to be built up in layers or segments by recording a passage

Figure 11.5: *Buchla synthesizer, 100 series, ca. 1963*

with the newly created sound onto tape, and then starting the process all over again to create a different patch for the next sound.

The first commercially produced synthesizers, which came onto the market in the early 1960s, were developed by close partnerships of engineers and composers (Robert Moog worked with Herb Deutsch and Donald Buchla with Morton Subotnick). Early commercial synthesizers were large, expensive modular systems designed for electronic music studios. They were extremely flexible but very complex to operate, requiring a room full of tape recorders and other equipment to piece together a composition. Many were also monophonic, meaning that only a single note could be played at any one time.

CONTROLLING THE PARAMETERS OF A SOUND

The synthesizer's ability to control each separate aspect of the sound was closely related to the development of Integral Serialism, in which the twelve-tone method determined every "parameter" of the music, including pitch, duration, articulation, and dynamics (see Chapter 10). The American composer Milton Babbitt was not only one of the earliest Integral Serialists, he was also one of the first composers to work intensively with the RCA Mark II. His *Philomel* (1964), for live soprano and tape, was written for Bethany Beardslee, whose voice is included on the tape along with the synthesized sounds. Both the voice and the tape part are precisely notated, reflecting Babbitt's interest in the synthesizer's ability to give the composer direct control over every detail of the performance. Based on a poem by John Hollander, *Philomel* uses the fragmentation and reconstruction of the voice, enmeshed in a tangled forest of electronic sounds, to retell the myth from Ovid's *Metamorphoses* of a brutalized woman who is transformed into a nightingale.

Stockhausen's *Electronic Study No. 2* had already exemplified the ideal of coordinating all aspects of a work by means of a single principle: he defined five harmonies, each made up of five frequencies, which he then used to construct the piece's five contrasting sections. With connections to the ideas of Henry Cowell and Joseph Schillinger (see Chapter 7), Stockhausen's essay "The Concept of Unity in Electronic Music" (1962) proposed a scientific basis for this approach by relating every musical parameter to the regular oscillation of a sound wave: "One must proceed from a basic concept of a *single, unified musical time*; and the different perceptual categories, such as color, harmony and melody, meter and rhythm, dynamics, and 'form,' must be regarded as corresponding to the different components of this unified time" (SR 182:1369–1370; 7/13:99–100). Thus pitch is determined by the fundamental frequency, such as A-440 (cycles per second), while timbre is produced by the relative strength of the overtones in the harmonic series at much faster speeds of vibration: A-880, E-1320, A-1760, C♯-2200, and so on. Rhythm and meter act as much slower cycles, while the large-scale structural points of the form occur on the slowest cycle.

Stockhausen explored analogies among harmony, timbre, and rhythm in pieces of electronic music, such as his *Kontakte* (Contacts, 1960), as well as in several instrumental works. In his massive *Gruppen* (Groups, 1957) for three orchestras and three conductors, he used the ratios between the frequencies of the overtones of a fundamental note to create different rhythmic subdivisions of a time span that could be layered on top of one another. This attention to overall effects and sound masses forecasts trends we will explore in Chapter 12.

SYNTHESIZERS AND TRADITIONAL MUSIC-MAKING

Whether synthesizers should be outfitted with conventional keyboards was a point of contention in the instruments' early years. Some felt that a keyboard would allow for standard tuning, integration with other instruments, and application of established keyboard performance techniques; others feared that the synthesizer's flexibility and distinctiveness would be sacrificed. A parallel debate concerned the use of synthesizers to duplicate the sounds of conventional instruments.

Morton Subotnick's *The Wild Bull* (1968) was created on the Buchla synthesizer, which, as can be seen in Figure 11.5, did not have a traditional keyboard. While some of the synthesized sounds recall a trumpet, a drum, or a bull's bellow, Subotnick was chiefly interested in creating new sound worlds. To that end, he emphasized the electronic origins of the sounds, using rapidly transforming timbres and gliding pitches not limited to conventional tuning. One of the most innovative aspects of *The Wild Bull* has since become so commonplace that it is easy to overlook: Commissioned by the Nonesuch record label, the piece was specifically intended to be "performed" on a home stereo over loudspeakers or headphones. Even its two-part form and overall length were determined by the capacity of a two-sided LP record. The popular success of Subotnick's piece can be attributed to its futuristic aspects, as well as to the way it reconnects with traditional compositional techniques. It begins, for example, with an amorphous passage, functioning like a slow introduction, that leads into a section featuring a developmental theme over a percussive accompaniment, with a strong pulse and clearly defined bass line.

A landmark in the history of the synthesizer and electronic music was the release of *Switched-On Bach* (1968), featuring well-known keyboard and orchestral works by J. S. Bach realized electronically by Wendy Carlos, who used a modular Moog system outfitted with a keyboard. Carlos's album was the first platinum-selling classical record and remained on *Billboard*'s Top 40 list for several months. As with its distinctive cover art—which depicted an eighteenth-century drawing room, someone dressed as Bach, and a Moog synthesizer—the point of the music was to show that the new sounds of the synthesizer could be accommodated to traditional musical styles and instrumental technique. In the liner notes, Moog himself wrote of Carlos's achievement as showing "that the medium of electronic music is eminently suited to the realization of much traditional music, and in doing so [Carlos] has firmly brought the electronic medium into the historical mainstream of music. This album is the most stunning breakthrough in electronic music to date."

The success of *Switched-On Bach* spawned similar projects using synthesizers to "update" the music of other composers and repertoires. It also brought the instrument to the attention of rock and jazz musicians, who began using synthesizers in the recording studio and in performance (Fig. 11.6). All of this suddenly created a market for the new instruments, and manufacturers responded to the demand by producing smaller synthesizers that sacrificed flexibility of programming for polyphonic capability and ease of use in live performance.

COMPUTER MUSIC

Both public and private investment in computer research accelerated during the Cold War. The first large-scale computer systems were developed to calculate ballistic missile trajectories and the design of nuclear weapons. But the technology was soon adapted to a wide range of nonmilitary applications, accelerating with the inventions of the transistor (1947) and microchip (1959). IBM

Figure 11.6: Keith Emerson performs on a large Moog synthesizer with Emerson, Lake & Palmer at the San Francisco Civic Center (1974)

produced the first computer for the business market in 1955; the user-friendly BASIC programming language was introduced in 1964.

In 1957 the engineer and musician Max Matthews, working at Bell Labs (a branch of AT&T), pioneered a programming language for creating sounds digitally and then converting the information into an analog signal that could be amplified and sent to a loudspeaker. By 1961 he had programmed a computer to sing "Daisy Bell," later immortalized in Stanley Kubrick's film *2001: A Space Odyssey* (1968) during the "death" scene of HAL, the spaceship's murderous computer. Several other computer music systems were developed by university-based composers, including FM (frequency modulation) synthesis, introduced in the 1970s by John Chowning at Stanford. Soon Yamaha and other major corporations began to take an interest in computer music. Industrial Light and Magic, a special effects company founded in 1975 by film director George Lucas, also became a major force in both digital sound and animation.

Pierre Boulez (see Chapter 10) spent some time in the early 1950s working with Pierre Schaeffer on *musique concrète*, but he soon grew dissatisfied with the lack of control over the sounds then available through studio techniques and turned his attention to electronic music. In 1977 he founded IRCAM *(Institut de Recherche et Coordination Acoustique/Musique,* or Institute for Research and Coordination Acoustic/Music), a state-sponsored research institute in Paris. The composers, performers, computer scientists, and engineers at IRCAM developed many new programs and sound technologies, including the digital 4x synthesizer, which Boulez featured in his *Répons* (Response, 1984) for small orchestra, six soloists, and synthesizer. Capable of sophisticated real-time applications, the 4x processed live sounds and sent them hurtling through space along elaborate sound routes (Fig. 11.7).

The computer music systems initially developed at IRCAM were complex and required composers to work with a tutor trained to operate the equipment. In the score of *NoaNoa* (1992; see Anthology 20) for flute and electronics, the Finnish composer Kaija Saariaho (b. 1952) acknowledges the programmer and engineer as members of her creative team. Using IRCAM's extensive computer music resources for analyzing and modeling instrumental timbre, reverberation, and spatial effects, Saariaho has explored many different ways of integrating live electronics into performance.

Unlike Davidovsky's *Synchronisms No. 6,* in which the performer must adapt to the prerecorded tape, *NoaNoa* gives the musician a great deal of control. Composed for the flutist Camilla Hoitenga, who also played some of the prerecorded flute sounds, the piece features many different types of interactivity, including real-time computer manipulation of the flute timbre and triggering by the flutist of reverberation effects and prerecorded sounds. Inspired in part by Spectralist approaches (see Chapter 12), Saariaho creates a sonic space that bridges the spheres of sound and noise, instruments and electronics, and harmony and timbre.

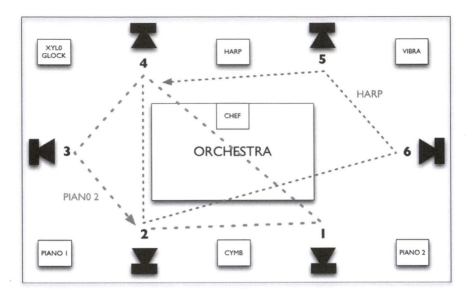

Figure 11.7: *Pierre Boulez,* Répons, *sound routes*

PORTABLE SYNTHESIZERS AND OTHER TECHNOLOGIES

As prices of computer chips plummeted, portable digital synthesizers appeared in the mid-1970s, with expensive units like the Synclavier soon followed by lower-priced instruments aimed at the rock and jazz markets. The E-mu Emulator (1982), the first commercial sampling keyboard, created sounds by recording and then modifying them, thus blurring the line between *musique concrète* and synthesized music. In addition to controlling all aspects of the sound, these powerful instruments had the added attraction of being immediately playable by traditionally trained keyboardists. Rather than creating sounds from scratch, however, many users relied on presets or purchased sound banks, thus sacrificing one of the defining characteristics of the original synthesizer.

Today, programmable synthesizers for tablets and smartphones can be purchased for a few dollars. Computer music's migration from large mainframes to programs designed for the desktop computer set the stage for the rapid spread of electronic music and digital home studios in the 1980s. Both the Musical Workstation program and the influential MAX-MSP software were developed at IRCAM. Another important breakthrough was the establishment in 1983 of the MIDI (Music Instrument Digital Interface) standard, which allowed computers, synthesizers, and keyboards from any manufacturer to interact. MIDI helped generate new forms of live electronic music, with "laptronica" ensembles like the Princeton Laptop Orchestra using music software and hardware to perform together either in the same space or over the Internet.

MIDI also facilitated the development of new interfaces for controlling sounds. Performance artist Laurie Anderson has employed devices that read gestures to trigger sounds, such as a full-body suit that responds to various dance movements. Tod Machover (b. 1953) and others working in the Media Lab at MIT have developed a range of hybrid acoustic-electronic "hyperinstruments," as well as radically new kinds of controllers resembling gloves and spheres. Machover's *Death and the Powers: The Robots' Opera* (see Chapter 1) features a massive chandelier-like sound sculpture that one of the characters plays to accompany her singing. New interfaces have figured in game technologies, including interactive musical games like Guitar Hero. In the spring of 2011 Adidas announced a shoe called the Megalizer, with built-in wireless sensors that trigger sampled sounds.

One of the most significant developments in electronic music has been its migration to smartphones and the Internet. Ringtones, which originated as a practical way for cell phone users to identify their phones, have become an integral part of the music business, fashion, and global consumer culture. With the development of phones capable of playing MP3s, many ringtones have been adapted from hit songs. Indeed, some composers write songs with that potential use in mind, while others specialize in composing new ringtones. As with Kurt Weill's media-specific art for the radio (see Chapter 5), ringtone composers willingly adapt to the technical and functional limitations of the medium.

In 2001 Golan Levin created the piece *Dialtones (A Telesymphony)*, which consists of ringtones sent to the phones of audience members, to be triggered at appropriate points in the performance. The smartphone's integration of video, sound, and the Internet has also made possible new forms of interactive multimedia art. In 1997 William Duckworth launched an Internet project called *Cathedral*, which disseminates software that allows listeners to participate from their own computers. Similar attempts to create a worldwide community include Ocarina, a program that turns a smartphone into a wind instrument capable of broadcasting over the Internet. Other musicians have been exploring YouTube as a medium for interactive composition and performance; for example, the Virtual Choir piece *Sleep* (2011) by Eric Whitacre was assembled from more than 2,000 individual performances submitted by singers around the world.

In an essay written in 1957, the American composer Elliott Carter (discussed further in Chapter 12) described the disorienting sense of liberation produced by electronic music, in the face of which "our present little musical world shrinks to a tiny system of timid sounds, our present instruments unresponsive, dull, and crude beside their colorful electronic counterparts, and even our best performers limited, slow to learn, and clumsy beside the nimble versatility of these electronic possibilities."

Carter likened the composer faced with this "vast world of possibilities" to someone who unexpectedly receives a lot of money and the leisure in which to spend it. With obvious relevance to the trajectories of order and chance discussed in Chapter 10, he writes that some respond to such windfalls by "hitting out at random, trying one course of action after another," while others adopt "some arbitrary system of action completely unrelated to the situation but which cuts down on the possibilities of choice." Yet despite Carter's anxieties, it was precisely the new ways of hearing and thinking about sound—made possible by Integral Serialism, Indeterminacy, and electronic music—that opened up for him and many others exciting new musical horizons that we will consider in Part IV.

FOR FURTHER READING

Bernstein, David, ed., *The San Francisco Tape Music Center: 1960s Counter Culture and the Avant Garde* (Berkeley and Los Angeles: University of California Press, 2008)

Collins, Nick and Julio d'Escriván, eds., *The Cambridge Companion to Electronic Music* (Cambridge: Cambridge University Press, 2007)

Holmes, Thom, *Electronic and Experimental Music* (New York: Routledge, 2002)

Katz, Mark, *Capturing Sound: How Technology Has Changed Music*, rev. ed. (Berkeley and Los Angeles: University of California Press, 2010)

Pinch, Trevor, and Frank Trocco, *Analog Days: The Invention and Impact of the Moog Synthesizer* (Cambridge, MA: Harvard University Press, 2002)

Riikonen, Taina, "Shaken or Stirred—Virtual Reverberation Spaces and Transformative Gender Identities in Kaija Saariaho's *NoaNoa* (1992) for Flute and Electronics," *Organised Sound* 8 (2003): 109–115

Simoni, Mary, ed., *Analytical Methods of Electroacoustic Music* (New York: Routledge, 2006)

Théberge, Paul, *Any Sound You Can Imagine: Making Music/Consuming Technology* (Middleton, CT: Wesleyan University Press, 1997)

Zak, Albin, *I Don't Sound Like Nobody: Remaking Music in 1950s America* (Ann Arbor: University of Michigan Press, 2010)

PART IV

From the 1960s to the Present

In Chapter 1 we considered the metaphors of tangled chaos and the blank
page to characterize the dizzying range of styles, slogans, and trends that
composers faced in the early decades of the twentieth century. The developments that we will explore in the final section of this book reflect a still more
extreme multiplicity of approaches. Displacing notions of a mainstream or a
widely shared culture, counter- and subcultures have proliferated in all aspects
of life, as has every form of transcultural hybridization.

While the globalization of the economy, technology, and media has been a
powerful homogenizing force, it has also facilitated a profusion of new voices
and perspectives. A defining feature of this heterogeneity—sometimes producing it, sometimes responding to it—has been the rise of new fundamental-
isms and the quest for a lost purity or simplicity. Some have responded to this
pervasive pluralism with a voluntary isolation, while others have attempted to
shout down or silence destabilizing voices and perspectives. Even among a class
of college music students, there has never been less common ground in musical backgrounds, experiences, or interests. Or to put it another way, the broad
influence of Musil's "sense of possibility," and the conviction that nothing has
to be the way it is, has never been stronger.

Part IV covers musical developments from the 1960s through the present.
While the trends considered in the previous chapters continued to play a central role, the social and cultural disruptions of the 1960s marked a significant
turning point as composers and musicians reengaged more directly with history, politics, and the world around them. Chapter 12 explores how composers
sought to move beyond Integral Serialism and Indeterminacy to create works
with richly expressive surfaces and textures. They employed new techniques for
working with sound masses and timbre, and created complex textures by piling
up of layers of independent lines.

In contrast to postwar efforts to make a clean break with the past, we will
see in Chapter 13 how composers used quotation and stylistic allusions to
reconstruct and deconstruct musical histories of all kinds in such trends as
Postmodernism and the New Romanticism. In Chapter 14 we focus on Minimalist
composers who responded to the seemingly limitless possibilities by reducing
music to its most basic elements and simple audible processes. The emergence
of Postminimalism, with its eclecticism and hybrid forms of music-making,
reflects the accelerating cycles of reaction and counterreaction. We conclude
in Chapter 15 with composers of the youngest generation who are questioning
many of the narratives that have shaped musical developments since the early
nineteenth century, while at the same time challenging long-established borders between musical traditions, music and other cultural forms, and composers and their audiences.

CHAPTER TWELVE

Texture, Timbre, Loops, and Layers

One of the most significant musical trends since World War II involves the de-emphasizing of melodic and harmonic motion, and even the significance of individual notes, to allow texture, timbre, rhythm, dynamics, and register to take center stage. The origins of what we will call "texture music" lie in electronic music, Integral Serialism, and Indeterminacy. But composers working in this broad category have developed a remarkable range of compositional techniques that draw upon an equally remarkable diversity of influences and inspirations. While pursuing very different expressive and stylistic ends, composers of texture music share a fascination with how we experience sounds as they move through time, building and fading, coalescing into stratified layers or thick clouds, or dissolving into particles.

From traditional musical perspectives, the works we will consider in this chapter are some of the most esoteric that we have encountered so far. Surprisingly, however, the emphasis on surfaces and timbre makes much texture music immediately expressive and effective. A clear measure of this ability to communicate a wide range of emotions, from transcendence to terror, is the ease with which the sounds of texture music have become part of popular culture. Inspired by works by György Ligeti and Luciano Berio, the Beatles brought an orchestra into the studio to improvise the surging sound masses in "A Day in the Life" (1967). Pieces by Ligeti and Krzysztof Penderecki have been featured in the soundtracks of Stanley Kubrick's *2001: A Space Odyssey* (1968), *The Shining* (1980), and *Eyes Wide Shut* (1999), and more recently in Kathryn Bigelow's *The Hurt Locker* (2008). It is now common for film composers to employ ambient textural effects in place of traditional leitmotivic character themes, as in scores by Thomas Newman (*American Beauty*, 1999) and James Newton Howard (*The Dark Knight*, 2008).

Texture music's accessibility can also be attributed to many composers' incorporation of a wide range of influences, including, as we shall see, non-Western traditions and popular styles. There are significant points of contact between textural approaches and Afro-diasporic forms of groove-based music, from funk to hip-hop and electronic dance music, in which the focus is more on rhythm, timbre, and shifting layers than on harmonic or melodic development. Lines have also blurred between popular and art music in the mass effects of layered distorted instruments employed by bands like My Bloody Valentine, Nine Inch Nails, and Sigur Rós, and works by composers like Rhys Chatham, who wrote *An Angel Moves Too Fast to See*, for 100 Electric Guitars, Electric Bass, and Drums (1989).

Texture music is thus not simply another "ism," but a more general manifestation of the new possibilities for creating form, structure, and expression when melodic development and harmonic progression play only a limited role. The categories of texture music we will consider here provide an overview of the trends that have been the most fertile and some of the composers associated with them. These subsets of texture music should not be seen as exclusionary; on the contrary, many composers have moved freely among them, sometimes embracing ideas from other post–World War II compositional trends as well. Similarly, much of the music we will be exploring in the following chapters has important textural elements.

ORIGINS OF TEXTURE MUSIC

One can hear anticipations of textural approaches throughout music history. In three- and four-voice organum by Perotinus from around 1200, sections are differentiated more by textural and rhythmic shifts than by changes in pitch content. In the early nineteenth century, Beethoven and Rossini wrote passages that rely on rhythm and dynamics to generate momentum; later in the century Wagner's astonishing Prelude to *Das Rheingold* was built on nearly five minutes of a sustained E♭-major triad. And as we have seen, throughout the first half of the twentieth century composers developed textural ways of working without functional harmonic progressions, including Debussy's techniques of varying "color and light," Schoenberg's tone-color melody, Stravinsky's explorations of rhythm and layering in the *Rite of Spring*, Berg's crescendo on a single note in *Wozzeck*, and Varèse's sound masses. Yet the emergence of texture music as a distinct category is inseparable from the postwar emphasis on experimentation and rebuilding music from the ground up, the technological tools and techniques for working with sound that emerged with electronic music and *musique concrète*, and ways of listening in terms of overall effects rather than individual events that were suggested by Integral Serialism and Indeterminacy.

Poème symphonique (Symphonic Poem, 1962) for 100 amplified metronomes, by the Hungarian-born composer György Ligeti (1923–2006), illustrates how texture music relates to some of these earlier trends as well as the crucial differences between them. As much a "happening" as a musical work, Ligeti's "score" consists of detailed instructions for every step of a performance, starting with how to acquire the pyramid-shaped mechanical metronomes the piece requires. Ten players each wind up ten metronomes, which are to be set at different speeds and amplified so that their sound fills the performance space. After a silence of several minutes—both an allusion to Cage's *4' 33"* (see Chapter 10) and a prolonged upbeat for the racket that is about to begin—a conductor signals for the wound-up metronomes to be set in motion. Beginning as an undifferentiated mass, like raindrops tapping on a metal roof, the texture slowly thins out as the metronomes run down. As we begin to hear individual ticking layers, it is possible to make out complex polyrhythms, which in turn become ever simpler until only a single pulse remains. The piece is over when the last metronome comes to a standstill.

Poème symphonique was in part a deliberate provocation of the audience—a planned television broadcast of the premiere in Holland was canceled as too controversial—as well as a parody of the seriousness with which other avant-garde composers took themselves and their systems. But Ligeti's piece was also an effort to move beyond the trajectories of order and chance discussed in Chapter 10. On the one hand, once the various tempi and the tensions of the clockwork mechanisms are set, the *Poème symphonique* is as strictly determined as a work of Integral Serialism. On the other hand, Ligeti left many aspects of the piece indeterminate, including the precise tempo of the individual parts. In so doing, he dramatized an argument he had made two years earlier about the underlying commonalities of Integral Serialism and Indeterminacy. In his essay "Metamorphoses of Musical Form," published in *Die Reihe* in 1960, Ligeti wrote, "There is really no basic difference between the results of automatism and the products of chance; total determinacy comes to be identical with total indeterminacy" (SR 184:1383; 7/15.113).

Echoing the teleological narrative posited by Schoenberg and his students for the evolution of twelve-tone music (see Chapter 7), Ligeti justified texture music as the inevitable outcome of the development of Western music since the Middle Ages. In the essay, he argued that extending the twelve-tone method to other musical parameters undermined the fundamental significance of the row as a series of intervals. Instead of individual notes and their relationships to each other, he observed that what we hear in Integral Serialism are "statistical prop-erties of form, e.g. relationships of register, the density and weave of the struc-ture" (SR 184:1379; 7/15:109). Ligeti had anticipated this way of hearing when he compared the sound of Pierre Boulez's *Structures I* to the patterns of light and dark created by city lights (see Chapter 10). Since both Integral Serialism and Indeterminacy inevitably lead to this "flattening out process," Ligeti asks, why not take the next step and work directly with surfaces, constellations of events, and global effects?

LIGETI'S SONOROUS TEXTURES AND MICROPOLYPHONY

Born into a Hungarian Jewish family, Ligeti studied music formally from an early age. During World War II several members of his family were killed in concentration camps, and he himself was conscripted into a forced-labor brigade, but managed to escape. After the war Ligeti adapted to the doctrine of Socialist Realism (see Chapter 9) imposed by Hungary's Soviet overlords, writing Bartók-inspired settings of folk songs and other ideologically accept-able works for public consumption. Meanwhile, he had already started experi-menting privately with sharply reduced pitch materials in works like his *Musica ricerata* (Music Research, 1951–53). The first of these 11 piano pieces presents a single note, A, in varying registers, rhythms, and dynamics, until a second note, D, is introduced at the very end. The second movement similarly uses only two pitches, adding a third at the conclusion; the process continues until all 12 pitches appear in the final piece.

After the short-lived Hungarian Revolution and subsequent Soviet crack-down in 1956, Ligeti fled to Austria and then to West Germany, where he became involved with electronic music and other trends. In 1961 he attracted international attention with his orchestral work *Atmosphères* (Atmospheres), which, as he wrote in a program note, demonstrated that it was possible to replace "the motivic-thematic approach" with sonorities "so dense that the individual interwoven instrumental voices are absorbed into the general tex-ture and lose their individuality." The work calls for a conventional orchestra, including a piano that is played directly on the strings. And while each part is precisely notated, one hears only vast, slowly shifting sound masses without any sense of meter or pulse. As *Atmosphères* unfolds, each section focuses on different aspects of texture, dynamics, register, and timbre. The piece begins with a softly sustained cloud of pitches in the middle register that gradually collapses into a cluster in the low strings. The second section expands the register while emphasizing timbral transformations as the various instrumental groups—first the strings, then the brass, followed by the woodwinds—crescendo to emerge from the mass.

The third section of *Atmosphères* uses strict procedures, including what Ligeti called the "micropolyphony" of closely spaced rhythmic and melodic canons, to create an intricate web of sound. Example 12.1 shows the music for the 14 first violins at Rehearsal C (the full score occupies 64 staves). The violins are divided into four groups, each of which oscillates between two pitches. Ligeti systematically increases the speed of the oscillation by subdividing each quarter note into ever-smaller parts, as similar processes unfold in the other instruments. All of this micropolyphonic activity takes place imperceptibly; as Ligeti explained, "The polyphonic structure does not actually come through, you cannot hear it; it remains hidden in a microscopic, underwater world, to us inaudible."

Ligeti brought such subliminal techniques to the surface in a series of works marked by frenetic mechanical activity, including *Continuum* for harpsichord (1968; see Anthology 21). He had employed the harpsichord for textural effects as part of large ensemble works, but he hadn't considered a solo piece until he

Example 12.1: *Györgi Ligeti,* Atmosphères, *Rehearsal C, excerpt, mm. 22–24, violin 1*

suddenly realized "that a harpsichord was really like some strange machine." Ligeti's childhood fascination with clocks and mechanical devices that fly out of control is reflected in his "meccanico" pieces such as *Poème symphonique* and the String Quartet No. 2 (1968), whose third movement is marked *Come un meccanismo di precisione* (like a precision mechanism). In *Continuum* Ligeti pushes both the mechanism of the instrument and the technique of the harpsichordist to the breaking point; he later mechanized the entire piece by preparing versions for mechanical organ and player piano.

Taking advantage of the harpsichord's two keyboards, *Continuum* begins with overlapping G–B♭ dyads played as fast as possible, creating the impression of a continuous sound. Figure 12.1 illustrates how Ligeti shapes the sound masses as they move through time by expanding the pitch content, shifting through different registers, and thickening the texture by layering ever more complex patterns that suddenly give way to moments of clarity.

In the midst of the mostly dissonant clusters, the striking introduction of a B-major triad, which morphs into B minor and then into a B-minor seventh chord, points to subsequent developments in Ligeti's music. In addition to reconnecting to tonality in various ways, he went on to engage with many different styles and traditions, including Minimalism, African music, quotation and collage (see Chapter 13), and the manic player piano works of Conlon Nancarrow (see p. 242).

TEXTURAL APPROACHES IN THE MUSIC OF STOCKHAUSEN AND BOULEZ

Ligeti was not alone in concluding that Integral Serialism and Indeterminacy offered new ways of working with masses of sound. As discussed in Chapter 11, Stockhausen began composing with textures in his *Gruppen* (Groups, 1957) for three orchestras, which consists of short sections, or "groups," each conceived as a musical object characterized by its overall qualities of duration, speed, intensity, and sonority. Stockhausen emphasizes the groups' contrasting and colliding textures by spatially separating the three ensembles and giving each its own conductor. In the early 1960s he extended the notion of working with groups to what he described as "moment form," first employed in the electronic piece *Kontakte* (Contacts, 1960). Instead of hearing passages in terms of where they come from and where they are going, moment form encourages listeners to focus on individual, self-sufficient units of time. Alluding to his teacher Olivier Messiaen's *Quartet for the End of Time*, Stockhausen wrote:

> This concentration on the present moment—on every present moment— can make a vertical cut, as it were, across horizontal time perception, extending out to a timelessness I call eternity. This is not an eternity that begins at the end of time, but an eternity that is present in every moment.

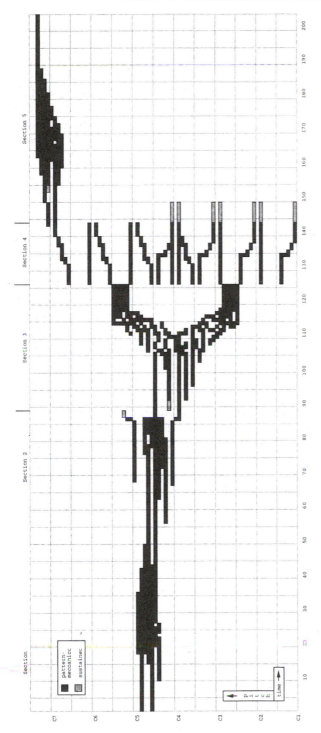

Figure 12.1: *Jane Piper Clendinning's analysis of Ligeti's* Continuum *for harpsichord*

As if to model this profound experience of the moment, his *Stimmung* (Voices, 1968), for six amplified solo voices, sustains a harmonic series for 75 minutes, with subtle timbral and textural changes produced by emphasizing the various overtones.

In addition to creating textural effects by precisely notating scores, both Stockhausen and Boulez—who, as we saw in Chapter 10, embraced some of Cage's innovations in the realm of chance music—used indeterminate means to create generalized sound masses. Boulez's *Eclat* (Brilliance, 1965) for chamber orchestra includes sections in which the conductor chooses the order of events, and others in which players are given pitches without rhythms and instructed to play "independently of the other instruments," in order to create floating moments of "amorphous time." By the end of the 1960s Stockhausen was writing scores such as *Aus den sieben Tagen* (From the Seven Days, 1968) consisting solely of written instructions for creating improvised textures. In a section entitled "Set Sail for the Sun," he instructs each member of the small ensemble to sustain a tone until they hear its individual vibrations, then to shift their attention to the overall mass of sound. All the players are then to bring their tones into "complete harmony" so that "the whole sound turns to gold, to pure, gently shimmering fire." As with Pauline Oliveros's *Sonic Meditations* (see Chapter 10), a performance of *From the Seven Days* becomes both ritual and theater.

MATHEMATICAL MODELS

In keeping with postwar efforts to align music with scientific modes of thinking, textural composers have been inspired by mathematical models derived from engineering, information theory, statistics, cybernetics, and chaos theory. Notable among the composers who prefigured such approaches was the American Conlon Nancarrow (1912–1997), who applied elaborate mathematical structures to an eclectic sound world that drew on jazz and blues piano styles. Nancarrow's Study No. 3 (1948), originally known as the Boogie-Woogie Suite, takes advantage of the player piano's precision to layer multiple ostinato patterns inspired by jazz virtuosos Art Tatum and Earl Hines, creating astonishing textures of interlocking polyrhythms.

Nancarrow explored the use of tempo canons, in which the speeds of the different voices were related according to ratios ranging from comparatively simple to mind-bogglingly complex. Nancarrow, who settled in Mexico in 1940, composed in relative obscurity for many decades until his works began to be recorded in the 1960s. His compositions and ideas influenced Ligeti and other composers, and anticipated the rhythmic complexities of the math rock associated with bands like Meshuggah and the electronic drum-and-bass music of Aphex Twin and Squarepusher.

XENAKIS AND STOCHASTIC PROCESSES

We encountered the Greek composer Iannis Xenakis in Chapter 11 in connection with Varèse's *Poème électronique* and the design of the Philips Pavilion at the 1958 Brussels World's Fair. Working with the architect Le Corbusier, Xenakis (1922–2001) used mathematical formulas for saddle-like shapes known as hyperbolic paraboloids to design the building's sweeping forms. He used the same formulas four years earlier to organize the surging masses of glissandi in his orchestral piece *Metastaseis* (Dialectical Transformations, 1954)—further evidence of his interest in fusing music, math, and architecture.

Trained as a civil engineer in Athens, Xenakis was active in the Greek resistance movement and fled to France after the war, where he worked in Le Corbusier's studio while studying composition with Darius Milhaud, Messiaen, and Pierre Schaeffer. Like Ligeti, Xenakis believed that Integral Serialism had opened up ways of hearing in terms of textures created by masses of notes. In his book *Formalized Music* (1963), he explained his conception of an integrated musical "space-time," which involved modeling mathematical probabilities for ongoing interactions of many indeterminate details. Xenakis compared such "stochastic" processes to "natural events such as the collision of hail or rain with surfaces, or the song of cicadas in a summer field" (SR 183:1374; 7/14:104). Thus his *Pithoprakta* (Actions by Probabilities, 1956), for two trombones, percussion, and strings, begins with scattered percussive sounds that gradually coalesce into complex textures. He was particularly interested in sonic phenomena, such as the sounds of a political demonstration involving hundreds of thousands of people, which could produce a "mass event" with a clearly articulated shape and form moving through time and space.

In the 1960s Xenakis began composing with computers. In addition to founding centers for "Mathematical and Automated Music" in Paris and at Indiana University, he developed a computer system in 1977 that converted drawings directly into sound, as with the score for *Mycenae-Alpha* (1978; Fig. 12.2). As the shifting shapes scroll past, they are translated into pitches in thin bands or clusters, complex mutating textures, and bursts of noise. Xenakis intended the system to make the act of composition accessible even to those without formal training; indeed, a free version known as HighC is currently available online. His software anticipated by many decades today's inexpensive graphic musical interfaces like Singing Fingers, developed at the MIT Media Lab, which enables children to finger-paint with sound.

SPECTRALISM AND ITS RESONANCES

In the 1970s a group of composers who became known as Spectralists began integrating mathematical models of timbre with principles of psychoacoustics to create luminous sound masses that surge through time and space. As with the

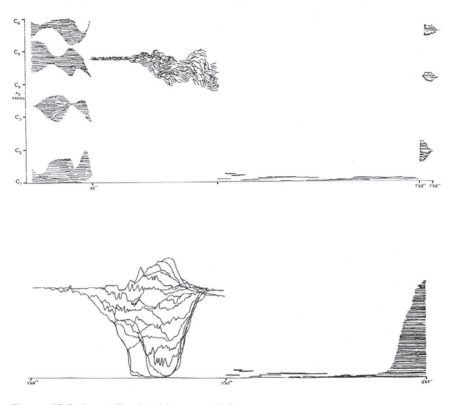

Figure 12.2: *Iannis Xenakis,* Mycenae-Alpha, *excerpt*

approaches to textural composition discussed earlier, Spectralism also emerged in part as a rejection of Integral Serialism and the various techniques that had been developed for controlling the individual musical parameters. As the British composer Julian Anderson has written, alluding to the creative process of Boulez's *Structures*: "the serial obsession with devising separate or related charts for pitch, duration, intensity, dynamics and timbre is replaced with a fondness for attempting to abolish the distinctions between these phenomena."

The Spectralists also differentiated themselves from both Integral Serialism and Indeterminacy by focusing on issues of the perceptibility of structure. The French-born composer and Messiaen student Tristan Murail (b. 1947), for example, has drawn on research in psychoacoustics and psychology to inform his compositions: "my material is neither the musical note nor musical sounds, but the sensation (sensation in a very general sense: that which is felt, in other words, perceived and interpreted) that is created by the note or sound."

As suggested by the emphasis on spectra, which could refer either to sound and timbre or to light and color, there are connections between the Spectralists and Impressionism (see Chapter 2). This is clear in Murail's *Vues aériennes*

(Aerial Views, 1986) for French horn, violin, cello, and piano. Inspired by Monet's paintings of Rouen Cathedral, capturing the play of light and shadow at different times of day, Murail "paints" four versions of the same musical object, the first seen in "morning light (clear light, very obtuse angles, maximum distortion)," the second as if through "light in the rain (soft-focus effect, sharper angles, slighter distortion)," and so on.

The often-noted quality of "acoustic glow" associated with many Spectralist works results from the close coordination of harmony (produced by the combination of individual pitches) and timbre (produced by the weighting and combination of overtones). This glow stands out vividly in *Partiels* (Partials, 1975), a piece for chamber orchestra by the French composer Gérard Grisey (1946–1998), who studied with Xenakis and Ligeti as well as Messiaen. Part of a cycle of works entitled *Les espaces acoustiques* (Acoustic Spaces, 1974–85), *Partiels* simulates the rich field of harmonics revealed through a spectrographic analysis of a low E played on a trombone (Ex. 12.2). The dramatic opening sonority and rhythmic motive are slowly destabilized over the course of the 22-minute-long piece as we experience the depths and variety hidden in a single sound.

Many Spectralist composers have been deeply involved with electronic music. Murail developed software at IRCAM for analyzing instrumental timbres and using the results to synthesize new sounds or modify live instruments. He also explored the inverse, that is the idea of imitating electronic effects with acoustic instruments: His orchestral work *Gondwana* (1980) re-creates the rich and shimmering bell sound of the analog ring modulator and some of the characteristic timbres of computer music synthesis. Murail's *Mémoire/Erosion* (Memory/Erosion, 1976), for horn and a small ensemble of strings, winds, and Ondes Martenot, imitates the increasingly chaotic effects of an analog tape-delay system (which creates echoes by sending the output of a tape machine back

Example 12.2: *Trombone harmonic series used for Gérard Grisey's* Partiels. *Arrows indicate microtonal intervals. As presented by François Rose.*

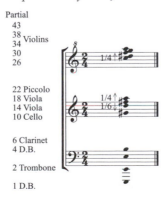

into the input). Beginning with a single note and its echoes, a complex cloud of sounds builds up gradually until it spins out of control, only to come to an abrupt stop, as if the composer had suddenly turned off the tape machine.

Other Spectralists have pursued different pathways. The Finnish composer Magnus Lindberg (b. 1958), a pupil of Grisey, began focusing on textures and the acoustic properties of harmonies as a result of his work at IRCAM in the 1980s. Lindberg also studied the works of Jean Sibelius (see Chapter 4), whose harmonies he describes as having a resonant, "almost spectral quality." Lindberg's music illustrates the connections between texture music and other recent trends. His virtuosic solo cello piece *Stroke* (1984) uses a host of extended techniques in playfully "decomposing" its dramatic opening gesture. The pervasive loops and layers in *Corrente* (1992) for chamber orchestra can be linked to Minimalism (see Chapter 14), while its quotations of Purcell, and Lindberg's use of passages from Mahler and Debussy in *Cantigas* (1999) for orchestra, exemplify the collage techniques discussed in Chapter 13.

Another Ligeti pupil, the Korean-born and Berlin-based Unsuk Chin (b. 1961), has employed Spectral ideas in pieces like *Xi* (Nucleus, 1998) for large ensemble and tape. Its soft opening sighs, synthesized at IRCAM from heavily manipulated piano pitches, gradually evolve into a richly textured haze of sound. Chin's opera *Alice in Wonderland* (2007) integrates textural approaches with more traditional techniques of melodic development. Chin has written of her works in terms of "a play of light and colours floating through the room and at the same time forming a fluid sound sculpture."

TIMBRE AND EXTENDED TECHNIQUES

PENDERECKI'S *THRENODY*

As timbre has taken center stage in textural composition, composers have begun to explore untraditional or "extended" performance techniques for instruments as well as the voice. Among the most influential works of texture music is *Threnody: To the Victims of Hiroshima* (1960) by the Polish composer Krzysztof Penderecki (b. 1933). Written for a 52-piece string orchestra, it opens with a series of shrieking clusters created by overlapping entrances of groups of instruments sounding their highest notes as loudly as possible. With a nod to Cage, Penderecki originally named the piece *8' 37"*, the length of the work as specified through its precise temporal graphic notation. After the first performances, he changed the title to *Threnody* (song of lament) for the victims of the American atomic bomb dropped on Japan in 1945, thus putting it in the category of Britten's *War Requiem* and other postwar memorial pieces. The change also reflects Penderecki's interest in connecting his music to political and social issues, an increasingly important factor over his long and prolific career.

The second page of Penderecki's score (Fig. 12.3) illustrates some of his novel string techniques and the new notational symbols that showed how to produce them. This passage begins with the violins, violas, and basses sustaining their opening clusters, some with the addition of a very slow quarter-tone vibrato. Meanwhile, each of the ten cellists is instructed to choose one of four sound patterns and play it as rapidly as possible during the 15-second block of time. Penderecki calls for various techniques of sound production, each with its own special symbol, such as bowing normally or with the wood, striking the instrument with fingertips or different parts of the bow, or playing on the short section of strings below the bridge. Instead of discrete notes and musical events, we hear a prickly sound mass moving through various registers as each section of the orchestra cycles through the patterns in turn. Penderecki also developed techniques for using contrasts in modes of sound reproduction to create large-scale form in a way analogous to the role of modulation in tonal music. Thus this passage of the *Threnody*, with its sharp attacks and highly active surface, is followed by a section that focuses on narrow clusters of sustained pitches that swell and contract.

NEW SOUNDS AND NEW INSTRUMENTS

Luciano Berio (see Chapters 11 and 13) wrote an innovative series of 14 solo *Sequenze* (Sequences, 1958–2002) employing a dramatically expanded field of instrumental and vocal timbres. Such explorations were possible only through partnerships between composers and performers who were willing to reimagine their instruments. Berio's *Sequenza No. 7* (1969) was dedicated to the pioneering oboe virtuoso Heinz Holliger, and mezzo-soprano Cathy Berberian inspired *Sequenza No. 3* (1966). Berberian further demonstrated her astonishing technique and vocal imagination in her own *Stripsody* (1966), a virtuosic showpiece that humorously brought to life the onomatopoetic sounds of comic strips.

We can see such dramatic expansions of sound in many areas of music making, including Jimi Hendrix's legendary performance of the *Star-Spangled Banner* at the 1969 Woodstock Festival, which used extensive feedback and distortion to envelop the melody in a wall of noise, while also enacting the sounds of "bombs bursting in air" to protest the Vietnam War (see Chapter 13). In the same year the American composer and jazz saxophonist Anthony Braxton (b. 1945) released *For Alto*, an album of improvisations for solo saxophone that unleashed surging masses of notes featuring extreme contrasts of register and dynamics, as well as multiphonics (a wind technique that produces two or more pitches sounding simultaneously). Braxton developed an elaborate system of sound classifications and notations for the extended techniques he used in his scores (Fig. 12.4). Influenced by Schoenberg and Stockhausen, Braxton was also shaped by his involvement in the 1960s with the Association for the Advancement of Creative

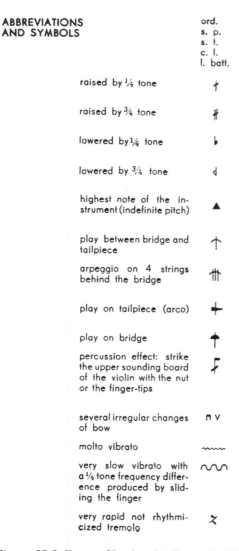

ABBREVIATIONS AND SYMBOLS

ord.
s. p.
s. t.
c. l.
l. batt.

raised by ¼ tone	
raised by ¾ tone	
lowered by ¼ tone	
lowered by ¾ tone	
highest note of the instrument (indefinite pitch)	
play between bridge and tailpiece	
arpeggio on 4 strings behind the bridge	
play on tailpiece (arco)	
play on bridge	
percussion effect: strike the upper sounding board of the violin with the nut or the finger-tips	
several irregular changes of bow	
molto vibrato	
very slow vibrato with a ¼ tone frequency difference produced by sliding the finger	
very rapid not rhythmicized tremolo	

Figure 12.3: *Krzysztof Penderecki,* Threnody: To the Victims of Hiroshima; *performance directions and p. 1 (facing)*

Musicians in Chicago, which developed distinctive black musical forms by fusing avant-garde jazz and new music. In a 1970 interview Braxton connected his use of challenging new sounds and techniques with this social and political agenda: "Consciousness is the most valuable thing that can be communicated right now—making people aware of themselves."

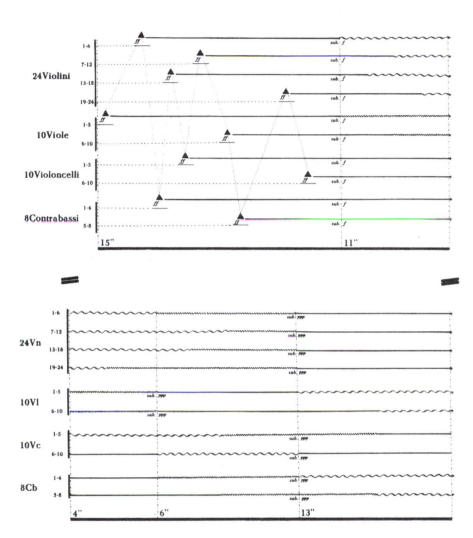

The German composer Helmut Lachenmann (b. 1935) has also challenged performers to break old habits by making the exploration of their instruments critical to the expressive meaning of his works. His cycle of piano pieces *Ein Kinderspiel für Klavier* (Child's Play for Piano, 1980) demonstrates the liberating potential of this idea. The fifth movement, *Shadow Dance*, requires

Figure 12.4: *Anthony Braxton,* Composition Notes, *Book B, ix, composition notes*

that the pianist silently hold down a low-register cluster while playing the top two pitches in repeating rhythms, resulting in shimmering, almost electronic resonances (Ex. 12.3). Later in the piece he introduces innovative ways of using the sustaining pedal to create rhythmic patterns in counterpoint with the ostinato in the right hand. Through such simple means, Lachenmann, who has described his music in terms of "instrumental *musique concrète*," asks us to question our self-imposed limitations and the potentially repressive power of convention. A similar transgressive impulse underlies *Játékok* (Games), an ongoing series of piano pieces by the Hungarian composer György Kurtág (b. 1926). In *Bored* (1979), Kurtág depicts a child distractedly putting off practicing through a playful exploration of the keyboard, including sweeping glissandi, brash clusters, and finally, as if newly discovered, two triads.

Example 12.3: *Helmut Lachenmann,* Shadow Dance, *from* Child's Play for Piano, *mm. 1–2*

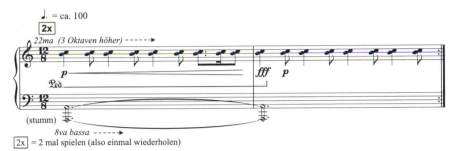

Some composers expanded the possibilities of timbre and texture still further by inventing totally new instruments. The American Harry Partch (1901–1974) dedicated much of his life to creating a hybrid art form drawing on many world traditions and involving music, drama, dance, and ritual. In his book *Genesis of a Music* (1949), he described his growing dissatisfaction beginning in the 1920s with virtually all the assumptions of Western music, in particular the limitations of equal temperament:

> The impulse to the growth and evolution of music is generated by the human ear, not by the piano keyboard, without which the harmony classes of this day and age would be inoperative. And the missing element which the human ear wants and needs most is a musical instrument capable of expressing an infinite range of ideas and of infinite mutability, so that ideas can first be tested, then proved or corrected.

In pursuit of this ideal, Partch developed various microtonal scales that could be played on adapted versions of traditional instruments; he also designed such novelties as suspended Cloud Chamber Bowls and the massive, xylophone-like Quadrangularis Reversum. These exotic-looking instruments, arranged on risers around the stage, provided both the accompaniment and the set for the ritualistic music theater work *Delusion of the Fury* (1969). Like some of the examples of extended techniques discussed earlier, Partch's highly individual body of work is notoriously difficult for others to re-create: after its premiere *Delusion of the Fury* was not performed again until 2007.

COMPOSING WITH LAYERS

In "Metamorphoses of Musical Form" Ligeti noted that serial works (like Stockhausen's *Gruppen*) and electronic music (where the early technologies required pieces to be built up in many stages on magnetic tape) exhibited a tendency toward "layer composition." Ligeti's characterization of this idea can be applied to a great deal of textural music written in many styles: "separate layers of various different types of configuration are pressed together into a simultaneous activity" (SR 184:1382; 7/15:112).

CARTER'S DRAMATIC INTERACTIONS

The American composer Elliott Carter (1908–2012) explored a wide range of different possibilities for creating rich and shifting textures through the layering of diverse elements. In a 1963 essay published in *Perspectives of New Music*, Carter presented an overview of the music he had been hearing at Darmstadt and other major European festivals. While critical of both Integral Serialism and Indeterminacy, he was attracted to the emerging approaches to texture. He noted that in contrast to faded and thin-sounding "one-note-at-a-time" music, works featuring "thick, packed, dissonant textures and vivid juxtapositions of whole clusters or constellations of notes seem to lead, these days, to livelier results."

Reflecting his remarkable longevity, Carter's music weaves together many different threads that we have been tracing throughout this book. Growing up in New York in the 1920s, Carter was steeped in music by Varèse, Cowell, Crawford, and especially Ives, whom he came to know well. Ives's use of musical Americana influenced Carter's brashly contrapuntal *Holiday Overture* (1944). After completing his master's degree at Harvard, Carter went to Paris in the early 1930s to study with Nadia Boulanger. Echoes of Milhaud and Stravinsky can be heard in his Primitivist ballet *Pocahontas* (1939), which was premiered on the same program as Copland's *Billy the Kid*, and Boulanger's teaching shaped his Neoclassical ballet *The Minotaur* (1947).

After the war, Carter's music changed direction as he expanded his harmonic palette under the influence of Berg, Bartók, and others. Still more important was his development of new approaches to rhythm and the temporal dimensions of his works, building on techniques developed by Cowell and Nancarrow (see p. 137), and his study of jazz, Balinese, Indian, and African music. To ensure structural continuity within a flexible rhythmic style, he developed the technique of metric modulation. Analogous to harmonic modulation from one key to another, metric modulation allows precise proportional shifts in the speed of the music's perceived pulse. Carter employed this technique in many works, including his String Quartet No. 5 (1995; see Anthology 22).

Carter also developed ways of giving individual layers distinctive rhythmic profiles, creating complex textures while preserving the individuality of the various voices. In large-scale works like the Double Concerto (1961), which features two timbrally distinct instrumental ensembles, he approached layering as if he were creating different characters in a drama who act out scenarios based on their own personalities and mannerisms. Dramatic interaction is central to the String Quartet No. 5; Carter described its form and content in terms of a chamber music rehearsal in which the players "try out fragments of what they later will play in the ensemble, then play it, and then stop abruptly to discuss how to improve it." He differentiates the four instrumental layers through the intervals they play, their dynamic levels, and their characteristic modes of sound production. Carter emphasizes special timbral effects like the snap pizzicato, where the plucked string is made to strike the fingerboard. Moreover, each of the quartet's main movements focuses on a single technique (such as harmonics, pizzicato, and legato), as if the characters had come to a momentary consensus about how to proceed.

STRATEGIES OF STRATIFICATION

Layered textural effects can be found in diverse musical contexts and in many different musical trends and styles. The British composer Harrison Birtwistle (b. 1934), for example, has described his music in terms of geological strata; the topographical layers in his orchestral piece *Earth Dances* (1986) are differentiated by means of rhythm, timbre, instrumentation, and diverse musical styles. An even more dramatic eclecticism defined the music of the Canadian-born American composer Henry Brant (1913–2008). Inspired by Ives's use of space in works like *The Unanswered Question* and the Fourth Symphony, in *Antiphony 1* (1953) Brant divides the orchestra into five ensembles—strings, French horns, muted brass, woodwinds, and percussion—that are placed as far apart as possible in the performance space. With connections to the use of quotation and collage we will consider in Chapter 13, in other pieces he created complex polyphonic textures by combining different styles and world music traditions; his *Meteor Farm* (1982) includes layers featuring gamelan, West African singing and drumming, Indian vocalists, a jazz band, orchestra, choruses, and soloists.

The Russian composer Sofiya Gubaydulina (b. 1931) uses textures and layers to create intensely expressive works, often infused with mysticism and religious symbolism. Extended techniques and microtonal effects play a key role in many of her pieces. In *Music for Flute and Strings* (1994), for example, the two layers of music are separated by a quarter tone, as if one were shadowing the other. In a 1995 interview she critiqued what she described as a pervasive overcomplication in twentieth-century music in the movement "from atonality and serialism to sonorism," paralleled by the limitless expansion of the world of possible sounds.

Rather than emphasizing still more new possibilities, Gubaydulina has worked "to cure the excessiveness of musical material" by carefully controlling rhythm, time, and form. The choral cycle *Now Always Snow* (1993) illustrates what she calls her "method of time structuring," a set of tools for shaping individual layers, controlling points of arrival, and determining the overall proportions of a piece, which are often based on the Fibonacci sequence. Her second violin concerto, *In tempus praesens* (For the Present Time, 2007), explores manifold ways of layering the solo line within heterophonic echoing effects, driving rhythmic clusters, and shimmering or skittering sound masses. Gubaydulina writes of trying to capture an intense and lasting experience of the present moment, one that is accessible "only in sleep, in the religious experience and in art."

As we will see in Chapter 14, the multiple ostinati of Minimalism and Postminimalism exemplify layer composition. The widespread use of music software such as Garage Band, Pro Tools, Reason, and Live has made it almost second nature for composers in some styles to stack up layers of repeating samples and loops. This is particularly true of hip-hop production; a transcription of the complex polyrhythmic groove used throughout Public Enemy's *Fight the Power* (1990) shows prominent samples of James Brown's voice and a much-sampled break from his *Funky Drummer*, along with over a dozen samples from Afrika Bambaataa, Sly and the Family Stone, and others (Ex. 12.4).

Example 12.4: *Public Enemy,* Fight the Power, *opening groove. Transcription by Robert Walser.*

That texture music ultimately represents a way of hearing and thinking about sound that can be applied to any context is clear from a piece like *9 Beet Stretch* (2002) by the Norwegian sound artist Leif Inge, which uses software to slow down a recording of Beethoven's Ninth Symphony so that it lasts 24 hours. The process results in slowly evolving masses of sound and shifting timbres, as if unveiling a work of texture music hidden between the notes in Beethoven's original score. A similar revelation takes place in Hans Zimmer's textural soundtrack for the movie *Inception* (2010), which features a sample of Edith Piaf's signature song "Non, je ne regrette rien" slowed down into an ominous, murky cluster. We will return in Chapter 15 to the breakdown of distinctions between composed works and the sounds of the world around us. In his book *The Tuning of the World* (1977), the Canadian composer R. Murray Schafer described our "soundscape" as a kind of ongoing texture music. "The world is always full of sounds," Schafer wrote. "They come from far and near, high and low; they are discrete and continuous, loud and soft, natural, human, and technological."

FOR FURTHER READING

Adlington, Robert, *The Music of Harrison Birtwistle* (Cambridge: Cambridge University Press, 2006)

Carter, Elliott, "Music and the Time Screen," in *Elliott Carter, Collected Essays and Lectures 1937–1995*, edited by Jonathan W. Bernard, 262–280 (Rochester: University of Rochester Press, 1997)

Drott, Eric Austin, "Ligeti in Fluxus," *Journal of Musicology* 21 (Spring 2004): 201–240

Fineberg, Joshua, ed., "Spectral Music I–II," *Contemporary Music Review* 19, nos. 2–3 (2000)

Gable, David, "Boulez's Two Cultures: The Post-War European Synthesis and Tradition," *Journal of the American Musicological Society* 43, no. 3 (Autumn 1990): 426–456

Gann, Kyle, *The Music of Conlon Nancarrow* (Cambridge: Cambridge University Press, 2006)

Lochhead, Judy, "Hearing Chaos," *American Music* 19, no. 2 (2001): 210–246

Mirka, Danuta, "To Cut the Gordian Knot: The Timbre System of Krzysztof Penderecki," *Journal of Music Theory* 45, no. 2 (2001): 435–456

Squibbs, Ronald, "Images of Sound in Xenakis's Mycenae Alpha," *Troisièmes journées d'informatique musicale (JIM 96) Conference Proceedings, Les cahiers du GREYC* 4 (1996): 208–218

Willson, Rachel Beckles, *Ligeti, Kurtág, and Hungarian Music during the Cold War* (Cambridge: Cambridge University Press, 2007)

CHAPTER THIRTEEN

Histories Recollected and Remade

Many of the postwar musical developments we have been exploring were driven by the conviction that the only way of moving forward was by leaving the past behind and starting anew. Composers adopted scientific models of experimentation, explored new instruments and technologies, submitted to strict systems or to chance, and searched for new approaches to sound and texture—all in the name of creating a music unencumbered by history, memory, and tradition. In the 1950s Stockhausen spoke of composing music "ex nihilo" by avoiding "everything which is familiar, generally known or reminiscent of music already composed." Yet beginning in the 1960s a growing number of composers decided that only by reengaging with the past could their music remain vital and relevant to the world around them. This chapter explores how composers have approached these recollected elements of the past through quotation, collage, and allusions to established styles.

Dating back at least to the origins of musical notation and polyphony, composers have made use of preexisting pieces and styles. In the preceding chapters we discussed examples of borrowing and stylistic allusion throughout the twentieth century. In this chapter we will see how the generation of composers who came of age after World War II pushed these ideas further than ever before, from jarring polystylistic juxtapositions within a work to seemingly wholesale restorations of earlier styles. The range of strategies is reflected in the many labels that have been used to characterize these trends, including Polystylism, Eclecticism, Postmodernism, the New Tonality, and the New Romanticism.

The shift in attitude toward earlier music after World War II can be attributed to the sense of historical rupture after 1945 that for many made the past seem like a foreign country, both alluring and strange. Hans Werner Henze, discussed further later, likened his use of elements of Romantic tonal harmony to adopting archaic forms of speech and forgotten words from earlier centuries: "one recalls them, even though they are no longer used. They mean something, but precisely what that meaning is seems to have slipped from our grasp." The different attitudes toward the past after the war were also shaped by the new context of the radically expanded possibilities opened up by serial, indeterminate, and electronic music. As Ligeti wrote:

> Now there is no taboo; everything is allowed. But one cannot simply go back to tonality, it's not the way. We must find a way of neither going back nor continuing the avant-garde. I am in a prison: one wall is the avant-garde, the other wall is the past, and I want to escape.

We might reframe Ligeti's longing for escape as another manifestation of Musil's "systems of happiness and balance" that people use to situate themselves in a changing world. And while there were those who maintained that any such stabilizing systems were illusory, many composers sought a new starting point through musical acts of remembering and reconstructing individual, political, national, and racial histories of all kinds. This new concern for tradition and identity was by no means limited to music; it has played an important role in many aspects of life and culture since the 1960s. That it is customary to speak now in plurals, of histories and musics, reflects the fact that interactions with the past have served widely divergent cultural and social agendas. We will see examples in this chapter of the use of history to both define and undermine identities of every kind, just as it has been used both to establish a mainstream and to question any sense of a single path forward.

THE PAST IN THE PRESENT

We live in an age of sampling, mashups, remakes, reruns, and retro fashions. Indeed, the past has become such an everyday presence in our lives that it may be hard to understand what was so startlingly novel about operas like *Die Soldaten* (The Soldiers, 1965), in which Bernd Alois Zimmermann employed historical forms and elements of jazz alongside quotations from Bach chorales; or Ligeti's *Le grand macabre* (The Grand Macabre, 1978), with its wildly farcical libretto and musical allusions to Monteverdi, Offenbach, Beethoven, and others. The Russian composer Alfred Schnittke, who coined the term Polystylism, composed works such as the Concerto Grosso No. 1 (1977), with its sardonically reworked quotations from Vivaldi, Mozart, and Beethoven. After earning recognition for texture music like the *Threnody: To the Victims of Hiroshima* (see Chapter 12), Krzysztof Penderecki surprised many with a series of works including the Symphony No. 2 (*Christmas*, 1980) and the *Polish Requiem* (1984, rev. 2005) that reconnect to tonality, Romanticism, and the sacred choral tradition. Even electronic music began to engage with the past with *Switched-On Bach* (1968), which was marketed as a demonstration of synthesizers joining the historical mainstream (see Chapter 11).

Among the most notable examples of this reengagement with history is the four-movement *Sinfonia* by Luciano Berio, composed in 1968 for the 125th anniversary of the New York Philharmonic (a fifth movement was added the following year). The work brings together an astonishing range of elements, above all in the third movement, *In Ruhig fliessender bewegung* (With a Peaceful Flowing Motion), which is based on the Scherzo of Mahler's Second Symphony. Berio wrote that Mahler's music "seems to carry all the weight of the last two centuries of musical history." Just how much heavier that weight had become for Berio is evident in the many quotations he superimposes on Mahler's score, including excerpts from Bach, Beethoven, Berlioz, Strauss, Ravel, Stravinsky, Berg, Boulez, and Stockhausen.

On top of this orchestral collage, a group of eight solo voices superimposes passages from Samuel Beckett's novel *The Unnamable* (1953), James Joyce's *Ulysses*, and urban graffiti. Although the sonic effect is chaotic, Berio's musical and textual quotations were carefully chosen to comment on each other and on the larger themes of the work. The passages by Beethoven (the *Scene by the Brook* from the *Pastoral* Symphony) and Berg (the drowning scene from *Wozzeck*), for example, echo the watery imagery of Mahler's song *St. Anthony's Sermon to the Fish*, which was the basis of his symphonic Scherzo.

Berio's rich web of allusions is apparent at the outset of the third movement. The first music we hear comes not from Mahler's Scherzo (which doesn't appear until Rehearsal 1) but from the crashing chord that begins the fourth movement of Schoenberg's Five Pieces for Orchestra (1909; see Chapter 3), whose programmatic title, *Peripetie* (Peripeteia), is announced immediately by the voices. Berio's evocation of peripeteia, the sudden reversal of fate in a Greek drama, suggests that he saw *Sinfonia* as a turning point, both in his artistic development and in contemporary music in general.

As the opening chord fades away, the flutes begin a passage from Mahler; but rather than the Second Symphony, as expected, we hear the opening six measures of the first movement of the Fourth Symphony. The voices note the confusion by announcing the tempo markings at the start of the Fourth—"nicht eilen, bitte" (don't rush, please) and "recht gemählich" (quite leisurely)—while Soprano 1 exclaims with bewilderment. Meanwhile, other instruments and voices introduce a passage from *Jeux de vagues* (Play of the Waves), the second movement of Debussy's *La mer* (The Sea), another quotation connected to the watery Mahler song. In these opening measures of Berio's piece, the quotations are identified by the voices; in measures 7–10 we even get a little summary in French of what we have heard so far: the phrases "fourth symphony" and "first part" refer to the quotation from the first movement of Mahler's Fourth, while "fourth part" alludes to the fourth movement of Schoenberg's Op. 16, and so on. But for the rest of the piece we are generally on our own. As we struggle to hold on in the midst of the confusion, the voices exhort us to "keep going," even as they ask, "Where now?" With its dense and complex surface, Berio's *Sinfonia* could be heard as texture music, but together with the mass effects there is a sense that the individual parts are striving to assert their own histories and identities.

QUOTATION, PROTEST, AND SOCIAL CHANGE

Berio's complex relationship to musical tradition was shaped by his early experiences in a family of professional musicians, as well as by Fascist suppression of contemporary music in Italy. Not until after the war, when he began his studies at the Milan Conservatory, did he hear works by Schoenberg, Stravinsky, and other Modernists; his first contact with twelve-tone music came through studies with Luigi Dallapiccola at the Berkshire Music Festival in Western Massachusetts. As is clear from his appearances in Chapters 11 and 12, Berio did not align himself with any single stance or orthodoxy. In addition to his involvement with electronic music and extended techniques, he pursued a lifelong interest in folk music. His cycle *Folk Songs* (1964), composed for Cathy Berberian, features small-ensemble tonal arrangements of songs from France, Italy, Azerbaijan, and the United States.

In an article that appeared in the summer of 1968—in the *Christian Science Monitor* newspaper rather than a specialist music journal like *Die Reihe*—Berio observed that never before had the average composer "come so dangerously close to becoming an extraneous, or merely decorative, figure in his own society." He acknowledged that music is powerless to stop wars or "lower the cost of bread"—phrases that he also includes in *Sinfonia*. Nevertheless, he wrote, "responsible composers" felt increasingly "compelled to challenge the meaning of and reasons for their work in relation to the world of events."

In referencing the "world of events," Berio was placing his music in the context of the radical and sometimes violent cultural, social, and political transformations that swept across the United States and Europe in the 1960s. In the second movement of *Sinfonia*, Berio paid tribute to Martin Luther King, Jr., who was assassinated in 1968: The slowly unfolding textures of *O King* are based on the phonemes of the slain civil rights leader's name. These years were marked by a long struggle against discrimination, including the passage of the 1964 Civil Rights Act. César Chavez organized migrant laborers in the National Farm Workers Association (1962), the National Organization for Women and the Black Panther Party were founded (1966), and the gay rights movement launched with the Stonewall riots in New York's Greenwich Village (1969). At the same time, the Vietnam War set off a tidal wave of student-led protest that crested in 1968. These years also saw the emergence of violent left-wing groups such as the Weather Underground in the United States and the Red Army Faction in West Germany, which advocated armed resistance against their governments.

Berio's plea for classical composers to become more politically engaged or risk obsolescence reflected the reality that musicians working in popular styles were leading the way in addressing social and political issues. Music associated with the American civil rights and antiwar movements surged to the top of the *Billboard* charts. Many of the protest songs that reached a mass audience in the 1960s were explicitly political, including Pete Seeger's "If I Had a Hammer," Bob Dylan's "Blowin' in the Wind," Sam Cooke's "A Change Is Gonna Come," Nina Simone's "Mississippi Goddam," and Barry Sadler's anti-antiwar "Ballad of the Green Berets." The 1968 Broadway opening of *Hair,* subtitled "The American Tribal Love-Rock Musical," confirmed that there was a mainstream market for the mores, politics, and values of the youth counterculture. The hippie movement, with its embrace of psychedelic drugs and music, free love, and radical politics, found immortality in the "Three Days of Peace and Music" of the 1969 Woodstock Festival in upstate New York.

To be sure, many of the works we encountered in previous chapters had significant political dimensions, but composers in the 1960s and 1970s felt driven to take a more explicitly political stance in their music. The question was, how? As was the case during the interwar years (see Chapter 7), composers debated how any kind of art directed to the "elite" audience of contemporary classical music could be dissident or oppositional. Some, like the American composer-conductor Leonard Bernstein (1918–1990), sought to straddle the worlds of classical music and Broadway. His hugely popular musical *West Side Story* (1957) retold *Romeo and Juliet* to dramatize tensions between white and Puerto Rican gangs in New York City. His *Mass: A Theatre Piece for Singers, Players, and Dancers* (1971) featured an eclectic score with rock and blues passages and an antiwar message so explicit that President Richard Nixon was advised to stay away from the premiere at the Kennedy Center. Others reached back to avant-garde movements early in the century, such as Dada, Futurism, and Surrealism, that commented on society more elliptically by challenging the traditional forms and institutions of the arts. In this context we can see that quoting familiar music and borrowing from past and present styles offered composers a solution to the challenge of making their music more broadly accessible and politically effective.

ELECTRONIC MUSIC

While it is customary to approach quotation in terms of instrumental music, the incorporation of recorded sounds in *musique concrète* has turned out to have just as important a legacy, thanks to the wide use of digital samples in many contemporary styles. Unlike *musique concrète*, where the point was to abstract sounds from their sources and focus solely on their musical qualities, in the works discussed here, as in hip-hop production and film scores, it is crucial that the listener recognize the meaning and origin of the sounds.

The Italian composer Luigi Nono (1924–1990) distanced himself from what he regarded as the ahistorical and apolitical stance of both Serialism and Indeterminacy. A committed Communist, he wrote a series of explicitly anti-Fascist, antiwar, and anticapitalist works. *La fabbrica illuminata* (The Illuminated Factory, 1964), for soprano and tape, concerns the exploitation of auto workers at a Fiat plant and was designed to be performed in factories as part of their protests. The tape part includes the manipulated sounds of machines and shouts of demonstrators. Nono described the work as a sonic "diary" of the workers' struggle; by using the sounds of their aural environment, he sought to be "semantically precise about today's man situated in the place of his slavery-liberation."

Such quotation of sounds from the real world has taken many forms. Reversing his earlier stance of expunging familiar "musical objects," Stockhausen in *Hymnen* (Hymns, 1967) engaged with what he described as the most familiar music imaginable by manipulating recordings of national anthems from around the world. In Japan, the composer Joji Yuasa incorporated into his *Voices Coming* (1969) recordings of Martin Luther King, Jr. and Asanuma Inejiro, the assassinated leader of the Japanese Socialist Party, in a section entitled *A Memorial for Two Men of Peace, Murdered*.

In *Sometimes* (1976), for tenor and tape, Olly Wilson (b. 1937) reworked the spiritual "Sometimes I Feel Like a Motherless Child" with an accompaniment of electronic sounds and the manipulated voice of the American tenor William Brown, for whom Wilson wrote the piece. At times the spiritual appears in its original form; in other passages it is hardly recognizable, but its emotional presence and message of transcending hopelessness inform the entire work.

Born and raised in St. Louis, Wilson has worked in classical performance, jazz, and electronic music, in addition to teaching composition at Oberlin and Berkeley. In both his electroacoustic compositions and his works for traditional instruments, Wilson has explored what he calls a "heterogenous sound ideal" shared by African-American and West African music that involves stratified layers of polyrhythms, rich and complex timbres, and the integration of the incidental sounds of the performance itself into the musical work.

In his 1974 article "The Significance of the Relationship of Afro-American Music and West African Music," Wilson compared an example from the Ghanian Ewe genre of Agbadza with James Brown's funk song "Superbad" (1970). Writing in 1972, at the height of the Black Power movement in the United States, Wilson argued that African-American composers had a special obligation to raise "the collective consciousness of black people" and instill a "renewed awareness of the power and significance of their culture." He described his use of electronic music as a tool for opening up different forms of perception and expression, to help others "gain new perspectives on their shared experiences" (SR 196:1423–1424; 7/27:153–154).

VOCAL AND INSTRUMENTAL MUSIC

Composers working in vocal and instrumental genres also began quoting and borrowing to engage with political and social issues, to reach a broader audience, and, like Berio and Nono, to separate themselves from the orthodoxies of Serialism and Indeterminacy. Growing up in Nazi Germany, the noted opera composer Hans Werner Henze (1926–2012) first encountered contemporary musical developments through the BBC broadcasts he heard as a prisoner of war in Britain. After studying twelve-tone composition at the first of the Darmstadt summer courses in 1946, he started in the 1960s to incorporate quotations in a series of explicitly Marxist and antiwar works. Henze's Sixth Symphony (1969), written while he was living in Havana, borrows from popular Cuban music as well as from a song associated with the anti-American National Liberation Front in South Vietnam. His *Voices* (1973), a collection of 22 protest songs for solo voices, small ensemble, and electronics, integrated popular, folk, and world music with serial and aleatoric techniques.

In similar fashion, the American composer Frederic Rzewski (b. 1938) created a set of 36 variations on a famous Chilean protest song in his virtuosic piano piece *The People United Will Never Be Defeated* (1975). The 50-minute-long piece, which includes other politically charged quotations such as Brecht and Eisler's "Solidarity Song" (1931), moves from the clear tonality of the opening theme to passages of great harmonic complexity and dissonance.

Another American composer, Lukas Foss (1922–2009), engaged musically with the violence that was so endemic to late-twentieth-century life. Like several of the Neoclassical works we considered in Chapter 6, his *Baroque Variations* (1967) is based on pieces by Handel, Scarlatti, and Bach, but he used the quotations to very different ends. In the third movement, *Phorion* (derived from the Greek word for "stolen goods"), he subjected Bach's famous keyboard Partita in E Minor to a series of increasingly extreme transformations, creating the effect, as he wrote, "of a cathedral being torn down." By the end of the movement only fragments of Bach's piece remain, nearly drowned out by percussion and the sounds of breaking glass (Ex. 13.1). And yet for Foss the point was not to embrace violence, but to send a message of nonviolence: "You are holding a mirror to people about violence, and in the arts, without harming anyone or anything. . . . Therefore the arts are extremely important in our age. They may be the ones to bring us out of war and destruction."

As Foss's *Phorion* illustrates, one of the ways in which composers made their music and its message more accessible and effective was by emphasizing the theatrical and visual dimensions of their works. The addition of recognizable quotations to Cage- and Fluxus-inspired performance (see Chapter 10) made possible more explicit commentaries on culture and society. The "instrumental theater" of Mauricio Kagel (1931–2008), who grew up in Argentina during the repressive régime of Juan Perón, challenged the aesthetic and political assumptions of both audiences and musicians. His *Ludwig van* (1970), created for the

Example 13.1: *Lukas Foss*, Baroque Variations, *movement 3*: On a Bach Prelude (Phorion), *Rehearsal 9, excerpt*

Duration: 4–5 seconds (no beats or cues)

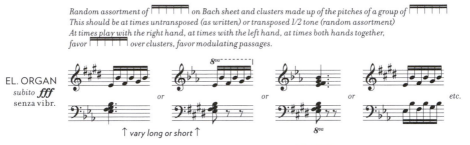

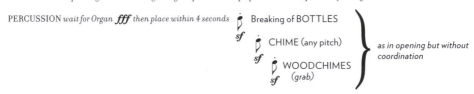

bicentennial of Beethoven's birth, is both an anti-authoritarian gesture and an acknowledgment of Beethoven's inescapable influence (Fig. 13.1). The piece began as a film representing various stages in the composer's life. One scene takes place in a room plastered with pages from Beethoven's scores, which musicians on the soundtrack frantically attempt to perform as the camera pans across the walls and furniture. The published score of *Ludwig van* was based on photographs of various objects in the room.

The music of the American composer George Crumb (b. 1929) brings together quotation, symbolic notation, and theatrical elements of staging and performance to engage with both contemporary issues and cosmic themes. Born into a musical family in Charleston, West Virginia, Crumb was exposed to a wide range of folk, classical, and world music styles. *Black Angels* (1970) for amplified string quartet, a commentary on the Vietnam War, evokes the tragedy of early death with a haunting passage from Schubert's *Death and the Maiden* Quartet. In *Ancient Voices of Children* (1970), Crumb sets a poem that Federico García Lorca wrote during the Spanish Civil War of the 1930s—"Each afternoon in Granada, a child dies each afternoon." The movement concludes with the sound of a toy piano playing a passage from Bach's *Notebook* for his daughter, Anna Magdalena, that gradually slows to a stop, like a music box running down.

Crumb's *Vox balaenae* (Voice of the Whale, 1971; see Anthology 23), for electric flute, electric cello, and electric piano, was connected to the emerging environmental movement. Rachel Carson's influential *Silent Spring* was published in 1962; the U.S Environmental Protection Agency was launched in 1970; and two

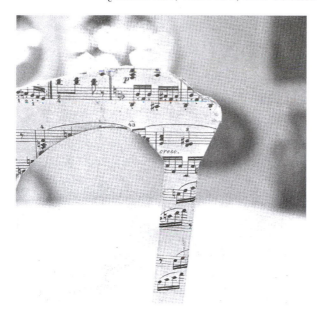

Figure 13.1: *Mauricio Kagel,* Ludwig Van, *excerpt*

years later the United Nations convened their first international Conference on the Human Environment. Inspired by recordings of humpback whales, Crumb re-creates the otherworldly sound of their song by having the flutist sing into the instrument while playing an elaborate vocalise. As specified in the score, the deep blue stage lighting and the black half-masks the musicians wear create the effect of a mystical and depersonalized ritual.

In *Voice of the Whale* Crumb integrates extremely eclectic materials, including allusions to the sounds of the Japanese shakuhachi flute and octatonic, triadic, and tonal passages. The opening *Vocalise* quotes the beginning of Strauss's *Also sprach Zarathustra*, with the imposing timpani part evoked by muting the bass strings on the piano. In keeping with the larger message of the work about mankind's destructive impact on the environment, Crumb reworks Strauss's opposition of C major and C minor to juxtapose two triads a tritone apart—first B major and F minor, and then B minor and F major when the passage recurs. Crumb thus invokes Strauss, Nietzsche, and the centuries-old notion of the tritone as the devil in music, transforming Zarathustra's heroic proclamation of the coming of the superman into an ominous warning.

The middle section, *Variations on Sea Time*, consists of a "Sea Theme" and five variations representing various geological eras, beginning with the Archeozoic when life first emerged. We hear another version of the *Zarathustra* quote at the end of variation 5 for the Cenozoic era, which covers the millions of years from the extinction of the dinosaurs up to our own human epoch. Crumb powerfully evokes the destruction of the whales in the closing *Sea-Nocturne* (. . . *for the end of time*). Written in what he described as the "luminous tonality of B major," the piece ends with ever-softer repetitions of a ten-note melody based on the "Sea Theme," marked "dying, dying . . . ," the last to be played silently in pantomime.

A similarly rich eclecticism characterizes the music of the American composer Anthony Davis (b. 1951). His opera *X: The Life and Times of Malcolm X* (1986) draws on a wide range of African-American jazz and popular styles to chart the trajectory of Malcolm's life from the 1920s to his assassination in 1965. Scored for a traditional orchestra augmented by a jazz ensemble, it includes both fully notated and improvisatory passages. Davis quotes his own music as well as the works of other musicians; Malcolm's conversion to Islam, for example, is accompanied by a passage from *A Love Supreme* (1964) by the jazz musician John Coltrane (1926–1967).

Davis synthesizes these ingredients with elements of gamelan music and a dissonant harmonic language evoking Berg, Bartók, and Stravinsky. His early musical experiences at Yale and Wesleyan focused on classical and world music; just as central was his involvement with jazz musicians connected with the Association for the Advancement of Creative Musicians, including Anthony Braxton, Leo Smith, and George Lewis.

Comparing his choice of subject matter to the role of Norse mythology in Wagner's operas, Davis has written many works that deal with "our American mythology," including the operas *Amistad* (1997), about the nineteenth-century slave ship uprising, and *Tania* (1991), about the kidnapping of Patricia Hearst by the Symbionese Liberation Army in 1974. He uses preexisting musical material to establish a context and foundation for his creative activities: "To me it's about developing a language, building upon the past, my past, my own personal language and means of expression." In writing music that engages with the past to influence the present, Davis has sought to differentiate himself from the Postmodernists, who he characterizes as putting marketability ahead of political content.

POSTMODERNISM

Postmodernism first entered the popular consciousness in the 1970s and 1980s, when, in place of gleaming glass skyscrapers representing the Modernist "International Style," architects like Robert Venturi, Philip Johnson, and Michael Graves began to design buildings that playfully incorporated disparate elements of earlier styles. But elements of Postmodernism have played a role in all the arts, as well as philosophy, religion, and even science. Influential philosophers of Postmodernism, including Jean-Francois Lyotard, have defined it as an "incredulity toward metanarratives" that have shaped so much of human thought and experience, including such foundational ideas as history, progress, and the autonomy of the individual. Among the "metanarratives" challenged by Postmodernism is the notion that an artwork has a fixed meaning determined by its author. Instead, Postmodernist thought shifts meaning from the act of creation to that of reception, which in turn depends on the multiplicity of our individual subjectivities and experiences.

Postmodernism's origins have been linked to the political upheavals of the 1960s, the rise of multinational capitalism, and the impact of the computer and the information age. Whether Postmodernism rejects or extends Modernism is a subject of ongoing debate, as is the question of its political implications and whether it serves or attacks the status quo. Not surprisingly, many different kinds of music have been labeled postmodern, including much of the music discussed here and in the five preceding chapters of this book. For our purposes, the idea of Postmodernism, like that of Modernism, is less useful as an explanatory category than as a starting point for discussion.

PASTICHE AND SIMULACRA

Postmodernist theories have been applied to music that features a flamboyant combination of styles, and that—unlike the works discussed above, which use quotation to anchor pieces in a historical or social context and to communicate a specific meaning determined by the composer—seem to embrace the impossibility of connecting with the past or with others. For the cultural theorist Frederic Jameson, Postmodernism reflects the pervasive commodification of our society, which has brought us to the point where "stylistic innovation is no longer possible, all that is left is to imitate dead styles, to speak through masks and with the voices of the styles in the imaginary museum." Works exemplifying this quality of "Postmodern pastiche" that results are sometimes marked by a deliberate blankness and emptiness, though individuals will respond very differently to such imitations of ostensibly "dead styles," depending on their own backgrounds and experiences.

The British composer Peter Maxwell Davies (b. 1934) has combined quotation and collage with vivid theatricality in works that, in Jameson's terms, seem drawn from a museum of dead styles. His *Missa L'homme armé*, first composed in 1968 and revised as a theater piece in 1971, incorporates fragments of an Agnus Dei from an anonymous fifteenth-century mass, which was itself based on a popular song of the day called "L'homme armé" (The Armed Man). Written for Davies's group The Fires of London, which used Schoenberg's *Pierrot lunaire* ensemble with an added percussionist, the piece features a vocalist who is instructed to act in an "extravagant, swaggering fashion," and who may be male or female, but "should be dressed as a Nun if taken by a man, or as a Monk if by a woman." With a Latin text comprised of biblical passages about the betrayal of Christ by Peter and Judas, the piece uses distorted quotations and allusions to many styles and eras to illustrate the difficulty of differentiating between truth and travesty.

Davies began composing the *Missa L'homme armé* as an arrangement of the surviving mass materials. Through what he describes as a process of "progressive splintering," he filtered passages of the original through "many varied stylistic 'mirrors.'" Along with manipulations using Indeterminacy and extended techniques, we hear a pastiche of styles, including a caricature of amateurish early music performance (Ex. 13.2a), a Baroque section disfigured by excessive ornamentation (Ex. 13.2b), and a grotesque foxtrot played on an out-of-tune-honky-tonk piano. In some performances the piano was replaced by the simulated sound of a scratchy 78-rpm recording, thus presenting us with an artificial copy of an obsolete technology reproducing a fake foxtrot played on a caricature of an instrument using musical material based on a distorted arrangement of a fragmentary and forgotten work.

For Davies, it still seems to matter that we differentiate between the fakes and the original. Indeed, the *Missa L'homme armé* ends with the speaker spouting

Example 13.2: *Peter Maxwell Davies*, Missa L'homme armé

(a) Rehearsal K, mm. 1–3

(b) Rehearsal K, mm. 8–11

accusations in Latin at the audience before storming out of the hall and slamming the door. Davies went on to a distinguished career as an upholder of the traditions of British music, recognized by his appointment in 2004 as Master of the Queen's Music. In pieces by other composers, however, the sense of irony and artificiality generated by multiple layers of copies and simulations is precisely the point.

Such works can be understood as "simulacra," an idea central to theories of Postmodernism. As theorized by the sociologist and philosopher Jean Baudrillard, a simulacrum can be thought of as a copy for which no original actually exists. Examples of this concept include the artist Jeff Koons's stainless steel replicas of balloon dogs from the 1990s, in which the relationship to an actual dog is very remote, and the photographer Cindy Sherman's series *Untitled Film Stills* (1977–80), which consists of self-portraits in stylized scenes from imagined "old movies." In a still more radical formulation, simulacra have been described as copies that displace the originals, an idea most vividly explored in the widely seen and discussed series of *Matrix* films (1999–2003), which depict a world of computer-generated virtual reality.

The idea of simulacra is useful for considering *Spillane* (1987), by the American composer John Zorn (b. 1953). Evoking the world of the Mike Hammer detective novels, *Spillane* rummages through the conventions and clichés of the genre, including a tough-guy voiceover that might have been taken from an old film noir. The first three minutes of Zorn's dizzying collage present a woman's blood-curdling scream, hints of "cool" bebop and hard-driving free jazz, the sounds of sirens and a barking dog, bump-and-grind strip club music, and retro-futuristic electronic effects. These snatches from different eras and traditions function less as direct quotations than as simulacra of styles. Zorn takes this idea still further in his 55-second-long *Speedfreaks* (1990) for saxophone, piano, bass, guitar, and vocalist. The transcription shown in Figure 13.2 consists of a sort of lead sheet indicating meter, harmonies, and rhythmic ideas. A different style is specified for every measure, including "oom-pah," "rockabilly," and "reggae."

DISLOCATING HIGH AND LOW

Along with Ives, Carter, and Stravinsky, Zorn cites as major influences Ennio Morricone, noted for his "Spaghetti Western" film scores, and the cartoon-music composer Carl Stalling, famous for his soundtracks for Looney Tunes and other Warner Brothers productions. Zorn has also compared his music, with its embodiment of the speed and multiplicity of contemporary experience, to the frantic pace of video games. That Zorn would reference both cartoons and video games points to one of the most important metanarratives challenged by Postmodernism: the hierarchies of high and low art.

Composers throughout history have borrowed from folk and popular forms, but almost always they have preserved a clear hierarchy between their

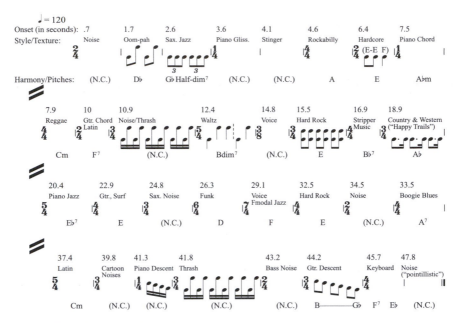

Figure 13.2: *John Zorn,* Speedfreaks

"cultivated" art form and the quoted music. Jean Cocteau insisted in *Cock and Harlequin* (see Chapter 6) that jazz and other popular entertainments could provide useful raw material for composers, but were not art in themselves. Since the 1960s, however, classical musicians and audiences have taken pop cultural forms more and more seriously. As a result, composers who borrow from popular styles are just as likely to seek to acquire prestige as they are to bestow it. Thus, for example, the Kronos String Quartet, founded in 1973 and famous for engaging with many different styles and traditions, helped define their edgy image through their signature arrangement of Jimi Hendrix's "Purple Haze."

The interactions between high and low have taken many forms over the last half-century. In the early 1960s the composer, conductor, and jazz scholar Gunther Schuller developed the idea of Third Stream music as a way of integrating classical music with jazz. Frank Zappa combined aspects of *musique concrète*, rock, and jazz in an aesthetic shaped by the music and writings of Edgard Varèse (see Chapter 5). Electric guitars and rock performance styles have appeared in the works of many composers, including the examples from Lukas Foss, Leonard Bernstein, and Rhys Chatham noted above, as well as pieces such as Steven Mackey's electric guitar concerto *Tuck and Roll* (2000). Mackey is one of many composers now active who started out as rock guitarists.

More recently, Zorn, jazz musician Uri Caine, sound artist Christian Marclay, and other composers have incorporated DJs, turntables, and live mixing into their works. The integration of high and low has also played an important role in sample-based music such as the "Plunderphonics" of Canadian composer John Oswald. Oswald's samples of Elvis Presley, Dolly Parton, and Led Zeppelin set the stage for later mashup artists like Girl Talk and Danger Mouse. A mix by the producer DJ Food called *Raiding the 20th Century* (2005) is a smorgasbord of more than 150 excerpts by Varèse, Schaeffer, Cage, the Beatles, Grandmaster Flash, James Brown, Kylie Minogue, Doctor Funnkenstein, and others.

Zorn wasn't the only composer inspired by comic strips; the American Michael Daugherty based *The Metropolis Symphony* (1993) on characters from the Superman comics. In the fourth movement, marked to be played "faster than a speeding bullet," Daugherty invokes the rapid contrasts of cartoon music to depict the perils faced by reporter Lois Lane, while the dense clusters of the third movement represent the explosion of Superman's home planet, Krypton. Opera composers in particular have been drawn to the sensational world of tabloid journalism, as in Richard Thomas's *Jerry Springer: The Opera* (2003), based on the television talk show. We will return in Chapter 15 to other examples of recent composers for whom the borders between high and low matter less and less.

MULTIPLE IDENTITIES

Zorn's career illustrates another phenomenon of Postmodernism: the increasing prevalence of composers who are comfortable working in different styles, for different audiences, and even under different names. With a background in classical, jazz, and popular music, Zorn has formed ensembles ranging from the hardcore rock band Naked City to the thrash band Painkiller and the "Radical Jewish" improvisatory jazz groups Masada and Electric Masada. Such multiple identities are common in the world of producers and DJs; in one of the most extreme cases, the German composer Uwe Schmidt has released music under more than 60 different aliases in styles including jazz and electronica, and as the fictitious Latin American dance band Señor Coconut, noted for its salsa and merengue covers of music by Kraftwerk.

The notion that identities are fluid has been linked to the impact of the Internet and social media, where it is common, and at times necessary, to adopt multiple personae, just as players of interactive games assume the identities of newly invented avatars to inhabit virtual worlds. Yet the sense of identities as constructed and interchangeable raises significant concerns in the real world. By challenging the fundamental concept of truth, some critics say, Postmodernism impedes political engagement and undermines the racial, national, and sexual identities that activists in the 1960s fought so hard to secure. Almost by definition, the use of multiple styles in pieces like *Missa L'homme armé*, *Spillane*, and *Speedfreaks* depends on stereotypes and clichés that, in turn, can shape and distort our experience of those styles and the people who make them.

REMAKING TRADITIONS

In his book *Music, the Arts, and Ideas* (1967), Leonard Meyer foresaw an era marked by "the persistence of a fluctuating stasis" in which, rather than the centuries-old tendency for styles to emerge and then go out of fashion, "an indefinite number of styles and idioms, techniques and movements, [would] coexist in each of the arts" (SR 211:1496; 7/42:226). Less accurately, Meyer predicted that critics and audiences would never accept a straightforward adoption of an earlier style, suggesting that such an approach, even if done creatively, would be regarded as "no more than a servile imitation." This claim has been challenged by composers like George Rochberg, whose rapprochement with the past was motivated by deep-rooted personal and artistic convictions.

In the immediate postwar years, Rochberg (1918–2005) established himself as a leading twelve-tone composer and theorist, while also exploring the implications of Indeterminacy. In the 1960s he began to quote Bach, Mozart, Mahler, Miles Davis, and others in works like *Music for a Magic Theater* (1965) for orchestra and *Nach Bach* (After Bach, 1966) for solo harpsichord. Both pieces feature a generally dissonant harmonic context in which familiar tonal passages fade in and out of focus like fragments from another world.

With his five-movement String Quartet No. 3 (1972), however, Rochberg struck off in a new direction. While the atonal harmonies of the outer movements recall Schoenberg and Bartók, the third movement is a newly composed tonal theme and variations in A major (Ex. 13.3). With its complex variation technique, stratospheric first violin part, and deeply contemplative tone, the movement seems to exist on a continuum somewhere between Beethoven's late string quartets and Mahler's Ninth Symphony. Rochberg raised the stakes

Example 13.3: *George Rochberg, String Quartet No. 3, movement 3, mm. 1–4*

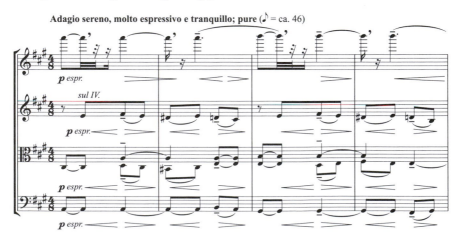

further by creating a freestanding version of the quartet's tonal centerpiece for string orchestra, which he called *Transcendental Variations* (1975).

Rochberg writes of being fiercely criticized as a "reactionary" and a "traitor" to the cause of contemporary music. He responded in turn by attacking the "dehumanized, morally devoid" scientific mindset of Modernism and the urge to forget the past that he associated with Serialism and Indeterminacy. In a program note for the Third Quartet, he argued that the past is indelibly stamped on our DNA. Only tonality can empower us to escape the "cultural pathology" of our time and embrace "what can only be called a *possibility*: contact with the tradition and means of the past, to re-emerge as a spiritual force with reactivated powers of melodic thought, rhythmic pulse, and large scale structure" (SR 213:1508; 7/44:238). Rochberg went on to produce a large body of works illustrating his concept of an *ars combinatoria*, or "art of combination," according to which composers should feel free to use any resources available to them, including tonality, atonality, and non-Western musics.

THE NEW ROMANTICISM

A significant number of composers since the 1980s have reintroduced tonality as part of their palette with much less anxiety—and backlash—than Rochberg. Many of these so-called New- or Neo-Romantics have embraced an overtly expressive idiom infused with the grand gestures and ambitions of the nineteenth century. The German composer Wolfgang Rihm, for example, has written many works that evoke German Romantic orchestral and Lieder traditions, just as his quotation-laden *Deus Passus* (2000), written for the 250th anniversary of Bach's death, evokes religious music of the eighteenth century. The Scottish composer James MacMillan has integrated textural approaches with lush tonality and soaring melodies in his dramatically intense sacred works, such as the cantata *Seven Last Words from the Cross* (1993) and the *St. John Passion* (2007) for chorus and orchestra.

A group of prolific American composers, including William Bolcom, David Del Tredici, Ned Rorem, John Harbison, Lowell Liebermann, and Jennifer Higdon, have similarly attracted broad audiences through powerfully expressive works that reflect their own individual syntheses of elements from past and present. In her cycle *Songs from Letters* (1989), Libby Larsen (b. 1950) sets passages from letters written at the end of the nineteenth century by Calamity Jane to her daughter, whose father was the famous gunfighter "Wild Bill" Hickok. In her program note about this "tender soul, a woman and pioneer on many frontiers," Larsen describes how Jane's attempt to explain her unconventional life sheds light on society in our own time. Reflecting Larsen's characterization of tonality as providing "pools of 'comfort' around a fundamental," the conclusion of the first song, "So Like Your Father's," places the accompanimental figure in different harmonic contexts, from poignant dissonance to gentle fourth chords (Ex. 13.4).

Example 13.4: *Libby Larsen*, Songs from Letters, *I, mm. 10–17*

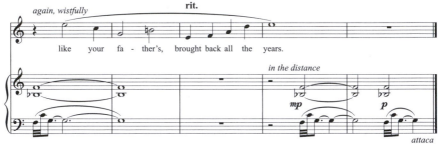

MAKING TRADITIONS IN EAST ASIA

A significant aspect of the renewed interest in reconnecting with history and tradition that took shape in the 1960s has been a recognition of the diversity of the world's musical cultures. As Berio wrote in his *Christian Science Monitor* essay, "A composer's awareness of the plurality of functions of his own tools forms the basis for his responsibility, just as, in everyday life, every man's responsibility begins with recognition of the multiplicity of human races, conditions, needs, and ideals." As we have seen, composers throughout the twentieth century borrowed from non-Western musical styles. In recent decades, composers and performers around the world have integrated their own musical traditions with the postwar trends we have been tracing as well as with popular music and jazz.

Such developments have been particularly significant in East Asia over the last half-century due to the multifaceted cultural politics of China, Korea, and Japan. By the early twentieth century Western classical music was officially championed in all three nations as a tool for modernizing society, often at the expense of indigenous musical traditions. The subsequent revival of interest in traditional music and instruments in these countries followed very different trajectories, reflecting changing attitudes toward westernization, modernization, and nationalism. Japan, for example, westernized aggressively after its defeat in World War II; not until 2002 did training on traditional Japanese musical instruments become part of the middle-school curriculum. In contrast, Western music was suppressed in China during the violent imposition of the Cultural Revolution of the 1960s and 1970s in favor of broadly accessible folk-based works.

East Asian composers have integrated traditional and Western music through quotation, allusion, and the combination of Western and Asian instruments and musical systems. Toru Takemitsu (1930–1996), a leading figure in postwar Japanese music, sought alternatives to Japanese music in the work of Debussy, Messiaen, and electronic techniques. When John Cage and pianist David Tudor were invited to visit Japan in 1962, their presence inspired an outpouring of indeterminate and Fluxus-inspired works by Takemitsu and others, including Toshi Ichiyanagi and Yuji Takahashi. In fact, Takemitsu claimed that it was Cage's interest in Japanese music that first inspired him to incorporate Japanese elements into his own work.

Takemitsu began composing *November Steps* (1967), a concerto for the traditional Japanese biwa (lute) and shakuhachi (flute), with the intention of demonstrating points of contact between Japanese and Western music, but he ended up emphasizing what he identified as fundamental differences between them in terms of sound, the passage of time, how one listens, and the basic conception of music: "We speak of essential elements in Western music—rhythm, melody, and harmony. Japanese music considers the quality of sound rather than melody."

Another major figure in the integration of East and West is the Chinese-born Chou Wen-chung, who came to the United States in 1946 to study with Varèse. Central to his teaching and composition has been the concept of a "re-merger" between Eastern and Western traditions to form a new mainstream. Chou helped a number of young Chinese composers come to the United States to establish their careers, including Tan Dun (see Chapter 15), Bright Sheng, Zhou Long, and Chen Yi.

Chen Yi (b. 1953) practiced piano and violin in secret before being sent to the countryside during the Cultural Revolution to work as a laborer. She later studied at the Central Conservatory in Beijing, where she became the first woman in China to earn a master's degree in composition. In her *Chinese Myths Cantata* (1996), Chen combines a contemporary Western idiom with instruments and subject matter drawn from Chinese art and literature. Her piano piece *Ba Ban* (1999; see Anthology 24) is based on the melody, characteristic rhythmic pattern, and form of the traditional Chinese instrumental piece from which the work takes its title. She integrates these elements with twelve-tone techniques developed through her studies with Chou Wen-chung and Mario Davidovsky. At times the rapid pentatonic figurations echo the exoticist fantasies of works like Debussy's *Pagodes* (see Chapter 2), but as the work unfolds *Ba Ban* uncovers layers of history documenting a rich and specific life story that takes us across continents and a half-century of experiences.

_____

Recalling the anxiety he felt in bringing together East and West in *November Steps*, Takemitsu wrote in 1989: "Today's young people do not share that ambivalence. Perhaps they have no sense of crisis; in fact, they handle two different traditions skillfully." As we will see in Chapter 15, such border crossings between cultures, histories, and traditions play an ever more central role in many aspects of contemporary musical life. While such developments always give rise to tensions and traumas, for many young composers, performers, and listeners today, it is the sense of crisis itself that seems a thing of the past.

FOR FURTHER READING

Banfield, William, *Musical Landscapes in Color: Conversations with Black American Composers* (Lanham, MD: Scarecrow Press, 2003)

Bernard, Jonathan W., "Tonal Traditions in Art Music Since 1960," in *The Cambridge History of American Music*, edited by David Nicholls, 535–566 (Cambridge: Cambridge University Press, 2004)

Bracket, John, *John Zorn, Tradition and Transgression* (Bloomington: Indiana University Press, 2008)

Foster, Hal, "Postmodernism: A Preface," in *The Anti-Aesthetic: Essays on Postmodern Culture*, edited by Hal Foster, ix–xvi (Seattle: Bay Press, 1983)

Gendron, Bernard, *Between Montmartre and the Mudd Club: Popular Music and the Avant-Garde* (Chicago and London: University of Chicago Press, 2002)

Hisama, Ellie M., "John Zorn and the Postmodern Condition," in *Locating East Asia in Western Art Music*, edited by Yayoi Uno Everett and Frederick Lau, 72–84 (Middletown, CT: Wesleyan University Press, 2004)

Hofer, Sonya, "I Am They: Technological Mediation, Shifting Conceptions of Identity, and Techno Music," *Convergence* 12, no. 3 (2006): 307–324

Kramer, Jonathan D., "Beyond Unity: Toward an Understanding of Musical Postmodernism," in *Concert Music, Rock, and Jazz Since 1945: Essays and Analytic Studies*, edited by Elizabeth West Marvin and Richard Hermann, 11–33 (Rochester: University of Rochester Press, 2002)

Li, Xiaole, "Chen Yi's Multicultural Approach in Ba Ban for Piano Solo," *Resonance: An Interdisciplinary Music Journal*, 2005, http://www.usc.edu/libraries/partners/resonance/2005/Spring/Xiaole/index.html (31 March 2012)

Lochhead, Judith, and Joseph Auner, *Postmodern Music/Postmodern Thought* (New York: Routledge, 2002)

Osmond-Smith, David, *Playing on Words* (London: Royal Musical Association, 1985)

Watkins, Glenn, *Pyramids at the Louvre: Music, Culture, and Collage, from Stravinsky to the Postmodernists* (Cambridge, MA: Harvard University Press, 1994)

CHAPTER FOURTEEN

Minimalism and Its Repercussions

In the musical world of the 1960s and 1970s, anything seemed possible. Chapter 13 considered a number of composers who responded to the absence of taboos by seeming to embrace all of music history in their works. At the same time, however, there were those who reacted by radically limiting the range of ideas and materials they explored in individual compositions. This movement, which became known as Minimalism, touches on all the postwar musical trends we have been discussing. But, as we can hear in *Four Organs* (1970) by Steve Reich, Minimalist music also marked a decisive break with what had come before (Ex. 14.1).

In place of the ametrical rhythms typical of serial, indeterminate, and texture music, maracas in *Four Organs* pound out a steady pulse throughout the 16-minute-long piece. As if to shut out the huge sound world available to him, Reich employs an austere, monochromatic timbral palette. Rejecting the fashion for constant change, *Four Organs* features incessant repetitions of a single chord that evolves only as each of the pitches is gradually lengthened. In contrast to the emancipated dissonances and atomized pitch structures of previous decades, Reich presents what he called "the longest V–I cadence in the history of Western Music," basing the piece on an E dominant eleventh chord that suggests a resolution to A. And unlike the cryptic techniques of serial, indeterminate, and texture music, Reich makes his structural devices audible for anyone who chooses to listen.

Example 14.1: *Steve Reich,* Four Organs, *mm. 1–4 (the steady eighth-note maraca part is not shown)*

All of this helps explain why Minimalism, although it has become one of the most influential trends in contemporary composition, has also been the most controversial. Consider this scathing review by Harold C. Schonberg, then the chief classical music critic for *The New York Times*, of a 1973 performance of *Four Organs*:

> An amused and, in some cases, vocally resentful audience listened to Reich's chordal manipulation and then started walking out in large numbers. The music is indeed a bore. There is no "content" in this kind of music, it is pure sound, and there is nothing to "understand" in it.
>
> What Reich has done is confuse an acoustic phenomenon with music. As such, *Four Organs* is non-music, just as so many minor baroque compositions, written in tonic-dominant formulae without a trace of personality, are non-music. Or as so much modern art is non-art—three white triangles against a white background, or something like that. Really it is "art" for people who are afraid of "art." Or do not understand what art really is. Or who are too emotionally inhibited to want to share the emotional and intellectual processes of a real creator's mind. *Four Organs* is baby stuff, written by an innocent for innocents.

Minimalism has provoked strong opposition not only from concert audiences and critics, but also from many musicians and composers affiliated with other contemporary trends. In many cases, the antipathy was mutual; Minimalist composers willingly separated themselves from both mainstream classical music culture and the new-music establishment by creating alternative models for building a career and for performing and disseminating their music.

Despite such strident opposition, Minimalism has attracted a large and passionately devoted cadre of fans. What began as a distinctively American fringe movement associated with the composers La Monte Young (b. 1935), Terry Riley (b. 1935), Steve Reich (b. 1936), and Philip Glass (b. 1937) is now a well-established international phenomenon. Minimalist composers have written successful operas and mainstream film scores, and have been featured in high-profile collaborations with jazz, rock, and world musicians. Minimalism's emphasis on loops and layers has made it particularly relevant to rap and electronic dance music producers.

Even in its early stages Minimalism as a movement was far from unified, and it is even less homogeneous today. In most cases the composers themselves rejected the label of Minimalism, or applied it to only a small part of their output. Yet it is this very diversity of interests and perspectives that has made Minimalism so influential, while allowing its founders to branch out in such unpredictable and distinctive ways.

ORIGINS AND LOCALES

In light of their subsequent "outsider" status, it is surprising that all four composers were products of major institutions and interacted with many of the figures we have encountered in previous chapters. Glass and Reich studied at the Juilliard School in New York City, Young and Riley at the University of California at Berkeley. Reich went on to do graduate work with Berio and Milhaud at Mills College in California. Glass traveled to Paris to study with Boulanger, while Young and Riley spent time with Stockhausen, Cage, and other avant-garde luminaries at Darmstadt. But although they could have joined the ranks of the established leaders of new music, they all ultimately chose different paths.

Rather than seeking commissions or teaching at a university or conservatory, Glass worked as a plumber, furniture mover, and taxi driver for ten years after returning to the United States in 1976. He used his earnings to pay for tours by his own Philip Glass Ensemble, the only group capable of or interested in performing his music at the time. Glass's first major success came with the five-hour-long opera *Einstein on the Beach* (1976), created in collaboration with stage director Robert Wilson. The abstract, nonlinear libretto, centering on Albert Einstein and the birth of the atomic age, features a hodgepodge of sometimes

nonsensical texts relating to current events and popular culture. After touring Europe with the piece in the summer of 1976, Glass rented the Metropolitan
Opera House in New York for two well-publicized performances that brought
wide attention to his highly amplified, very fast, and extremely repetitive music.

Reich likewise founded his own ensemble, Steve Reich and Musicians, whose
first recording appeared in 1969. Nine years later his *Music for 18 Musicians*, on the
German jazz label ECM, sold over 100,000 copies and was even named one of
the ten best pop albums of the year. In an interview published in 1987, Reich
explained why he felt so strongly about separating himself from the postwar
European avant-garde and their American followers:

> Stockhausen, Berio, and Boulez were portraying in very honest terms what it
> was like to pick up the pieces of a bombed-out continent after World War II.
> But for some American in 1948 or 1958 or 1968—in the *real* context of tailfins,
> Chuck Berry, and millions of burgers sold—to *pretend* that instead we're *really*
> going to have the dark-brown *Angst* of Vienna is a *lie*, a musical lie, and I think
> these people are musical liars and their work isn't worth [*snaps fingers*] *that!*

MINIMALISM AND THE COUNTERCULTURE

For the Minimalist composers, and even more for their early audiences, an
important context for their music was the emerging counterculture. Glass
writes of coming of age in the 1960s, the era of "civil rights, pop music, and
drugs," and realizing that his friends who were popular musicians were "living in a very connected way with their culture, and many of us wanted to have
the same connection in our work." In New York City, Glass gravitated toward the
hip downtown neighborhood of SoHo, as opposed to the more academic uptown
scene centered around Juilliard and Columbia University. Reich, Young, and
Riley thrived in the countercultural Mecca of San Francisco, distinguished by
its openness to non-Western musics, Eastern religions, and psychedelic drugs.

The *New York Times* review of *Four Organs* suggested that the point of the piece
was for the listener "to saturate himself in pure sound, concentrating, departing
to other spheres on a cloud of musical zen." Indeed, *trance music* was a popular
synonym for Minimalism in the early years, reflecting the genre's association
with new forms of spirituality and chemically altered consciousness. While
drug culture did not play a major role in early Minimalism, there were specific
references to hallucinogens in pieces like Riley's *Mescalin Mix* (1963), which filtered the sounds of laughter, voices, and soft piano chords through psychedelic
tape echo effects.

Minimalism's connection to the countercultural ethos is further evident in
Riley's *In C* (1964), whose participatory character had much in common with the
loosely structured Fluxus and performance art "happenings" of the late 1950s
and early 1960s. According to Morton Subotnick, who played in the premiere

of the piece at the San Francisco Tape Music Center, police showed up on the day of the performance to investigate a fire code violation and a report that the participants were into "drugs and nude dancing." He recalled that the audience was garbed in the colorful manner of the "psychedelic dress-up era," with Riley wearing a "floppy purple bow tie and orange pants."

Young wrote a set of pieces in 1960 in Berkeley and New York entitled *Compositions 1960*, which consisted of Cage- and Fluxus-inspired written instructions for a liberating merger of art and life. *No. 10*, for example, directed the performers to "draw a straight line and follow it," while *No. 5* anticipated the flower power imagery of the mid-1960s: "Turn a butterfly (or any number of butterflies) loose in the performance area. When the composition is over, be sure to allow the butterfly to fly away outside. . . ." *Compositions 1960* also show early signs of the interest in drones that would become central to Young's distinctive approach to Minimalism, as in *No. 7*, which consists of a B–F♯ perfect fifth "to be held a long time."

RILEY'S *IN C*

In C was the first Minimalist piece to attract wide attention, reaching many through the recording released four years later on Columbia Records. The work consists of 53 figures, ranging from two notes to extended melodies, to be performed by any number of players (Riley suggests approximately 35) on any instruments, including voice (Ex. 14.2). The musicians can repeat each figure as many times as they choose and wait as long as they want before moving on to the next one; the result resembles a slowly shifting mobile of diverse sounds pulsating together as it moves. In place of a conductor, the ensemble is "led" by a person playing the optional eighth-note pulse on the top two Cs of a piano or mallet instrument.

In C was meant to be a communal exercise rather than a display of anarchy. The piece, which usually lasts between 20 minutes and an hour depending on how many times the figures are repeated, works best when the musicians listen to one another carefully, sometimes asserting their own voices and other times stepping back to focus on the polyrhythmic combinations of the patterns.

In C illustrates the cornucopia of ingredients that came together in early Minimalism. Like Reich's *Four Organs*, there are echoes of serialism in the way the content and order of the figures are strictly defined. There are also indeterminate aspects in the scoring and length of the piece and the ways the figures come together. Riley's incorporation of the basic elements of tonality, exemplified by the stylized opening figure with its grace note and major third, reveals an affinity with the New Romanticism (see Chapter 13), while the overall effect is comparable to the texture music of Penderecki and Ligeti (see Chapter 12). But the work's cheeky, back-to-basics title provides a clue to Riley's provocative iconoclasm: with its bright, steady pulse and relentless repetitions, *In C* thumbs its nose at music that takes itself too seriously.

Example 14.2: *Terry Riley,* In C, *excerpts 1–15*

MINIMALIST ART AND MUSICAL PROCESSES

The free-wheeling sprawl of Riley's *In C* shows that early Minimalist music was hardly minimal in every respect. The same can be said of contemporaneous Minimalist art, from which the label for the musical style is borrowed. Indeed, the four composers we have been discussing were closely connected to the Minimalist painters, sculptors, and filmmakers who rose to prominence in the 1960s. Just as Minimalist composers reacted against the music of the previous generation, Minimalist artists like Sol LeWitt, Frank Stella, and Donald Judd distanced themselves from the emotionally charged canvases of the Abstract Expressionists like Jackson Pollock, opting for a radical simplification of materials, cool emotional affect, smooth surfaces, and a focus on the object rather than the creating or viewing subject.

In Minimalist art the emphasis is often on the pattern of an arrangement rather than any intrinsic meaning or interest in the parts themselves. *Rainbow Pickett* (1964) by Judy Chicago, for example, consists of six beams of decreasing sizes leaning against a wall at the same angle; as the beams get smaller, their colors grow progressively warmer, from cool blues to orange and ochre (Fig. 14.1). Sol LeWitt designed a series of more than 100 "wall drawings" consisting solely of patterns of lines, which he communicated by means of instructions intended to be realized by other artists in multiple locations. *Wall Drawing 56* (1970), for example, describes a square "divided horizontally and vertically into four equal parts, each with lines in four directions superimposed progressively."

Many early Minimalist scores present similar repetitions of a single musical "object"; Reich, for example, created pieces using a chord (*Four Organs*), a rhythm (*Clapping Music*, 1972), and a tape loop (*Come Out*, 1966). In each, Reich arranges these simple objects into slowly evolving patterns. As described in his essay "Music as a Gradual Process" (1968), for Reich a musical process had four essential characteristics: First, the process should determine all the details of a work as well as its overall form. Second, the process should be perceptible to the listener, in contrast to the hidden structural devices in serial and indeterminate music. Third, the process should be gradual and invite close and sustained attention. Fourth, once set in motion, the process should run by itself, without needing input from the composer or performer.

To illustrate the idea of a gradual process, Reich offered the image of "pulling back a swing, releasing it, and observing it gradually come to rest." He turned this analogy into a piece with *Pendulum Music* (1968), which consists of two to four microphones suspended by their cables to swing freely in front of an equal number of loudspeakers. The performers start the microphones swinging in broad arcs and adjust the amplifier level so that a burst of feedback is produced when a microphone passes in front of a speaker. Once the process is under way, the performers are instructed to sit down and join the audience in listening to the shifting rhythmic patterns until all the microphones have come to rest and are producing continuous feedback. The piece ends with the theatrical gesture of the performers pulling out the amplifiers' power cords.

PHASE SHIFTING

The most important musical process in Reich's work is what he called "phase shifting," a reference to the mathematical formula that shifts the curve horizontally in a graph of a sine wave. In a musical context, phase shifting involves placing a simple repeating pattern in different combinations with itself. Reich compares the idea to traditional canonic technique, but with the distance between the leading and the following voice being infinitely variable. He discovered the process accidentally while working with tape loops; when he played identical loops simultaneously on two tape decks, the equipment's slight differences in speed caused one loop to move very gradually ahead of the other. One of the most influential of Reich's works is the tape piece *Come Out*, which is based

Figure 14.1: *Judy Chicago,* Rainbow Pickett *(1964)*

on a short tape loop of the phrase "Come out to show them." The words were taken from a recorded interview with Daniel Hamm, one of six black teenagers arrested and convicted for the murder of a white shop owner in the 1964 Harlem riots. Reich's work, which was written for a benefit concert to support efforts advocating a retrial of the "Harlem Six," uses an excerpt of Hamm's account of being beaten while in police custody.

Reich applied phase shifting to live performance in a series of pieces including *Clapping Music* for two people clapping, *Piano Phase* (1967) for two pianos, and *Violin Phase* (1967; see Anthology 25), which can be performed either by four violinists or by one live player and three prerecorded parts. *Violin Phase* begins with a one-measure repeating pattern played by two violins (one of which may be prerecorded); when the lead violinist increases the tempo slightly, the two layers slowly drift out of phase. Performing the phasing process takes considerable practice and discipline, especially to avoid the tendency to move ahead too quickly or to fall back into synchronization.

For Reich the phasing process was a revelation. Starting with a simple musical idea, it produced rich and varied rhythms, melodies, harmonies, timbres, and textures. Early in the phasing process of *Come Out*, for example, the effects are primarily acoustic and timbral as the repeating words, "Come out to show them," stretch out and echo. As the two loops move further apart, we start to focus on the melody of the speech, the shifting rhythmic patterns, and the percussive timbres of the consonants. When the number of layers is doubled to four and then again to eight, the voices turn into a richly pulsing texture.

In *Come Out* it is the listener's job to pay attention to the "resultant patterns" produced by the musical process, but in *Violin Phase* the lead violinist is instructed at several points to bring out the rhythms, melodies, and harmonies that he or she notices. Reich writes in his program note:

> As one listens to the repetition of the several violins, one may hear first the lower tones forming one or several patterns, then the higher notes are noticed forming another, then the notes in the middle may attach themselves to the lower tones to form still another. All these patterns are really there; they are created by the interlocking of two, three, four violins all playing the same repeating pattern out of phase with each other.

Although conceptually *Violin Phase* depends on tape music techniques, it also points to the increasing importance of live performers in Reich's works. With this piece, Reich began to approach composing through an intensive rehearsal process in which he often played alongside the performers and benefited from their insights. In his preface to the score Reich indicates that the violinists Shem Guibbory and Paul Zukofsky contributed several of the resulting patterns that he incorporated into the work.

We can hear a slightly more complicated process in Reich's *Music for Mallet Instruments, Voices, and Organ* (1973; Ex. 14.3). Here, the fourth marimba gradually assembles an out-of-phase version of the ostinato played by the third marimba, starting with one note, then two, then three, and so on, until the pattern (shifted three eighth notes ahead) is completed. Starting at Rehearsal 2, glockenspiel 2 uses the same process to reconstruct the pattern of glockenspiel 1, shifted five eighth notes ahead. While the percussion instruments are busily employed in these efforts, Reich initiates another process of systematically lengthening the chords in the voices and organ, recalling the technique he used in *Four Organs*.

PROCESS MUSIC, RITUAL, AND POLITICS

For both performers and audiences, the "process" works of Reich, Young, Glass, and Riley require a focus and concentration that Reich described as "a particular liberating and impersonal kind of ritual. Focusing in on the musical process makes possible that shift of attention away from *he* and *she* and *you* and *me* outwards towards *it*." The objectivity, strictness, and impersonal nature of this formulation of process music relate to both serial and indeterminate music. But Reich is careful to differentiate the audibility of his musical processes from the "hidden structural devices" of pieces like Boulez's *Structures* and Cage's *Music of Changes* (see Chapter 10). He similarly contrasted his attraction to an "impersonal" compositional approach with Cage's goal of removing his likes and dislikes from the act of composition: "What I wanted to do was to come up with a piece of music that I loved intensely, that was completely personal, exactly what I wanted in every detail, but that was arrived at by impersonal means. I compose the material, decide the process it's going to be run through—but once those initial choices have been made, it runs by itself."

While some do indeed experience the ritualistic aspect of process music as liberating, both Minimalist music and art have been criticized for being shallow, limiting, and even coercive. Writing in 1984, George Rochberg (see Chapter 13) linked Minimalism with both Modernism and Postmodern "Tower of Babel" pluralism: "Much of what still goes by the name of 'music' is either simply sound-generation or soul-less complexity or mindless minimalism." In his book *The Minimal Self* (1984), the historian Christopher Lasch attacked Minimalist art as retreating from history and responsibility. In its focus on objective surfaces, he argued, Minimalism "not only denies the reality of inner experience but denies the reality of surrounding objects as well. It annihilates the subject and object alike."

One of the harshest criticisms of Minimalism came from Elliott Carter in 1982, who was also responding to what he heard as an element of coercion: "About one minute of minimalism is a lot, because it is all the same. One also hears constant repetition in the speeches of Hitler and in advertising. It has its dangerous aspects." It is thus striking that while Rochberg critiques Minimalism for its links to a "soul-less" insular Modernism, from Carter's perspective it

Example 14.3: *Steve Reich,* Music for Mallet Instruments, Voices, and Organ, *mm. 1A–E and 2A–D*

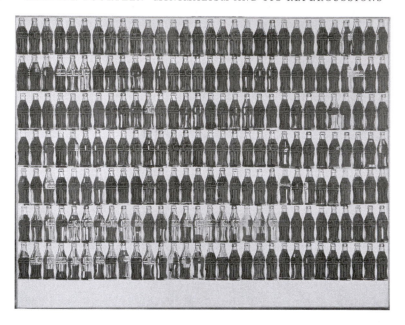

Figure 14.2: *Andy Warhol,* Green Coca-Cola Bottles *(1962)*

is Minimalism's similarities to the unceasing repetitions of propaganda and advertising in consumer culture that should provoke our distrust.

One could compare, for example, Reich's constant repetitions of the cheery E dominant eleventh chord on four portable electric organs to the pop art repetitions of Andy Warhol's *Green Coca-Cola Bottles* (1962; Fig. 14.2). But viewers and listeners must decide for themselves whether these works represent a cynical acquiescence to commercialization, a critique thereof, or just as a fresh way of looking at a familiar object. As we will see, Minimalism draws on a wide range of styles and sources. How we interpret the ramifications of these connections, for our understanding of the music or of the composers, will depend upon our own perspectives and cultural contexts.

MINIMALIST SOURCES

POP ART AND FOUND OBJECTS

In addition to the basic principle of repetition, pop art provided musical Minimalism with a model for incorporating found objects and readymades (a term coined by the French artist Marcel Duchamp for everyday objects presented as art). Just as Warhol turned Coke bottles and Campbell's soup cans into works of art, and Robert Rauschenberg integrated shells, fabric, and everyday objects into his "combine" paintings, so Minimalist composers built some of their works from recorded voices and sounds, as well as techniques and materials borrowed from other traditions.

The most pervasive found objects in Minimalism are major and minor triads, scales, and arpeggios. Indeed, one could characterize the score of Riley's *In C* as a collection of tonal objects that are combined and repurposed in unexpected ways. The presence of tonal materials in early Minimalist works often produces an initial sense of familiarity; in most cases, however, the music has little to do with functional harmony. Rather than writing tonal music, Minimalist composers used the building blocks of tonality as raw material for pieces based on very different musical processes. It was this defamiliarization of everyday tonal materials that seems to have most provoked early audiences, who often found it difficult to hear beyond what seemed to be endless repetitions of the most basic musical ideas.

In their later works, however, Glass, Reich, and John Adams (see p. 293) introduced more traditional approaches to harmony. In an interview published in 1995, Glass challenged the centrality of atonality in narratives of twentieth-century music: "It now seems to me that the mainstream was tonal music, if you think about Shostakovich, Sibelius, Strauss, and Copland. When we look at the major literature from the perspective of the ninth decade in the twentieth century, it seems that twentieth-century music is tonal music. But there were moments when it didn't appear that way." In contrast to the objectivity and coolness of many of Glass's pieces discussed above, the return to tonality in his later music brought it closer to an expressive Neo-Romantic idiom. In his scores for major Hollywood films, including *The Hours* (2002) and *The Illusionist* (2006), Glass packs a strong emotional punch by reinterpreting his characteristic arpeggios and scales using functional harmonic progressions.

MODAL JAZZ

Modal jazz—which features long melodies over static or slowly moving modal harmonies—was another major influence on Minimalism, especially for Young, Reich, and Riley. Along with its musical qualities, the countercultural status of jazz as a symbol of liberation and "coolness" was part of its appeal. Reich has written of his time at Mills College in the 1960s, where he studied serialism and the music of Webern with Berio by day, then went to hear John Coltrane's modal jazz by night. This influence is obvious in the opening harmony of Reich's *Music for Mallet Instruments, Voices, and Organ* (see Ex. 14.3), which recalls the opening of Miles Davis's *So What*, from the legendary recording *Kind of Blue* (1959). While Davis's passage is based on a D-minor seventh chord as part of a D Dorian scale, Reich uses an F-minor seventh chord within an F Dorian framework. Both pieces feature, as Reich noted of Coltrane's music, "a lot of notes and very few changes of harmony."

Reich credits his integral involvement in the performance of his own music to the experience of playing jazz. Jazz also offered a model for incorporating input from other performers into his work, and one that was more in line with his notions of improvisation than was Cage's Indeterminacy. Furthermore, many performers who collaborated with Minimalist composers had jazz backgrounds and brought those sensibilities to the extensive rehearsal process through which many works were composed.

WORLD MUSIC

Just as Coltrane and other modal jazz composers drew influences from Africa, India, and the Middle East, the early Minimalists had extensive exposure to or training in non-Western music. Young attributes his interest in sustained sounds in part to the drones of Indian music he heard on recordings when he was a student at UCLA. Beginning in the late 1960s, both he and Riley devoted themselves to a long-term study of Indian vocal techniques. Reich spent the summer of 1970 in Ghana studying Ewe drumming with the master drummer Gideon Alorwoyie, and later investigated the Balinese gamelan. Before traveling to India and North Africa, Glass had transcribed music by the Indian sitar player and composer Ravi Shankar for the score to the film *Chappaqua* (1966).

In some cases, non-Western influences are evident on the surface of Minimalist music, as with the gamelan-like percussion and stratified layers in Reich's *Music for Mallet Instruments, Voices, and Organ*. Riley has featured North Indian and Middle Eastern musical influences in works like his programmatic string quartet *Salome Dances for Peace* (1987). But the Minimalists also sought to separate themselves from earlier Exoticist composers by arguing that they were more interested in new ideas about musical structure than in simply borrowing the sounds of other traditions.

Reich based many works on the 12-beat bell pattern typical of West African Ewe music, with its built-in ambiguities concerning the location of the downbeat and possibilities of division into groups of four or six beats. In the Ewe genre of Agbadza, complex polyrhythms are produced by the layering of short rhythmic patterns in instruments and vocal parts, each suggesting alternative downbeats and metric subdivisions (Reich's transcription of one passage is given in Ex. 14.4). The Ewe bell pattern is particularly clear in Reich's *Clapping Music* and *Music for Pieces of Wood* (1973), but it also plays a role in *Violin Phase*, which consists of a 12-beat pattern divided asymmetrically in the measure. As with the complex layers of Ewe music, Reich's phase pieces build rhythmic excitement by superimposing out-of-phase patterns that force the listener to continually reexamine the overall metric context.

In his early studies of Indian music, Glass was particularly inspired by additive rhythms. To accompany the Hindustani vocal genre of *dhrupad*, for example,

Example 14.4: *Transcription of Agbadza by Steve Reich, from "Gahu—A Dance of the Ewe Tribe in Ghana." The bell pattern appears in the top line.*

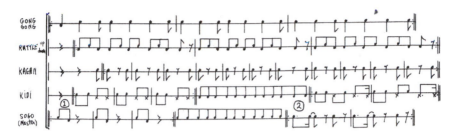

tabla players build up complex patterns by combining small units (typically of two to five beats each) in a steady pulse, as in the typical 12-beat (4+4+2+2) and 14-beat (5+2+3+4) patterns. In Glass's *1 + 1* (1967), the musician taps an amplified tabletop, creating rhythmic patterns based on the addition or subtraction of two units: two sixteenths plus a quarter note, and a single quarter note (Ex. 14.5). Glass extended the additive rhythmic technique to scales and arpeggios in his *Music in Similar Motion* (1969), which consists of blazingly fast patterns that expand and contract unpredictably. In his stage works, such as the operas *Einstein on the Beach* and *Satyagraha* (1980), Glass uses additive techniques to create extended rhythmic cycles. He applied these techniques not only to the musical material but to the libretto and stage action as well, governing them by similar repetitive patterns and processes.

TECHNOLOGY AND MULTIMEDIA

Among the most distinctive features of early Minimalism was the composers' use of electronic instruments and amplified sound. Among the put-downs in the *New York Times* critique of Reich's *Four Organs* was the disdainful comment on the use of a "quartet of tiny electric organs." Yet electronic keyboards were ideally suited for handling the rhythmic and endurance demands of early Minimalism. Amplification also made it possible for Glass and others to perform works in a variety of venues, from small art galleries to the Metropolitan Opera House, with a relatively small, portable, and inexpensive ensemble. Early on,

Example 14.5: *Philip Glass, 1 + 1, excerpt*

Glass came to regard his sound engineer, Kurt Munkacsi, as an integral member of the group. Glass went on to feature electronic keyboards in his soundtracks for films such as *Koyaanisqatsi* (1982), with its dizzying patterns and accelerated city scenes and cloudscapes.

The impact of technology on Minimalism goes far beyond questions of instruments and timbre; as with Minimalist art and pop art, technological processes and the techniques and materials of mass production suggested new ways of working, thinking, and hearing. Young cites among the inspirations for his interest in drones the experience of singing and whistling over the sound of a lathe while working in his high school machine shop. In some cases Young's drones were produced by traditional instruments, as with the *Well-Tuned Piano* (1964) which features long-sustained harmonies emphasizing the bright resonance of just intonation. But drones created technologically became increasingly important with Young's ongoing series of installations called *Dream House*, which began in the late 1960s. Created in collaboration with the artist Marian Zazeela, *Dream House* combines lighting effects, projections, and highly amplified sine waves that interact in changing ways with each other and with the resonant frequencies of the spaces as the listener moves through the rooms.

Riley began using tape loops, tape delay, and multitracking in the early 1960s, creating psychedelic echo effects that transformed the voice of a single instrument into a rich, swirling mass of sound. He describes *In C* as the sounds of layered tape loops re-created with live instruments. Another example of his ongoing exploration of technology is the piece *Sun Rings* (2002), written for the Kronos Quartet on commission from the National Aeronautics and Space Administration (NASA), which includes a choir, live processing of sounds, and an elaborate multimedia production featuring images from outer space.

As we have seen with Reich's early tape loop pieces like *Come Out*, technology has played a crucial role in his music, offering not only tools and ideas, but also an aesthetic stance; he has described the yoga-like discipline required to perform phase-shifting music as "imitating machines." Reich started working with digital sampling technologies in the 1980s, writing pieces that generate melodies and rhythms from the repetition of recorded voices and sounds. He also has collaborated with the video artist Beryl Korot in a series of innovative music theater works that combined looping images and sounds. In Reich's later music, these and other processes served works that engage directly with historical and current events, thus linking him to the politically motivated use of quotations in electronic music discussed in Chapter 13. Reich's *Different Trains* (1988) is based on the voices of Holocaust survivors, while *The Cave* (1994) transforms audio and video recordings of Israelis, Palestinians, and Americans reflecting on the biblical figure of Abraham. In *Three Tales* (2001), Reich takes technology itself as his subject, drawing on archival films, recorded speech, and images concerning the *Hindenburg* explosion, nuclear weapons testing on the Bikini atoll, and the implications of cloning and artificial intelligence.

PATHWAYS OF POSTMINIMALISM

Composers in many styles soon began adapting and extending the sounds, techniques, and ideas of Minimalism. A number of labels, including "Postminimalism," "Totalism," and "Maximalism," have been used to describe the works of composers whose music foregrounds a strong pulse, constant repetition, and very gradual changes, but in which the other defining elements of early Minimalism—namely, audible processes and a reduction in musical material—play a lesser role.

While early Minimalist composers tended to distill disparate influences into works with a unified tone, a rich eclecticism is often central to the meaning of works by Postminimalists like the American composer John Adams (b. 1947). Adams has written pieces that integrate many different styles and influences, including popular song, the jazz piano music of Jelly Roll Morton, the player piano works of Conlon Nancarrow (see Chapter 12), the idealized folk idiom of Charles Ives (see Chapter 4), and the cosmopolitan culture of the West Coast. Starting with his *Shaker Loops* (1978) for string ensemble and *Phrygian Gates* (1978) for piano, which use the techniques of early Minimalism—a steady pulse, tape-loop–inspired repetition, and slowly evolving processes—Adams introduced elements of nineteenth-century chromatic harmony to create a more lushly expressive idiom. Adams described his orchestral piece *Harmonielehre* (Theory of Harmony, 1985), which takes its title from Schoenberg's 1911 treatise, as a manifestation of his desire to reach out and embrace "all that harmony that we weren't supposed to touch."

Adams also engaged with history and politics in a series of influential and often controversial operas, including *Nixon in China* (1987), based on President Richard Nixon's groundbreaking visit to Communist China in 1972; *The Death of Klinghoffer* (1991), which depicts the murder of a Jewish passenger by Palestinian terrorists during the 1985 hijacking of the *Achille Lauro* cruise ship; and *Doctor Atomic* (2005), which focuses on the physicist J. Robert Oppenheimer and the detonation of the first atomic bomb in 1945.

The libretto for *Doctor Atomic*, assembled by the stage director Peter Sellars from historical documents and memoirs, explores the enormous pressures and moral dilemmas Oppenheimer and his colleagues faced in unleashing such destructive force. *Doctor Atomic* also evokes the early stages of the Cold War and the doctrine of "mutually assured destruction" (see Chapter 9). The opera alludes to suspicions faced by Oppenheimer and some of the other scientists due to their earlier leftist sympathies. Adams cites Cold War science fiction films as an important inspiration for the work: "a typical plot would involve a nuclear explosion in the desert—in Nevada perhaps. This would result in some disturbing phenomenon, something frightening and threatening. Nature would go awry, or a monster would appear."

Illustrating the eclectic combination of elements associated with Postminimalism, the music of *Doctor Atomic* includes passages with Minimalist rhythms and repetitive patterns, *musique concrète* to represent the storm and the sounds of machines, and a Neo-Romantic harmonic language. There are many allusions to the history of opera, starting with the large performing forces of the orchestra, chorus, and soloists. The libretto draws on poetry that was important to Oppenheimer, including passages from the nineteenth-century French poet Charles Baudelaire and the ancient Sanskrit epic, the *Bhagavad Gita*. A sonnet by the seventeenth-century English poet John Donne provides the searing text for the aria *Batter my heart*, which Oppenheimer sings as he stands alone in front of the bomb he has created the night before its detonation (see Anthology 26; Opera Sampler). *Batter my heart* amplifies what Adams describes as "Oppenheimer's enormous historical awareness" with the "archaic feel" of the D-minor chord sequences and the slow, stately form of the seventeenth-century chaconne. Adams also alludes to the vocal music of Donne's era in the rhythmic gestures used to express the text, and he evokes pieces like "Dido's Lament" from Henry Purcell's opera *Dido and Aeneas* in the flexible interaction between the lyrical melody and the repeating harmonic sequence and descending bass lines.

POSTMINIMALIST FUSIONS

Like the Minimalists, Postminimalist composers have drawn on many sources while forging links to diverse styles and traditions. The Dutch composer Louis Andriessen (b. 1939) has integrated Minimalism's pulse, repetition, and process into a more dissonant idiom with echoes of Stravinsky, Bartók, and Shostakovich. Andriessen, who studied with Berio and cites Cage, Frank Zappa, and jazz composer and saxophonist Ornette Coleman as influences, identifies hearing the Columbia recording of Riley's *In C* as a turning point in his development. His *Hoketus* (1977), for two matching ensembles of wind, percussion, and amplified instruments, uses the medieval hocket technique in which a musical line is divided between two parts. The slow, shifting rhythmic patterns and chromatic harmonies build relentlessly to a massive climax.

The American composer Phil Kline (b. 1953) extended the basic idea of Riley's *In C* in his "participatory sound sculpture" *Unsilent Night* (1992). The electronic score consists of multiple layers of loops and textures that were originally distributed via cassette, and later by CD and MP3 files, to be played on boom boxes carried by the participants through city streets. First performed as a sort of Postminimalist caroling party in Greenwich Village, the 45-minute-long piece is now a holiday fixture around the world. Another homage to *In C* is Darren Solomon's web-based work *In B♭ 2.0* (2009), which allows the user to combine short passages of music submitted via YouTube by musicians playing acoustic and electronic instruments in response to the request: "Sing or play an instrument, in B♭ major. Simple, floating textures work best, with no tempo or groove. Leave lots of silence between phrases."

Among the most prominent Postminimalists are several composers associated with the New York–based new-music organization Bang on a Can: Michael Gordon, David Lang, Julia Wolfe, and Evan Ziporyn. Known for their wildly eclectic "marathon concerts," these composers have infused their works with elements of world music, in particular gamelan (see the discussion of Ziporyn in Chapter 15), as well as virtuosic bebop jazz and the aggressive energy of rock. Gordon's multimedia projects include his score for *Decasia* (2001), Bill Morrison's haunting film based on decaying fragments of found footage.

Postminimalism has extended and intensified the crossover of sounds, ideas, and styles that was important to the emergence of Minimalism. La Monte Young worked with filmmaker and musician Tony Conrad and with John Cale, who went on to become a founding member of the art-rock band The Velvet Underground. Cale later collaborated with Riley on the improvisatory rock album *Church of Anthrax* (1971). Reich worked with jazz guitarist Pat Metheny on *Electric Counterpoint* (1987), a prominent sample from which was featured in The Orb's widely heard dance track *Little Fluffy Clouds* (1990). The British electronic duo Orbital adapted Reich's tape loop technique in their *Time Becomes* (1993), creating a phase piece based on a vocal sample from *Star Trek: The Next Generation*. We can also hear a Postminimalist homage to Reich in the ambient electronic piece *Music 4 No Musicians* (1997) by Coldcut. A sample of Reich's *Come Out* is featured in the 2004 song "America's Most Blunted" by the rapper MF Doom and producer Mad Lib; their source was not the original but a remix from 1999 by Japanese DJ Ken Ishii. Glass's *Low Symphony* (1992) adapts songs from the 1977 album *Low* by David Bowie and Brian Eno. Eno, a producer for U2 and many others, used tape loops, phasing, and echo effects in his *Music for Airports* (1978). Together with software designer Peter Chilvers, Eno has created a series of interactive multimedia applications such as Bloom (2008) that allow users to create their own Postminimalist music in real time.

"HOLY MINIMALISM"

We can hear very different formulations of Postminimalism in the music of three composers who are sometimes grouped under the label of "Holy" or "Sacred Minimalism": from Poland, Henryk Górecki; from Britain, John Tavener; and from Estonia, Arvo Pärt. Early in their careers all three composers explored the trends we have been considering, including Serialism, texture music, and quotation and collage, before striking out in new directions in the late 1960s and early 1970s. Inspired in part by the sound and techniques of Minimalism, they adopted a radically simplified musical vocabulary, anchored in tonality and modality and strongly tinged with religiosity and mysticism. Like the Minimalists, they have reached broad audiences through recordings. The 1992 Nonesuch recording of Górecki's hauntingly contemplative Third Symphony (*Symphony of Sorrowful Songs*, 1976), featuring the soprano Dawn Upshaw, went on to become one of the best-selling classical recordings of all time.

Pärt (b. 1935) came of age as a composer in Soviet-controlled Estonia, where his interest in twelve-tone music and other new techniques brought him into conflict with the authorities. Later his sacred work provoked similar trouble, and he immigrated to Germany in 1980. We can hear Minimalism's influences in Pärt's "tintinnabuli" style, which he introduced in the piano piece *Für Alina* (1976). Taking cues from Minimalism, Pärt applies gradual musical processes to simple diatonic pitch collections, but he was also inspired by the centuries-old practice of "change ringing," in which church bells are rung in elaborate patterns over extended cycles. The opening of the Kyrie of Pärt's *Berliner Messe* (Berlin Mass, 1997) demonstrates the basic principles of the tintinnabuli technique, homorhythmically combining diatonic scales with arpeggiations of a triad (Ex. 14.6). Thus in measure 3 the sopranos sing the notes of a G-minor triad while the altos sing a descending scale from D to G. Throughout the movement the vocal phrases are answered in the same fashion by the organ, which

Example 14.6: *Arvo Pärt, Kyrie, from* Berlin Mass, *mm. 1–4*

sustains a G pedal. Within the piece's serene and contemplative atmosphere, Pärt creates contrast and a sense of progression with varied rhythms, dynamics, and textures.

Here and in other works, Pärt draws connections with the long history of sacred choral music not only by setting the Ordinary of the Catholic Mass, but also by employing medieval techniques such as isorhythm and fauxbourdon, while his melodic style is inspired by Gregorian chant.

The success of Holy Minimalism owes much to the renewed popularity of chant and New Age spirituality in the late twentieth century. In 1995 the Choir of King's College, Cambridge released a recording of works by Tavener, Górecki, and Pärt interleaved with performances of plainchant; the previous year an album of chant recordings made in a Spanish monastery by the Benedictine monks of Santo Domingo sold millions of copies worldwide. Another measure of the broad interest in chant was its surprising appearance in electronic dance music, such as the samples of chant recordings used in Enigma's *MCMXC a.D* (released in "anno Domini" 1990).

Here and in other works, Pärt's music and its contexts symbolize the astonishing and often bewildering heterogeneity that characterizes Western musical culture at the turn of the twenty-first century. But the idea that such an incongruous combination of elements—Postminimalist techniques used by a devout Russian Orthodox composer from Estonia, marketed to audiences involved with medievalism, New Age spirituality, and rave culture—could coexist in one piece no longer seems particularly unusual. While Bartók, Stravinsky, and Ligeti responded to a similar sense of overwhelming diversity in terms of "tangled chaos," a terror of "the infinitude of possibilities," and the breakdown of "taboos," in the new century such border crossings between styles, audiences, and traditions are likely to be perceived as just the way things are, as we will see in Chapter 15.

FOR FURTHER READING

Bernard, Jonathan W., "Minimalism, Postminimalism, and the Resurgence of Tonality in Recent American Music," *American Music* 21, no. 1 (2003): 112–133

Cohn, Richard, "Transpositional Combination of Beat-Class Sets in Steve Reich's Phase-Shifting Music," *Perspectives of New Music* 30, no. 2 (1992): 146–177

Duckworth, William, *Sound and Light: La Monte Young and Marian Zazeela* (New York: Associated University Press, 2009)

Fink, Robert, "(Post-)minimalism 1970–2000: The Search for a New Mainstream," in *The Cambridge History of Twentieth-Century Music*, edited by Nicholas Cook and Anthony Pople, 539–556 (Cambridge: Cambridge University Press, 2004)

Gann, Kyle, *American Music in the Twentieth Century* (New York: Schirmer, 1997)

Glass, Philip, and Robert T. Jones, *Music by Philip Glass* (New York: Harper and Row, 1987)

Gopinath, Sumanth, "The Problem of the Political in Steve Reich's *Come Out*," in Robert Adlington, *Sound Commitments: Avant-garde Music and the Sixties*, 121–144 (Oxford: Oxford University Press, 2009)

Hillier, Paul, *Arvo Pärt* (Oxford: Oxford University Press, 1997)

Joseph, Branden W., *Beyond the Dream Syndicate: Tony Conrad and the Arts after Cage* (New York: Zone Books, 2011)

Locke, David, "The Metric Matrix: Simultaneous Multidimensionality in African Music," *Analytical Approaches to World Music Journal* 1, no. 1 (2011)

Potter, Keith, *Four Musical Minimalists: La Monte Young, Terry Riley, Steve Reich, Philip Glass* (Cambridge: Cambridge University Press, 2000)

Trochimczyk, Maja, *The Music of Louis Andriessen* (New York: Routledge, 2002)

CHAPTER FIFTEEN

Border Crossings

We began our discussion of musical developments in the early decades of the twentieth century with Robert Musil's formulation of the "sense of possibility." Musil was writing in the context of the external and internal "loss of cohesion" that accompanied the splintering of the Austro-Hungarian Empire and modernity's profound transformations of many aspects of daily life. As we consider some of the directions taken by composers, performers, and audiences in the early twenty-first century, it becomes clear that the pace of change in the world around us and within us continues to accelerate, rendering "systems of happiness and balance" to help us maintain our equilibrium more necessary than ever.

A short list of the major events and trends of the past 25 years includes the end of the Cold War (signaled by the fall of the Berlin Wall in 1989 and the peaceful dissolution of the Soviet Union in 1991); the creation of the European Union in 1993 and the emergence of China, India, and Brazil as new world economic powers; the rapid formation of vast global networks of wealth, information, and communication (Google was founded in 1998 and Facebook in 2004); and the final mapping of the human genome in 2003. Based on new discoveries in quantum mechanics, cosmologists now maintain that our universe is only one of an infinite number of parallel universes in which every possibility has been realized. Add to this a growing awareness of climate change, the rise of global terrorism, the resurgence of new forms of nationalism and fundamentalism, and the construction of new walls and lines of demarcation, and it becomes clear that many of the real and imaginary boundaries that have shaped the lives of people around the globe over the past century have been comprehensively redrawn. Indeed, just as some historians have argued for a "long nineteenth century" lasting from 1789 to 1914, the momentous changes around 1991 have given rise to the notion of the "Short Century," based on the belief that a "short twentieth century" (1914–1991) has already given way to a new epoch.

As Leonard Meyer predicted in 1967 (see Chapter 13), our era of "fluctuating stasis" has produced many composers who continue to explore all the various -isms and styles we have investigated in this book. At the same time, border crossings of every kind have opened up new possibilities for music-making. All the examples cited below have precedents in the twentieth century and previous epochs. Yet in each case it can be argued that the very different contexts of our time give them all new meanings and implications. As John Adams noted in 1998, "We're in a kind of post-style era. Composers my age and younger, we are not writing in one, highly defined, overarching expression, like Steve Reich or Luciano Berio would write."

The emerging generation of composers and performers has much less invested in the old battles, historical narratives, and anxieties than their elders do. Musil's "possibilist" notion that things "could probably just as well be otherwise" would now strike many as self-evident. And while as many voices as ever are clamoring that things have to be the way they are, their uniformity of perspective and ultimate authority have never been less. On the contrary, contemporary composers must establish a direction and context for their music in the absence of either traditional constraints or supports that allowed previous generations to attract attention and be heard.

GLOBAL ENCOUNTERS

The most obvious examples of border crossings today are the countless forms of transnational, post-national, and post-colonial music-making that we noted in our brief discussion of world music traditions at the end of Chapter 13. Despite legitimate concerns about the homogenizing force of global media and communications, there is clear evidence of the resilience of local traditions, alongside the emergence of hybrid cross-cultural forms of music-making. The Austrian-born Lukas Ligeti (b. 1965), the son of Györgi Ligeti, founded the band Burkina Electric, which features the West African singer and composer Mai Lingani. A percussionist with a background in jazz and computer music, Ligeti describes the band's style as "electronic dance club music, related to Western DJ culture, but using elements of traditional music, in this case from Burkina Faso." The proliferation of local hip-hop dialects around the world signals trends that also appear in electronic music, jazz, and other genres.

Another border-crossing figure is Osvaldo Golijov (b. 1960), who was born into a Russian-Jewish family in Argentina and spent his early twenties in Israel before coming to the United States in 1986 to study with George Crumb (see Chapter 13). Golijov has worked with rock, jazz, folk, and classical musicians, and among the early influences he cites are classical chamber music, Jewish liturgical and Klezmer music, and the new tango style of the Argentinean composer Astor Piazzola. Golijov's lullaby for voice and piano *Lúa descolorida* (Moon, Colorless, 2002), based on a text by the Galician poet Rosalía de Castro, alludes to the melismatic vocal lines in François Couperin's *Leçons de ténèbres* (1714), the luminous harmonies of Franz Schubert's C-Major String Quintet (1828), and the rhythms and harmonies of Spanish dance.

As never before, such transnational border crossings are moving in both directions. For example, the Javanese gamelan composer and ethnomusicologist Rahayu Supanggah (b. 1949) studied in Paris and has collaborated with artists and musicians in Europe and the United States; he and stage director Robert Wilson created *I La Galigo* (2004), a theatrical work based on the ancient Indonesian epic. Reversing this trajectory, the American composer Evan Ziporyn (b. 1959) based his opera *A House in Bali* (2009) on a memoir by Colin McPhee (see Chapter 8) and his own study of gamelan music. Premiered in Bali, the work combines newly composed music for a gamelan ensemble with rock-inflected, Postminimalist passages performed by a small group of strings, electric guitar, keyboards, and percussion.

MUSIC IN-BETWEEN

Popular music elements feature prominently in the works of many composers, such as the British composer Thomas Adès (b. 1971). In his chamber opera *Powder Her Face* (1995), Adès alludes to 1930s popular song, tango, and twentieth-century opera styles from Berg to Weill; he has also drawn on electronic dance music in his rave-inspired "Ecstasio," from his orchestral work *Asyla* (1997). But our new epoch is defined still more clearly by the movement of composers, performers, and audiences across the traditional boundaries separating popular, avant-garde, indie, jazz, folk, and classical music. Indeed, the clear hierarchy that once demarcated such categories is steadily disintegrating.

Unlike the Postmodernists of the late twentieth century, who tended to keep all musical languages at an ironic distance, many composers today feel at home in more than one milieu. The American composer Nico Muhly (b. 1981) has written orchestral works for major orchestras and scores for *The Reader* (2008) and other films, all while collaborating with such diverse musicians as Björk, Grizzly Bear, and Antony and the Johnsons. In "The Only Tune," from his wide-ranging CD *Mothertongue* (2008), Muhly and the folk musician Sam Amidon reconceive the folk song "The Wind and the Rain" in various avant-garde transformations before concluding with an ethereal arrangement featuring fiddle, guitar, and celesta.

Other notable figures developing this in-between zone include DJ Spooky, Missy Mazzoli, Bryce Dessner, Daniel Bernard Roumain, Mica Levi, Sufjan Stevens, Joanna Newsom, Yo-Yo Ma, and Chris Thile.

Festivals, performance venues, and record labels facilitate such border crossings by offering a common ground where audiences of different tastes and backgrounds can come together. A 2011 concert presented by the New York–based Wordless Music organization included György Ligeti's Chamber Concerto; the Philip Glass/David Bowie/Brian Eno Symphony No. 4, *Heroes*; and the premiere of an orchestral work called *Doghouse* by Radiohead guitarist Jonny Greenwood. The 2009 album *Central Market* by Tyondai Braxton, guitarist and singer for the rock band Battles and the son of Anthony Braxton, includes rock songs, playfully eclectic orchestral compositions, textural electronic works, and Postminimalist loop-based pieces.

Film scores have played a particularly important role in blurring the distinctions between "serious" and "popular" compositions. John Corigliano (b. 1938), who has been a significant force in American music since the 1970s, arranged his Neo-Romantic score for the film *The Red Violin* (1998) as a freestanding Suite for Violin and Orchestra (2000). The Chinese composer Tan Dun (b. 1957), now residing in the United States, has emerged as a leading transnational figure on the strength of pieces like the *Symphony 1997: Heaven Earth Mankind*, commissioned to celebrate the reunification of Hong Kong with China, and his scores for the martial arts film *Crouching Tiger, Hidden Dragon* (2000) and *Hero* (2002).

Here, too, the influence goes both ways, as in the Austrian composer Olga Neuwirth's (b. 1968) opera *Lost Highway* (2003), based on the film of that name by David Lynch. The work begins with an ominously swelling drone that builds to a sudden orchestral outburst, evoking Lynch's long opening credit sequence, which shows a car's headlights hurtling through a deserted nighttime landscape. This climax gives way to layered loops of electric guitar, strings, winds, and sampled voices, before the live singers finally appear. The staging of *Lost Highway* includes video projections and recorded sounds, as well as electronically manipulated live instrumental and vocal parts. Neuwirth speaks of being inspired by the "rapidly changing visual and auditive perspectives" in the film to create an experience of "innumerable (architectural and emotional) spaces inside and outside."

MULTIMEDIA AND SOUND ART

As exemplified by Neuwirth's film-inspired opera, border crossings among the arts are another flourishing area of creativity. Works involving sounds, images, words, and movements go by a number of labels, including "sound art," "new media," "intermedia," and "dynamic media." Created by artists who don't necessarily think of themselves as composers, presented mostly outside of traditional concert halls, and directed at audiences who may not even think they are listening to music, such works nevertheless make sound an integral part of the expe-rience. The notion that music is a subcategory of the broader spheres of sound, touch, and space situates composition within the emerging realms of sound studies, auditory culture, architectural acoustics, and aural geographies.

Many pieces attempt to break down the distinctions between composed works and the sounds of the world around us. In *Traffic Mantra* (1992) by the American sound artist Bruce Odland (b. 1952), the ambient noises themselves comprise the work. Installed in Trajan's Forum in Rome, the piece amplified the noise of pass-ing traffic and filtered it through the various resonances of ancient clay amphorae in the site to create constantly shifting "pools of harmonics." The form of the work was determined by the constantly changing sonic environment and traffic pat-terns, which varied from periods of frantic activity to more sporadic events during the night. The Spanish sound artist Francisco López (b. 1964) has produced a large body of works and installations that feature extended "field recordings" of natural and man-made soundscapes. While he acknowledges his debt to Cage, he has also strongly critiqued what he calls Cage's "devious version of the classical procedural paradigm," which ultimately keeps the focus on the composer and compositional procedures, rather than on a direct and immersive engagement with sounds.

Seeking an ecology of music, other artists have constructed pieces out of ele-ments particular to a certain place and time. John Luther Adams (b. 1953) has created sound-and-light installations like *The Place Where You Go to Listen* (2004) that respond to the seismic activity, aurora borealis, and other natural forces of the Alaskan environment where he makes his home. The San Francisco–based composer and intermedia artist Pamela Z (b. 1956) has participated in the *Elastic City Walks* project in New York, in which artists in many forms lead small groups of participants through the city. Her piece *Site Reading* (2011) is described as:

> a walk that creates musical scores from the graphic features (micro and macro) of downtown Manhattan. Participants will form a roving experi-mental sound and performance ensemble that will interpret and play the neighborhood's building facades, sidewalk hardware, public art and street markings to make a contrapuntal, chance-based chorus.

With computer applications such as *Ambience*, anyone can experience personal-ized environmental soundscapes with recordings of diverse environments from a California beach to a busy marketplace in Morocco.

MUSIC, SCIENCE, AND TECHNOLOGY

Paralleling the expansion of musical works to involve our various senses, con-temporary composition is being further transformed by new fusions of music, technology, and science. Many composers are working with digital samples, such as Annie Gosfield (b. 1960) in *The Harmony of the Body-Machine* (2003) for cello and electronics, which features sampled sounds of band saws, metal presses, and pile drivers. Others are making the technology part of the piece, as with the *1-Bit Symphony* (2010) by composer, artist, and programmer Tristan Perich (b. 1982). It consists of an electronic circuit with a headphone jack assembled inside a clear plastic CD case that performs his five-movement symphony for 1-bit electronic sounds.

Research centers such as the MIT Media Lab, the Stanford Center for Computer Research in Music and Acoustics, and IRCAM (see Chapter 11) are creating new constellations of composers, performers, engineers, and scientists. The availability of tools such as functional magnetic resonance imaging (fMRI) now makes it possible to observe in real time how the brain responds to music. As more and more people bridge the disciplinary divide between the arts and sciences, research has flourished in the areas of music cognition, music therapy, and the relationships between music and language. Composer-theorist David Cope has developed an artificial intelligence system that both analyzes and composes music in the styles of Bach, Beethoven, Mozart, Mahler, and Scott Joplin. A number of programs are being used to model and shape listeners' preferences (such as the Music Genome Project, which drives Pandora's personalized Internet radio); others are being designed in the search for formulas that will make it possible to compose a surefire hit.

Our daily lives are shaped by interactions with multimedia technologies like computers, gaming systems, smartphones, and home theaters, which provide tools to work with sound, images, words, and movement. As the science fiction fantasies of human-computer cyborgs and lifelike androids seem ever more possible, artists and scholars have explored the far-reaching implications of the idea of the "posthuman." The notion that the essence of our consciousness and selves is nothing but an informational pattern that will eventually be transferable into immortal machines is the subject of Machover's *Death and the Powers,* whose operabots are depicted on the front cover of this book (see Chapter 1). What these transcendental and apocalyptic possibilities mean for how we interact with each other and our natural environment is an increasingly urgent subject for debate.

ARTIST AND AUDIENCE

One of Walter Benjamin's most prescient observations in *The Work of Art in the Age of Mechanical Reproduction* (1936; see Chapter 5) concerned the breakdown of the distinction between "author and public." Unlike previous centuries, when "a small number of writers were confronted by many thousands of readers," Benjamin observed that in the early twentieth century the expansion of opportunities for publication had made it possible for an increasing number of readers to become writers. In the age of Web 2.0, interactive social media, and user-generated content, the proliferation of authorship has reached unprecedented levels.

In various spheres of music, traditional channels for education and career building still play a central role. At the same time, the burgeoning border crossings between artist and audience, expert and amateur, production and consumption, and original and remix are redefining what it means to be a composer, performer, or listener. Particularly in the areas of electronic music and multimedia, easy-to-use hardware and software and free distribution via the Internet have fueled creativity worldwide, including, no doubt, by many who are reading this book right now.

To be sure, the border crossings we have discussed have both positive and negative ramifications. Just as Benjamin wrote of the "destructive and cathartic" implications of art in "the age of mechanical reproduction," we can observe, along with the many gains brought by current trends, much that is being swept away in musical traditions around the world. Reaching across musical boundaries can be done in a spirit of cooperation, cross-fertilization, and reciprocity, but it can also be viewed as trespassing, appropriation, and colonization. Similarly, the act of crossing borders can divide people and cultures just as easily as it can unite them. For anyone engaging with music today in any form, whether as listener, composer, performer, scholar, teacher, student, business person, or most likely some combination of those roles, the challenge is to define and defend your own path forward.

Musil posited the dangerous, provocative, and stimulating "sense of possibility" as the opposite of "a sense of reality" and the "unquestioned belief that things are as they should be." And yet, as we have seen with the border crossings noted here, as well as with all the extraordinary, disturbing, and exhilarating music considered in previous chapters, the boundaries between a sense of possibility and a sense of reality are becoming ever more open to question.

FOR FURTHER READING

Auner, Joseph, "'Sing It for Me': Posthuman Ventriloquism in Recent Popular Music," *Journal of the Royal Musical Association* 128, no. 1 (2003): 98–122

Condry, Ian, *Hip Hop Japan* (Durham: Duke University Press, 2006)

Cope, David, *Virtual Music: Computer Synthesis of Musical Style* (Cambridge: MIT Press, 2001)

Corona, Ignacio, and Alejandro L. Madrid, *Postnational Musical Identities: Cultural Production, Distribution, and Consumption in a Globalized Scenario* (Lanham, MD: Lexington Books, 2008)

Demers, Joanna, *Listening through the Noise: The Aesthetics of Experimental Electronic Music* (Oxford: Oxford University Press, 2010)

Gopinath, Sumanth, and Jason Stanyek, *Oxford Handbook of Mobile Music Studies* (Oxford: Oxford University Press, 2013)

Hobsbawm, Eric, and Antonio Polito, *On the Edge of the New Century*, translated by Allan Cameron (New York: The New Press, 2000)

LaBelle, Brandon, *Background Noise: Perspectives on Sound Art* (New York: Continuum, 2006)

Levitin, Daniel, *This Is Your Brain on Music* (New York: Penguin, 2006)

Levitz, Tamara, et. al "Colloquy: Musicology Beyond Borders?" *Journal of the American Musicology Society* 65, no. 3 (2012): 821–861.

Licht, Alan, "Sound Art: Origins, Development and Ambiguities," *Organised Sound* 14, no. 1 (2009), 3–10

Metzer, David, *Musical Modernism at the Turn of the Twenty-First Century* (Cambridge: Cambridge University Press, 2009)

Patel, Aniruddh, *Music, Language, and the Brain* (New York: Oxford University Press, 2008)

Scherzinger, Martin, "'Art' Music in a Cross-Cultural Context: The Case of Africa," in *The Cambridge History of Twentieth-Century Music,* edited by Nicholas Cook and Anthony Pople, 584–614 (Cambridge: Cambridge University Press, 2004)

Sheppard, W. Anthony, "Blurring the Boundaries: Tan Dun's Tinte and The First Emperor," *Journal of Musicology* 26, no. 3 (2009): 285–326

GLOSSARY

absolute music Music, usually instrumental, that is independent of words, drama, visual images, or anything representational; it expresses ideas that are only musical in nature.

accidental A sign that calls for altering the pitch of a note: a ♯ raises the pitch a half step, a ♭ lowers it a half step, and a ♮ cancels a previous accidental.

acoustics Branch of physics concerned with the properties, production, transmission, and aural reception of sound.

additive rhythm Rhythmic patterns built up by the addition of small units (in contrast to rhythms based on the subdivision of a regular beat).

aleatory Composed using chance procedures, from the Latin alea, "dice."

antiphonal Adjective describing a manner of performance in which two or more groups alternate.

aria Lyrical number for solo voice in an opera or oratorio.

arpeggio Chord in which the individual pitches are sounded one after another instead of simultaneously.

articulation Any of various ways a note can be performed, for example, with a sharp attack or connected to the previous note; usually indicated by special notational symbols.

atonal, atonality Terms for music that avoids establishing a central pitch or tonal center.

augmentation Statement of a theme in longer note values, often twice as slow as the original.

augmented second The interval of a major second expanded from two half steps to three; for example, C♮ to D♯.

avant-garde Term for art that is iconoclastic, irreverent, antagonistic, and nihilistic, seeking to overthrow established aesthetics.

barline Vertical line used in a musical score to indicate a division between measures.

Baroque Period of music history from about 1600 to about 1750, overlapping the late Renaissance and early Classical periods.

beat Unit of regular pulsation in musical time.

blue note Slight drop or slide in pitch on the third, fifth, or seventh degree of a major scale, common in blues and jazz.

brass instrument Wind instrument with a cup-shaped mouthpiece, a tube that flares into a bell, and slides or valves to vary the pitch.

cadence Melodic or harmonic succession that closes a musical phrase, section, or composition.

canon Composition in which the voices enter successively at determined pitch and time

A1

intervals, all performing the same melody. Double canons have two pairs of voices based on different melodies; with a canon in contrary motion the answering melody is in inversion.

cantata Multimovement work for solo singers, chorus, and instrumentalists, based on a lyric or dramatic poetic narrative.

chaconne Form, originating in the Baroque period, in which variations unfold over a repeated bass line.

chamber music Music for a group of up to about ten players, with one person to a part.

chamber orchestra A small orchestra, often with one person to a part.

chance Approach to composing music pioneered by John Cage, in which some of the decisions normally made by the composer are instead determined through random procedures, such as flipping coins.

character piece Short piece, usually for piano and often in ternary form, that projects a single principal mood or spirit, often conveyed by its title.

chorale Strophic hymn in the Lutheran tradition, intended to be sung by the congregation.

chord Combination of three or more pitches, heard simultaneously.

chromatic scale Scale built of all twelve pitches in the octave.

chromaticism Musical vocabulary employing all or most of the chromatic pitches, originally as an expansion of a major or minor key.

Classical Musical idiom of the mid- to late eighteenth century, generally characterized by an emphasis on melody over relatively light accompaniment; simple, clearly articulated harmonic plans; periodic phrasing; clearly delineated forms based on contrast between themes, between keys, between stable and unstable passages, and between sections with different functions; and contrasts of mood, style, and figuration within movements as well as between them.

cluster A tightly packed group of three or more notes played together, usually separated by half steps or whole steps.

coda Final part of an instrumental movement, usually coming after the standard parts of the form are completed.

common practice General term to describe widely shared conventions in Western music from ca. 1600 to ca. 1900 for structuring harmony and melody, including functional harmonic progressions, voice-leading techniques, and the treatment of dissonance.

concert aria Aria for voice and orchestra written for performance as an independent composition.

concerto Instrumental work in several movements for solo instrument and orchestra; a concerto grosso features two or more soloists.

conservatory School that specializes in teaching music.

conductor Person who, by means of gestures, leads performances of musical ensembles.

consonance Combination of pitches that provides a sense of stability in music.

counterpoint The art of combining two or more melodic lines in a single texture.

cyclic form Musical structure in which thematic material from one movement recurs in a later movement, often at the end of the work.

decadence In the late nineteenth century, originally a pejorative label for an artistic style characterized by a perceived decline of moral and ethical standards; the name was later adopted by many artists and writers.

development In sonata form, the second section, in which the thematic material is fragmented and modulates through a range of keys.

diatonic Built from the seven pitches of a major or minor scale.

diminished seventh chord Chord built of a diminished triad and a diminished seventh, occurring naturally on the raised seventh step of a minor scale.

diminution Statement of a theme in shorter note values, often twice as fast as the original.

dissonance Combination of pitches that sounds unstable, in need of resolution.

dominant In tonal music, the pitch a perfect fifth above the tonic, or the chord based on that note.

dominant seventh chord The chord form that occurs naturally on the dominant of a major key, consisting of a major triad and a minor seventh.

Dorian A mode based on the pattern of whole steps and half steps w–h–w–w–w–h–w. Using the white notes on the piano keyboard, this mode can be played D–E–F–G–A–B–C–D.

double stop The playing of two pitches simultaneously on a bowed string instrument.

drone A note or notes sustained throughout an entire piece or section.

dynamics Element of musical expression relating to the degree of loudness or softness, or volume, of a sound.

English horn Double-reed woodwind instrument, larger and lower in range than the oboe.

etude An instrumental piece designed to develop a particular skill or performing technique.

exoticism In music, a style in which the rhythms, melodies, or instrumentation are designed to evoke the atmosphere of foreign countries or cultures.

exposition Opening section of sonata form, in which the principal thematic material is presented. The first theme group is in the tonic key, and the second is generally in the dominant or the relative major.

fauxbourdon Style of polyphony in the early Renaissance, in which two voices are written, moving mostly in parallel sixths and ending each phrase on an octave, while a third unwritten voice is sung in parallel perfect fourths below the upper voice.

fermata Symbol placed over a note, chord, or rest indicating it is to be sustained longer than the indicated time value, at the performer's discretion.

figured bass A form of notation for keyboard or other accompanimental instrument in which the bass line is supplied with numbers or flat or sharp signs to indicate the appropriate chord to be played.

finale Last movement of an instrumental work, or the last, extended section of an act in an opera.

folk music Music of unknown authorship from a particular region or people, passed down through oral tradition.

form Structure and design in music, based on repetition, contrast, and variation.

foxtrot A popular style of dance music that originated in America in the early twentieth century.

free jazz An experimental jazz style introduced in the 1960s by Ornette Coleman, using improvisation that disregards the standard forms and conventions of jazz.

fugato A passage of imitative counterpoint that evokes fugal techniques within a larger work.

fugue Polyphonic form in which one or more themes or "subjects" are treated in imitative counterpoint. In a double fugue two different themes or "subjects" are developed simultaneously.

functional harmony Conventions governing common-practice tonality that created expectations for which chords were mostly likely to follow in a chord progression.

gamelan Indonesian ensemble of instruments, including gongs, bronze metallophones, and drums, usually along with solo wind and string instruments.

genre (1) Type or category of musical composition, such as sonata or symphony. (2) A more general classification of a type of art or music characterized by a set of conventions and expectations.

Gesamtkunstwerk (German, "total artwork") Term coined by Richard Wagner for an opera in which poetry, scenic design, staging, action, and music all work together toward one artistic expression.

gigue Stylized dance movement of a standard Baroque suite.

glissando A slide from one pitch to another, in contrast to discrete steps of a scale.

habanera Moderate duple-meter dance of Cuban origin, based on a characteristic rhythmic figure, and popular in the nineteenth century.

half-diminished seventh chord Chord constructed of a diminished triad and a minor seventh, most commonly encountered in the minor mode as a ii^7 harmony that leads to the dominant (V).

half step Distance between two adjacent pitches on a piano.

harmonic progression Series of chords that are directed toward a harmonic goal, usually a stable, consonant sonority.

harmonic series The higher overtones or partials produced by a vibrating string or column of air above the fundamental pitch, with frequencies based on the ratios $\frac{1}{2}$, $\frac{1}{3}$, $\frac{1}{4}$, etc.

harmonic sequence A melodic-harmonic pattern that is restated successively at different pitch levels.

harmony Aspect of music that pertains to simultaneous combinations of notes, the intervals and chords that result, the succession of chords, and the underlying principles.

harpsichord Keyboard instrument, originally in use between the fifteenth and eighteenth centuries, in which the strings are plucked by quills instead of being struck with hammers like the piano; returned to regular use in the 1920s in association with Neoclassicism.

heterophony Music or musical texture in which a melody is performed by two or more parts simultaneously in more than one way, for example, one voice performing it simply, and the other with embellishments.

hexachord Set of six pitches. In twelve-tone theory, the first six or last six notes in the row.

homophony Musical texture in which all voices move together in essentially the same rhythm.

homorhythmic Having the same rhythm, as when several voices or parts move together.

hymn Song in praise of God, often involving congregational participation.

Indeterminacy An approach to composition, pioneered by John Cage, in which the composer leaves certain aspects of the music unspecified or up to the performer.

interval Relationship or distance between two pitches.

inversion (1) In a melody or twelve-tone row, reversing the upward or downward direction of each interval while maintaining its size; or the new melody or row form that results. (2) In harmony, a distribution of the notes in a chord so that a note other than the root is the lowest note. (3) In counterpoint, reversing the relative position of two melodies, so that the one that had been lower is now above the other.

isorhythm Repetition of an extended pattern of durations throughout a section or an entire composition.

just intonation A system of tuning notes in the scale common in the Renaissance, in which most (but not all) thirds, sixths, perfect fourths, and perfect fifths are in perfect tune, as opposed to adjusted slightly as in equal temperament.

key In tonal music, the organization of pitches and chords around a central pitch, the tonic.

key signature Sharps or flats placed at the beginning of a piece to show the key or tonal center of a work.

leading tone The seventh degree in a major or minor scale; it has a strong tendency to move to the tonic.

leitmotive (German, "leading motive") In Wagner's operas, a short theme associated with a character, idea, object, or place, which returns continually in different transformations.

libretto Text of an opera or oratorio.

lied (German, "song"; plural, *lieder*) A setting of a poem for solo singer or several singers, with the accompaniment of a piano, sometimes supplemented by other instruments.

liturgy The body of texts to be spoken or sung, and ritual actions to be performed, in a religious service.

major scale Scale consisting of seven different pitches in a specific pattern of whole and half steps. It differs from a minor scale primarily in that the interval between the second and third pitches is a whole step.

mass Musical setting of the texts from the Mass service of the Catholic Church; usually in five movements, consisting of the Kyrie, Gloria, Credo, Sanctus, and Agnus Dei.

measure Recurring temporal unit containing a fixed number of beats, indicated on the musical staff by barlines.

melody Succession of pitches, usually in several phrases, perceived as a coherent, self-contained structure.

melisma A long melodic passage sung to a single syllable of text.

meter Recurring patterns of strong and weak beats, dividing musical time into units of equal duration; duple meter has two beats per measure, and triple has three. Music with a clearly defined meter is considered metric; music without regular meter is considered ametric.

Mighty Handful Group of five Russian composers in the later nineteenth century, including Mily Balakirev, Aleksandr Borodin, César Cui, Modest Musorgsky, and Nikolay Rimsky-Korsakov, who fostered a distinctly Russian art music.

metronome Mechanical or electrical device used to indicate tempo by sounding regular beats at adjustable speeds.

microtonal Music using intervals smaller than a half step.

minor scale Scale consisting of seven different pitches in a specific pattern of whole and half steps. It differs from the major scale primarily in that the interval between the second and third pitches is a half step.

minstrelsy Popular form of musical theater in the United States during the mid-nineteenth century, in which white performers blackened their faces and impersonated African Americans.

mode (1) A scale or melody type, identified by the particular intervallic relationships among the notes in the mode. (2) In particular, one of the eight (later twelve) scale or melody types recognized by church musicians and theorists beginning in the Middle Ages.

modulation In tonal music, a gradual change from one key to another within a section of a movement.

monophonic Consisting of a single unaccompanied melodic line.

motive Short melodic or rhythmic idea; the smallest fragment of a theme that forms a recognizable unit.

movement Complete, self-contained segment of a larger musical work.

Musikdrama (German, "music drama") Term often applied to Wagner's mature operas, suggesting a carefully planned coordination of music, words, and scenic presentation.

nationalism Attitude or outlook that posits an identity for a group of people through characteristics such as common language, shared culture, historical tradition and institutions, and musical elements derived from folk or indigenous styles.

natural horn Ancestor of the modern French horn, characterized by a lack of valves.

New Orleans jazz Leading style of jazz just after World War I, which centers on group variation of a given tune, either improvised or in the style of improvisation.

nocturne (French, "night piece") Type of character piece, with slow tempo, flowing accompaniment, and broad lyrical melodies.

octatonic scale Scale composed of alternating half and whole steps, favored by some late-nineteenth- and early-twentieth-century Russian composers.

octave Interval between two pitches seven diatonic pitches apart; the lower note vibrates half as fast as the upper.

opera Musical stage work that is generally sung throughout, combining vocal and instrumental music with poetry and drama, acting and pantomime, and scenery and costumes.

opera house Theater or hall where opera is regularly performed, usually designed to accommodate an orchestra, sets, and other stage equipment.

operetta Broad term for light opera in which musical numbers are interspersed with spoken dialogue.

oratorio Large-scale genre originating in the Baroque, with a libretto of religious or serious character; similar to opera but unstaged; performed by solo voices, chorus, and orchestra.

orchestra Performing group generally consisting of groups or "sections" of string instruments, with single, paired, or multiple woodwind, brass, and percussion instruments.

orchestration The study or practice of writing music for instruments, or adapting for orchestra music composed for another medium.

organicism Process in which all the parts of a musical work derive from a single source and relate to each other and to the whole.

organum One of several styles of early polyphony from the ninth through thirteenth centuries, involving the addition of one or more voices to an existing chant.

Orientalism Term describing a Western view of a non-Western or non-European culture from a position of superiority and prejudice; in Western music, the use of non-Western or exotic elements, sometimes implying their lesser status.

ostinato Short melodic or rhythmic pattern that is repeated persistently throughout a piece or section.

overtone Constituent higher pitch that is part of a sounding tone: any instrumental or vocal pitch produces a characteristic set of overtones that help create the tone color or timbre.

passacaglia Baroque genre of variations over a repeating bass line or harmonic progression.

patronage Sponsorship of an artist or a musician, undertaken in the nineteenth century primarily by a member of the aristocracy or middle class.

pedal point Low sustained note or drone.

pentachord Set of five pitches.

pentatonic scale Five-note pattern (usually scale degrees 1-2-3-5-6) used in some non-Western musics and adopted by Western composers in the nineteenth and twentieth centuries.

perfect cadence Cadence that moves from a dominant to a tonic harmony, with chords in root position.

phrase Unit of a melody or of a succession of notes that has a distinct beginning and ending and is followed by a pause or other articulation.

Phrygian mode A mode based on the pattern of whole steps and half steps h–w–w–w–h–w–w. Using the white notes on the piano keyboard this mode can be played E–F–G–A–B–C–D–E.

piano quartet Chamber ensemble of piano, violin, viola, and cello, or a composition written for that ensemble.

piano trio Chamber ensemble of piano, violin, and cello, or a composition written for that ensemble.

pitch-class Any one of the twelve notes of the chromatic scale, in any octave, and including its enharmonic equivalents (C♯ and D♭, etc.)

pitch-class set (or **set**) A collection of pitch classes that preserves its intervallic content when transposed, inverted, or reordered.

pizzicato Performance direction to pluck a string of a bowed instrument with the finger.

plainchant Monophonic, unmeasured vocal melody, usually part of the liturgy of the early Roman Catholic Church.

polymeter The simultaneous use of two or more meters, each in a different layer of the music (such as melody and accompaniment).

polymodal The simultaneous use of two or more modes, each in a different layer of the music (such as melody and accompaniment).

polyphony Musical texture featuring two or more lines or voices.

polytonality The simultaneous use of two or more keys, each in a different layer of the music (such as melody and accompaniment).

prelude (1) An instrumental movement preceding an opera or other large-scale vocal work. (2) An independent short piece for piano or other solo instrument.

program music Instrumental music based on a narrative or a poetic idea, which is often explained in an accompanying text or program that is meant to be read by the listener before or during the performance.

quarter-tone A microtonal interval that divides a half step in two.

quotation Borrowing of a passage from a specific work, as opposed to allusion, which implies reference to a style or type of work.

ragtime American popular musical style from around 1900 that features syncopated rhythm against a regular, marchlike bass.

range Distance between the lowest and highest pitches of a melody, an instrument, or a voice.

realism Mid-nineteenth-century movement in the arts that stressed naturalistic depiction of people, situations, and objects; in music, often an emphasis on naturalistic opera plots or declamation of a sung text.

recapitulation In sonata form, the third section, where material from the exposition is restated, now in the tonic key.

recital Concert given by one or two performers.

recitative Speechlike type of singing, with minimal accompaniment, that follows the natural rhythms of the text; used in opera and oratorio.

register The relative placement of a pitch in terms of the overall range from low to high.

relative major Scale or key whose initial note lies a minor third above the tonic of a minor scale, with which it shares all pitches.

relative minor Scale or key whose initial note lies a minor third below the tonic of a major scale, with which it shares all pitches.

rhythm A particular pattern of short and long durations.

ricercare (1) In the early to mid-sixteenth century, a prelude in the style of an improvisation. (2) From the late sixteenth century on, an instrumental piece that treats one or more subjects in imitation.

Romanticism A nineteenth-century reaction against Enlightenment values of rationality and universality, celebrating subjectivity, spontaneity, and the power of emotions; in music, associated with a turn to smaller and more flexible forms, as well as increased chromaticism and melodic expressivity.

rondo Musical form in which the first section recurs, usually in the tonic, between subsidiary sections.

rubato Technique common in nineteenth-century music in which the performer holds back or accelerates the written note values.

sacred music Religious or spiritual music, for church or devotional use.

scale Series of pitches arranged in ascending or descending order according to a specific pattern of intervals. Scale degree refers to the position of an individual pitch in the scale.

score The written form of a musical composition, containing musical notation as well as verbal and graphic indications for performance.

scherzo Composition in ternary (ABA) form, usually in triple meter; often part of a multimovement chamber or orchestral work.

secondary dominant Dominant chord that resolves to or is directed toward a harmony that is not the tonic.

sequence Restatement of a musical idea or motive at a different pitch level.

serenade Multimovement work for large instrumental ensemble, usually lighter in mood than a symphony.

seventh chord Four-note combination consisting of a triad with another third added on top, spanning a seventh between its lowest and highest pitches.

Singspiel Genre of opera in Austria and Germany featuring spoken dialogue interspersed with arias, ensembles, and choruses.

sonata Work for solo instrument or ensemble; especially, multimovement work for piano or for other solo instrument with piano.

sonata form The design of the opening movement of most multimovement instrumental works from the later eighteenth through the nineteenth centuries, consisting of themes that are stated in the first section (exposition), developed in the second section (development), and restated and transformed in the third section (recapitulation).

song cycle Group of art songs or lieder meant to be performed in succession, usually tracing a story or narrative.

spiritual Type of religious song that originated among slaves of the American South and was passed down through oral tradition.

stretto A section in a fugue where statements of the subject follow each other more closely than in the exposition.

string quartet Chamber music ensemble consisting of two violins, viola, and cello, or a multimovement composition for this ensemble.

strophic Song or aria structure in which the same music is repeated for every stanza (strophe) of the poem.

subdominant In tonal music, the pitch a perfect fourth above the tonic, or the chord based on that pitch.

suite Multimovement work made up of a series of contrasting movements, usually dance-inspired and all in the same key.

Symbolism Movement originating in French literature in the late nineteenth century in which events, feelings, or objects are presented by suggestion and allusion; in music, associated with composers' blurring of harmonic, melodic, and formal structures.

symphonic poem Term coined by Franz Liszt for a one-movement work for orchestra that conveys a poetic idea, story, scene, or succession of moods.

symphony Large work for orchestra, usually in four movements.

syncopation Temporary shifting of the accent to a weak beat or a weak part of a beat.

temperament Any system of tuning notes in the scale in which pitches are adjusted to make most or all intervals sound well, though perhaps not in perfect tune.

tempo Speed of a musical composition, or the designation of such in a musical score.

ternary form Musical form comprising three sections, with the outer sections being essentially the same, contrasting with a middle section: ABA.

tetrachord Set of four pitches.

texture (1) A description of the number of distinct musical lines in a work and their relationship; e.g., monophonic, homophonic, polyphonic, etc. (2) A more general characterization of the overall effect produced by the interaction of melody, harmony, rhythm, register, timbre, and dynamics.

thematic transformation Presentation of a recurring motif that keeps its basic shape and contour but returns in varied mood, instrumentation, meter, or tempo, often in connection with a program.

theme Melody or other well-defined musical element used as basis for a composition or movement; in a fugue, the theme is often called the subject.

theme and variations See **variation form**.

through-composed Descriptive term for songs that are composed from beginning to end, without repetitions of large sections.

timbre The sound quality or character that distinguishes one voice or instrument from another.

Tin Pan Alley (1) Jocular name for a district in New York City where numerous publishers specializing in popular songs were located from the 1880s through the 1950s. (2) Styles of American popular song from that era.

tonality The system by which a piece of music is organized around a central note, chord, and key (the tonic), to which all the other notes and keys in the piece are subordinate.

tone poem Term coined by Richard Strauss to describe his one-movement orchestral works in the tradition of the symphonic poem.

tonic (1) The first and central pitch of a scale. (2) The main key area in which a piece or movement begins and ends and to which all other keys are subordinate.

transposition The process of moving a theme, twelve-tone row, or musical passage to start on a higher or lower pitch while preserving its intervallic structure.

tremolo Rapid repetition of a tone or alternation of two pitches.

triad Common chord type consisting of three pitches, normally a third and a fifth apart. The common forms are major, minor, diminished, and augmented.

trio (1) Piece for three players or singers. (2) The second of two alternating sections in a minuet or scherzo movement.

triplet Group of three equal-valued notes played in the time of two.

"Tristan" chord The first chord heard in the Prelude to Wagner's *Tristan und Isolde*, a dissonant chord that recurs throughout the opera and also became widely known and quoted by other composers.

tritone Interval spanning three whole steps or six half steps, such as F to B, and a component of the diminished seventh chord.

variation form, variations Musical form that presents a series of transformations of a theme, usually preserving the length and phrasing but altering melody or harmony. Also referred to as theme and variations.

vibrato Small, rapid fluctuation of pitch used as an expressive device to intensify a sound.

virtuoso Performer of extraordinary technical ability.

vocalise A vocal passage without words.

waltz Ballroom dance type in triple meter; in the nineteenth century, often a character piece for piano.

whole-tone scale (or **whole-tone collection**) A scale consisting of only whole steps.

whole step Musical interval equal to two half steps.

woodwind Musical instrument that produces sound when the player blows air through a mouthpiece that has a sharp edge or a reed, causing the air to vibrate in a resonating column.

CHAPTER 1

2. SR 198:1438; 7/29:168: Throughout the text, these citations refer to *Strunk's Source Readings in Music History*, Leo Treitler, general editor (New York: W. W. Norton, 1998). The first reference is to selection and page number in the one-volume edition. The second is to the volume in the seven-volume set, with selection and page number: in this case, volume 7 (*The Twentieth Century,* ed. Robert P. Morgan), selection 29, page 168.

2. "if this is music of the future": Nicolas Slonimsky, *Lexicon of Musical Invective: Critical Assaults on Composers since Beethoven's Time* (Seattle: University of Washington Press, 1974), 153.

2. "to cast out my musical gods": Alex Ross, *The Rest Is Noise: Listening to the Twentieth Century* (New York: Farrar, Straus, and Giroux, 2007), 160.

2–3. "All the tangled chaos": László Somfai, *Béla Bartók: Composition, Concepts, and Autograph Sources* (Berkeley and Los Angeles: University of California Press, 1996), 11.

3. "As for myself": Igor Stravinsky, *Poetics of Music* (Cambridge, MA: Harvard University Press, 1977), 63.

5. "Whoever has it does not say": Robert Musil, *The Man Without Qualities*, trans. Sophie Wilkins (New York: Knopf, 1995), 11 (translation slightly modified and emphasis added).

8. "I said to myself": Alma Mahler-Werfel, *Diaries, 1898–1902*, ed. Antony Beaumont (Ithaca: Cornell University Press, 1999), 99.

8. "every meaningful work": Luciano Berio, "The Composer on His Work: Meditation on a Twelve-Tone Horse," in *Classic Essays on Twentieth-Century Music: A Continuing Symposium*, ed. Richard Kostelanetz and Joseph Darby (New York: Schirmer, 1996), 168.

11. "There is something": Musil, *The Man Without Qualities*, 11.

CHAPTER 2

17. "Some passages of it": Deryck Cooke, *Gustav Mahler: An Introduction to His Music* (Cambridge: Cambridge University Press, 1994), 61.

18. "I want to sing": Stefan Jarociński: *Debussy: Impressionism and Symbolism*, trans. Rollo Myers (London: Eulenberg, 1976), 96.

18. "the loss of cohesion": Robert Musil, *The Man Without Qualities*, trans. Sophie Wilkins (New York: Knopf, 1995), 575.

19. "Looked at closely": Musil, *The Man Without Qualities*, 574.

20. "For me everything": Hugo von Hofmannsthal, *The Whole Difference: Selected Writings of Hugo von Hofmannsthal*, ed. J. D. McClatchy (Princeton: Princeton University Press, 2008), 74.

21. "Herr Klimt's latest": Peter Vergo, *Art in Vienna, 1898–1918: Klimt, Kokoschka, Schiele and Their Contemporaries* (Ithaca: Cornell University Press, 1986), 58.

21. "thrice homeless": Cooke, *Gustav Mahler*, 7.

21. "To me 'symphony' means": Peter Franklin, *Mahler: Symphony No. 3* (Cambridge: Cambridge University Press, 1991), 37.

22. "Introduction: 'Pan awakes.'": Ibid., 24–25.

22. "like playing with building blocks": Constantin Floros, *Gustav Mahler: The Symphonies* (Portland: Amadeus Press, 2000), 25.

23. "His father, apparently a brutal person": Norman Lebrecht, *Mahler Remembered* (New York: Norton, 1987), 283.

23. "Everyone knows by now": Knud Martner, ed., *Gustav Mahler: Selected Letters* (New York: Farrar, Straus, and Giroux, 1979), 189.

24. "The Viennese novelist Stefan Zweig": Stefan Zweig, *The World of Yesterday* (Lincoln: University of Nebraska Press, 1964) 64–65.

24. "An unbelievable jumble": Alma Mahler-Werfel, *Diaries, 1898–1902*, ed. Antony Beaumont (Ithaca: Cornell University Press, 1999), 345.

25. "Away with the whole 'woman's movement'": Otto Weininger, *Sex and Character* (New York: G. P. Putnam's Sons, 1906), 71.

25. "Why are boys *taught*": Mahler-Werfel, *Diaries*, 394 and 202.

25. "Her strongest challenge came from Gustav": Henry-Louis de La Grange, *Gustav Mahler* (New York: Doubleday, 1973), 668.

26. "One asks oneself": François Lesure, ed., *Debussy Letters* (Cambridge, MA: Harvard University Press, 1987), 306.

27. "from the direct and the palpable": Stéphane Mallarmé, "Crisis in Poetry," in *Modernism: An Anthology of Sources and Documents*, ed. Vassiliki Kolocotroni (Chicago: University of Chicago Press, 1998), 127.

27. "the desires and dreams": William Austin, *Debussy: Prelude to "The Afternoon of a Faun"* (New York: Norton, 1970), 14, 23.

29. "all the various impressions": Nigel Simeone, "Debussy and Expression," in *The Cambridge Companion to Debussy*, ed. Simon Trezise (Cambridge: Cambridge University Press, 2003), 104.

29. "collect impressions": Leon Botstein, "Beyond the Illusions of Realism: Painting and Debussy's Break with Tradition," in *Debussy and His World*, ed. Jane Fulcher (Princeton: Princeton University Press, 2001), 161.

33. "Will it not mean a diminution": Evan Eisenberg, *The Recording Angel: Music, Records, and Culture from Aristotle to Zappa* (New Haven: Yale University Press, 2005), 44–45.

CHAPTER 3

36. "unbelievably showy": Alma Mahler-Werfel, *Diaries 1898–1902*, ed. Antony Beaumont (Ithaca: Cornell University Press, 1999), 350.

36. "a methodical negation of all": Nicolas Slonimsky, *Lexicon of Musical Invective: Critical Assaults on Composers since Beethoven's Time* (Seattle: University of Washington Press, 1974), 148.

36. "Now that I have set out": Joseph Auner, *A Schoenberg Reader: Documents of a Life* (New Haven: Yale University Press, 2003), 78.

36. "Laws apparently prevail here": Arnold Schoenberg, *Theory of Harmony*, trans. Roy E. Carter (Berkeley: University of California Press, 1983), 421.

37. "know *consciously* the laws": Arnold Schoenberg, *Style and Idea*, ed. Leonard Stein (1950; reprint, Berkeley: University of California Press, 2010), 218.

37. "not a single word is known": Robert Morgan, "Secret Languages: The Roots of Musical Modernism," *Critical Inquiry* 10, no. 3 (1984): 444.

40. "We will destroy the museums": Filippo Tommaso Marinetti, "The Founding and Manifesto of Futurism 1909," *Modernism: An Anthology of Sources and Documents*, ed. Vassiliki Kolocotroni (Chicago: University of Chicago Press, 1998), 251.

42. "But whereas Mahler used": Charles Youmans, "The Private Intellectual Context of Richard Strauss's *Also sprach Zarathustra*," *19th-Century Music* 22, no. 2 (1998), 103.

44. "At certain times the masses": Daniel Albright, *Modernism and Music: An Anthology of Sources* (Chicago: University of Chicago Press, 2004), 234.

44. "A 1912 article that appeared": Leonid Saba-neiev, "Scriabin's Prometheus," in *The Blaue Reiter Almanac*, ed. Wassily Kandinsky and Franz Marc. New Documentary Edition, ed. Klaus Lankheit (New York: Viking Press, 1974), 134.

45. "It seemed to me": Simon Morrison, "Skry-abin and the Impossible," *Journal of the American Musicological Society* 51, no. 2 (1998): 311.

46. "There are many sections": Auner, *Schoenberg Reader*, 56.

47. "sounds as if someone": Albright, *Modernism and Music*, 7.

50. "the disturbing intervention": Schoenberg, "Franz Liszt's Work and Being," in *Style and Idea*, 444.

50. "The independent progress": Auner, *Schoenberg Reader*, 88.

51. "But it also resulted": Schoenberg, "Brahms the Progressive," in *Style and Idea*, 415.

CHAPTER 4

57. "What does the Lowell Folk Festival": *Boston Phoenix*, July 24, 2009.

57. "a confrontation with another culture": Cited in Greil Marcus, *The Old, Weird America*. Liner notes to *Anthology of American Folk Music*, Smithsonian Folkways Recordings, Washington, D.C., 1997.

59. "We recognize these [tones]": Matti Huttunen, "The National Composer and the Idea of Finnishness: Sibelius and the Formation of Finnish Musical Style," in *The Cambridge Companion to Sibelius*, ed. Daniel Grimley (Cambridge: Cambridge University Press, 2004), 8.

59. "In a letter of 1911": Ibid., 13.

61. "They circled over me": James Hepokoski, *Sibelius: Symphony No. 5* (Cambridge: Cambridge University Press, 1993), 36.

62. "If the Yankee can reflect": J. Peter Burkholder, *Charles Ives: The Ideas Behind the Music* (New Haven: Yale University Press, 1985), 15.

62. "Why tonality as such": Charles Ives, "Some Quarter Tone Impressions" (1920), reprinted in *Essays Before a Sonata*, ed. Howard Boatwright (New York: Norton, 1999), 117.

64. "Well, I'll say two things here": John Kirkpatrick, ed., *Charles E. Ives: Memos* (New York: Norton, 1972), 131.

65. "The musicologist Cecil Gray": Cecil Gray, *A Survey of Contemporary Music* (London: Oxford University Press, 1924), 187.

65. "a picture of the development": Sigmund Freud, *The Interpretation of Dreams* (New York: Avon, 1965), 588.

66. "Stravinsky . . . is entirely unable": Rutland Boughton, *Musical Times*, London, June 1929, in *The Lexicon of Musical Invective*, ed. Nicolas Slonimsky (Seattle: University of Washington Press, 1965), 203.

67. "Rather than any sort": Eric Walter White, *Stravinsky: The Composer and His Works* (Berkeley: University of California Press, 1979), 72.

67. "A German musician will be able": Béla Bartók, "On the Significance of Folk Music," in *Contemporary Composers on Contemporary Music*, ed. Elliott Schwartz (New York: Holt, Rinehart and Winston, 1967), 79.

68. "the brotherhood of peoples": David Schneider, *Bartók, Hungary, and the Renewal of Tradition: Case Studies in the Intersection of Modernity and Nationality* (Berkeley: University of California Press, 2006), 186.

68. "indications of individual intervals": Alexander Rehding, "Wax Cylinder Revolutions." *Musical Quarterly* 88 (2005): 132.

70. "In his ghostwritten *Autobiography*": Richard Taruskin, "Russian Folk Melodies in *The Rite of Spring*." *Journal of the American Musicological Society* 33, no. 3 (1980): 502–503.

72. "Nationalist artists are faced with": Richard Taruskin, *Stravinsky and the Russian Traditions: A Biography of the Works through Mavra* (Berkeley: University of California Press, 1996), 516.

72. "In his article": Igor Stravinsky, "What I Wished to Express in *The Rite of Spring*," in *Modernism and Music: An Anthology of Sources*, ed. Daniel Albright (Berkeley: University of California Press, 2004), 238.

73. "It is the life of the stones": Jann Pasler, "Music and Spectacle in *Petrushka* and *The Rite of Spring*," in *Confronting Stravinsky: Man, Musician, and Modernist*, ed. Jann Pasler (Berkeley: University of California Press, 1987), 69–70.

76. "the sense of many people living": Peter Burkholder, *All Made of Tunes: Charles Ives and*

the Uses of Musical Borrowing (New Haven: Yale University Press, 1995), 263.

PART II

80. "the spells exerted by *Le sacre*": Glenn Watkins, *Soundings* (New York: Schirmer, 1995), 312.

CHAPTER 5

82. "But even the open-minded Janáček": Leoš Janáček, "Basta!" in *Janáček's Uncollected Essays on Music*, ed. Mirka Zemanová (New York: Marion Boyars, 1993), 224, 226.

85. "I was born in 1881": Stefan Zweig, *The World of Yesterday* (Lincoln: University of Nebraska Press, 1964), xviii.

86. "I take out one of the books": Erich Maria Remarque, *All Quiet on the Western Front*, trans. A. W. Wheen (New York: Fawcett Crest, 1958), 173.

86. "There is great destructive": Tristan Tzara, "From *Dada Manifesto, 1918*," in *Modernism: An Anthology of Sources and Documents*, ed. Vassiliki Kolocotroni (Chicago: University of Chicago Press, 1998), 279.

87. "Nowadays the world is rotten": Liner notes to Ute Lemper, *Berlin Cabaret Songs*, London G2 52849 (1996).

88. "justifiably learned to mistrust": Max Brod, "Women and the New Objectivity," in *The Weimar Republic Sourcebook*, ed. Anton Kaes (Berkeley: University of California Press, 1994), 205.

88. "The music Antheil liked best": George Antheil, *Bad Boy of Music* (Hollywood: Samuel French, 1990), 29.

88. "Stravinsky became a standard bearer": Igor Stravinsky, "An Autobiography," in *Modernism and Music: An Anthology of Sources*, ed. Daniel Albright (Chicago: University of Chicago Press, 2004), 282.

89. "Now, I go back to Bach": Scott Messing, *Neoclassicism in Music: From the Genesis of the Concept through the Schoenberg/Stravinsky Polemic* (Ann Arbor: UMI Research Press, 1988), 142.

90. "We can see the artistic significance": Liner notes to Kurt Weill and Paul Hindemith, *Der Lind-*

berghflug, first version, conducted by Hermann Scherchen, Capriccio 60012-1 (1990).

91. "Observe how this crazy funnel": Hermann Hesse, *Steppenwolf* (New York: Holt, 1990), 212–213.

91. "For the first time in world history": Walter Benjamin, "The Work of Art in the Age of Mechanical Reproduction," in *Illuminations*, ed. Hannah Arendt (Glasgow: Fontana/Collins, 1970), 226.

92. "play this piece very ferociously": Glenn Watkins, *Soundings: Music in the Twentieth Century* (New York: Schirmer Books, 1995), 289.

94. "Varèse used the language": Carol Oja, *Making Music Modern: New York in the 1920s* (Oxford: Oxford University Press, 2000), 3, 42.

94. "Antheil described the work": George Antheil, *Ballet mécanique* (New York: Schirmer, 2003), vi.

95. "The architect Le Corbusier's remark": Joel Dinerstein, *Swinging the Machine: Modernity, Technology, and African-American Culture Between the World Wars* (Amherst and Boston: University of Massachusetts Press, 2003), 3.

100. "The new music was extremely subtle": Darius Milhaud, "My First Encounter with Jazz," in *Contemporary Composers on Contemporary Music*, ed. Elliott Schwartz (New York: Holt, Rinehart, and Winston, 1967), 36.

100. "In his view Negro music": George Antheil, "The Negro on the Spiral, or A Method of Negro Music," in Albright, ed., *Modernism and Music*, 391.

101. "Showing these completely soulless machines": Ernst Krenek, *Exploring Music*, trans. Margaret Shenfield (London: Calder and Boyars, 1966), 23–24.

CHAPTER 6

106. "Satie's music, Auric writes": George Auric, prefatory note, in Erik Satie, *Parade* (Mineola, NY: Dover, 2000), xii.

107. "He was dismissed": Robert Orledge, *Satie the Composer* (Cambridge: Cambridge University Press, 1990), xx.

107. "Boredom disguises itself": François Lesure, ed., *Debussy Letters* (Cambridge, MA: Harvard University Press, 1987), 196.

109. "a sort of apotheosis": Deborah Mawer, "Ballet and the Apotheosis of the Dance," in *The Cambridge Companion to Ravel*, ed. Deborah Mawer (Cambridge: Cambridge University Press, 2000), 150.

110. "Despite Satie's plea": Orledge, *Satie the Composer*, 143.

111. "All of his thought": Richard Taruskin, "Back to Whom? Neoclassicism as Ideology." *19th-Century Music* 16, no. 3 (1993): 293.

111. "tantamount to a signature": Eric Walter White, *Stravinsky: The Composer and His Works* (Berkeley: University of California Press, 1979), 323.

112. "The clarity and simplicity": Josef Wulf, *Musik im Dritten Reich: Eine Dokumentation* (Gütersloh: Sigbert Mohn Verlag, 1963), 235 (author's translation).

112. "It is by no means easy": Sergei Prokofiev, "That Path of Soviet Music," in *Contemporary Composers on Contemporary Music*, ed. Elliott Schwartz and Barney Childs (New York: Holt, Rinehart and Winston, 1967), 100.

113. "Further minimizing emotional expression": Glenn Watkins, *Pyramids at the Louvre: Music, Culture, and Collage from Stravinsky to the Postmodernists* (Cambridge, MA: Harvard University Press, 1994), 357.

113. "What a joy it is": Igor Stravinsky, *An Autobiography* (New York: Norton, 1936), 128.

114. "I'm an advocate of architecture": Walsh, *Stravinsky: A Creative Spring: Russia and France, 1882–1934* (Berkeley: University of California Press, 1999), 500.

115. "I began without preconceptions": Igor Stravinsky and Robert Craft, "Expositions and Developments," in *Modernism and Music: An Anthology of Sources*, ed. Daniel Albright (Chicago: University of Chicago Press, 2004), 284–285.

116. "This is no doubt the kind": Virgil Thomson, "The Only Twentieth-Century Aesthetic?," in *Music in the Western World*, ed. Piero Weiss and Richard Taruskin (Belmont, CA: Wadsworth Group, 1984), 475.

116. "In an essay from 1923": Darius Milhaud, "Polytonality," in Weiss and Taruskin, eds., *Music in the Western World*, 474.

117. "not an 'emotive' work": Igor Stravinsky, "The New Objectivity," in Weiss and Taruskin, eds., *Music in the Western World*, 459.

118. "Poulenc wrote of the work": Nancy Lynn Perloff, *Art and the Everyday: Popular Entertainment and the Circle of Satie* (Oxford: Oxford University Press, 1991), 100.

118. "Without any transition": Darius Milhaud, "Notes Without Music," in Schwartz and Childs, eds., *Contemporary Composers on Contemporary Music*, 36.

120. "one among us who best embodies": Bernard Gendron, *Between Montmartre and the Mudd Club: Popular Music and the Avant-Garde* (Chicago and London: University of Chicago Press, 2002), 114.

120. "a mechanism like everything else": Laura Rosenstock, "Léger: The Creation of the World," in *"Primitivism" in 20th Century Art*, ed. William Rubin (New York: Museum of Modern Art, 1984), 482.

122. "He read it attentively": Carl Schmidt, *Entrancing Music: A Documented Biography of Francis Poulenc* (New York: Pendragon, 2001), 41.

CHAPTER 7

125. "Schoenberg experienced the collapse": Joseph Auner, *A Schoenberg Reader: Documents of a Life* (New Haven: Yale University Press, 203), 161.

125. "reminiscent of the fairest": Ibid., 183.

126. "Nationalistic musicians regard me as *international*": Ibid., 242.

128. "In Divine Creation": Arnold Schoenberg, "Composition with Twelve Tones," in *Style and Idea: Selected Writings of Arnold Schoenberg*, trans. L. Black, ed. L. Stein (Berkeley: University of California Press, 2010), 215.

131. "And Schoenberg gets mad": Joan Allen Smith, *Schoenberg and His Circle: A Viennese Portrait* (New York: Schirmer, 1986), 216.

131. "It's my belief": Anton Webern, *The Path to the New Music*, ed. Willi Reich (Bryn Mawr: Theodore Presser, 1963), 42.

132. "Considerations of symmetry": Webern, *Path to the New Music*, 54.

134. "subjected to every conceivable combination": Alban Berg, "The Musical Forms in My Opera *Wozzeck*," in Douglas Jarman, *Alban Berg, Wozzeck* (Cambridge: Cambridge University Press, 1989), 151.

136. "truly new music which": Schoenberg, "National Music," in *Style and Idea*, 174.

137. "In his book *New Musical Resources*": Henry Cowell, *New Musical Resources*, ed. David Nicholls (Cambridge: Cambridge University Press, 1996), xi.

138. "not only music and the arts": Joseph Schillinger, *The Schillinger System of Musical Composition*, 2 vols. (New York: Carl Fisher, 1946), 1:24.

140. "a heterophony of dynamics": Judith Tick, *Ruth Crawford: A Composer's Search for American Music* (New York: Oxford University Press, 1997), 357.

140. "There is therefore a sort of dissonance": Ibid., 360.

140. "I also vent my spleen": Ellie Hisama, *Gendering Musical Modernism: The Music of Ruth Crawford, Marion Bauer, and Miriam Gideon* (Cambridge: Cambridge University Press, 2001), 38.

142. "I never created new theories": Benjamin Suchoff, ed., *Béla Bartók Essays* (Lincoln: University of Nebraska Press, 1992), 376.

143. "While the idea is comparable": Ibid., 365–366.

144. "This rule of construction": Paul Hindemith, *A Composer's World* (Cambridge, MA: Harvard University Press, 1952), 140.

144. "Music, as long as it exists": Paul Hindemith, *Theory*, Book 1 of *The Craft of Musical Composition* (New York: Associated Music Publishers, 1942), 22.

145. "the supreme condition for your participation": Hindemith, *Composer's World*, 143.

CHAPTER 8

148. "like a ghost wandering": Alex Ross, *The Rest Is Noise: Listening to the Twentieth Century* (New York: Farrar, Straus, and Giroux, 2007), 160.

148. "I have been thinking so much": Christopher Mark, "The Later Orchestral Music (1910–34)," in *The Cambridge Companion to Elgar*, ed. Daniel M. Grimly and Julian Rushton (Cambridge: Cambridge University Press, 2004), 166.

150. "constituted of syllables and vocalises": Gerard Béhague, *Heitor Villa-Lobos: The Search for Brazil's Musical Soul* (Austin: University of Texas Press, 1994), 90.

152. "Through singing songs and commemorative hymns": Simon Wright, *Villa-Lobos* (Oxford: Oxford University Press, 1992), 108.

152. "Patriotism in music": Liss M. Peppercorn, *The World of Villa-Lobos in Pictures and Documents* (Aldershot: Scolar Press, 1996), 177.

154. "His goal as a storyteller": J. R. R. Tolkien, *Tree and Leaf* (New York: Houghton Mifflin, 1965), 37.

154. "the stuff of plainsong and folk-song": Cited in Robert Stradling and Meirion Hughes, *The English Musical Renaissance 1840–1940: Constructing a National Music* (Manchester and New York: Routledge, 2001), 138.

154. "They have behind them": Alain Frogley, "National Characters and the Reception of Vaughan Williams," in *Vaughan Williams Studies*, ed. Alain Frogley (Cambridge: Cambridge University Press, 1996), 11.

156. "hoped that the cultivation of folk music": Judith Tick, "Historical Introduction: The Salvation of Writing Things Down," in Ruth Crawford Seeger, *The Music of American Folk Song*, ed. Larry Polansky with Judith Tick (Rochester: University of Rochester Press, 2001), xxiv–xxv.

157. "The collection of essays": Henry Cowell, ed., *American Composers on American Music: A Symposium* (New York: Frederick Ungar, 1962), 13.

158. "entirely new public for music": Elizabeth B. Crist, *Music for the Common Man: Aaron Copland During the Depression and War* (New York: Oxford University Press, 2005), 5.

158. "rather like coming upon an unexpected city": Aaron Copland, "The Composer in Industrial America," in *Music in the Western World*, ed. Piero Weiss and Richard Taruskin (Belmont, CA: Wadsworth Group, 1984), 492.

159. "Jazz played a big role": Aaron Copland and Vivian Perlis, *Copland 1900–1942* (New York: St. Martins, 1994), 134.

159. "But by the mid-1930s": Carol J. Oja, "Marc Blitzstein's *The Cradle Will Rock* and Mass-Song Style of the 1930s," *Musical Quarterly* 73 (1989): 452.

160. "I'm just an Irish, Negro": Lisa Barg, "Paul Robeson's Ballad for Americans: Race and Cultural Politics of 'People's Music.'" *Journal of the Society for American Music* 2 (2008): 43.

160. "wider mutual appreciation of the music": Deane L. Root, "The Pan American Association of Composers (1928–1934)." *Anuario Interamericano de Investigacion Musical* 8 (1972): 51.

162. "Our music possesses exoticism": William Grant Still, "An Afro-American Composer's Point of View," in Cowell, *American Composers on American Music*, 183.

162. "An American Negro has formed a concept": Catherine Parsons Smith, *William Grant Still* (Urbana and Chicago: University of Illinois Press, 2008), 52.

162. "Jazz (as one black form)": William C. Banfield, *Musical Landscapes in Color: Conversations with Black American Composers* (Lanham, Maryland: Scarecrow, 2003), 7.

163. "Everyone carries within him": Carol Oja, *Colin McPhee: Composer in Two Worlds* (Washington and London: Smithsonian Institute Press, 1990), 144.

164. "Although *Tabuh-tabuhan* makes much use": Quoted in Douglas Young, "Colin McPhee's Music: 'Tabuh-Tabuhan,'" *Tempo* 159 (1986): 16.

164. "like the stirrings of a thousand bells": Colin McPhee, *A House in Bali* (New York: John Day, 1947), 2.

166. "I wondered at their natural ease": McPhee, *House in Bali*, 38.

174. "I ask myself why": Michael Kennedy, *Richard Strauss: Man, Musician, Enigma* (Cambridge: Cambridge University Press, 2006), 387.

175. "To be twenty or twenty-five": M. J. Grant, *Serial Music, Serial Aesthetics: Compositional Theory in Post-War Europe* (Cambridge: Cambridge University Press, 2001), 12.

178. "It is not a *Requiem*": Mervyn Cooke, *Britten: War Requiem* (Cambridge: Cambridge University Press, 1996), 78

178. "Since I believe that there is": Ibid., 15.

179. "I couldn't be alone": Lloyd Whitesell, "Men with a Past: Music and the 'Anxiety of Influence,'" *19th-Century Music* 18, no. 2 (1994): 156.

179. "accept their loneliness": Philip Brett, "Keeping the Straight Line Intact? Britten's Relation to Folksong, Purcell, and His English Predecessors," *Music and Sexuality in Britten, Selected Essays*, ed. George Haggerty (Berkeley: University of California Press, 2006), 158.

180. "There are many dangers": Benjamin Britten, "On Winning the First Aspen Award." *Contemporary Composers on Contemporary Music*, ed. Elliott Schwartz and Barney Childs (New York: Holt, Rinehart and Winston, 1967), 118.

183. "You cannot change the natural evolution": Joseph Auner, *A Schoenberg Reader: Documents of a Life* (New Haven: Yale University Press, 2003), 341.

PART III

170. "that I was part of a new epoch": Karlheinz Stockhausen, *Towards a Cosmic Music* (Salisbury: Element Books, 1989), 10.

170. "In 1945–1946 nothing was ready": Pierre Boulez, *Orientations*, ed. Jean-Jacques Nattiez (Cambridge, MA: Harvard University Press, 1986), 445.

CHAPTER 9

172. "The awful ruin of Europe": James W. Muller, *Churchill's "Iron Curtain" Speech Fifty Years Later* (Columbia: University of Missouri Press, 1999), 3.

174. "winning over the entire people": Michael P. Steinberg, "Richard Strauss and the Question," in *Richard Strauss and His World*, ed. Bryan Gilliam (Princeton: Princeton University Press, 1992), 169.

183. "mood of suspicion, ill-will": Elizabeth B. Crist, *Music for the Common Man: Aaron Copland During the Depression and War* (Oxford: Oxford University Press, 2005), 194.

184. "I started thinking that if": David Fanning, *Shostakovich: String Quartet No. 8* (Aldershot: Ashgate, 2004), 145.

184. "The quartet also uses themes": Ibid., 145–146.

185. "Scholars have argued that *Lady Macbeth*": Richard Taruskin, *The Early Twentieth Century*, vol. 4 of *The Oxford History of Western Music* (Oxford: Oxford University Press, 2005), 787.

186. "a creative method based on": Ibid., 775ff.

186. "I wanted to convey": Laurel Fay, *Shostakovich: A Life* (Oxford: Oxford University Press, 2000), 102.

187. "try again and again to create": Ibid., 160.

188. "The shackled genius Shostakovich": Ibid., 270.

188. "Tormented by grievous bondage": Adapted from Fanning, *Shostakovich: String Quartet No. 8*, 141.

188. "It is a pseudo-tragic quartet": Ibid., 146.

188. "to influence the world": Ibid., 159.

CHAPTER 10

191. "a bombed-out city": John Cage, "Forerunners of Modern Music," cited in *The Boulez-Cage Correspondence*, ed. Jean-Jacques Nattiez (Cambridge: Cambridge University Press, 1993), 40.

191. "the construction of devices for composing music": L. B. Meyer, "Meaning in Music and Information Theory," *Journal of Aesthetics and Art Criticism* 15 (1957): 412, 421.

191. "Just as a layman": Milton Babbitt, "The Composer as Specialist," in *Music in the Western World: A History in Documents*, ed. Piero Weiss and Richard Taruskin (Belmont, CA: Wadsworth, 1984), 531.

192. "For twelve years we have been": M. J. Grant, *Serial Music, Serial Aesthetics: Compositional Theory in Post-War Europe* (Cambridge: Cambridge University Press, 2005), 39.

192. "the mightiest of fortresses": Martin Brody, "'Music for the Masses': Milton Babbitt's Cold War Music Theory," *Musical Quarterly* 77, no. 2 (1993): 167.

192. as "a gesture of liberation from Value": Caroline Jones, "Finishing School: John Cage and the Abstract Expressionist Ego," *Critical Inquiry* 19, no. 4 (1993): 641.

192. "Contemporary music *only* is taught": Amy C. Beal, *New Music, New Allies: American Experimental Music in West Germany from the Zero Hour to Reunification* (Berkeley: University of California Press, 2006), 39.

193. "a real hero . . . doomed": Igor Stravinsky "[Foreword]," *Die Reihe* 2 (Original German Edition, 1955; English Edition, Bryn Mawr: Theodore Presser, 1958): vii.

193. "derive the structure from the material": Pierre Boulez, "Schoenberg Is Dead," in Weiss and Taruskin, eds., *Music in the Western World*, 507–508.

195. "He heard these structures": Siglind Bruhn, *Messiaen's Language of Mystical Love* (New York: Garland, 1998), 85.

196. "Boulez's Second Piano Sonata (1948) first brought": David Gable, "Ramifying Connections: An Interview with Pierre Boulez," *Journal of Musicology* 4, no. 1 (1985–1986): 111.

197. "What is inorganic is this": György Ligeti, "Pierre Boulez," *Die Reihe* 4 (Original German Edition 1958; English Edition, Bryn Mawr: Theodore Presser, 1960): 39–40.

197. "the individual lights are indeed": Ibid., 61.

197. "The network of possibilities": Cited in Felix Salzer, ed., *Settling New Scores: Music Manuscripts from the Paul Sacher Stiftung* (Mainz: Schott, 1998), 94.

197. "Based on three poems by the French Surrealist": Ligeti, "Pierre Boulez," 62.

198. "we are always ready to go": Gable, "Ramifying Connections," 112.

199. "a completely autonomous conception": Milton Babbitt, "Some Aspects of Twelve-Tone Composition," in *The Collected Essays of Milton Babbitt*, ed. Stephen Peles (Princeton: Princeton University Press, 2003), 40.

200. "I am widening the possibilities": Pierre Boulez, in Nattiez, *Boulez-Cage Correspondence*, 150.

200. "What they thought was silence": Kyle Gann, *No Such Thing as Silence: John Cage's 4'33"* (New Haven: Yale University Press, 2010), 4.

202. "magnetic tape music makes it": John Cage, "A History of Experimental Music in the United States," in *Silence*, by John Cage (Middletown, CT: Wesleyan University Press, 1961), 70.

203. "Any sound makes sense": George Lewis, *A Power Stronger Than Itself: The AACM and American Experimental Music* (Chicago: University of Chicago Press, 2008), 41.

203. "Around 1950, inspired by his studies": John Cage, "Composition: To Describe the Process of Composition used in *Music of Changes* and *Imaginary Landscape, No. 4*," in *Silence*, 59.

203. "By making moves on the charts": John Cage, in Nattiez, *Boulez-Cage Correspondence*, 94.

204. "are musicians and not painters": Pierre Boulez, in Nattiez, *Boulez-Cage Correspondence*, 116.

206. "opened up the door": Fred Orton and Gavin Bryars, "Morton Feldman Interview," *Studio International*, November 1976: 244–248.

206. "imitating nature in the manner": Steven Johnson, "Jasper Johns and Morton Feldman," in Steven Johnson, *The New York Schools of Music and the Visual Arts* (New York: Routledge, 2002), 224.

207. "the literature and 'traditions'": Cage, "Composition," in *Silence*, 59.

207. "When this freedom is given": Judy Lochhead, "Controlling Liberation: David Tudor and the 'Experimental' Sound Ideal," paper presented at the Getty Research Institute Symposium "The Art of David Tudor," May 2001.

208. "Our business in living is to become": David Bernstein, "Cage and Asia: History and Sources," *The Cambridge Companion to Cage*, ed. David Nicholls (Cambridge: Cambridge University Press, 2002), 49.

208. "I said that since the sounds": John Cage, "Indeterminacy," *Die Reihe* 5, Reports/Analyses (Original German Edition 1959; English Edition, Bryn Mawr: Theodore Presser, 1961), 116.

208. "a live friction sound piece": Amy Beal, *New Music, New Allies: American Experimental Music from the Zero Hour to Reunification* (Berkeley: University of California Press, 2006), 118.

209. "seemed to float in the air": "Pauline Oliveros," in *Talking Music: Conversations with John Cage, Philip Glass, Laurie Anderson, and Five Generations of American Experimental Composers*, ed. William Duckworth (New York: Da Capo, 1999), 162.

209. "Any number of persons": Cited in Roberta Lindsey, "Pauline Oliveros," in *The New Historical Anthology of Music by Women*, ed. James Briscoe (Bloomington: Indiana University Press, 2004), 454.

209. "as a sort of microcosm": "Meredith Monk," in Duckworth, *Talking Music*, 366.

210. "One seeks desperately to dominate": Pierre Boulez, *Notes of An Apprenticeship*, ed. Paule Thévenin, trans. Herbert Weinstock (New York: Knopf, 1968), 40.

210. "effects of chaos": Gable, "Ramifying Connections," 111.

CHAPTER 11

212. "We are astonished": H. H. Stuckenschmidt, "The Third Stage," *Die Reihe* 1 (Original German Edition 1955; English Edition, Bryn Mawr: Theodore Presser, 1958), 12–13.

213. "We realized that the historical": Karlheinz Stockhausen, "Two Lectures," *Die Reihe* 5 (Original German Edition 1958; English Edition, Bryn Mawr: Theodore Presser, 1961): 59.

214. "A sudden chorus of whoops": Thomas Pynchon, *The Crying of Lot 49* (New York: Harper Collins, 1999), 34.

214. "music has evidently become": John Backus, "*Die Reihe*: A Scientific Evaluation," *Perspectives of New Music* 1 (1962): 160.

215. "mankind viewed itself in contrast to nature": M. J. Grant, *Serial Music, Serial Aesthetics: Compositional Theory in Post-War Europe* (Cambridge: Cambridge University Press, 2005), 33.

217. "The moment man ceased": Jacques Barzun, "Introductory Remarks to a Program of Works Produced at the Columbia-Princeton Electronic Music Center," in *Audio Culture: Readings in Modern Music*, ed. Christoph Cox and Daniel Warner (New York: Continuum, 2006), 369.

217. "work very much like painters": Howard Taubman, "U.S. Music of Today Played at Concert," *The New York Times*, October 29, 1952.

220. "singing, chanting, droning": Amy C. Beal, "Music Is a Universal Human Right: Musica Elettronica Viva," in *Sound Commitments: Avant-Garde Music and the Sixties*, ed. Robert Adlington (Oxford: Oxford University Press, 2009), 109.

222. "the public concert as we know it": Glenn Gould, "The Prospects of Recording," in *Classic Essays on Twentieth-Century Music: A Continuing Symposium*, ed. Richard Kostelanetz and David Darby (New York: Schirmer, 1996), 54.

222. "we have called our music": Timothy D. Taylor, *Strange Sounds: Music, Technology, and Culture* (New York: Routledge, 2011), 45.

223. "Repetition was the basic tool": Daniel Teruggi, "Technology and musique concrète: The Technical Developments of the Groupe de Recherches Musicales and Their Implication

in Musical Composition," *Organised Sound* 12, no. 3 (2007): 213.

224. "For Schaeffer, a work qualified": Taylor, *Strange Sounds*, 46.

224. "a revolutionary invention": Peter J. Schmelz, "From Scriabin to Pink Floyd: The ANS Synthesizer and the Politics of Music between Thaw and Stagnation," in Adlington, *Sound Commitments*, 260.

232. "hitting out at random": Elliott Carter, "Sound and Silence in Time: A Contemporary Approach to the Elements of Music," in *Elliott Carter: A Centennial Portrait in Letters and Documents*, ed. Felix Meyer and Anne C. Shreffler (Woodbridge: Boydell, 2008), 132.

CHAPTER 12

239. "The polyphonic structure does not": Cited in Amy Bauer, "'Tone-Color, Movement, Changing Harmonic Planes': Cognition, Constraints, and Conceptual Blends in Modernist Music," in *The Pleasure of Modernist Music: Listening, Meaning, Intention, Ideology*, ed. Arved Ashby (Rochester: University of Rochester Press, 2004), 121.

240. "that a harpsichord was really": Jane Piper Clendinning, "The Pattern-Meccanico Compositions of Györgi Ligeti," *Perspectives of New Music* 31, no. 1 (1993): 194.

240. "This concentration on the present moment": Jonathan D. Kramer, "Moment Form in Twentieth Century Music," *Musical Quarterly* 64, no. 2 (1978): 179.

244. "the serial obsession with devising separate": Julian Anderson, "A Provisional History of Spectral Music," *Contemporary Music Review* 19 (2000): 8.

244. "my material is neither the musical note": Cited in Claudy Malherbe, "Seeing Light as Color; Hearing Sound as Timbre," *Contemporary Music Review* 19 (2000): 18.

245. "Inspired by Monet's paintings": Tristan Murail, composer's webpage, www.tristanmurail.com (accessed July 10, 2011).

246. "Lindberg also studied the works": Julian Anderson, "Sibelius and Contemporary Music," in *The Cambridge Companion to Sibelius*, ed. Daniel M. Grimley (Cambridge University Press, 2004), 207–208.

246. "a play of light and colours": Unsuk Chin, composer page on Boosey and Hawkes website, www.boosey.com (accessed July 10, 2011).

248. "Consciousness is the most valuable thing": Cited in Ronald M. Radano, *New Musical Figurations: Anthony Braxton's Cultural Critique* (Chicago: University of Chicago Press, 1993), 178–179.

251. "The impulse to the growth": Harry Partch, *Genesis of a Music: An Account of a Creative Work, Its Roots and Its Fulfillment*, 2nd ed. (New York: Da Capo Press, 1974), 95.

252. "thick, packed, dissonant": Elliott Carter, "Letter from Europe," *Perspectives of New Music* 1, no. 2 (Spring 1963): 201.

253. "try out fragments": Elliott Carter, cited in David Schiff, *The Music of Elliott Carter*, 2nd ed. (Ithaca: Cornell University Press, 1998), 92.

254. "only in sleep, in the religious experience": Sofiya Gubaydulina, program note to *In tempus praesens*.

255. "The world is always full of sounds": R. Murray Schafer, "Music and the Soundscape," in *Classic Essays on Twentieth Century Music: A Continuing Symposium*, ed. Richard Kostelanetz and Joseph Darby (New York: Schirmer Books, 1996), 231.

CHAPTER 13

257. "everything which is familiar": David Metzer, *Quotation and Cultural Meaning in Twentieth-Century Music* (Cambridge: Cambridge University Press, 2003), 140.

258. "one recalls them": Cited in Arnold Whittall, *Exploring Twentieth-Century Music: Tradition and Innovation* (Cambridge: Cambridge University Press, 2003), 132.

258. "Now there is no taboo": Cited in Alex Ross, *The Rest Is Noise: Listening to the Twentieth Century* (New York: Farrar, Straus and Giroux, 2007), 465.

259. "seems to carry all the weight": Liner notes to Luciano Berio, *Sinfonia: Findrücke*, Erato 1986.

260. "compelled to challenge the meaning": Luciano Berio, "The Composer on His Work: Meditation on a Twelve-Tone Horse," in *Classic Essays on Twentieth-Century Music: A Continuing Symposium*, ed. Richard Kostelanetz and Joseph Darby (New York: Schirmer, 1996), 168.

262. "semantically precise about today's man": Luigi Nono, program note, *The Luigi Nono Archives*, www.luiginono.it (accessed July 27, 2012).

263. "You are holding a mirror to people": Lukas Foss, "Foss Talks about Stolen Goods and the Mystique of the New," *Music and Artists* 3 (1970): 35.

266. "To me it's about developing": Anthony Davis, interview in *American Composers: Dialogues on Contemporary Music*, ed. Edward Strickland (Bloomington: Indiana University Press, 1991), 73, 80.

266. "incredulity toward metanarratives": Jean-François Lyotard, "Answering the Question: What Is Postmodernism?" in *The Post-Modern Reader*, ed. Charles Jencks (New York: St. Martin's Press, 1992), 138.

267. "stylistic innovation is no longer possible": Fredric Jameson, "Postmodernism and Consumer Society," in *The Anti-Aesthetic: Essays on Postmodern Culture*, ed. Hal Foster (Seattle: Bay Press, 1991), 115.

268. "Through what he describes as a process": Peter Maxwell Davies, program note to *Missa L'homme armé*.

272. "no more than a servile imitation": Leonard B Meyer, *Music, the Arts, and Ideas: Patterns and Predictions in Twentieth-Century Culture* (Chicago: University of Chicago Press, 1967), 194.

273. "He responded in turn by attacking": George Rochberg, *The Aesthetics of Survival: A Composer's View of Twentieth-Century Music* (Ann Arbor: University of Michigan Press, 2004), 140.

274. "A composer's awareness of the plurality": Luciano Berio, "The Composer on His Work," in Kostelanetz and Darby, *Classic Essays*, 169.

275. "We speak of essential elements": Toru Takemitsu, "Sound of East, Sound of West," in *Confronting Silence: Selected Writings* (Berkeley: Fallen Leaf Press, 1995), 65.

276. "Today's young people do not share": Ibid., 67.

CHAPTER 14

279. "What Reich has done is confuse": Harold C. Schonberg, "Carter, Cage, Reich . . . Speak to Me," *The New York Times*, 4 February 1973, 119.

281. "Stockhausen, Berio, and Boulez": Steve Reich, interview in *American Composers: Dialogues on Contemporary Music*, ed. Edward Strickland (Bloomington: Indiana University Press, 1991), 46.

281. "civil rights, pop music, and drugs": Philip Glass, interview in *Talking Music: Conversations with John Cage, Philip Glass, Laurie Anderson, and Five Generations of American Experimental Composers*, ed. William Duckworth (New York: Da Capo Press, 1999), 337.

282. "psychedelic dress-up era": Cited in the liner notes to Terry Riley, *In C: 25th Anniversary Concert*. New Albion Records, 1995.

282. "Turn a butterfly": K. Robert Schwartz, *Minimalists* (New York: Phaidon Press, 2008), 31.

283. "divided horizontally and vertically": Cited in Sol LeWitt, "A Wall Drawing Retrospective," *Massachusetts Museum of Contemporary Art*, www.massmoca.org (accessed July 30, 2012).

284. "Fourth, once set in motion": Steve Reich, "Music as a Gradual Process," in *Writings on Music: 1965–2000*, ed. Paul Hillier (Oxford: Oxford University Press, 2002), 34–36.

285. "As one listens to the repetition": Steve Reich, "Violin Phase (1967)," in Hillier, *Writings*, 26.

286. "a particular liberating": Steve Reich, "Music as a Gradual Process," in Hillier, *Writings*, 36.

286. "What I wanted to do": Steve Reich, "Excerpts from and Interview in *Art Forum*," in Hillier, *Writings*, 33.

286. "Much of what still goes by the name": George Rochberg, "Can the Arts Survive Modernism? (A Discussion of the Characteristics, History, and Legacy of Modernism)," *Critical Inquiry* 11, no. 2 (1984): 332.

286. "not only denies the reality": Cited in Amy Lynn Wlodarski, "The Testimonial Aesthetics of Different Trains," *Journal of the American Musicological Society* 63, no. 1 (2010): 108.

286. "About one minute of minimalism is a lot": Cited in Robert Fink, *Repeating Ourselves: American Minimal Music as Cultural Practice* (Berkeley: University of California Press, 2005), 63.

289. "It now seems to me that the mainstream": Philip Glass, interview in *Talking Music: Conversations with John Cage, Philip Glass, Laurie*

Anderson, and *Five Generations of American Experimental Composers*, ed. William Duckworth (New York: Da Capo Press, 1999), 325.

289. "a lot of notes": Cited in Steve Reich, "Introduction," in *Writings*, ed. Hillier, 9.

292. "he has described the yoga-like discipline": Reich, "*Piano Phase* (1967)" and "*Four Organs*—an End to Electronics," in *Writings*, 24, 45.

293. "all that harmony": Cited in Alex Ross, "The Harmonist," in *The John Adams Reader: Essential Writings on an American Composer*, ed. Thomas May (Portland: Amadeus Press, 2006), 37.

294. "a typical plot would involve a nuclear explosion": "John Adams on Doctor Atomic: Interview by Thomas May," in May, *The John Adams Reader*, 225.

294. "'Batter my heart' amplifies 'Oppenheimer's'": Ibid., 233.

295. "Sing or play an instrument": Darren Solomon, "FAQ," *In Bb 2.0*, www.inbflat.net (accessed August 4, 2011).

CHAPTER 15

300. "We're in a kind of post-style era": Cited in Robert Fink, "(Post-)minimalism 1970–2000: The Search for a New Mainstream," in *The Cambridge History of Twentieth-Century Music*, ed. Nicholas Cook and Anthony Pople (Cambridge: Cambridge University Press, 2004), 539.

300. "electronic dance club music": Lukas Ligeti, "Secret Instruments, Secret Destinations," in *Arcana II: Musicians on Music*, ed. John Zorn (New York: Hips Road, 2007), 145.

302. "rapidly changing visual and auditive perspectives": Olga Neuwirth, "Afterthoughts on *Lost Highway:* A *Waiting for Godot*' of Passion and Proximity—A Test Arrangement about Futility." Liner notes to Olga Neuwirth, *Lost Highway*, Kairos (2006).

303. "Installed in Trajan's Forum": Bruce Odland, composer's webpage, www.o-a.info (accessed July 10, 2011).

303. "devious version of the classical": Francisco López, "Cagean Philosophy: A Devious Version of the Classical Procedural Paradigm," *The Official Francisco López Website*, 1996, www.franciscolopez.net (accessed August 1, 2012).

303. "a walk that creates musical scores": Elastic City webpage, www.elastic-city.com (accessed August 13, 2011).

CREDITS

SCORES AND MUSICAL EXAMPLES

37 Arnold Schoenberg, Op. 11, No. 3. © Copyright 1910, 1938 by Universal Edition A.G., Wien/UE 2991. Reprinted with permission. **51** Webern, *Four Pieces*, Op. 7, for violin and piano. Used with kind permission of European American Music Distributors Company, U.S. and Canadian agent for Universal Edition, AG, Vienna **74** *The Rite of Spring* by Igor Stravinsky. Copyright 1912, 1921 by Hawkes and Son (London) Ltd. Reprinted by permission. **84** Kurt Weill, *Der Lindberghflug*. Text by Bertolt Brecht. Copyright © 1929 by European American Music Corporatio (for the U.S.A., Canada, and other British revesionary territories) and Universal Edition AG, Vienna (for all other countries). Copyright © renewed. All rights reserved. Used by permission of European American Music Corporation and by Universal Edition AG, Vienna **96–97** From *Hyperprism*, Music by Edgard Varese. Copyright © 1986 Casa Ricordi—Milano. Tous droits reserves pour tous pays. Reproduced by kind permission of MGB Hal Leonard s.r.l. **119** From *La creation du monde*, opus 81a (bars 1–10), music by Darius Milhaud. Copyright © 1929 Éditions Max Eschig. Tous droits reserves pour tous pays. Reproduced by kind permission of MGB Hal Leonard s.r.l. **129** Arnold Schoenberg, Op. 33a. © Copyright 1910, 1938 by Universal Edition A.G., Wien/UE 2991 Klavierstuck op. 33a. Reprinted with permission. **133** Webern, *Symphony*, Op. 21. Copyright © 1929 by Universal Edition AG, Vienna. Copyright © renewed. All rights reserved. Used by permission of European American Music Distributors Company, U.S. and Canadian agent for Universal Edition AG, Vienna **135** Berg, *Violin Concerto*. Copyright © 1936 by Universal Edition AG, Vienna. Copyright © renewed. All rights reserved. Used by permission of European American Music Distributors Company, U.S. and Canadian agent for Universal Edition AG, Vienna **136** Berg, *Violin Concerto*. Copyright © 1936 by Universal Edition AG, Vienna. Copyright © renewed. All rights reserved. Used by permission of European American Music Distributors Company, U.S. and Canadian agent for Universal Edition AG, Vienna **138** Henry Cowell, *Fabric*. Copyright © 1922 (renewed) by Associated Music Publishers, Inc. (BMI) International Copyright Secured. All rights reserved. Reprinted by permission. **141** *String Quartet 1931* by Ruth Crawford Seeger. Copyright © 1941 by Merion

PHOTOGRAPHS AND FIGURES

INDEX

Note: Page numbers in *italics* indicate illustrations or musical examples.

A25